Hellenic Studies 82

HOMERIC IMAGERY
AND
THE NATURAL ENVIRONMENT

Recent Titles in the Hellenic Studies Series

HOMERIC IMAGERY

AND

THE NATURAL ENVIRONMENT

by
William Brockliss

CENTER FOR HELLENIC STUDIES
Trustees for Harvard University
Washington, DC
Distributed by Harvard University Press
Cambridge, Massachusetts, and London, England
2019

Homeric Imagery and the Natural Environment
   By William Brockliss
Copyright © 2019 Center for Hellenic Studies, Trustees for Harvard University
All Rights Reserved.
Published by Center for Hellenic Studies, Trustees for Harvard University,
   Washington, D.C.
Distributed by Harvard University Press, Cambridge, Massachusetts and
   London, England
Printed by Maple Press, York, PA
Cover Design: Joni Godlove
Production: Kerri Cox Sullivan

EDITORIAL TEAM
Senior Advisers: W. Robert Connor, Gloria Ferrari Pinney, Albert Henrichs†,
   James O'Donnell, Bernd Seidensticker
Editorial Board: Gregory Nagy (Editor-in-Chief), Casey Dué (Executive Editor),
   Mary Ebbott (Executive Editor), Scott Johnson, Olga Levaniouk, Leonard
   Muellner
Production Manager for Publications: Jill Curry Robbins
Web Producer: Noel Spencer
Multimedia Producer: Mark Tomasko

ISBN 978-0-674-98735-7

Elenei, soției mele scumpe

Contents

Contents

Color plates follow page 248.

Preface

But Athena daughter of Zeus made him
Taller and broader to look at; and from his head
She sent down curly locks, like the flower of the hyacinth.
As when some man pours gold around silver,
A skilled man, whom Hephaestus and Pallas Athena taught
Every kind of craft—he achieves graceful works—
So she poured grace on his head and shoulders.

Odyssey 6.229–235 ≈ 23.156–162

This book, which offers a study of Homeric metaphor and of its engagements with the Greek natural environment, arose from an interest in the multifarious and highly developed vegetal imagery of archaic Greek poetry. Many of the relevant images from non-Homeric genres demand close analysis and discussion—and I have drawn on a number of such images in the chapters below. But I found myself time and again being struck by the vegetal imagery of Homeric poetry and, in particular, by its floral images, such as the image of hyacinthine hair quoted above. Seeking explanations for these striking images, I found that they could, in part, be traced to characteristics of the Greek flora. But of course, the characteristics of a given flora do not determine the kinds of vegetal images that poets of a given region will develop. Rather, as we can see from comparison with other archaic Greek genres, the vegetal images of Homeric poetry reflect particular choices on the part of the Homeric poets: in forming their imagery these poets drew on particular aspects of the Greek natural environment, such as the sudden, colorful blooms of the Greek spring.

A full investigation of Homeric imagery and of its cultural and natural milieux would not have been possible without the assistance and advice of a very large number of friends and experts. Though it is impossible to name them all here, I take the opportunity now to thank Victor Bers, Ann Hanson, Pauline LeVen, and Irene Peirano for their help with the initial stages of the project; Verity Harte for her guidance on Presocratic philosophy; Jay Fisher,

Brian Joseph, Douglas Adams, and James Mallory for their thoughts on historical linguistics; Dimitri Gutas (on Theophrastos), Michael Donoghue (the natural environments of Greece and the Mediterranean), and Emily Greenwood (literary theory). Discussions with Fabian Horn and Richard Buxton have refined my understanding of cognitive approaches to metaphor and of metaphor more generally.

I have also benefited greatly from interactions with colleagues and students, both at Brigham Young University and at my current home, the University of Wisconsin-Madison. My analysis of gender in the Homeric poems and in other archaic Greek poetry (Part I) has been significantly strengthened through discussions with colleagues in the Classics department at UW-Madison, including Alex Dressler and Laura McClure. I have learned much from the ecocritics George Handley and Chip Oscarson at Brigham Young, and from my colleagues in the UW-Madison Center for Culture, History, and Environment. At UW-Madison I have had the opportunity to develop some of my ideas further through discussions with students in my classes on Classics and the natural environment, and ancient monsters—the latter having particular relevance to my discussion of death in Part III of this study.

I am particularly grateful to the Loeb Classical Library Foundation, whose generous support helped me to complete this project; to Elizabeth Minchin, who has twice read and offered advice on versions of it at short notice; to Jonathan Burgess for his comments on my Introduction; to Egbert Bakker, whose wise and insightful guidance was indispensable both during the first stage of this project (its incarnation as a Yale PhD thesis, 2011) and in its later instantiations; to Patricia Rosenmeyer, who has very generously given of her time in looking over a number of different versions of this text; to Jeff Beneker, for his assistance with the latter stages of the project; to Amy Hendrix and Claire Trivax for their help in preparing this manuscript; to Kerri Cox Sullivan (production); and to Jill Curry Robbins, Casey Dué Hackman, Mary Ebbott, Leonard Muellner, and Gregory Nagy at the Center for Hellenic Studies. But most of all, I would like to thank my wife, Elena, to whom this book is dedicated, for her support, patience, and love.

For the most part, I have used the more common, Latinized versions of Greek names: Achilles rather than Akhilleus, Hera rather than Herē. I have however retained Greek forms where Latinized versions would appear awkward (I refer, for instance, to Aphrodite and Helios).

Madison, WI
May 2019

Introduction

THE IMAGES OF FLOWERS, TREES, AND OTHER PLANTS that we find in the poetry of a given region represent particular responses to a particular flora with particular characteristics familiar to those who live in that region. Therefore, if we are to achieve a proper understanding of the operations of such images and of the ways in which they would have been received by audiences and readers, we need to gain a sense of the characteristics of the relevant natural environments. These natural environments may differ from those with which we ourselves are familiar; accordingly, it is imperative that we set aside preconceptions formed on the basis of such familiar environments and focus instead on the natural phenomena peculiar to the region that we are studying. But it is necessary also to identify the specific choices made by poets of that region as they engage with their natural environments. We should bear in mind that the characteristics of these environments do not determine the poets' choices: rather, the relevant natural phenomena provide the palette on which poets of the region draw in order to form their vegetal images.

This book provides a case-study for how we might investigate a particular body of poetic imagery and its engagements with the natural environments of a particular region. I shall be exploring the vegetal imagery of Homeric poetry and especially its images of flowers. We shall also consider comparanda from other archaic Greek genres that can help set in relief the particular choices made by the Homeric poets in their interactions with their natural environments. Such an investigation marks a clear departure from previous studies which, with the exception of a few brief articles, have not treated Homeric poetry as a response to a particular flora.[1] And even those that have done so have not set the Homeric poems against other kinds of Greek poetry; they have neglected, then, to reveal the particular choices of the Homeric poets in their engagements with the natural world.

---

[1] For exceptions, see Irwin 1984, 1990, 1994, 1997; also those sections of Motte 1971 that discuss the Homeric poems.

By recognizing Homeric poetry as a particular response to a particular natural environment, we can derive new insights into the ways in which listeners would have engaged with it, and at the same time facilitate new readings of the Homeric poems. As we shall see, in forming their vegetal images the Homeric poets responded to the sorts of natural phenomena that would have been familiar to audiences from their own environments. And the most striking examples of such imagery—the associations of flowers with the concepts of deception, disorder, and the monstrousness of death—drew on some of the most striking characteristics of the Greek flora: the brief, diverse blooms of the Greek spring.

The Greek Natural Environment

The Homeric poets and their counterparts in other genres of archaic Greek poetry experienced vegetation in the world around them, and it was on the basis of such experiences that they formed their images of flowers, trees, and other plants. In order to investigate such images, then, we need to gain an understanding both of the general characteristics of the archaic Greek natural environment and also of the particular characteristics of the plants that would have been familiar to early audiences.

In order to identify a particular plant in an archaic Greek poem, we should attempt where possible to match it with a modern equivalent, since our knowledge of modern Greek flowers is more secure than our knowledge of their ancient equivalents. On the basis of linguistic continuities and/or cognates, we are frequently able to identify at least the genus of a plant in a given passage of Homeric poetry: it is, for instance, highly probable that the Homeric term νάρκισσος refers to a plant of the genus *Narcissus*, or that the various occurrences of the Greek noun ἴον point to a violet of one sort or another (genus *Viola*). Similarly, the term δρῦς is very likely to refer to trees of the genus *Quercus* (oak). In some cases this is as far as we can and should go, since a given floral or arboreal lexeme in a given context may not have suggested a particular species to Homeric audiences. The term "species" is, after all, a modern botanical concept based ultimately on reproductive qualities, and poets and their audiences might have other properties in mind, which were common to more than one modern species.

That said, the plants in some of the passages that we shall study resemble a restricted range of species within a genus, or even one particular species. For instance, the description of the many-headed narcissus in the *Hymn to Demeter* may well evoke the *Narcissus tazetta*, which unlike most other members of the genus *Narcissus* has multiple heads; another possibility is the many-headed

N. papyraceus.[2] We should, however, bear in mind that artistic evocations of plants are not the sorts of disinterested descriptions that we might find (or hope to find) in scientific writings. While it is perfectly possible that a given ancient text alludes to one or two particular modern species, the Homeric poets may have manipulated the characteristics of those species to their particular artistic ends. In Chapter 2, for instance, I show that the narcissus described in the *Hymn to Demeter* is an artificially enhanced plant with exaggerated blooms, which helps to explain its special attraction for Korē.

Turning to the general qualities of Greek vegetation, we have good reasons to suppose that the major characteristics of the modern Greek flora identified by botanists were also features of archaic Greece. I shall explain what these characteristics are and offer justifications for assuming that they held good for archaic Greece also.

One of the most striking qualities of the modern Greek flora is its great diversity, and in particular the diversity of its flowering plants: see Plates 1 and 2. Anthony Huxley and William Taylor describe modern Greece as "a country marvellously rich in flowers: it has a flora of at least 6,000 species, many of them endemic."[3] Hellmut Baumann likewise counts "more than 6,000 species ... making Greece floristically the richest country in Europe."[4] Britain, by contrast, is home to around 2,300 flowering plants.[5] It seems probable that human activity will have had an impact on the flora of Greece since archaic times. Some endemic species will have been lost to fire, deforestation, and agricultural activities.[6] At the same time, however, some non-native species will have been introduced as a result of contact with other botanical regions.[7] The archaic landscape would therefore have hosted fewer non-native species of flowering plant than the contemporary landscape, but more endemic species.[8] It is very likely, then, that

[2]   See Chapters 2, 4, and 9 below. For the *Narcissus tazetta*, see Murr 1969:248–249, Huxley and Taylor 1977:153, and Polunin 1980:502; for *N. papyraceus*, Polunin 1980:502.

[3]   Huxley and Taylor 1977:6.

[4]   Baumann 1993:10. Similar figures are cited by Polunin in his survey of the Balkan flora, including that of Greece (Polunin 1980:22–23). On the diversity of the Greek flora, see also Pignatti 1983:154 and Voliotis 1984. For a discussion of the geological and botanical reasons for such diversity, see Polunin 1980:22–28.

[5]   Baumann 1993:10. See also Hughes 2014:17–18, who offers the figure 2,113.

[6]   See Pignatti 1983; also Polunin 1980:26 on man's impact on the flora of Greece over the last 10,000 years.

[7]   For the introduction of new species through human activities, see Broodbank 2013:71 on the botanical history of the Mediterranean as a whole.

[8]   Scholars differ over the extent of such changes, with some stressing continuities between the ancient and modern flora. Horden and Purcell (2000:328–330) for instance, citing Rackham and Moody 1996:123–139, note the "increasingly powerful case for very substantial overall stability" in Mediterranean vegetation over the last 3,000 years of history. Rackham and Moody, for their part, trace broad continuities in the history of the vegetation of Crete and of Greece more

the archaic Greek landscape like its modern equivalent boasted exceptional botanical diversity.[9]

A second characteristic of the modern Greek flora is the suddenness and brevity of the blooming of its flowers—a stark contrast with the gentler blooming periods of Britain or much of North America.[10] André Motte refers to the blooming of flowers in the Greek spring as "le moment exquis de l'éclosion printanière."[11] Huxley and Taylor describe how "by early March the Greek winter is giving way to the Greek spring with bewildering, almost explosive speed."[12] A second burst of color opens the summer: "[a] rough indication that summer has begun is given by the final, almost explosive flowering of the annual flowers which abound everywhere."[13] Similarly, Oleg Polunin notes the "short-lived flush of brightly coloured annuals and bulbous plants, followed by another flush when the rains return in early winter."[14] Plate 3 suggests the vibrancy of this "short-lived flush" at Mycenae, the most powerful Greek city in the world of the Homeric epics.[15]

---

generally from the late Bronze Age to the present. The descriptions of Greek vegetation in the *Odyssey* (esp. 19.439–443: a boar lies in the thick undergrowth) and in writers such Theophrastus, Xenophon (*Cynegeticus*), and Pausanias remind them of the current Greek landscape, which is dominated by maquis (low, dense shrubbery) rather than woodland.

[9] On the estimation of the plant biologist and Mediterranean expert Michael Donoghue (personal communication), diversity is probably somewhat greater in modern Greece than it would have been in ancient Greece: while some species will have become restricted to, e.g., montane zones, a number of weed species have been introduced from Asia. Ancient Greece would also, however, have hosted a comparatively diverse flora.

[10] These phenomena will be more familiar to inhabitants of Mediterranean-like environments such as California. Nevertheless, the botanical diversity of the Mediterranean itself, to be discussed below, exceeds that of other similar environments: see Broodbank 2013:70 and, more generally, Broodbank 2013:54–81 on the uniqueness of the Mediterranean region.

[11] Motte 1971:10.

[12] Huxley and Taylor 1977:21. See Höhfeld 2008:39 on the flora of the Troad: "Wenn man nach den mediterranen Winterregen im Frühjahr durch die Feldfluren der Troas streift, erlebt man im saftigen Grün des Winterweizens *die faszinierende Blütenexplosion in Weiß und Rot* von Margeriten und Klatschmohn, die mit ihren kräftigen Tönen die Landschaft *für wenige Wochen* in *ein rauschendes Farbenfest* verwandeln—leider nur kurz, ehe sich die Flur wieder unter unbarmherziger Hitze und Trockenheit in ihr blassbraunes Sommerkleid hüllt." ("If you roam the fields of the Troad in spring after the Mediterranean winter rains, you experience among the lush green of the winter wheat *the fascinating explosion of white and red blooms* of daisies and corn poppies, which *for a few weeks* transform the landscape with their strong tones into *a glittering feast of color*—unfortunately only briefly, before the field once more wraps itself in its pale brown summer cloak as a result of the merciless heat and drought"; my emphases).

[13] Huxley and Taylor 1977:24.

[14] Polunin 1980:30–31. See also p. 37 on the "burst of colour" in the Greek phrygana (the low shrubbery typical of Greece). See also Braudel 1972:233 on spring in the Mediterranean region, including Greece: "Of real springtime there is little or none; perhaps a short week that brings out leaves and flowers."

[15] Something of the brevity of the Greek spring bloom is suggested by the fact that on a visit to the same location on 29 March 2015 (in a different year, but nineteen days later in March than the original visit), the slope depicted in Plate 3—south-facing and hence exposed to the sun—was

Such phenomena are the result of longstanding climatic conditions. As Polunin points out, the sudden, short-lived blooms of the Greek flora are a response to the mild winters and hot, dry summers of Greece and of the Mediterranean region as a whole:[16] the mildness of winter allows, and the heat of summer necessitates, a quick, early spring bloom. As Fernand Braudel observes, the alternation between wet winters and hot, dry summers, which defines the Mediterranean climate, is determined by the influence of the Atlantic in the winter and of the Sahara in the summer.[17] And these conditions have obtained for millennia. Cyprian Broodbank observes that the contemporary climate of the region dates from the period 3,500–2,200 BCE, which "witnessed a drying of the Mediterranean's climate, and the beginnings of the regime familiar to us today."[18] Taking a still longer view, Sandro Pignatti argues that these basic characteristics of the Mediterranean climate were established towards the end of the Tertiary Cretaceous period, i.e., around 65 million years ago.[19] In comparison, the gap between modern and archaic Greece is an eye-blink in the history of the landscape.

---

very much past peak. By contrast, more shaded areas at the bottom of the slope were considerably more advanced in their bloom than on my earlier visit.

[16] Cf. Polunin 1980:30–31. Höhfeld (2008:39) offers a similar explanation for the springtime "Blütenexplosion" in the Troad: see the quotation in n12 above. On the hot summers and mild winters of the Mediterranean region, including Greece, see also Horden and Purcell 2000:12–13, and Broodbank 2013:56: "The technical definition of a Mediterranean climate is a particular variety of semi-arid regime in which the winter rainfall predominates (ideally threefold) over summer levels, and where summers are hot, and winters mild to cool." For the characteristics of the Mediterranean climate, see also Hughes 2014:9–10.

[17] Braudel 1972:232–234; 2001:15–18.

[18] Broodbank 2013, esp. 41–44, 262–264, 506–507, and 600. The quotation is taken from p. 80. It is true that some scholars have argued that significant fluctuations occurred in the climate of the Bronze and Iron Age Mediterranean. For instance, Weiss 1982, Neumann 1993, and Kaniewski et al. 2010 explain the fall of the major Bronze Age civilizations of the eastern Mediterranean in terms of climatic crises. However, as Finné et al. (2011) point out in their survey of such studies, the evidence for these crises is at best inconclusive. Scholars have applied findings from one geographical area to the Mediterranean basin as a whole or have drawn on only one type of evidence for the ancient climate. What is more, when two or more such studies are compared, we find contradictions between them: for instance, while Weiss attributes late Bronze Age migrations to drought, Neumann suggests that they resulted from flooding. Given the conflicting climatic evidence for the Mediterranean as a whole, it is likely that, as Horden and Purcell (2000) observe, any climatic fluctuations were localized and temporary. We would not expect such fluctuations to have had a significant impact on the metaphorical systems of the Homeric poems, which developed over a long period of time and spread to a considerable range of Greek-speaking locales. For these reasons, I explore the origins of Homeric floral imagery by focusing on the more enduring and more general characteristics of the Mediterranean environment, which have after all remained consistent: over the last few millennia Mediterranean summers may at times have been hotter and drier, but they have nevertheless alternated with relatively mild winters.

[19] Pignatti 1983:151–152.

Given the persistence of the general characteristics of the Greek natural environment, it is unsurprising to find that ancient writers such as the Hesiodic poets or Theophrastus portray climatic conditions resembling those of modern Greece. The archaic Greeks, if the *Works and Days* is anything to go by, experienced hot summers and early springs similar to those described by modern botanists. Spring for the Hesiodic poets begins after the rising of Arcturus (*Works and Days* 564–570), i.e., in late February.[20] By the time the Pleiades appear in mid-May it is already hot enough that the farmer is tempted to enjoy shady seats, when he should be busying himself with the harvest (571–576).[21] At its height the Dog Star dries out the body and the head, and a man has to retreat to the shade to drink wine (582–596).[22] From the classical period, the botanist Theophrastus describes conditions and times of Greek plant growth in terms resembling Polunin's descriptions of modern Greece. Spring, with its moisture and warmth, is best for growth (*De Causis Plantarum* 1.13.5), but autumn, with its similar climatic conditions, is also good (1.13.7). Moreover, mild (καλοί) winters at the proper time make an essential contribution both to good growth and to the formation of fruit (2.1.2–4).[23]

Though neither the Hesiodic poets nor Theophrastus focuses specifically on flowering periods, we can, on the basis of this evidence for the similarity of ancient and modern climates and growing conditions, assume that the archaic Greek flora was, like that of modern Greece, remarkable for the sudden blooming of its spring flowers. I shall argue that this, probably the most striking characteristic of the archaic Greek flora, provided the basis for the Homeric associations of flowers with shifting, deceptive appearance (Part I) and with challenges or changes to the established order of the cosmos (Part II).

Homeric Poetry

We have established one of the two poles of our investigation—the characteristics of the archaic Greek natural environment. As we have seen, we can be confident that the general characteristics of the archaic Greek flora were similar to those of its modern equivalent; we have also observed that it is possible to identify the particular genera and (sometimes) species of plants in our texts. I turn now to the second major constituent of my study—the poems of the

---

[20] Cf. Most 2006:133n32.

[21] For the appearance of the Pleiades in mid-May, see Most 2006:135n34.

[22] Cf. *Aspis* 393–401: the heroes Cycnus and Heracles fought at the time when the cicada sings and Sirius dries out the flesh. For a description of the parching heat of the Greek summer, see also Alcaeus 347 Voigt.

[23] For the effect of climatic conditions on growth, see more generally *De Causis Plantarum* 2.1.1–3.8.

Homeric corpus. It might seem at first sight that considerably less needs to be said, by way of definition, about the Homeric poems than about the characteristics of the Greek flora; nevertheless, it is necessary to make clear which poems I am treating as Homeric and how I understand the place of those poems in the culture of archaic Greece, the time period that will form the focus of my study.

Such matters have after all been the subject of considerable debate among scholars. For Richard Janko or Martin West, something like our texts of the Homeric epics and hymns were composed at particular times in the archaic period. Janko, on the basis of linguistic evidence from the poems themselves, assigns approximate dates to the individual Homeric poems and separates out the Homeric corpus as we have it (both the *Homeric Hymns* and the Homeric epics) into a series of historical moments. At these particular times, in Janko's opinion, orally trained poets dictated poems resembling our Homeric texts to scribes.[24]

West argues that two separate seventh-century poets composed the *Iliad* and *Odyssey*, and that their compositions can be reconstructed from the manuscript tradition of the epics. Like Janko he believes that these poets were trained in the oral tradition of Homeric poetry; but he contends that they composed the epics in written form and then edited their texts over a prolonged period of time.[25] He attributes the composition of the hymns and poems of the Epic Cycle to other poets of the archaic period working in the same tradition.[26] For both Janko and West, these archaic Greek compositions served as the models for subsequent versions of the poems, whether textual or oral.

Like West, scholars such as Gregory Nagy treat as Homeric the hymns, the *Iliad*, the *Odyssey* and the poems of the Epic Cycle (or to be more precise, the archaic precursors of the poems with which we are familiar). Moreover, like Janko and West such scholars explore the relationship of the texts of Homeric poetry with the oral tradition. But for the most part their conclusions depart significantly from those of Janko and West: they treat Homeric poetry—at least in the archaic period—as a fluid phenomenon, multiform in its instantiations in performance. Nagy, for instance, argues that the Homeric epics were first written down, by means of dictation, in the archaic period. To that extent he echoes the arguments of Janko, though he prefers a date later in the archaic period for these first recordings—ca. 550 BCE. Unlike Janko, however, he argues that such texts did not play an important role in the development of Homeric poetry. Granted, they may have influenced the *koinai* texts associated in the classical period with the Panathenaea in Athens. But according to Nagy they had no

---

[24] Janko 1982, 1998.
[25] West 2011, 2014.
[26] See, for instance, West 2011:7, 81 on the hymns and 2013:26–40 on the Epic Cycle.

impact on the wider performance tradition of Homeric poetry, which continued to exhibit fluidity down to the third century BCE.[27]

I follow all these scholars in attributing to the same poetic tradition not only the major epics and the hymns (which appear to have served as preludes to epic recitation), but also, insofar as we have evidence for the sorts of images found in them, the poems of the Epic Cycle.[28] I shall refer to all these works—not merely the major epics and hymns—as "Homeric." As I shall show, such terminology is justified not merely by their treating the same stock of Trojan myth but also by their development of a common metaphorical system.[29]

As we have seen, it is unclear to what degree the poems we possess might or might not have resembled particular performance versions and/or texts of the archaic age. Nevertheless, we can at least treat them as representative of the *sorts* of things that would have been found in the Homeric poems at that time. After all, both scholars such as Nagy and critics of Nagy such as Janko or West would agree that Homeric *diction*, if not the Homeric *texts*, became more or less fixed over the course of the archaic period—a period of Panhellenic interaction in which the multi-dialectical strands of the Homeric tradition coalesced.[30]

I shall therefore treat our texts of the Homeric epics, hymns, and Epic Cycle as reflexes of a unified poetic system potentially subject to multifarious instantiations in performance—that is, as products of the system of Homeric poetics that coalesced over the course of the archaic period.[31] This poetic system embraced not only the formulae, type-scenes, and plot structures that were the focus of classic studies by Milman Parry and Albert Lord, but also, as scholars such as William Scott, Leonard Muellner, and Casey Dué have shown, the similes

---

[27] For the dictation of the Homeric epics ca. 550 BCE, see Nagy 1996. For the lack of impact that these texts had on Homeric performance traditions and for the fluidity of the Homeric epics in the performance cultures of archaic Greece, see Nagy 1996:29–63 and Nagy 2004 (Nagy's "evolutionary model" for the development of the Homeric poems). For similar conceptions of the history of Homeric poetry, see González 2013.

[28] Justifications for this approach are revealed in Part I, where I demonstrate commonalities between the metaphorical systems of poems such as the *Hymn to Demeter*, the *Odyssey* and the *Cypria*. For the *Homeric Hymns* as preludes to epic recitals, see Parker 1991:1 and n5, Richardson 1974:3–4, Càssola 1975:xii–xvi, as well as the internal evidence for such a relationship between the hymns and epics: *Odyssey* 8 and *Hymn to Apollo* 158–161 (Demodocus/the Delian Maidens sing songs of both gods and men); *Hymn* 31.18–19 and 32.18–20 (the poet closes his hymn with a promise to sing of heroes).

[29] For relationships between the Homeric epics and the Trojan Cycle, which are the focus of neoanalytical studies of Homeric poetry, see for instance Burgess 2001 and 2009.

[30] See Nagy's description of the eighth century BCE as the "pan-Hellenic" stage of Homeric epic (1996:39–42, 52–54), or his distinction between Homeric text (addressed in the first part of his 2004 monograph) and language (addressed in the second).

[31] For the Epic Cycle as a reflex of the Homeric poetic system, see Bernabé 2015 on the close similarities between the language of the cycle and that of the major epics.

employed by the Homeric poets.[32] We shall see, moreover, that not only similes but also other figures of speech are subject to relatively consistent treatment across the Homeric corpus. It would appear, then, that they are likewise constituents of this system.

Interactions between Homeric Poetry and the Natural Environment

This book, then, will focus on passages from the Homeric epics, *Homeric Hymns*, and Epic Cycle and on the sorts of natural phenomena explored above. But we also need a model for how these two elements of my study—Homeric poetry and the Greek natural environment—might have interacted with one another. The breakthroughs in the cognitive study of metaphor in the work of George Lakoff, Mark Johnson, and Mark Turner offer us a promising methodology for such an investigation. With the slight modifications set out below (the broader definition of the term "metaphor"; the greater emphasis on distinctions between the metaphors of different poetic genres), their insights can be applied to the sorts of Homeric passages that we shall consider.

Lakoff and his collaborators help us to understand how metaphor interacts with concrete elements of our worlds, such as the characteristics of our natural environments, and thereby enhances our understanding of more abstract concepts. In *Metaphors We Live By*, Lakoff and Johnson argue that metaphor is not merely a linguistic phenomenon: in fact, metaphorical expressions reflect conceptual associations in the mind of the speaker. With metaphor we associate more abstract concepts, which might prove difficult to understand on their own, with more concrete concepts drawn from our bodies or physical environments. In *More than Cool Reason*, Lakoff and Turner go on to show that even the more unusual metaphorical expressions that we find in poetry are formed on the basis of conceptual associations that are likewise grounded in our physical experience of the world.[33]

As Lakoff and Turner point out, plants are among those elements of the physical environment that are "at least partly, if not totally, understood on their own terms," i.e., without the aid of metaphor.[34] Unsurprisingly, then, the concrete concepts drawn from our observations of and interactions with plants are an extremely important source of metaphor, whether poetic or otherwise: they form the basis of associations with more abstract concepts and thereby

---

[32]   Parry 1971:1–190, Lord 2000, Scott 1974, 2009, Muellner 1990, Dué 2010. See also Ready 2018 on simile patterns shared by different performers of Homeric poetry.

[33]   Lakoff and Johnson 2003; Lakoff and Turner 1989.

[34]   Lakoff and Turner 1989:135.

help us to understand those concepts. In one common system of metaphor, Anglophone poets imagine human life cycles in terms of the more concrete, more readily observable processes of a plant's life cycle. Within that metaphorical system, flowers, in particular, are associated with the beauty and flourishing of youth.[35] For instance, Shakespeare's eighteenth sonnet reminds us that "Rough winds do shake the darling buds of May, / And summer's lease hath all too short a date ..." (lines 4–5).[36] At other times different aspects of flowers are accessed in metaphor, such as lightness, scent, or their associations with the natural as opposed to the artificial.[37]

Building on such scholarship, I shall treat Homeric floral images as expressions of conceptual associations between more abstract concepts such as death and more concrete concepts drawn from the natural environments that would have been familiar to early audiences. And I shall study the ways in which such associations would have helped those audiences to understand the abstract concepts in question.

My approach, however, distinguishes itself from that of Lakoff, Johnson, and Turner in two respects. Firstly, while my discussion follows their insight that metaphors express mental associations between more abstract and more concrete concepts (e.g., death and flowers), and many of the linguistic expressions of such associations that I shall discuss match the sorts of examples analyzed by those scholars, I also consider metaphorical expressions that are broader in scope than those studied by Lakoff and his collaborators. They investigate linguistic expressions where one thing is directly described in terms of another within the syntax of a sentence or phrase—such as, "Man that is born of woman ... cometh forth like a flower, and is cut down."[38] As is clear from this example, Lakoff et al. treat similes alongside metaphors in the classic sense, on the understanding that both kinds of image reflect associations of an abstract with a more concrete concept.[39] My study likewise incorporates a number of

---

[35] Lakoff and Turner 1989, esp. 12–17.

[36] I quote Sonnet 18 from Burrow 2002:417.

[37] Lakoff and Turner 1989:144–154. For other applications of the work of Lakoff and his school to the study of Greek poetic imagery, cf. Hopman 2012, Horn 2015a and b, and Eckerman forthcoming (drawing on Lakoff and Johnson 2003), Budelmann and LeVen 2014, and Horn 2015b (drawing on Fauconnier and Turner 2002). For cognitive approaches to ancient Greek imagery more generally, cf. Minchin 2001:132–160, Crowther 2003, and Tsagalis 2012:271–372.

[38] Job 14:1–2, cited by Lakoff and Turner (1989:14).

[39] Recent psycholinguistic research has explored possible differences between similes and metaphors. For instance, Chiappe and Kennedy (1999) and Chiappe, Kennedy, and Smykowski (2003) argue that metaphors typically state more apt comparisons than similes; cf. Ready 2008 for applications of such ideas to Homeric poetry (see also Ready 2004 on Catullus poem 61). Other papers have asked whether similes and metaphors serve as comparisons or categorization statements. (If the latter, they would not only juxtapose the tenor and the vehicle

similes. In Chapter 2, for instance, I discuss passages in which Odysseus' hair is said to be "like a hyacinth" (*Odyssey* 6.231, 23.158), and in Chapter 9 I examine a simile comparing Ilioneus' head with that of a poppy (*Iliad* 14.496–500).

But although metaphors and similes in the classic sense are of interest to me, in Parts I and II I shall also be concerned with associations of vegetal images with the themes explored by whole passages. As will become clear, such large-scale metaphorical expressions are an important component of Homeric poetry: in fact, if we do not take them into account, we vastly underestimate the richness of Homeric metaphor. To give an example, descriptions of bodies with a seductive, deceptive appearance in the Homeric poems are accompanied in a number of instances by descriptions of flowers. Odysseus' hyacinthine hair facilitates his re-seduction of Penelope, albeit in the guise of a younger man. The narcissus in the *Hymn to Demeter* is the double of "flower-faced" Korē, and it rouses her autoerotic desires; but she is unaware of its special, divine qualities, which draw her to the flower (see Chapter 2). The concepts of flowers, seduction, and deception are thereby associated with one another.

Even though these sorts of image are not considered by Lakoff, Johnson, and Turner, their dynamics follow the model discussed by those scholars. As with similes or metaphors in the classic sense, these larger-scale images are linguistic expressions reflecting underlying conceptual associations. For instance, in the passages from the *Odyssey* and the *Hymn to Demeter* mentioned above, the Homeric poets were employing the characteristics of a concrete object, the flower, to aid and enhance listeners' understanding of the concepts of seduction

---

but also be making the claim that the tenor belongs in a higher-order category, of which the vehicle is a prototypical example. For example, the metaphor "cigarettes are time-bombs" would state that cigarettes belong in a higher-order category of things liable to kill you in time [Glucksberg and Keysar 1990, 1993]). Scholars such as Ortony (1979, 1993b) and Chiappe and Kennedy (2000) have argued that both similes and metaphors make comparisons. Glucksberg and Keysar (1990, 1993), however, contend that both are categorization statements. Other studies suggest that similes offer comparisons, but that metaphors make categorization claims (cf. Haught 2013, Glucksberg and Haught 2006). Bowdle and Gentner (2005) have provided a way to reconcile these different approaches. They suggest that novel metaphors, like similes, are understood as comparisons; metaphors are only processed as categorization statements once they have become conventionalized. Given the attention that it pays to novel metaphors, Bowdle's and Gentner's study represents a promising way to approach poetic images, which tend to be among the more novel figures of speech in a given language. Their findings are, moreover, consistent with those of Lakoff and Turner. All four scholars agree that a poetic metaphor or a poetic simile represents an encounter between the tenor and the vehicle, with no extra higher-order category implied. And while Bowdle and Gentner point to occasional exceptions (such as "a soldier is a pawn"), they are broadly agreement with Lakoff's and Turner's contention that both metaphors and similes associate a more abstract with a more concrete concept (p. 200).

and deception.[40] In this way, such broader-scale comparisons would count as metaphors in the sense understood by Lakoff and his colleagues. Nevertheless, I wish to avoid confusion with the more common usage of the term "metaphor" to refer to associations of two concepts at the level of a sentence. For that reason I shall use the words "image(s)" and "imagery" to refer to all the different kinds of metaphorical expression in Homeric poetry, all of which would have helped audiences to understand more abstract concepts in terms of concrete concepts drawn from the Greek natural environment.

My emphasis on the peculiarities of Homeric metaphor represents a second departure from the work of Lakoff and his colleagues. Lakoff and Turner are at pains to show that the same basic conceptual associations underlie metaphors from different spheres of language use. Accordingly, while they acknowledge that poets manipulate metaphor in novel ways, they place greater stress on commonalities between poetic and non-poetic metaphor, or between the work of one poet and another. The evidence from archaic Greek poetry that we shall consider, however, draws our attention to distinctions between the metaphorical systems of different genres, which in turn reflect contrasting engagements with the Greek natural environment.

Such distinctions are apparent both in explorations of particular concepts and in the general outlook of Homeric and other archaic Greek poetry. For instance, both the Homeric poets and their elegiac counterparts associate flowers with death. But while the relevant elegiac images emphasize the brevity of life, Homeric floral images explore the monstrous otherness of death. And the two genres illustrate these different aspects of death by drawing on different characteristics of Greek flowers. The elegiac images focus on the brief blooms of the Greek spring, but the equivalent Homeric images associate flowers with exceptional fertility, a quality shared with the monsters of the Hesiodic tradition. What is more, the different sets of Homeric images that we shall study, when considered together, suggest a darker, more pessimistic conception of the human condition than we find in other genres: while lyric poets celebrate beauty and elegiac poets advertise the joys of youth, the Homeric poets, through their interactions with the natural environment, draw attention to the concepts of deception, instability, and horror.

---

[40] This broader definition of the "metaphorical" is in keeping with Buxton's (2004) discussion of "similes and other likenesses" in Homeric poetry. While exploring metaphors and similes in the usual sense of those terms, he also notes a broader "sense of equivalence between … narrated phenomena" (p. 147), such as Calypso's grove or Laertes' orchards, and the main action of the *Odyssey*. I shall consider both these descriptions of vegetation in my discussion of the Homeric imagery of civic order and its opposite (Part II). See also Hopman's (2012) discussion of metaphor in different representations of Scylla, including that which we find in the *Odyssey*. Most of Hopman's examples are of larger scale associations within the structure of a given portion of narrative.

Overview of the Argument

Each part of this book centers around associations of Homeric vegetal imagery with one particular concept or pair of concepts—erotic bodies, order and disorder, and death—and seeks to explain such associations in terms of the particular characteristics of the Greek natural environment. But in order to cast light on the particular choices of the Homeric poets, I also study equivalent images from other archaic Greek genres. Like the Homeric poems, the poetry of these genres developed through long traditions of oral performance, which continued into the archaic period.[41] Comparison of imagery from these genres with that of the Homeric poems suggests the different options that were available to archaic Greek poets in their engagements with natural phenomena. I have focused in each case on whichever genre presents the most abundant comparanda for the relevant Homeric images.

Part I explores images of flowers and eroticism in Homeric poetry and defines them against the equivalent images from archaic Greek lyric. Both genres associate flowers with physically attractive bodies; there are, however, clear distinctions between the developments of these associations in Homeric poetry and Greek lyric that imply two different constructions of eroticism, based on two different responses to natural phenomena and on two different relationships between the viewer and the viewed.

I elucidate such distinctions by referring both to the characteristics of Greek flowers and to modern theories of the gaze.[42] The lyric poets tend to cast the beloved who is associated with flowers as the object of the gaze, and such an objectifying gaze is reminiscent of the filmic gaze explored by Laura Mulvey. But in Homeric poetry the erotic bodies associated with flowers are also deceptive: they present a misleading appearance to the viewer and thereby spur her/him to adopt a certain course of action. Odysseus' "hyacinthine hair" in *Odyssey* 23, for instance, gives him the appearance of the young man who left for Troy twenty years ago and thereby helps persuade Penelope to accept him as her husband. The very deceptiveness of these erotic bodies goes some way to balancing the subjectivity of viewer and viewed: such descriptions of viewing resemble Lacanian accounts of the gaze, according to which the world looks back at the viewer and undermines her/his control of the scene.

As we shall see, these Homeric images constituted a distinctive response to the characteristics of flowers in the Greek natural environment. The floral imagery of erotic bodies in Greek lyric responded to the experience of viewing

---

[41] See Nagy 1974 and 1990 on the oral tradition of Greek lyric, 1982 on Hesiodic poetry, and 1985:46–50 on Greek elegy.

[42] Lacan 1977, esp. 95–96; Mulvey 1989a and b.

flowers and judging them beautiful. The Homeric poets, by contrast, drew on the shifting vistas of extremely diverse but short-lived surfaces of flowers seen in the Greek spring and early summer to provide an image for the attractive but temporary appearances of seductive, deceptive bodies.

Part II analyzes images that describe the cosmos and human society, and explores the relationships between them. Firstly, both the Hesiodic and the Homeric poets associate plants and pillars with order in the cosmos. But while the relevant Hesiodic images would have helped audiences to understand the actual structure of the cosmos, the equivalent Homeric images offer more general evocations of the stability and permanence of cosmic order. The Homeric poets also set their associations of trees, pillars, and cosmic order against floral imagery associated with challenges or changes to that order. In *Iliad* 14, for example, floral imagery marks the moment when Hera disables Zeus, the ruler of the universe, but the tree on which Sleep settles in the same passage suggests the divine order that he is about to undermine.

I go on to study vegetal images of civic order and its opposite, which provide a complement to the equivalent cosmic imagery. Both the Homeric and the Hesiodic poets associate flourishing trees with orderly communities. But again there are clear distinctions between the developments of such images in the two genres. The Hesiodic poets associate well-ordered cities with flourishing vegetation in general—both floral and arboreal. The Homeric poets, however, associate civic order not merely with trees, but more specifically with trees managed by human hands—especially the orderly plantings found in orchards. By contrast, uncivilized lands in Homeric poetry are associated with wild vegetation.

I further consider the manner in which these Homeric images of civic and cosmic order engaged with Greek perceptions of the natural environment. These different Homeric associations reflect beliefs about vegetal growth that, if ancient scientific and philosophical writings are any guide (especially those of the Presocratics and Theophrastus), would have been familiar to archaic Greek audiences. The cosmic imagery of trees and flowers reflected a contrast between the sudden growth of flowering plants, perceived as spontaneous, and the more regular growths of trees in forests. The equivalent civic imagery drew on the distinction between uncontrolled growths of plants in the wild and trees managed with the techniques of arboriculture.

In Part III, I discuss the Homeric floral imagery of death and engage in particular with Christiane Sourvinou-Inwood's and Jean-Pierre Vernant's explorations of death in archaic Greece. According to Sourvinou-Inwood the archaic period saw a gradual supplanting of an acceptance of death as part of life with a fear of death as something horrific.[43] I suggest that, rather than the

---

[43] Sourvinou-Inwood 1995.

one conception succeeding the other, both conceptions were present in early Greek culture and were instantiated in a dialogue between two different poetic genres. While for the elegiac poets death is a part (albeit an unwelcome part) of life, the Homeric poets depict death as something horrific.

More specifically, I suggest that unlike the equivalent images in other genres of Greek poetry these Homeric floral images evoke the monstrous disorder of death—a concept that Vernant associates with the mask of the Gorgon in *Odyssey* 11.[44] As we shall see, images both in *Odyssey* 11 and in other Odyssean passages associate flowers with the dissolution of bodily form and with a loss of the orderly distinctions that undergird the identity of the living individual. What is more, images such as the flowery meadows of the *Odyssey* or the poppy simile for the death of Gorgythion (whose name recalls the monstrous Gorgon) evoke the irregular fertility that the Greeks attributed both to monsters and flowers. And much as the fertility of Hesiodic monsters threatens the good order of the cosmos, the Homeric poets associate flowers with challenges or changes to cosmic and civic order (cf. Part II). Such associations of flowers, which echo those of Hesiodic monsters, reinforce allusions to the monstrous disorder of death in the relevant Homeric passages.

Lastly, I discuss the contribution of Homeric vegetal imagery and of its particular engagements with the natural environment to the Homeric corpus as a whole (Conclusion). In particular, I note that the choices of the Homeric poets in forming their floral images accord with the pessimistic tone of much of the Homeric corpus. Certain aspects of the Greek flora enabled the Homeric poets to associate flowers with negative concepts—deception, disorder, death, and monstrosity: the strikingly fertile but short-lived growths of flowers in the Greek spring contributed to associations of Homeric images with shifting and hence untrustworthy surfaces, and with ungoverned or monstrous fertility. But as we can see from other genres, these choices were not forced on the Homeric poets. The archaic lyric poets emphasized instead the beauty of flowers and thereby the beauty of the attractive youths associated with those flowers; the elegiac poets drew on the short-lived beauty of Greek flowers in order to celebrate the brief joys of youth. As I shall suggest, the choice of the Homeric poets to focus on more negative concepts in their floral imagery is indicative of their interest in the darker sides of human experience. Their compositions explore the untrustworthy nature of appearances, the instabilities latent in human communities or the cosmos as a whole, and the special horrors of the battlefield.

---

[44] Vernant 1991a, 1991b, 1996.

PART ONE

FLOWERS AND EROTIC BODIES

Preamble

THE FIRST PART OF THIS STUDY FOCUSES ON VEGETAL IMAGES of the erotic or, more specifically, on associations of flowers and erotic bodies. Most of the surviving examples of floral images of the erotic in archaic Greek poetry are to be found in the corpus of Greek lyric; accordingly, I shall draw on that genre to set in relief the particular choices of the Homeric poets in forming their own images of flowers and erotic bodies. As we shall see, while lyric poets develop imagery that subordinates erotic bodies associated with flowers to the gaze and evaluation of the speaker, Homeric poetry attributes seductive and deceptive qualities to such erotic bodies and thereby challenges the viewer's control over the scene.

Since the distinctions between the floral images of erotic bodies in the two genres depend in large part on different configurations of viewing and subjectivity, we can gain a clearer idea of those distinctions by drawing on the work of scholars who have analyzed such themes. I shall focus on the theories of Laura Mulvey and Jacques Lacan, which, though originally developed for the study of mainstream cinema (Mulvey) or in the context of Lacanian psychoanalysis, have proven central to a number of recent discussions of the gaze in classical literature. For Mulvey, the filmic gaze establishes dichotomies of viewer and viewed, of dominance and passivity, of masculine and feminine. In a seminal article from 1975, Mulvey argues that the filmic gaze is gendered masculine through its association with male characters and its objectification of female characters. Both the gaze of the camera and the gaze of male characters take women as their passive objects. In turn, the spectator is encouraged to channel her/his gaze through these viewpoints, and a masculine, dominating, and unreciprocated gaze is facilitated, which gratifies the erotic desire of the male viewer for a non-threatening, passive portrayal of the female. In this way, the imagery of mainstream film indulges the erotic fantasies of the male viewer.[1]

While the filmic gaze described by Mulvey operates in only one direction, from viewing subject to viewed object, Lacan characterizes the gaze as an exchange between the subject and the world, and a disturbing exchange at that. In his best-known illustration of this phenomenon, he recalls an encounter with a boy from a Breton fishing village, Petit-Jean. On catching sight of a sardine tin floating on the sea, Petit-Jean jokes *"You see that can? Do you see it? Well, it doesn't see you!"* Lacan, though, has the unnerving sense that the can is, in fact, looking back at him: "if what Petit-Jean said to me, namely, that the can did not see me, had any meaning, it was because in a sense, it was looking at me, all the same."

This experience upsets Lacan's sense of his centrality to the scene before his eyes and challenges his belief in the overriding importance of his own subjectivity. Previously, without reflecting on it, he was treating his surroundings—both human and nonhuman—as the passive contents of a "picture" that he himself controlled and that was subject to his judgement. But the feeling that the sardine tin is looking at him brings with it a realization antithetical to such beliefs. The tin is closely tied to the difficult work of Petit-Jean and the other fishermen, and its glinting surface reminds Lacan that he himself has no place in such activities. The "gaze" of the tin, then, gives him the sense that he is being judged as alien to the scene. He extrapolates from this experience the fact that, whenever he views the world, he can never view himself and is therefore always alien to the scene before his eyes. He is viewed by the very things that make up his visual field, and his subjective evaluation of them is always matched by their (competing) evaluation of him.[2]

Mulvey's and Lacan's theories of the gaze have had an important influence on studies of ancient epic and ancient lyric. But we can arrive at new conclusions regarding their relevance to these genres if we focus specifically on floral images and on their interactions with the characteristics of Greek flowers. Scholars such as Elizabeth Sutherland and Ellen Greene have identified a Mulveyan gaze in the work of male lyric poets (specifically those of the Roman tradition): according to Sutherland and Greene, the gaze of the poet's male persona dominates its female objects. As in Mulvey's analysis of film, this objectification of the female beloved and her subordination to the poet's gaze

---

[1] Mulvey 1989b. In a second article, however (1989a), Mulvey qualifies her conclusions. She asks why it is that female viewers are still able to experience pleasure when viewing films, even when the filmic gaze is so strongly associated with the masculine and the passivization of the feminine. She suggests that such viewers, while watching a film, identify with active male chararacters and the masculine gaze as much as with the objectified females.

[2] Lacan 1977:95–96; quotations from p. 95; italics in the original.

respond to male erotic desires. While male fantasies of the objectified female are given visual form in films, these lyric poems reflect such fantasies in their verbal descriptions. Eva Stehle argues that the poetry of Sappho undermines such objectifications of the female. Her poems, according to Stehle, assign the role of gazing subject to female personae and characters, and thereby suggest the possibility of equality in erotic relationships.[3] My studies, however, suggest that similarly unequal dynamics of the gaze are operative in the floral images of Sappho and of her male counterparts. And this is the case whether the gazing subject or desired object happen to be male or female.

By contrast, we shall find that the depiction of the gaze in Homeric floral images of the erotic more closely resembles the dynamics described by Lacan. In making this observation, my findings to some extent coincide with Helen Lovatt's on ancient epic in general. Lovatt derives the theoretical parameters for her discussion of the gaze partly from the work of Mulvey and Lacan.[4] She resists a straightforward equation of the epic gaze with the masculine gaze described by Mulvey and identifies a female gaze that operates "from the margins" and that is able to challenge even the direct power of the divine gaze. One realm in which this female gaze operates is in dreams, where it is associated with "deception, emotion and insubstantiality." This female gaze disrupts the dominance of the male gaze and of male subjectivity, like the disruptive contents of the visual field described by Lacan.[5]

The evidence that we shall discuss below accords in two respects with the dynamics described by Lovatt: the erotic bodies of Homeric poetry are associated with deception, and their deceptive qualities challenge the dominance of the viewer. There are, however, important distinctions to be drawn between my findings and those of Lovatt. The erotic bodies in question may belong to characters of either gender, and those viewing them may likewise be male or female. Homeric floral images, then, are associated with a less unequal dynamics of the gaze than that which we find in the equivalent passages of Greek lyric, but not necessarily with a female challenge to male dominance.

What we are dealing with, then, is not so much a contrast between male and female poets, or between male and female viewers as a general distinction between two archaic Greek genres. In the floral imagery of archaic Greek lyric, we find dichotomies of desiring subject and desired object, of (dominant)

[3] Stehle 1996, Sutherland 2003, Greene 2010:37–92.

[4] Lovatt 2013, esp. pp. 7–9. In common with Lovatt's book and a recent study of the *Odyssey* (Grethlein 2018), I draw on Mulvey's explorations of the dynamics of the gaze without incorporating her psychoanalytic terminology. Cf. Lovatt 2013:8: "The superstructure of [Mulvey's] argument may retain its strength, even if we do not accept the Freudian underpinnings."

[5] Lovatt 2013, esp. pp. 206–251; quotations from pp. 216 and 260.

viewer and (passive) viewed similar to those identified by Mulvey—though the gender dynamics of the gaze in the relevant passages are somewhat more fluid than those that Mulvey discovers in film. While the object of the gaze may be a beautiful girl or a beautiful boy, the viewer is for the most part gendered masculine, much like the viewers that Mulvey analyzes. In poems of Sappho that present floral images of erotic bodies the speaking subject is feminine, but the operations of the gaze otherwise resemble the unequal dynamics described by Mulvey. In both the work of Sappho and that of her male counterparts, erotic bodies decked with flowers are described as the object of the gaze and in no way threaten the subjectivity of the one who looks. The speaker claims the right to describe and to evaluate the object of her/his desires, but the beloved is allowed no corresponding opportunity to express a perspective on the scene. The speaker may also situate the beloved in an erotic space of her/his own imagining, such as the grove of Aphrodite in Ibycus fr. 282C(i) Campbell. The verbal imagery of these compositions provides an analog to the visual images discussed by Mulvey, to the extent that it reflects the erotic desires of the viewer and suggests an unequal relationship between viewer and viewed.

Conversely, Homeric floral images of the erotic suggest some degree of reciprocity between the one who gazes and the recipient of the gaze, but this reciprocity also poses a challenge to the subjectivity of the viewer. For these reasons the operations of the gaze in the relevant passages resemble those described by Lacan. Like Lacan's sardine can, the deceptions carried out by erotic bodies in the passages from Homeric poetry that we shall study challenge the subjectivity of viewers and the uniqueness of their perspectives on the scene.

And in fact, viewers' control of the scene is undermined to a greater extent than in the episode described by Lacan: their very agency is called into question. In the Judgement of Paris from the *Cypria*, for instance, Paris looks at Aphrodite's body, decked with flowery robes, and is seduced by her charms and by her offer of the hand of Helen. But when he judges Aphrodite the winner of the beauty contest, he has no sense that he is also choosing the destruction of Troy: in fact, the abduction of Helen will act as the catalyst for the Trojan War.[6] Korē sees a reflection of her own beauty in the narcissus; but she misses its special, divine qualities, which are designed to lead her astray. Unlike Lacan himself, Paris and Korē are overcome at the moment of encountering these objects of their vision—their conscious reflection on the operation of deception comes only later in their respective stories. They are fooled into performing actions that prove detrimental to their own interests: it is not merely that their subjectivity is called into question but that their agency is circumscribed.

---

[6] For Zeus' plan to bring about the Trojan War, cf. *Cypria* fr. 1 Bernabé and Proclus' summary of the *Cypria* at Bernabé 1996:38–39, lines 4–7.

In this way, the floral images of Greek lyric and Homeric poetry not only present contrasting associations of flowers and erotic bodies, but thereby also create a dialogue between two different conceptions of eroticism and the gaze.[7] And these two sets of floral images represent two contrasting engagements with the Greek natural environment. Both the Greek lyric poets and their Homeric counterparts drew on perceptions of the beauty of flowers to conceptualize the attractiveness of desirable youths.[8] In addition, the lyric descriptions of erotic bodies reflect interactions with the natural environment in which flowers are the object of the evaluative gaze of the viewer. Homeric poetry, however, draws on other characteristics of flowers. The Homeric poets focused on the many-colored, shifting surfaces of flowers in the Greek spring, which masked the normally arid appearance of the Greek landscape.

In both cases, through their engagements with the natural environments familiar to early audiences, these poets, in accordance with the analysis of metaphor of Lakoff, Johnson, and Turner, used more concrete concepts to explain more abstract concepts.[9] Specifically, they drew on more concrete concepts associated with flowers in the Greek natural environment to help their audiences to understand more abstract concepts associated with erotic bodies, such as beauty, deception, and seduction. Both the Homeric poets and their lyric counterparts drew on the palette of characteristics presented by the Greek flora to illustrate their particular perspectives on the erotic.

---

[7]   For the presentation of a distinct conception of eroticism in a particular Greek genre, cf. Konstan 1994 on the Greek novel. According to Konstan, Greek novels, as opposed to other kinds of ancient literature, are remarkable for their symmetrical depictions of eroticism, which focus on the relationships between a young man and a young woman. We shall not find such erotic symmetry in images from either of the two genres that we shall discuss in Part I, but the Homeric depictions of challenges to the dominance of the viewer by seductive, deceptive bodies bring us closer to such a phenomenon than the stricter dichotomies of viewer and viewed that are described in the equivalent imagery from Greek lyric.

[8]   It is not, however, immediately obvious which aspects of flowers the Greeks would have found beautiful. While modern westerners tend to think of flowers predominantly in terms of hue, ancient viewers may have responded more readily to other qualities. Irwin (1994), for instance, observes the use of the epithet ῥοδοδάκτυλος/βροδοδάκτυλος ("rosy-fingered") for phenomena as dissimilar in hue as the Dawn (Homeric epic) and the moon (Sappho fr. 96.8 Voigt), and suggests that this adjective, along with the similar term ῥοδόπηχυς ("rosy-armed") evoked not rosy hue but delicacy and fragrance—of flowers, goddesses, and nubile girls. Cf. Irwin 1974, where she argues that in archaic and classical poetry color terms can pick out qualities such as value (i.e., brightness or darkness) or surface sheen. See also Elliger 1975:96–102 on the lack of terms for hue in Homeric poetry.

[9]   Lakoff and Johnson 2003, Lakoff and Turner 1989.

1

Flowers, Subjectivity, and the Gaze
The Erotic Imagery of Greek Lyric

THE IMAGERY OF ARCHAIC GREEK LYRIC offers our most promising comparandum for Homeric treatments of flowers and erotic bodies; accordingly, I would like to consider relevant images from the lyric corpus before turning to the Homeric images that will form the focus of my study.[1] The bodies decked with flowers in Greek lyric tend to be objectified by the gaze of the speaker, like the female bodies subjected to the desiring gaze in Laura Mulvey's analysis of film.[2] They are subject moreover to the speaker's judgement—much as one might experience flowers in the natural environment and judge them to be beautiful. And such dynamics are operative not only in the floral images of male lyric poets, but also in the equivalent images from the poems of Sappho.

I would like to start by considering the works of some male lyric poets, which given the gender dynamics in play offer the clearest parallels for the analysis of film in Mulvey's article and thereby give us the clearest indication of the relevance of her ideas to the depiction of the gaze in archaic Greek lyric. Poets such as Ibycus and Anacreon cast erotic bodies adorned with flowers—whether those

---

[1]   As stated in my Introduction, I treat archaic Greek lyric and Homeric poetry as contemporaneous performance traditions, however it is that the texts from those traditions came to be written down. See Nagy 1974 and 1990 on Greek lyric; 1996:29–63 and 2004 on Homeric poetry. As a further consequence of the great frequency of floral images of the erotic in Greek lyric, if we are to treat even a representative sample of such images we must consider evidence from that genre at somewhat greater length than in the case of the examples from Hesiodic and elegiac poetry that I consider in Parts II and III.

[2]   Mulvey 1989b. Calame (2016) points to later lyric poems that suggest something more like the Lacanian conception of the gaze. In Pindar fr. 123 Snell-Maehler, from the classical period, the beloved looks back at the speaker and the speaker describes the effect that the boy's gaze has on him. An element of the speaker's visual field, then, looks back at him and thus objectifies him; we might compare the sardine tin that returns Lacan's gaze.

of girls or boys—as the objects of the evaluative gaze of the speaker, which, in the absence of indications to the contrary, we would understand to be a male persona adopted by the male poet. Therefore, although the gender of the objectified beloved varies, the gaze in each case is gendered masculine, as with the filmic gaze described by Mulvey. For instance, the speaker in Ibycus fr. 282C(i) Campbell describes a boy (παιδ]ίσκον) who is reared, decked in flowers, and blessed with beauty by the goddess Grace:[3]

>   ὦ Χά-
> ρις, ῥόδων ἔ]θρεψας αὐτὸν ἐν κάλυξιν
> Ἀφροδίτας] ἀμφὶ ναόν·
> στέφαν]ον εὐώδη με δεῖ
> 10   λέγην, ὅσω]ν ἔχρ[ι]σε θωπά-
> ζοισα παιδ]ίσκον· τέρεν δὲ
> κάλλος ὠ]πάσαν θεαί.

Ibycus fr. 282C(i) Campbell Vol. III, lines 6–12

>   O Grace,
> You [r]aised him in [rose]-cups
> Around the temple [of Aphrodite];
> I must [speak] of his fragrant
> 10   Garla]nd, [from how man]y things
> In fla[ttery] she ano[i]nted the boy; goddesses
> [En]dowed him with tender [beauty].

If David Campbell's reconstruction is correct, the speaker imagines an erotic space—a grove holy to Aphrodite—and places the boy within it. Both the boy and the grove, then, are perceived through the mind's eye—the imaginative gaze—of the speaker. Allusions to flowers, moreover, associate the different objects of the speaker's gaze with one another: flower-cups surround the temple and the child, and the boy himself wears a garland, presumably made

---

3   For similar themes, see Ibycus fr. 288 Campbell, where Euryalus is described as the stock of the Graces, reared by Aphrodite and Persuasion amid roses. In this poem, however, the involvement of the Olympian goddess Aphrodite in the boy's rearing (as opposed to Grace, a personification of human quality, in Ibycus fr. 282C(i)) threatens to blur the distinction between the speaker as subject and the boy as object: listeners might have wondered whether this powerful deity fostered the boy's beauty in order to manipulate the speaker's desires. For a god's dominance over the speaking subject in archaic Greek lyric see also Sappho 1.1–4 ("Sappho" pleads with Aphrodite not to "conquer [her] spirit") and fr. 47 Voigt (Love shakes the speaker's mind like a wind falling on mountain oaks).

up of flowers.[4] Indeed, the floral elements of the scene appear to complement the beauty (κάλλος) of the boy, which, if we follow Campbell's reconstruction, is the focus of line 12.

The speaker's gaze and judgement establish clear subject and object roles in his relation with the child. And the speaker's perspective on the boy is emphasized by the inclusion of the adjective τέρεν, "tender," which conveys his assessment of the boy's beauty. In addition, the speaker describes the boy's garland as "fragrant" (εὐώδη). And given the close associations between the boy and the flowers in this scene, the speaker's evaluation of the garland suggests at the same time an evaluation of the boy—he is associated with the fine fragrance of the garland. In this way the boy, the garland, and the flowers mentioned in lines 7–8 are all subordinated to the judgement of the speaker. The speaker objectifies the beloved, as one might objectify flowers that one views. By contrast, no mention is made of the boy's perspective on the scene. The speaker, then, claims the sole right to view and to evaluate what he sees, and to that extent dominates the beloved.

The speaker's dominating gaze is, moreover, associated with the masculine gender. We assume that the character of the speaker is a male persona adopted by the male poet Ibycus, and this impression is reinforced shortly after the lines quoted above. The first person intrudes and is associated with the masculine participle ἰαύων: β]αρύνομαι δὲ γυῖα, / [πολλὰ δ' ἀ]γρύπνο[υ]ς ἰαύων / [νύκτας ὁρμ]αίνω φρε[νί ("my limbs are [h]eavy, / and sleeping [w]akef[u]l [nights] / I [pon]der many things in my mi[nd]," 14–16). It would seem, then, that we have something similar to the filmic gaze described by Mulvey: the gaze is gendered as masculine, and through it an adult, male persona exercises dominance over the object of his imagination.[5]

The speaker in Anacreon fr. 1 Leo establishes a similar dominance over the figure that he describes. He depicts a child of beautiful complexion (καλλιπρό[σ] ωπε) who is somehow associated with fields of hyacinth (ὑακιν[θίνας ἀρ]ούρας) haunted by Aphrodite.[6] As with Ibycus' boy, this child is set in a space of the speaker's own imagining. And again, it is likely that early audiences would have understood the speaker to be male. Without further indications we would assume this is a male persona adopted by the male poet Anacreon:

---

4   Cf. Sappho fr. 94 Voigt, discussed below.
5   The term ὁρμαίνω might qualify the notion of the speaker's dominance. The verb can suggest anxiety: see LSJ s.v. ὁρμαίνω I.1: "revolve anxiously in the mind." Therefore, even though the speaker objectifies the beloved through his gaze and his evaluative comments, he might nonetheless be subject to the effects of ἔρως.
6   For discussion of the plants to which the term ὑάκινθος might refer, see Chapter 2 n42 below.

οὐδε...[.]ς . φ . .α . [. . .] . . [
φοβερὰς δ' ἔχεις πρὸς ἄλλωι
φρένας, ὦ καλλιπρό[c]ωπε παίδ[ων.

—

καί σε δοκέει μὲν ἐ[ν δόμοιϲι
5   πυκινῶϲ ἔχουϲα [μήτηρ
ἀτιτάλλειν· c[ὺ δέ . . . .] . . . [. . . .

—

τὰς ὑακιν[θίναc ἀρ]ούρας,
ἵ]να Κύπρις ἐκ λεπάδνων
. . . .]'[.]α[.κ]ατέδηcεν ἵππουc·
  —]

10 . . . . . .] δ' ἐν μέcωι κατῆξας
ὀμάδ]ωι, δι' ἄϲϲα πολλοί
πολ]ιητέων φρένας ἐπτόεαται
  —]
λεωφ]όρε, λεωρόρ' Ἡρο[τ]ίμη

Anacreon fr. 1 Leo

And not ...
You have a timorous mind in the presence
Of another, o fair-fa[c]ed of gir[ls;

—

And [your mother] seems
5   To nurture you, holding you close
A[t home; b[ut] y[ou...

—

The hyacin[thine fi]elds
Whe]re Cypris... from their yoke-straps
. . . . b]ound her horses.
  —]
10 . . . . . .] coming down into the middle
Of the cro]wd, because the minds
Of many [ci]tizens are aflutter
  —]
Public thoroughf]are, public thoroughfare, Hero[t]ima

We are lacking portions of the poem; accordingly, we cannot be certain of the exact implications of each of the surviving details—and I indicate as much with the alternatives that I offer below. Nevertheless, there can be little doubt that the child associated with flowers in lines 1–8 is subject to the judgement of the speaker. That the addressee is subordinate to the speaker is firstly suggested in the opening lines by her inclusion amongst girls or children (παίδων). Moreover, as in Ibycus fr. 282C(i) Campbell, there are indications in this poem of the speaker's assessment of the child. The phrase φοβερὰς ... φρένας ("timorous mind," lines 2–3) suggests either that she appears coy or that she is genuinely fearful. The speaker goes on to mention how things seem to him (δοκέει, 4): namely, that the girl is subject to the solicitous attentions of a second female, probably her mother (4–6).[7] Lines 6–9 appear to locate the girl in the meadows of Aphrodite, goddess of love and eroticism, and thus to associate her with the sphere of the erotic. Such associations carry two possible implications, both of which give a sense of the girl's subordination to the judgement of the speaker. Perhaps he judges her to be attractive despite her bashfulness (her "timorous mind"): she is the object of his erotic desire. Alternatively, he may suggest the girl's active involvement in erotic encounters: on this second reading, the bashfulness of the opening lines was only for show.[8]

If the Herotima referred to at the end of the poem is the same person as this child, then lines 9–13 would reinforce the impression of the addressee's subordination to the poet's persona.[9] The dominance of the speaker becomes

---

[7] Gentili 1958:44 and 181; Campbell 1982–1993 Vol. II, pp. 40–41. If Campbell is right in restoring the words c[ὺ δέ in line 6, these words might have introduced a reference to the girl's thoughts and intentions: e.g., "you yearn for ... hyacinthine fields." But a more neutral phrase such as "you wander [the fields]" is just as possible.

[8] If we follow Rosenmeyer (2004:173–177), the descriptions of horses and a hyacinthine meadow reflect a masculine perspective on Herotima and on the question of her innocence. She argues that from a Greek male perspective such as that of the speaker the girl's presence in hyacinthine fields and among horses would probably carry suggestions of sexual availability that would undercut the timidity ascribed to her in the opening lines. She distinguishes between the perspective of the male speaker, who sees such dalliance as unambiguous erotic display, and the perspective of the girl herself, for whom it represents the first explorations of a youthful, innocent eroticism. For suggestions of sexual availability here, see Gentili 1958:182–194, who associates the "hyacinthine fields" of Anacreon's poem with Aphrodite and specifically (p. 184) with her portrayal in *Cypria* fr. 4 Bernabé, where, as we shall see (Chapter 2 below), the goddess dons clothes dipped in hyacinth, crocus, narcissus, and rose.

[9] For the identification of Herotima with the child of line 3, see Gentili 1958:180–194, Serrao 1968, Kurke 1999:191–195, and Leo 2015:33–48. Not all critics have accepted this identification. Some scholars, taking into account the apparent contrast between the tone of the opening lines and that of the closing lines, have divided this poem into two separate compositions. Campbell (1982–1993 Vol. II p. 41), for instance, translates ὦ καλλιπρό[c]ωπε παίδ[ων (line 3) as "you lovely-faced boy," and suggests that the reference to Herotima in line 13 opens a new poem. Apart from the change in tone, however, there is no clear indication that we are dealing with two separate youths. And there are positive reasons for regarding the poem as a unity. For one thing, the different components of the poem can, in fact, be reconciled with one another if we suppose that it depicts different stages in a life story, or contrasts (bashful) appearance with (coy) reality:

particularly clear in line 13: he scornfully dismisses Herotima as λεωφόρος. The term is otherwise used of public thoroughfares—that is, of places through which many pass.[10] Probably, we are to imagine a prostitute—either the prostitute that the innocent girl Herotima eventually becomes (if her earlier bashfulness was genuine), or that she has been all along (if it was only for show).[11] If Herotima and the child of lines 1–8 are indeed one and the same, we would have a depiction of subject/object relations that recalls Mulvey's description of the dynamics of the gaze still more strikingly than Ibycus' poem: a male speaker claims the right to gaze at a female character and renders her unthreatening to the point that she is the object of his scorn.

We should now see if similar dynamics of the gaze are identifiable also in other lyric poems that associate erotic bodies with flowers. But before we can make such a move there is an important question that we need to address. A large number of the other instances of floral images of the erotic in extant archaic lyric are to be found in the poems of Sappho. But it has been a point of contention among critics to what extent we can treat Sappho's poems no less than those of her male contemporaries as representative of the genre of lyric, particularly when it comes to her explorations of eroticism, gender, and subjectivity.

Several scholars have argued for the uniqueness of Sappho's depiction of eroticism. Lyn Wilson, for instance, regards Sappho as an unparalleled voice of female erotic subjectivity, whose verse could not have been composed by a male poet, while Jane Snyder identifies a specifically lesbian eroticism in Sappho's poetry, which differs from the masculine homoeroticism of her poetic contemporaries.[12] Jack Winkler for his part argues that Sappho's poetry occupies a private register that focuses on women's erotic experience; according to him, her poetry rejects masculine obsessions with domination and submission in

---

see above. For another thing, the minds of the populace, all aflutter in line 12, echo the (apparently?) timorous mind of the girl in line 2. The terms of the debate, with relevant bibliography, are set out by Gentili 1958:180–194 and Leo 2015:33–35.

[10] For the semantics of the term λεωφόρος, see Leo 2015 *ad loc.*, LSJ s.v. and *Iliad* 15.682: λαοφόρον καθ' ὁδόν ("along the public-bearing way"). On the scornful tone of the poem, see Gentili 1958:189 and 191, and Serrao 1968:50.

[11] See Kurke 1999:191–195. For the poem as an account of Herotima's life story, see Serrao 1968. Leo (2015:34–35) objects to this interpretation on the grounds that δοκέει in line 4 is a present-tense verb and so is not likely to refer to Herotima's past. For this reason he concludes that the poem contrasts appearance (Herotima's innocence) with reality (her sexual availability).

[12] Wilson 1996; Snyder 1997, esp. 79–95. For the unparalleled erotic subjectivities of Sappho's poetry, see also Stehle (Stigers) 1981. In his response to Wilson's book, Lardinois (1998) shows that many of the features of Sappho's verse believed by Wilson to be unique are, in fact, paralleled in the work of male lyric poets.

favor of a shared subjectivity.[13] Similarly, Eva Stehle in *Performance and Gender* identifies a phenomenon of "intersubjectivity" in Sappho's poems: her poetry for female addressees encourages different readers to take on different roles, including that of the poet herself, and thereby to imagine themselves as both "desirer and desired." According to Stehle, such depictions of eroticism distinguish Sappho from her male contemporaries in the genre of lyric.[14] In "Sappho's Gaze" Stehle associates a shared subjectivity more specifically with the operations of the gaze—and hence with one of the key themes of my own discussion. Stehle suggests that Sappho's poetry disrupts the sort of normative masculinity of the gaze that is identified by Mulvey, thus encouraging her female listeners to fantasize heterosexual relationships where they enjoy an equality of subjectivity with a male partner.[15]

Other scholars have treated Sappho's inclusion in the genre of lyric as largely unproblematic. Franco Ferrari for instance agrees with Winkler that Sappho's poetry embodies an intense subjectivity; however, he sees this as an indication not of a specifically feminine eroticism, but rather as "no different from what

[13] Winkler 1990:162–187, 1996. For Winkler this aspect of Sappho's verse represents, in particular, a subversion of the concerns of Homeric poetry: she is able to repurpose masculine, martial discourse of the Homeric poems in her own more egalitarian depictions of eroticism. On dialogues between Sappho's poetry and Homeric poetry, see Rissman 1983 and Rosenmeyer 1997. For Sappho's reuse of Homeric poetry in portrayals of a more egalitarian eroticism, see also duBois 1995. On Sappho's subversion of masculine notions of dominance, cf. Skinner 1993, who focuses on the "bilateral and egalitarian" (p. 133) homosexual relationships enabled by challenges to patriarchal social dynamics, both on the part of Sappho and of other female authors. Bowman's (2004) reply to Skinner, however, echoes arguments of critics such as Lardinois and Ferrari (for which see below): she asserts that "female-authored poetry" does not "display ... subjective modes differing appreciably from those of male-authored poetry" (p. 8).

[14] Stehle 1997:262–318, with quotation from p. 302; see also Stehle 2009. This quotation is a comment specifically on fr. 96 Voigt, a poem that will be discussed below. Stehle and other critics have also pointed to Sappho 1.19–24 for evidence of the interchangeability of roles in Sappho. At first sight, Aphrodite appears to be depicting an asymmetrical eroticism: she seems to promise that the object of Sappho's desire "will love" (φιλήϲει, 23), "even if she is not willing" (κωὐκ ἐθέλοιϲα, 24): for suggestions of an asymmetrical relationship in these lines, see duBois 1995:9 and Wilson 1996:25. Stehle (2009:298), Greene (2008:25–29), and Purves (2014:193–194), however, point out that the subject of lines 21–24 is left unspecified and that the verbs there have no grammatical object. These lines might, then, suggest the interchangeability of the two roles—neither partner is marked definitively as the object of pursuit. Ferrari (2017) argues that line 24 should read κωὐκ ἐθέλοιϲαν and that lines 21–24 refer to a later time, when a girl who is currently unwilling to accept Sappho's advances will love another girl, who will herself be unwilling (ἐθέλοιϲαν). If that is the case, the verb φιλήϲει has an object, but lines 21–24 suggest an interchange of roles—of pursuer and pursued—over time.

[15] Stehle 1996. Similar arguments for Sappho's challenge to the masculine dominance of the gaze are offered by de Jean 1987 and Greene 2002. In an article from 2008, however, Greene nuances her arguments for the uniqueness of Sappho's poetry, arguing that she "bring[s] the passions of women into dialogue with male literary tradition" (p. 43).

we encounter in the rest of Greek lyric poetry from the seventh century to the fifth."[16] André Lardinois likens Sappho's lesbian eroticism to the homoeroticism of her male counterparts, describing her as "a kind of female pederast" (which he understands in terms of social practice rather than personal inclination).[17] Likewise Claude Calame identifies similar relationships between the "I" of the poet's persona and the beloved, both in Sappho's poems and in those of her male contemporaries.[18]

Consideration of Sappho's floral images alongside those of her male counterparts gives us the opportunity to lend some, albeit qualified, support to the arguments of critics such as Ferrari, Lardinois, and Calame. This is not, of course, to say that Sappho's other imagery is compatible with that of her male contemporaries: such a conclusion could only be based on a detailed survey of her whole corpus of poetry. But the evidence presented below suggests that if we focus on Sappho's floral imagery of the erotic and on the dynamics of the gaze in the relevant poems, it is legitimate to treat them alongside those of her male counterparts, and that we can therefore use the floral imagery of archaic Greek lyric, including that of Sappho, as a comparandum for the Homeric images that we shall consider in the next chapter. Several of Sappho's poems cast desirable bodies associated with flowers as the objects of the speaker's gaze: to this extent her verse resembles that of poets such as Ibycus and Anacreon when they depict desirable youths. We are reminded of the uni-directional gaze that Mulvey identifies in film or that Elizabeth Sutherland and Ellen Greene find in the work of male lyric poets of the Roman tradition.[19]

We should, however, firstly acknowledge examples of floral imagery from Sappho's verse that appear to cast doubt on arguments for her objectification

---

[16]   Ferrari 2010:13.

[17]   Lardinois 1989, with quotation from p. 18. Elsewhere, Lardinois acknowledges "important differences of tone and subject matter between Sappho and most male poets" (1996:171) and finds that some of Sappho's poems draw on genres otherwise associated with women, such as laments or hymns to goddesses (2001). Nevertheless, he argues for similarities between the performance contexts of Sappho' poems and those of the male lyric poet Alcman (1996).

[18]   Calame 1997:255–258, 1999:23–27, 2016. Calame argues that the beloved, who refuses her/his favors, dominates the lover, who is in the grip of passion: see also n2 above. But the asymmetries of the gaze operate in the opposite direction in the poems that we shall study. For arguments for the similarity of Sappho's verse to that of male lyric poets, see also Boehringer and Chabod 2017; Bowman 2004, cited in n13 above; Parker 1993; Nagy 1990 (esp. p. 94, with n60). Nagy regards Sappho's poetry as one instantiation among several of an archaic lyric song culture. Parker, for his part, argues that placing Sappho in her own peculiar category, even if intended as praise, in fact perpetuates the attribution of normativity and subjectivity to the masculine and subversion or perversity to the feminine—she is treated not as a poet but a female poet, as if that were necessarily a different kind of thing. In fact, Parker contends, Sappho's poetry is fully representative of the typical concerns and performance contexts of the (predominantly male) genre of lyric.

[19]   Sutherland 2003, Greene 2010: see the Preamble to Part I.

of the desirable girls associated with such images. Critics have, for instance, found evidence of reciprocal relationships in Sappho fr. 2 Voigt. Winkler and Stehle both adduce this poem as evidence for their view that Sappho's poetry expresses a uniquely feminine eroticism, which eschews the masculine rhetoric of domination and submission. In the opening lines, the speaker—presumably representing Sappho's own persona in this poem—invites Aphrodite to a sacred place (ναῦον / ἄγνον, fr. 2.1-2 Voigt) and goes on to describe a grove of roses and apple-trees sacred to that goddess:

5   ἐν δ' ὕδωρ ψῦχρο⌊ν⌋ ⎢ κελάδει δι' ὕϲδων
       μαλίνων, ⎢ βρόδοιϲι δὲ παῖϲ ὁ χῶροϲ
       ἐϲκί⎢αϲτ', αἰθυϲϲομένων δὲ φύλλων ⎢
          κῶμα †καταιριον·

       ἐν δὲ λείμων ⎢ ἱππόβοτοϲ τέθαλε
10   †τωτ...(.)ιριν ⎢νοιϲ† ἄνθεϲιν...

                                Sappho fr. 2.5–10 Voigt

5   In it cool water resounds through the apple
       Boughs, and the whole place is shaded
       With roses, and there is deep ... sleep
          As leaves quiver;

       In it a horse-trodden meadow blooms
10   ... with spring(?) flowers...

Stehle offers fr. 2 as an example of how "description" in Sappho's poetry "is often very sensuous and very unspecific," and believes that the emphasis on senses other than sight in the poem helps to break down the distinction between viewing subject and viewed object.[20] According to Winkler, the fragment depicts a feminine eroticism that is explored in the worship of the goddess: "Virtually every word suggests a sensuous ecstasy in the service of Kyprian Aphrodite (apples, roses, quivering followed by repose, meadow for grazing, spring flowers, honey, nectar, flowing)." Sappho is guiding her audience towards an experience that is at once sacred and sexual: she "is providing a way to experience [cultic] ceremonies, to infuse the celebrants' participation with memories of lesbian sexuality."[21] Wilson distinguishes the poem from a fragment of lyric by a male

---

[20] Stehle 1996:220.
[21] Winkler 1990:186 = 1996:108. Cf. Stehle (Stigers) 1977:92–93, who reads the grove as an image of the adolescent anticipation of sexual experience: it is "a haven of that threshold state of unconsummated erotic eagerness."

poet, Ibycus fr. 286 Campbell. That fragment describes an untouched garden (κῆπος ἀκήρατος) of the Maidens, only to contrast it with the violent assaults of love, which are likened to stormwinds and lightning. Wilson reads this image as an evocation of a masculine eroticism of "violence and disorder," creating "binary oppositions" that are absent from Sappho's poem, which focuses instead on feminine experiences of the erotic and the divine.[22] On these readings, then, images of roses and other flowers in Sappho fr. 2 evoke a shared, feminine eroticism, through which all might experience subjectivity.

There is, however, an important reason to hesitate before identifying a reciprocal eroticism in this poem: there are no references in the surviving lines to a group of women who might share such an experience. The first-person speaker may have been an explicit presence in this poem. If David Campbell's reconstruction is correct, the opening lines introduce this speaker, with the pronoun μ(οι), "to/for me." But nowhere in the extant lines of the poem do we hear of female companions who share this space with her. We cannot, then, be sure that erotic relationships between mortals are being depicted; nor, *a fortiori*, that the poet's persona here attributes a shared subjectivity to such relationships and does not exercise dominance over their perspectives. All that can be said for certain is that the speaker calls Aphrodite to a flowery grove (lines 13–16). If we stick to the details of this particular poem, then, we can only infer that a space sacred to the goddess is being described.[23]

We could also consider fr. 96 Voigt, which has been cited by Snyder and Stehle as a depiction of a reciprocal relationship. Atthis' girlfriend stands out among the women of Lydia as the rosy-fingered moon outshines the stars; its light spreads over fields of roses, chervil, and melilot in flower. We might imagine that Atthis' beloved causes less attractive girls around her to bloom in borrowed radiance, just as the flowers in the fields bloom under the moonlight. In this way, the poem suggests the beauty shared by the moon and the girl, or perhaps their common hue and delicacy:[24]

---

[22] Wilson 1996:39–42, with quotations from p. 39. On the unity of religious and erotic experience in this and other fragments of Sappho, see McEvilley 2008:50–64, esp. 63–64.

[23] Quite possibly, we should imagine a cultic setting for performances of the poem. As Ferrari (2010:151–154) notes, Aphrodite was often worshiped in groves and gardens; see also Elliger 1975:179. But if multiple worshipers attended such a performance, this does not imply that other women besides the speaker are present in the scene described in the poem: perhaps the speaker pictures herself as the only worshiper. Cf. Lardinois 1996: poems of Sappho focused on a single speaker's emotions might be performed in public settings.

[24] Cf. Irwin 1994, who sees βροδοδάκτυλος in this poem as a reference to delicacy, and Waern 1999, who believes that it describes a rosy hue.

νῦν δὲ Λύδαιϲιν ἐμπρέπεται γυναί-
   κεϲϲιν ὤϲ ποτ' ἀελίω
      δύντοϲ ἀ βροδοδάκτυλοϲ <ϲελάννα>
πάντα περ<ρ>έχοιϲ' ἄϲτρα· φάοϲ δ' ἐπί-
10   ϲχει θάλαϲϲαν ἐπ' ἀλμύραν
      ἴϲωϲ καὶ πολυανθέμοιϲ ἀρούραιϲ·
ἀ δ' <ἐ>έρϲα κάλα κέχυται, τεθά-
   λαιϲι δὲ βρόδα κἄπαλ' ἄν-
      θρυϲκα καὶ μελίλωτοϲ ἀνθεμώδηϲ·

Sappho fr. 96.6–14 Voigt

Now she stands out among the Lydian women
   As the rosy-fingered <moon>,
      When once the sun has set,
Out<s>hining all the stars; it sends its light
10   Equally over the salt sea
      And to the many-flowered fields;
The lovely <d>ew is poured out, and roses flourish
   And tender chervil
      And blooming melilot.

These lines evoke not only the beauty of Atthis' girlfriend, but also the erotic bond shared by the two girls. According to Snyder the allusions to roses, the moon, tenderness (κἄπαλ', 13), and dew (<ἐ>έρϲα, 12) combine to suggest a "female sexuality."[25] On this sort of reading, the two girls would express that sexuality in their attraction for one another. Moreover, the focus on the moon may suggest a reciprocity of longing, experienced by Atthis and the absent girl: one can imagine both girls gazing up at it as they yearn for each other, lying alone at night.[26]

There is evidence, then, of a reciprocal relationship between Atthis and her girlfriend—perhaps an example of the sort of "intersubjectivity" described by Stehle.[27] Nevertheless, it is not clear to what extent the girls' own perspectives dominate these lines. True, the poem does not emphasize the perspective of the poet (or, more strictly, of her persona): there are no first-person singular

---

[25] Snyder 1997:49–52; quotation from p. 51. For associations of dew with femininity, see θῆλυς ἐέρϲη ("the female dew") at *Odyssey* 5.467.

[26] For this interpretation, see Hague 1984:30 with bibliography (though this is a position from which Hague distances herself).

[27] See Stehle's own reading of the poem (1997:300–302).

statements in what survives of the composition. But it does, in fact, introduce first-person plural verbs and pronouns—ὤομεν ("we ... ," line 3), ἄμμ- ("us," 18); perhaps also α ̣μι ("us[?]," 21). Given the fragmentary nature of the text, it is impossible to be sure, but the speakers may have focalized the scene described in lines 6–14. If so, the scene and the girls within it would be the objects of the speakers' imaginative gaze; what is more, the adjectives "lovely" (κάλα, 12) and "tender" (ἄπαλα, 13) would reflect the speakers' evaluation of the scene and of the girls within it. To that extent, the speakers would establish dominance over the pair. In this fragment, then, we detect an erotic reciprocity between Atthis and her beloved within the scene; but at the same time those girls no less than the rest of the scene may be the objects of the speakers' imaginative gaze.

The speaker's point of view dominates more clearly in poems where both the poet's persona and a female companion of the poet are present. As we shall see, the female viewer in these poems establishes a relationship with the desirable girl similar to that of Anacreon's or Ibycus' personae with the objects of their gaze. These poems of Sappho suggest an asymmetrical dynamic, not so much through the actions described as through an emphasis on the perspective of the poet. Although the gazing subject is female, the description of the gaze in these scenes resembles the unequal dynamics that Mulvey identifies in film.[28]

In fr. 94, for instance, Sappho's persona recalls how a girl, standing next to her, wreathed her tender neck with garlands of violets and roses:

> πό[λλοιc γὰρ cτεφάν]οιc ἴων
> καὶ βρ[όδων ...]κίων τ' ὔμοι
> κα.. [– 7 –]πὰρ' ἔμοι π<ε>ρεθήκα<ο>
> 15 καὶ πό|λλαιc ὐπα ̱θύμιδαc
> πλέκ|ταιc ἀμφ' ἀ ̱πάλαι δέραι
> ἀνθέων ἐ[– 6 –] πεποημέναιc ...
>
> Sappho fr. 94.12–17 Voigt

> Fo[r with many wrea]ths of violets
> And of r[oses], and equally of ...
> ... you g<a>rlande<d> yourself by me

---

[28] We might infer that such a gendering of the gaze offers a challenge to the patriarchal gender structures of archaic Greek societies in which—as in the films discussed by Mulvey—men would normally claim the right to view and evaluate the objects of their vision: cf. Mulvey 1989a on the ability of female viewers to appropriate the male gaze when watching films. Nevertheless, it is also possible that archaic Greek poems emphasizing a woman's gaze and hence her subjectivity would not have this kind of socially subversive effect in an archaic Greek context. As Lardinois (2001:80) points out, it may be that female self-expression was limited to particular contexts sanctioned by the patriarchal culture at large (such as laments or songs for goddesses), and Sappho's poetry may reflect such contexts.

15 And with many plaits of a nosegay
Made ... of flowers
Around your tender neck ...

The poem opens with expressions of anguish: in the first line, the first-person speaker, or perhaps the girl with whom she is speaking, recalls the pain of their parting and expresses the wish to die (τεθνάκην δ' ἀδόλωc θέλω); the girl then stresses how terribly they have both suffered, and explains that she leaves "Sappho" against her will (4–5; the girl addresses Sappho by name in line 5). In the lines quoted above, evocations of garlands, ointments, and a soft bed suggest a relationship of physical eroticism between these two speakers. With such evidence in mind, Winkler argues that these lines depict "a loving progression of intimacy, moving in space—down along the body—and in time—to increasing sexual closeness: from flowers wreathed on the head to flowers wound around the neck to stroking the body with oil to soft bedclothes and the full satisfaction of desire."[29]

However, these suggestions of a shared eroticism exist in tension with the dynamics of the gaze in the poem. The scene is focalized through the eyes of the first-person speaker: these lines present the scene as it appeared to "Sappho"—that is, to the persona of the poet in this poem. The relationship of seeing subject and seen object, then, resembles that found in the poems of Ibycus and Anacreon studied above. What is more, as in Ibycus fr. 282C(i) the first-person speaker's evaluation of the object of desire is suggested through the use of an adjective: from her perspective the girl's neck is tender, ἀⲓπάλαι, much as Ibycus' speaker admired the "tender [beauty]" (τέρεν ... [κάλλοc]) of the boy. The gaze in this poem is, then, uni-directional like the filmic gaze explored by Mulvey.

In other fragments asymmetrical relationships are described without any suggestion of a shared eroticism. For instance, in fr. 132 the lovely Cleis is said to have a beauty like golden flowers:

Ἔcτι μοι κάλα πάιc χρυcίοιcιν ἀνθέμοιcιν
ἐμφέρη<ν> ἔχοιcα μόρφαν Κλέιc < > ἀγαπάτα,
ἀντὶ τᾶc ἐγωὐδὲ Λυδίαν παῖcαν οὐδ᾽ ἐράνναν ...

Sappho fr. 132.1–3 Voigt

I have a beautiful girl, with form lik<e>
Golden flowers, Cleis,
In return for whom I ... not ... all lovely Lydia ...

---

29 Winkler 1990:186 = 1996:107. Stehle 1996:220 cites fr. 94 among Sappho's "description[s]" that are "both very sensuous and very unspecific."

The girl in this poem may well be Sappho's own daughter.[30] But even if this is the case, her relationship to the poet's persona closely resembles that of the poet and beloved in other erotic lyric from archaic Greece. Firstly, as in such poetry, the description focuses on the visual and attributes the gaze to the first-person speaker. These lines emphasize Cleis' beauty rather than, for instance, her laughter or her skill at dancing, and as in fr. 96 the poet has evoked visual features of the natural environment to give her audiences a sense of this beauty.[31] Much as flowers in the natural environment would at other times have been the passive objects of Sappho's or her listeners' vision, the girl is merely the object of the speaker's gaze. Secondly, as in other archaic lyric the first-person speaker claims the license to evaluate such an object of the gaze. While the adjective ἀγαπάτα, "beloved" or "desirable,"[32] possesses positive connotations, it nonetheless reflects the speaker's perspective and not that of the girl, who is thus the object both of Sappho's gaze and of her evaluative comments. Thirdly, in addition to being objectified in this way, Cleis is described as a πάις. This term is reserved for children and slaves in wider Greek culture, but is often used for the object of desire in lyric, as we have seen in both Ibycus' and Anacreon's poems.[33]

Fr. 122 Voigt likewise casts a girl as the object of Sappho's gaze, and again she is referred to as a πάις. In Athenaeus' citation of the fragment (12.554b), the poet is said explicitly to have *seen* the girl gathering flowers: Cαπφώ φησιν ἰδεῖν ἄνθε᾽ ἀμέργοισαν παῖδ᾽ ἄγαν ἀπάλαν. Presumably, then, the tenderness of the girl was focalized through the persona of the poet in the version of the poem known to Athenaeus. The girl is evaluated from Sappho's perspective, and the focus is on her body rather than the flowers that she is gathering. The key phrase is ἄγαν ἀπάλαν: "*too* tender." Sappho judges not only that the girl is physically attractive (ἀπάλαν), but also that she is, for some reason, *too* attractive.[34]

---

[30] Two *testimonia* (1 and 2 Campbell) inform us that Sappho had a child by the name of Cleis.

[31] The simile may have suggested to them landscapes with which they were familiar: as Waern points out (1999:174), Lesbos is bathed in golden flowers each spring.

[32] LSJ s.v. II.1 and 2.

[33] Ibycus fr. 282C(i).11 Campbell (παιδ[ίσκον); Anacreon fr. 1.3 Leo (ὦ καλλιπρό[c]ωπε παίδ[ων). See also Ferrari 2010:33–37 on παῖδες in Sappho. For the connotations of the Greek term παῖς more generally, see LSJ s.v. I–II (children), III (slaves): the term refers to a subordinate with respect to descent, age, or social class.

[34] Cf. Stehle (Stigers) 1977:93: she is "too inviting to be doing something as exposed as picking flowers." Athenaeus adduces Sappho fr. 122 alongside the myth of Korē to show that flower-gathering is a natural activity for those who believe themselves to be attractive. We cannot be certain that Sappho shares Athenaeus' assessment of the scene in fr. 122—that the girl was advertising her own attractiveness; we know only that the poet herself judges her to be attractive. Perhaps she is too attractive for an onlooker to resist, or perhaps her attractiveness threatens to expose her to the sort of dangers associated with flowery meadows in poems such as the *Hymn to Demeter*, which we shall discuss in the next chapter. Nevertheless, there is a contrast to be

We have found, then, similarities between Sappho's floral images of the erotic and those of her male contemporaries. At least in those poems where Sappho's persona is a clear presence, the desirable girl is the object of the viewer's gaze, much like the desirable youths in the poems of Ibycus and Anacreon.[35] Moreover, in the work of all these poets the beloved is the object of the speaker's evaluation, much as audiences would themselves have viewed flowers in the natural environment and judged them to be beautiful or fragrant. The unequal dynamics of the gaze resemble those described by Mulvey, but the gender relations depicted in these poems do not accord with Mulvey's observations: the desiring viewer dominates the desired, whatever the gender of the two parties. In these compositions, inequality inheres in the nature of the erotic gaze, rather than in the power relations between the two genders.

---

drawn between the handling of the association of flowers and erotic bodies in this fragment and in Homeric poems, such as the *Hymn*. As we shall see, Korē claims a kind of agency through the apparently autoerotic act of plucking a flower that is her own double; but we have no evidence of such agency on the part of Sappho's girl.

[35] The "new" (as opposed to "newest") Sappho offers an interesting inversion of such tropes. The narrator's own ageing body becomes the object of her imaginative gaze. It contrasts not only with the bodies of the "violet-bosomed Muses" (Μοίσαν ἰ]οκ[ό]λπων, line 1) but also, by implication, with the bodies of the young girls who are associated with the goddesses. Similarly, the ageing body of Tithonus in the last four lines contrasts with that of "rosy-armed Dawn" (βροδόπαχυν Αὔων, 9). On the gaze and on the dynamics of youth and age in this poem, see Bierl 2016. For a text of the "new" Sappho, West 2005:6.

2

Fantasizing the Narcissus, Gilding the Hyacinth

Flowers, Seduction, and Deception in Homeric Poetry

HAVING STUDIED FLORAL IMAGES OF THE EROTIC that were developed by the archaic lyric poets, we turn now to the equivalent Homeric images. By comparing these two genres we can set in relief the particular choices made by the Homeric poets in their development of such imagery. As we have seen, in Greek lyric the gaze of the poet's persona objectifies erotic bodies associated with flowers, in a manner similar to the uni-directional filmic gaze described by Laura Mulvey. But the Homeric associations of flowers and erotic bodies suggest rather different dynamics of viewing, more reminiscent of Jacques Lacan's account of the gaze.[1]

The Homeric images that we shall study hail from very different contexts in the Homeric corpus; nevertheless they share certain basic characteristics. In all of the scenes that we shall consider, flowers are associated with erotic bodies that are in some way seductive and deceptive. Unlike their equivalents in Greek lyric, these erotic bodies both exercise an erotic attraction over the viewer and at the same time mislead her/him (cf. Latin *sē-ducere*). They conceal their true nature and/or hide dangers from the viewer; such concealments, moreover, further the aims of a third party.

In two of the relevant scenes, the deception of the viewer places her/him in peril but at the same time furthers the plans of Zeus. The narcissus in the *Hymn to Demeter* doubles the body of the "flower-faced" Korē. But she fails to notice that it is an artificially enhanced plant designed to rouse her autoerotic desires. She is, moreover, unaware of the dangers associated with the plant: in fact, her plucking of it will precipitate her abduction by Hades. This, in turn, is in accordance with the will of Zeus, who wishes to provide his brother with a bride.

---

[1] Mulvey 1989b, Lacan 1977.

In the *Cypria*, Paris, seduced by Aphrodite and her flowery robes, declares her the winner in a beauty contest. But he is unaware that in choosing her and in accepting her offer of Helen, he will provide the catalyst for the Trojan War and thereby ensure the destruction of his own city, Troy. And again, while this represents a calamity for the viewer, the fall of Troy will further the plans of Zeus.

In the scenes that we shall discuss from the *Odyssey*, the viewer is deceived but not placed in danger. As with Korē in the *Hymn to Demeter*, Nausicaa and Penelope in *Odyssey* 6 and 23 are misled by enhancements to the object of their gaze: they fail to notice Athena's improvements to Odysseus' appearance, which include the "hyacinthine" hair of a younger man, more in keeping with their desires. Unlike Korē or Paris, neither Penelope nor Nausicaa are endangered by this deception: this is, then, the visual equivalent of a white lie. But even so, both become the unwitting instruments of Athena's plans: firstly the goddess uses Nausicaa to win a homecoming for Odysseus, and later she helps bring about his reunion with Penelope.

In this way, the erotic bodies associated with flowers in the relevant scenes influence the viewer in a manner unparalleled by the erotic bodies associated with flowers in the lyric poems that we have discussed. And unlike Mulvey's filmic viewers or the speaker in the poems of Ibycus, Anacreon, and Sappho discussed in Chapter 1, the viewer is not able to achieve complete dominance over them.

Rather, as with Lacan's description of viewing, these objects of the gaze undermine the viewer's control of the scene. As mentioned in the Preamble to Part I, Lacan recalls an experience on a Breton fishing boat that helped to draw his attention to his own lack of control over the contents of his visual field. The feeling that a glinting sardine tin was looking back at him reminded him that his was not the only perspective on the scene: those things that he had been treating simply as the objects of his vision might in fact be viewing and evaluating him. And he goes on to generalize this experience to all acts of viewing: the viewer is always subject to the gaze and evaluation of those things that he himself views.[2] Similarly, the deceptive qualities of the erotic bodies that we shall study below suggest the incompleteness of the viewer's knowledge and the inadequacy of the her/his assessment of the scene. Korē, Paris and Penelope gaze on the objects of their desire, but they misunderstand their true significance. As in Lacan's Breton tale, the contents of these characters' visual fields offer a challenge to the centrality and dominance of their perspectives.

---

[2]   Lacan 1977:95–96.

The Exaggerated Charms of the Narcissus: The Deception of Korē in the *Hymn to Demeter*

Our first example of Homeric associations of flowers with seductive, deceptive bodies is offered by the *Homeric Hymn to Demeter*. The opening lines of the hymn depict the girl Korē picking flowers with her companions, the daughters of Oceanus. But all is not as it seems in this meadow. The goddess Gaia has, in fact, sent up one particular flower as a trick (δόλος) for Korē. This plant, the narcissus, exhibits miraculous qualities: it possesses a hundred heads and a scent that fills heaven, earth, and the sea. The "flower-faced" (καλυκῶπις) Korē is captivated by it; she reaches out eagerly to pluck it. But as soon as she does so, the earth gapes wide; the god of the dead, Hades, rushes up from the lower world and seizes her, apparently to be his bride. For Zeus, so we are told, had granted him the girl.

Earlier studies have drawn our attention to the erotic aspects of this scene. A review of such scholarship in light of the details presented by the hymn will help us to appreciate the nature of the eroticism being described: Korē's desire is best explained as an autoerotic attraction towards the narcissus, which is described as her double. Yet in order to understand why the narcissus qualifies as a δόλος, a trick, we need also to consider its relationship with flowers in the natural environments familiar to early audiences. Though Korē fails to realize this, the narcissus is an exaggerated version of such a plant. It possesses special qualities that rouse her desires and lure her to the flower. Moreover, unbeknownst to Korē this attractive flower conceals dangers behind it: by plucking it, she facilitates her abduction by the lord of the dead. In this way, as with the Lacanian account of the gaze, elements of Korē's visual field—namely, the deceptive qualities of the narcissus—undermine the dominance of her perspective on the scene.

Several scholars have identified erotic dimensions in Korē's and her companions' activities, but they have offered contrasting viewpoints on the nature of the eroticism being described. In what follows I consider three readings of the hymn that, when taken together, encompass the full range of such viewpoints. According to the first reading, Korē's innocent play falls victim to Hades' heteroerotic exploitation; the second scholar argues that Korē and her companions experience homoerotic desire for one another; the third contends that Korē herself expresses an autoerotic desire. Even if it is surprising from a modern perspective, this last explanation best accounts for the details of the hymn.

Firstly, Patricia Rosenmeyer distinguishes between two different perspectives on expressions of eroticism in poems such as the *Hymn to Demeter* that describe girls playing in flowery meadows: these expressions are interpreted in one way by the girls themselves and in quite another by male characters, male poets, and/or male audience members. Rosenmeyer regards the flowery meadows of the hymn and of other Greek poems as "a place of awakening sexual awareness," but not as settings for the mature expression of adult desire. As in other poems with comparable imagery, the hymn describes the actions of the girls as "play": the narrator refers to Korē as "playing" (παίζουσαν, 5), and as Korē recalls the scene in conversation with her mother, she remembers that "we were playing" (παίζομεν, 425). Such "play" "is ... both innocent and suggestive, meaning different things to different people"—that is, to the girls themselves, on the one hand, and to adult male poets and listeners, on the other.[3]

Susan Deacy likewise distinguishes between the heteroerotic desire of the male intruder, Hades, and the desires of the girls. She points out that there is no evidence that the erotic desire expressed by the girls in the hymn is a desire for heterosexual experiences; we are told only that they desire the meadows themselves.[4] And Korē and her companions not only desire the flowers but are specifically likened to the flowers that they pluck. Early in the hymn the narrator identifies Korē as the "flower-faced girl" (καλυκώπιδι κούρη, 8) at the moment she plucks the narcissus. In this way, the narcissus is portrayed as her double. Likewise, in her own description of the scene later in the poem, Korē gives her companions floral names and epithets. These girls, Ῥοδεία (419), Ῥοδόπη (422), and Ὠκυρόη καλυκῶπις (420), are like the flowers—the ῥόδεας κάλυκας ("rose-cups," 427)—of the meadow on which they are standing. Deacy interprets the girls' picking of these flowers, their own doubles, as expressions of their desire for one another—their homosocial "play" shades into homoeroticism.[5] She argues that Korē's desires can be interpreted in a similar fashion. As she points out, the external narrator's focus on Korē's eagerness to pluck

---

[3] Rosenmeyer 2004, with quotations from pp. 176 and 177. On the innocence of Korē's desire see also Arthur (Katz) (1994:237): Korē's/Persephone's eagerness to pluck the flower, together with her acceptance of a pomegranate seed later in the hymn (lines 371–374) suggest a "youthful naiveté," which is easily exploited by the dangers posed by Hades: "Persephone's easy seduction by these symbols indicates her greater susceptibility to the dangers and pleasures of sexuality with the male." For the distinctions between male and female perspectives on the action of the hymn, cf. DeBloois 1997, who points out that female characters such as Demeter see the abduction of Korē as a rape or as a kind of death, but Zeus and Hades regard it as a marriage. For the associations of the abduction of Korē with death, see Chapter 9 and the discussion of Stehle's argument below.

[4] Deacy 2013; to quote her analysis of depictions of Europa's abduction by Zeus in poetry and visual art, Europa's "desire ... is for the sexualised meadow rather than for the Zeus-bull who intrudes into that sensuous space" (p. 401). For the story of Europa, see also n18 below.

[5] What Deacy describes, then, is something akin to the eroticized groves, the havens of mutual female eroticism, that Winkler (1996) finds in Sappho's poetry. See Chapter 1 for discussion of flowers and eroticism in Sappho, and of Winkler's analysis thereof.

the narcissus contrasts with Korē's own description of the scene, in which she dwells at length on her many companions and on the many flowers of the meadow (*Hymn to Demeter* 417–430). Deacy believes that Korē's speech offers a more accurate insight into her desires than the words of the narrator. According to Deacy, Korē's speech suggests that she feels desire for the flowers and for her companions in general, rather than for the narcissus in particular.

Eva Stehle arrives at a rather different understanding of Korē's desires. She interprets the desire of the "flower-faced" Korē for the narcissus, her own double, as an expression of a youthful autoeroticism. But rather than being valorized as innocent play, this eroticism is cast in a negative light: it is portrayed as a narcissistic and sterile desire, which fittingly ends in a kind of death—in her abduction by the lord of the Underworld.[6] I would hesitate before associating Korē's desires with sterility: most importantly, it does not seem to be the case that she desires anything like the near-death that she experiences at Hades' hands.[7] Like Deacy, then, I would distinguish between Korē's desires and Hades'. Nevertheless there are reasons to recommend Stehle's autoerotic reading of Korē's actions over Deacy's homoerotic reading.

In particular, Korē's description of her own actions can readily be reconciled with that of the narrator, whose juxtaposition of the narcissus and the "flower-faced girl" has suggested an autoerotic desire. Firstly, Korē's juxtaposition of the ῥόδεας κάλυκας ("rose-cups," 427) with the names Ῥοδεία (419), Ῥοδόπη (422), and Ὠκυρόη καλυκῶπις (420) would be consistent with Deacy's idea that the girls are assimilated to the meadow in general and that their attraction to the flowers suggests a homoerotic desire for one another. But it would also accord with Stehle's reading of eroticism in the hymn: perhaps we should infer that each girl is assimilated to a particular flower in the meadow and that her desire for that flower is suggestive of autoeroticism.

Secondly, while both the narrator and Korē mention the many flowers of the meadow in their accounts of the abduction, each focuses ultimately on the narcissus (lines 8–16, 428–429) and on Korē's eagerness as she plucks it: according to the narrator, Korē seizes it "with both hands" (15); in her own words, she plucked it "for joy" (περὶ χάρματι, 429). Like the narrator, then, Korē foregrounds her desire for one particular flower, rather than for the flowers of the meadow in general. Even though the narrator's and Korē's accounts diverge in other respects (see below), her speech is consistent with the

---

[6] Stehle (Stigers) 1977, esp. 94–96. For other interpretations of the erotic dimensions of Korē's actions, see Lincoln 1981:71–90, Arthur (Katz) 1994, Calame 1999:154–155, and Suter 2002:40–41 and 54–56. Like Stehle, Suter identifies autoerotic dimensions in the scene: "Persephone finds herself desirable and wants to possess herself in the flower" (p. 55).

[7] For Korē's near-death in the hymn, see also Chapter 9 below and n3 above.

narrator's autoerotic interpretation of the scene and leaves that intepretation unchallenged.

Stehle, then, gives the most promising account of the erotic aspects of this scene, and her reading will help us in our understanding of the operations of seduction and deception in the hymn. But as mentioned above, to gain a full appreciation of the workings of such themes, we need also to compare the narcissus—this "trick" sent up by Gaia—with flowers in the Greek natural environment. As we shall see, the flower's divergence from the natural characteristics of narcissi opens up space for different perspectives on the plant: Rosenmeyer and Deacy are right, then, to point to the existence of different viewpoints on the action of the hymn. Most importantly, Korē's perspective would have differed from that of early audiences. Korē, mistakenly, accepts the narcissus as a regular element of the natural environment. But listeners would have understood that its attractive qualities far exceed those of narcissi in the real world.[8] And it is these special qualities that lure her to pluck the flower and thereby to expose herself to danger.

The narrator makes the unusual qualities of the narcissus clear when s/he first describes the flower. The wonderful bloom and scent of the plant far surpass those of real narcissi. A hundred flowers grow from the one root; they possess a scent that causes all heaven, the earth, and the sea to rejoice:

> νάρκισσόν θ᾽, ὃν φῦσε δόλον καλυκώπιδι κούρῃ
> Γαῖα Διὸς βουλῇσι, χαριζομένη πολυδέκτῃ
> 10 θαυμαστὸν γανόωντα, σέβας τότε πᾶσιν ἰδέσθαι
> ἀθανάτοις τε θεοῖς ἠδὲ θνητοῖς ἀνθρώποις·
> τοῦ καὶ ἀπὸ ῥίζης ἑκατὸν κάρα ἐξεπεφύκει,
> κῶζ᾽ ἥδιστ᾽ ὀδμή, πᾶς δ᾽ οὐρανὸς εὐρὺς ὕπερθε
> γαῖά τε πᾶσ᾽ ἐγέλασσε καὶ ἁλμυρὸν οἶδμα θαλάσσης.

Hymn to Demeter 8–14

> ... and a narcissus, which, as a trick for the flower-faced girl,
> Gaia sent up, by the counsels of Zeus, as a favor to the Lord-of-
>   Many
> 10 wonderful, shining, an object of awe then
>   for all the immortal gods and mortal men to see,
>   and from its roots a hundred heads had grown,

---

[8] Elliger (1975:160–161) is possibly the only other critic to have noted the contrast between flowers in the Greek natural environment and the representation of the narcissus in the hymn. He observes that the "Steigerung der Blütenpracht" (p. 161; cf. *Hymn to Demeter* 10–11) of the plant elicits a heightened response on the part of viewers, both mortal and immortal.

and the sweetest smell arose, and all the wide heaven above,
and all the earth, and the salt swell of the sea laughed.

As Josef Murr suggests, the Homeric poets here may have had in mind the *Narcissus tazetta*, a Greek plant "of intoxicating scent with a luxurious inflorescence of golden flowers."[9] But even if this is right, the Homeric poets have nevertheless manipulated the characteristics of such a plant. The inflorescence of the species is indeed "luxurious," but no specimen from the natural world would have anything close to a hundred heads: clusters of three to eighteen are the norm.[10] Another possibility is the many-headed *Narcissus papyraceus*; this species, however, boasts a maximum of twenty flower-heads.[11] In either case, then, the abundant blooms of the plant would represent a clear exaggeration of anything that would be found in the Greek natural environment. Likewise, despite its "intoxicating scent," no real narcissus would possess such a powerful fragrance as to fill the whole earth, heaven, and the sea.

Details in the narrative would have encouraged audiences to trace the plant's preternatural qualities to divine origins—to view it as a special creation that could only grow by the gods' dispensation. It is said to have grown "in accordance with the plans of Zeus" (Διὸς βουλῆσι, line 9). We learn of these plans in lines 2–3: Zeus intends to give Korē, presumably as a bride, to his brother Hades. For the first stage of his scheme, he employs the goddess Gaia—not merely "the earth" but the personified "Earth"—to send up the narcissus. The divinely inspired plant evokes a sense of religious awe: it is an object of reverence (σέβας) and wonder (θαυμαστόν), and gives off a divine radiance (γανόωντα), all qualities that would have suggested the presence of divinity to early audiences.[12] But Korē herself does not pick up on these clues. The very characteristics that would have alerted listeners to the divinity of the plant overwhelm her senses. Wondering at (θαμβήσασ', 15) the wondrous plant (θαυμαστόν, 10), she seizes it.

In her report of her abduction towards the end of the hymn, she still shows no awareness of the plant's divine origins:

---

9   Murr 1969:248: "von betäubendem Wohlgeruche mit einer üppigen Dolde gelblicher Blüten." On the scent of the *Narcissus tazetta*, see Huxley and Taylor 1977:153: the flowers are "very fragrant."

10 Huxley and Taylor 1977:153 and Polunin 1980:502. See Plate 4 for an example of such a plant.

11 Polunin 1980:502. My own study of specimens of the genus *Narcissus* at the Herbarium of the Royal Botanical Gardens, Kew suggests that examples with more than nine heads are rare: of the 917 specimens that I surveyed (the majority of the Kew collection), only fourteen had more than nine heads; none had more than fifteen. For further discussion of the many-headedness of Korē's narcissus, see Chapter 9.

12 For the divine connotations of θαῦμα, see Prier 1989:84–97. Motte (1971:35), commenting on the *Hymn to Demeter*, notes that an encounter with a θαυμαστός object evoked the sorts of emotions that the Greeks experienced in the face of the sacred. The term γάνος conveys "une intuition de la nature scintillante et magicienne ..." (Motte 1971:431; cf. Jeanmaire 1939:436).

425   πάιζομεν ἠδ’ ἄνθεα δρέπομεν χείρεσσ’ ἐρόεντα,
      μίγδα κρόκον τ’ ἀγανὸν καὶ ἀγαλλίδας ἠδ’ ὑάκινθον
      καὶ ῥόδεας κάλυκας καὶ λείρια, θαῦμα ἰδέσθαι,
      νάρκισσόν θ’ ὃν ἔφυσ’ ὥς περ κρόκον εὐρεῖα χθών.
      αὐτὰρ ἐγὼ δρεπόμην περὶ χάρματι, γαῖα δ’ ἔνερθε
430   χώρησεν, τῇ δ’ ἔκθορ’ ἄναξ κρατερὸς πολυδέγμων.

Hymn to Demeter 425–430

425   We were playing and plucking lovely flowers with our hands,
      Mixedly, gentle saffron, irises, hyacinth,
      Rose-cups, and lilies, a wonder to behold,
      And a narcissus, which the wide earth sent up like saffron.
      And I plucked it for joy, and the earth opened beneath,
430   And there the mighty lord who welcomes many leapt out.

As noted above, both Korē and the narrator focus on the narcissus and on Korē's eagerness in plucking it. But there are also differences in the ways in which they describe the flower, and these contrasts reveal her ignorance of the plant's divine origins. The narrator in lines 8–10 attributes the growth of the flower to a willful goddess, Gaia, who sends it up in accordance with Zeus' plan and in order to please Hades: νάρκισσόν θ’, ὃν φῦσε δόλον καλυκώπιδι κούρῃ / Γαῖα Διὸς βουλῇσι χαριζομένη πολυδέκτῃ / θαυμαστὸν γανόωντα ("a narcissus, which, as a trick for the flower-faced girl, / Gaia [Earth] sent up, by the counsels of Zeus, as a favor to the Lord-of-Many, / wonderful, shining ..."). Korē likewise describes the earth sending up the narcissus:[13] νάρκισσόν θ’ ὃν ἔφυσ’ ὥς περ κρόκον εὐρεῖα χθών ("a narcissus, which the wide earth sent up like saffron," 428). But there is no indication that she has in mind the goddess Earth, since unlike the narrator she makes no reference to any divinity's intentions.[14]

What is more, while the narrator suggests the divine qualities of the flower, there is no indication that Korē perceives them. The narrator makes clear that the narcissus, in particular, is θαυμαστὸν γανόωντα, σέβας τότε πᾶσιν ἰδέσθαι ("wondrous, shining, an object of awe then for all ...") and, through the echo of the related roots θαυμ- and θαμβ- in lines 10 and 15, implies that the wondrousness of the narcissus directly causes Korē's eager reaction. As noted above, the root θαυμ- would have alerted audiences to the divine origins and

---

[13]   For the implications of the use of φύω in this passage, see chapter 6 below.

[14]   Moreover, in describing the emergence of the narcissus Korē employs the lexeme χθών rather than Γαῖα/γαῖα, the regular term for the goddess Earth in early hexameter; cf. *Theogony* 159–166 (Earth enlists the help of her children against Heaven); 493–495 (Earth deceives Cronus); 821 (Earth sends up Typhoeus). For parallels between the birth of Typhoeus and the growth of the narcissus, see Chapter 9 below.

characteristics of the flower. Korē for her part focuses on the narcissus and remembers her own eagerness in plucking it—she seized it περὶ χάρματι ("for joy," 429). She acknowledges, then, her particular attraction to the flower. But her words in lines 425–428 suggest that she does not see it as a divine growth beside the natural growths of the rest of the meadow. For Korē all the flowers of the meadow are a θαῦμα ἰδέσθαι, "a wonder to behold" (427); and she notices neither the particular wondrousness of the narcissus nor its divine characteristics. Moreover, by likening the narcissus to saffron in line 428 (ὥς περ κρόκον "like saffron") she assimilates it to the first flower that she lists (κρόκον, 426)—that is, to one of the regular flowers of the meadow.[15]

There is a contrast, then, between the narrator's and Korē's perspectives on the narcissus. And we should remember this contrast when we analyze the operations of erotic desire in the hymn. As noted above, the narrator at line 8 describes the narcissus as a double of Korē, who is called "flower-faced" (καλυκῶπις) in the same line. As Stehle points out, the narrator's description of Korē's eagerness to pluck this double of herself suggests an autoerotic desire: she is attracted to the narcissus as a reflection of her own charms. Korē's own account, as we have seen, is consistent with this idea of autoerotic attraction: she focuses on the narcissus and remembers her eagerness in plucking it. But early audiences would have known from the narrator's description that this is a specially enhanced flower. Gaia has endowed it with additional charms that heighten Korē's desires and increase its attractions for her. Given that Korē is unaware of these special qualities, her interaction with the narcissus constitutes at once an autoerotic seduction and a deception.

There is more to be said, however, about the way in which the narcissus qualifies as a δόλος, a trick. Korē is unaware of the preternatural qualities of the plant; but she is also unaware of the dangers to which she is exposed by its attractions. These dangers are revealed at the moment she plucks the flower. Both the narrator and Korē make clear that her plucking the narcissus creates an opening through which Hades is able to rush up from the Underworld and abduct her:

> ἡ δ' ἄρα θαμβήσασ' ὠρέξατο χερσὶν ἄμ' ἄμφω
> καλὸν ἄθυρμα λαβεῖν· χάνε δὲ χθὼν εὐρυάγυια
> Νύσιον ἄμ' πεδίον τῇ ὄρουσεν ἄναξ πολυδέγμων...

Hymn to Demeter 15–17

---

[15] Cf. *Hymn to Demeter* 177–178: the narrator likens the hair of the daughters of Celeus to the saffron flower (χαῖται ... κροκηΐῳ ἄνθει ὁμοῖαι). Their hair has not been enhanced by the gods; Korē's description of the narcissus as "like saffron" likewise suggests a regular flower. By contrast, as we shall see the hyacinthine hair of Odysseus in *Odyssey* 6 and 23 is the result of divine intervention.

> Wondering at it she reached for it with both hands
> To seize the lovely toy; the earth of the wide ways gaped
> Along the Nysian Plain where the lord who welcomes many rose up
>
> ...

αὐτὰρ ἐγὼ δρεπόμην περὶ χάρματι, γαῖα δ' ἔνερθε
χώρησεν, τῇ δ' ἔκθορ' ἄναξ κρατερὸς πολυδέγμων.

Hymn to Demeter 429–430

> But I was plucking it for joy, and the earth opened
> Beneath, and there the mighty lord who welcomes many leapt up.

It is unclear whether Hades views Korē's expression of autoerotic desire as an excuse for his violent, heteroerotic action, or indeed whether the kind of dynamics described by Rosenmeyer are operative here—namely, that Hades interprets Korē's action as a kind of erotic invitation. But it is certainly the case that Korē's eager plucking of the flower, her own double, precipitates the abduction by opening up a pathway between the upper and lower worlds.[16] What appears to be an act of autoerotic desire on Korē's part exposes her to the exploitative, heteroerotic intentions of a male character: the consequences of the abduction are, at best, a forced marriage and, at worst, a rape.[17] By juxtaposing Hades' action with her unwillingness in line 19 (ἁρπάξας ἀέκουσαν, "snatching one who was unwilling"), the narrator makes clear that Korē would not have chosen such a consummation of her desires.

If we bear in mind all the elements of the scene that we have noted thus far—Korē's eagerness to pluck the flower; Hades' abduction of the unwilling Korē; the divine characteristics of the narcissus; and Korē's lack of awareness of her flower's divine characteristics—the full operations of seduction and deception in this episode of the hymn become clear. Korē is lured into an expression of autoerotic desire by the enhanced characteristics of the flower; but she would have been more cautious had she known the dreadful consequences of her action. And she is not granted the consummation of her desires but rather suffers an altogether different mode of sexual experience (violent, heteroerotic). In this way, audiences of the hymn would have received a dark and exploitative vision of the art of seduction.[18]

---

[16] For the narcissus as a path between worlds, see Chapter 4 below.

[17] On the tale of the hymn as a rape, cf. Lincoln 1981:78, DeBloois 1997, and Deacy 2013.

[18] A fragment of Hesiodic poetry offers a partial parallel for this Homeric scene. In fr. 140 MW, from the *Catalogue of Women*, Zeus spies Europa gathering flowers and is struck with desire for her. With the intention of seducing her, he transforms himself into a bull and breathes on her with saffron breath (κρόκον ἔπνει). Having thus deceived her, he is able to mount her (ἀπατήσας

Aphrodite's Flowery Accoutrements:
The Deception of Paris in the *Cypria*

As we have seen, the seductive, deceptive narcissus doubles the body of Korē: its special qualities heighten her autoerotic desires. In the other examples of Homeric imagery that we shall discuss, flowers are associated more directly with bodies that are in some way seductive and deceptive. One of the relevant passages derives from an episode early in the *Cypria*, in which Aphrodite prepares for the Judgement of Paris. The Graces and Seasons deck her body in clothes dipped in flowers:

> εἵματα μὲν χροῒ ἕστο, τά οἱ Χάριτές τε καὶ Ὧραι
> ποίησαν καὶ ἔβαψαν ἐν ἄνθεσιν εἰαρινοῖσι,
> οἷα φέρουσ' ὧραι, ἔν τε κρόκωι ἔν θ' ὑακίνθωι
> ἔν τε ἴωι θαλέθοντι ῥόδου τ' ἐνὶ ἄνθεϊ καλῶι
> 5   ἡδέι νεκταρέωι, ἔν τ' ἀμβροσίαις καλύκεσσιν
> αἰθέσι ναρκίσσου καλλιπνόου· ὣδ' Ἀφροδίτη
> ὥραις παντοίαις τεθυωμένα εἵματα ἕστο.

Cypria fr. 4 Bernabé

> Her flesh was clothed with clothes that the Graces and Seasons
> Made for her and dipped in spring flowers
> Such as the seasons bear, in saffron and hyacinth
> And flourishing violet, and the beautiful, sweet, nectared
> 5   Flower of the rose, and the shining, ambrosial
> Cups of the beautifully scented narcissus; thus Aphrodite was clothed
> With robes perfumed with every kind of season.

The adornments described in this passage play an important role in the seduction of Paris: their charms help persuade him to choose Aphrodite in her beauty contest with Hera and Athena. Paris however is unaware of the dangers that lie behind such a choice. He believes that he is simply identifying the most beautiful goddess and taking as his reward the hand of Helen. But in fact, his choice furthers the plans of Zeus. As we learn from *Cypria* fr. 1 and Proclus' summary of the poem, Zeus has hatched a plan to bring about the Trojan War and thereby to reduce the earth's population.[19] And this plan is put into effect immediately

---

ἐβάστασε). Quotations of Hesiodic poetry are from West 1966, 1978, and Merkelbach and West 1967. For the story of Europa, see also n4 above.

[19]   Proclus at Bernabé 1996:38–39 lines 4–7. See also the D-scholium to *Iliad* 1.5 (van Thiel 2000 p. 5, lines 8–13 of the scholium).

after Paris makes his choice. Listeners would have recognized that, in choosing Aphrodite, Paris unwittingly opts for the destruction of his own city.

The fragment quoted above, then, describes Aphrodite's preparations for a crucial moment in the Trojan Cycle; even so, it has been largely neglected by critics.[20] Jasper Griffin, one of the few critics to engage closely with it, discusses it only to disparage its style relative to passages of the Homeric hymns and major epics: these lines are a "conscious attempt to compose in a richly ornamental manner," reflected both in a careless use of epithets and in an over-expansive catalogue of flowers. He finds such stylistic inadequacies to be typical of the Epic Cycle as opposed to the Homeric hymns and major epics.[21]

Yet these lines do not deserve to be dismissed in this fashion. The description of flowers in *Cypria* fr. 4 would not be out of place in other Homeric poems: in fact, it resembles a Homeric flower catalogue that we have already encountered—the list of flowers at the opening of the *Hymn to Demeter*. What is more, rather than constituting empty verbiage, the epithets used would have helped audiences to imagine the impact of Aphrodite's accoutrements on Paris and thereby to understand the workings of seduction in this scene.

The rose, the crocus, the hyacinth, and the violet, listed in *Cypria* fr. 4, are also found in the description of the flowers that Korē and her companions are picking at *Hymn to Demeter* 6–7.[22] Both passages present a rich catalogue of the sorts of flowers that early audiences would have witnessed in the Greek natural environment. From these catalogues listeners would have gained a sense of the charms of the meadow in the *Hymn to Demeter* and of Aphrodite's accoutrements in our lines from the *Cypria*.[23] On this evidence, we would not be justified in excluding *Cypria* fr. 4 from the canon of Homeric poetry simply because it presents an extensive list of flowers.

Furthermore, the epithets employed in this passage serve a positive function: they suggest the sensual qualities of the flowers in which Aphrodite's robes are dipped and, by extension, the effect that her appearance will have on Paris. In lines 4–5, for instance, we proceed from an allusion to the visual

---

[20] Where *Cypria* fr. 4 Bernabé is mentioned, it tends to be adduced as a comparandum for other, better known and better loved passages within or beyond the Homeric corpus, which likewise associate flowers and the erotic; see Faulkner 2008:20n62, Scheid and Svenbro 1996:57–58, Janko 1994 on *Iliad* 14.172–174, Maggiuli 1989:187.

[21] Griffin 1977:50–51.

[22] The crocus and hyacinth are also paired at *Iliad* 14.348 and at *Hymn to Pan* 25 (see Chapter 4 and 5 below, respectively).

[23] For the close relationship of *Cypria* fr. 4 Bernabé with other passages of Homeric poetry, see Bernabé 1996 ad loc., West 2013:75–76, and Sammons 2017:185–186. West stresses the conventionality of the diction of these lines. For instance, he notes parallels between the flowers mentioned in this fragment of the *Cypria* and those described in two of the passages that I discuss elsewhere in Part I: the opening of the *Hymn to Demeter* (above) and the Διὸς ἀπάτη (Chapter 4 below).

effect of the rose (καλῷ, "beautiful") to descriptions of its scent (ἡδέι, "sweet"; νεκταρέωι, "nectared").[24] The adjective ἀμβροσίαις, which describes the cups of the narcissus in line 5, may likewise evoke their scent:[25] after all, the related noun, ἀμβροσίη, refers to sweet-smelling ointments. At *Odyssey* 4.445–446, for instance, it is the sweet-scented unguent that enables Menelaus and his men to block out the stench of Proteus' seals.[26] If we follow Bernabé's reconstruction, in line 6 further emphasis is placed on the visual qualities of the narcissus-cups with the adjective αἴθεσι, "shining." Finally, the descriptions of Aphrodite's clothes as τεθυωμένα ("perfumed") and, again if Bernabé's text is correct, of the narcissus itself as καλλιπνόου ("beautifully blowing/scented") echo the earlier references to sweet scents.[27]

These epithets, through their cumulative effect, suggest the impact that Aphrodite's appearance will have on Paris. Her clothes take on the scents of these flowers and thereby enhance the charms of Aphrodite's own body. And owing to the close association between the flowers, the clothes, and the goddess in these lines, the allusions to the beauty of the rose and the narcissus would have encouraged listeners to imagine the beauty of the clothes and of the goddess herself. Audiences would moreover have understood that these flowery robes help persuade Paris to choose Aphrodite in the contest between her, Hera, and Athena.[28] After all, they would have familiar with other episodes from Homeric poetry, such as the Διὸς ἀπάτη in *Iliad* 14, where goddesses don special clothing in order to seduce male characters.[29] As with those scenes, the sensuous experience offered by Aphrodite's body, decked with flowery robes, and the victory that it affords her in the beauty contest amount to a seduction.[30]

But in choosing Aphrodite, Paris is also the victim of a deception.[31] As we have seen, in plucking the narcissus, Korē unwittingly exposes herself to

---

[24] For ἡδύς as a reference to scent in Homeric poetry, cf. *Odyssey* 4.446, 9.210, and 12.369.

[25] The adjective ἀμβρόσιος frequently describes divine garments in Homeric poetry, including as here the robes of Aphrodite (*Iliad* 5.338). For other such descriptions of divine clothing, see *Iliad* 14.178, 21.507, 24.341, *Odyssey* 1.97, 5.45.

[26] The term ἀμβροσίη also refers to the unguent with which Hera anoints herself in preparation for the Διὸς ἀπάτη (14.170); on Hera's preparations for the Διὸς ἀπάτη, see also Chapter 3 below. For ἀμβροσίη as an ointment, cf. 16.670 and 680, where Apollo anoints the body of Sarpedon.

[27] See Bernabé 1996 ad loc. on the different attempts to emend the reading καλλιρρόου that is preserved in our manuscripts.

[28] As with the narcissus in the *Hymn to Demeter*, the divine origins of the flowers in these lines suggest that they will have a greater impact on the senses than flowers of the same names from the Greek natural environment. The narcissus is created specially by the goddess Gaia; here, the divine Graces and Seasons prepare Aphrodite's robes.

[29] For the Διὸς ἀπάτη, see Chapter 3 below.

[30] For the Judgement of Paris as a seduction scene, see Currie 2016:154 and Sammons 2017:186.

[31] A similar scene from Hesiodic poetry is explicitly marked as a deception: at *Theogony* 589 and *Works and Days* 83, Pandora is described as δόλον αἰπὺν, ἀμήχανον ἀνθρώπων, "a sheer trick,

danger. Similarly, Paris makes his choice unaware of the dangers that lie behind the seductive appearance of Aphrodite's body—dangers that would have been well known to early listeners. We get a sense of such dangers and also of Paris' ignorance of them when we bear in mind the context of this fragment in the *Cypria*. The opening of the poem anticipates the broader scheme of events in which Paris will eventually be caught up: in fr. 1 Bernabé, Zeus plans the Trojan War out of pity for the earth, which was overburdened by its human population. According to the D scholium to *Iliad* 1.5, this plan includes two key elements: the marriage of Thetis with a mortal and the birth of a beautiful daughter:[32] Zeus will father the beautiful Helen, and Thetis will marry the mortal Peleus.

Both events are important prerequisites for the war. As a result of the marriage the pre-eminent hero of the Trojan War, Achilles, will be born. And at the wedding ceremony itself, as we learn from Proclus' summary of the *Cypria*, the goddess Eris stirs up a quarrel between Athena, Hera, and Aphrodite over which of them is most beautiful.[33] The goddesses then repair to Ida to be judged by Paris. Paris chooses Aphrodite, but at the same time he accepts her offer of Zeus' beautiful daughter, Helen. Dual prophecies emphasize the consequences of his choice: Paris' siblings Helenus and Cassandra offer pronouncements περὶ τῶν μελλόντων, "about the things to come." And their predictions are borne out in the ensuing narrative. As a result of Aphrodite's promise, Paris abducts Helen and thus provides the catalyst for war between the Greeks and the Trojans, since Helen happens to be the wife of the Greek king Menelaus.[34]

Therefore, if this evidence is anything to go by, ancient audiences familiar with the *Cypria* would have known that in making the choice of Aphrodite and

---

impossible for mankind." In preparation for the seduction and deception of Epimetheus and of men more generally, the Seasons (*Works and Days* 74–75) wreathe her "with spring flowers" (ἄνθεσιν εἰαρινοῖσιν). The same phrase is used in connection with the Graces and the Seasons at *Cypria* fr. 4.2 Bernabé. If lines 576–577 belong to the *Theogony* (see West 1966 ad loc. for reasons to doubt their authenticity), then Pandora is decked with flowery wreaths in that poem also, this time by Athena. For the resemblances between these accounts of the preparation of Pandora and the Homeric seduction scenes that we are studying in this chapter, see Richardson 1974:38, West 1978 on *Works and Days* 73–75 and 2013:75, Holmberg 1990:74n75. There is also one other Hesiodic scene that offers a partial parallel for these Homeric scenes: see n18 above.

[32] Van Thiel 2000:5, lines 11–12 of the scholium to the words Διὸς δ' ἐτελείετο βουλή.

[33] West 2013:68–70.

[34] Proclus' summary of the *Cypria* at Bernabé 1996:38–40 lines 4–26, with quotation from lines 9–11. Unfortunately his summary is too threadbare for us to be sure quite how Zeus engineers these events in the version(s) of the *Cypria* known to Proclus. If Paris is to choose Helen and thereby provide the catalyst for the war, Eris must provoke the quarrel that leads to the Judgement of Paris, and Aphrodite must make her offer of Helen's hand. But Proclus passes straight from a description of Zeus' plans to an allusion to Eris' presence at the wedding of Peleus and Thetis, without explaining the connection between the two elements of the story (Bernabé 1996:38–39 lines 4–7). Likewise, he fails to explain how Zeus ensures that Aphrodite offers Helen to Paris.

in accepting her offer of Helen Paris will bring about the Trojan War and hence the destruction of his own city. Our surviving fragments of the *Cypria* suggest, however, that he was unaware of any serious consequences at the time of his choice:[35] he simply followed his lusts. We have already observed the powerful effect that Aphrodite's accoutrements would have on him. Paris' desires are further roused by the promise of her mortal double, Helen: προκρίνει τὴν Ἀφροδίτην ἐπαρθεὶς τοῖς Ἑλένης γάμοις: "he chooses Aphrodite, excited by [the prospect of] marriage with Helen."[36] The *Iliad* offers a still blunter assessment of Paris' motives: he made his choice on the basis of the "licentiousness" offered to him by Aphrodite—τὴν δ' ᾔνησ' ἥ οἱ πόρε μαχλοσύνην ἀλεγεινήν ("he praised her who was offering him grievous licentiousness," 24.30).[37]

But the order of events in Proclus' summary suggests that, if Paris discovers the consequences of his choice, he does so only after he has already prepared for his expedition to Sparta to abduct Helen. Spurred on by Aphrodite, Paris fits out his ships for the voyage; Helenus then reveals what is to come: "then at Aphrodite's suggestion he constructs ships, and Helenus prophesies to them about the coming events" (ἔπειτα δὲ Ἀφροδίτης ὑποθεμένης ναυπηγεῖται, καὶ Ἕλενος περὶ τῶν μελλόντων αὐτοῖς προθεσπίζει).[38] Helenus apparently addresses the Trojans in general (cf. αὐτοῖς); if this is so, Paris would probably be among those who hear the prophecy.

We have seen, then, that like the narcissus in the *Hymn to Demeter* Aphrodite's body in *Cypria* fr. 4 is associated with an erotic deception. As in the hymn, flowers are associated with enhanced appearances that arouse the desires of the viewer; as in the hymn, the viewer is mistaken as to what s/he is, in fact, choosing. And like the narcissus in the *Hymn to Demeter*, Aphrodite's erotic appearance, enhanced by her preparations in *Cypria* fr. 4, both hides dangers behind it and lures Paris towards those dangers. In both poems, the Homeric poets made

---

[35] Aphrodite may also be the unwitting instrument of Zeus' plans in this episode, as she is in her *Homeric Hymn*: see Sammons 2017:188. For Aphrodite's ignorance in the hymn, see also Chapter 3 n13 below.

[36] Proclus' summary of the *Cypria* at Bernabé 1996:39 line 8. On Helen as a double for Aphrodite, see Brillet-Dubois 2011:110 on this passage of the *Cypria*, and Clader 1976:53–54, Stehle 1996:196, and Brillet-Dubois 2001:258–259 on Homeric poetry in general.

[37] The adjective ἀλεγεινήν, "grievous," suggests the dire consequences of Paris' lusts, both for himself and for the Trojans in general: see Richardson 1993 ad loc.

[38] Bernabé 1996:39 lines 9–10. The architect Harmonides, who built the ships for Paris, was likewise unaware of the consequences of his actions—both for the Trojans and for himself: "he fashioned the equal ships for Alexander, / the beginnings of evil, which became an evil thing for the Trojans / and for himself, since he knew nothing of the pronouncements from the gods" (Ἀλεξάνδρῳ τεκτήνατο νῆας ἐΐσας / ἀρχεκάκους, αἳ πᾶσι κακὸν Τρώεσσι γένοντο / οἷ τ' αὐτῷ, ἐπεὶ οὔ τι θεῶν ἐκ θέσφατα ᾔδη, *Iliad* 5.62–64). The ships are mentioned in connection with Harmonides' personal tragedy: he loses his son Phereclus in the war (59–68).

such perils clear to their audiences through references to the plans of Zeus and then by a description of the events that follow from the seduction of an unwary youth: Korē plucks the narcissus and is abducted by Hades; Paris accepts Aphrodite's offer of Helen, and her abduction brings about the Trojan War. But the *Cypria*, by including Helenus' and Cassandra's prophecies of things to come, places still greater emphasis on the connection between a youth's choice and its unpleasant consequences.

Odysseus' Hyacinthine Hair: Erotic Encounters with Nausicaa and Penelope

While Aphrodite's preparations for the Judgement of Paris occur near the beginning of the Trojan cycle, the last two images that we shall consider are found towards the end of the stories of Troy. In both cases the goddess Athena grants her favorite, Odysseus, hyacinthine hair, and in both cases the relevant images carry associations with seduction and deception. Odysseus' hyacinthine hair seduces Nausicaa in Book 6 and Penelope in Book 23 by presenting them with an image of the sort of man each desires: Nausicaa sees the sort of young man that she hopes to marry; Penelope sees an image of Odysseus as he was when he left for Troy.

Athena prepares for the seduction and deception of Nausicaa from the moment of Odysseus' arrival in the girl's homeland, Scheria. Firstly, she appears to Nausicaa in a dream to suggest an expedition to the washing-places, on the grounds that she is now of an age to marry and should wash her clothes in preparation (25–40). This is already an act of deception. Athena does not intend to provide Nausicaa with a suitable match; rather, she plans to use her good graces to gain Odysseus entrance to the Phaeacian court and thereby to win him a passage home: Athena is "plotting a return journey for great-hearted Odysseus" (νόστον Ὀδυσσῆϊ μεγαλήτορι μητιόωσα, 14). Spurred on by the dream, but suspecting nothing of Athena's intentions, Nausicaa appeals to her father king Alcinous for the use of a carriage. Yet she is unwilling to admit to him that she has thoughts of marriage: she pretends instead that she is concerned for her unmarried brothers, who need fine clothes to attend dances, presumably with a view to their own marriages (57–65). Alcinous, however, understands Nausicaa's true wishes and grants her the carriage (66–67).[39] Athena thus succeeds in sending Nausicaa off to a remote place with thoughts of marriage in her mind; and it is there that she will meet Odysseus.

---

[39] "Thus she spoke; for she felt ashamed to mention her flourishing marriage / to her dear father; but he understood everything and answered authoritatively" ("Ὣς ἔφατ᾽· αἴδετο γὰρ θαλερὸν γάμον ἐξονομῆναι / πατρὶ φίλῳ· ὁ δὲ πάντα νόει καὶ ἀμείβετο μύθῳ· 6.66–67).

When, a little later, Nausicaa encounters Odysseus, his appearance is far from appealing: he emerges from the undergrowth caked with salt and clutching only a branch to cover his nakedness (127–129, 137).[40] Nevertheless, Athena must ensure that Nausicaa thinks of him as a potential husband if she is to help this stranger to reach the Phaeacian city. Accordingly, when he retires to refresh himself Athena enhances his appearance: she makes him taller and broader to look at, pours grace on his head and shoulders, and sends down locks from his head, like the flower of the hyacinth:

> τὸν μὲν Ἀθηναίη θῆκεν Διὸς ἐκγεγυῖα,
> 230 μείζονά τ' εἰσιδέειν καὶ πάσσονα, κἀδ' δὲ κάρητος
> οὔλας ἧκε κόμας, ὑακινθίνῳ ἄνθει ὁμοίας.
> ὡς δ' ὅτε τις χρυσὸν περιχεύεται ἀργύρῳ ἀνὴρ
> ἴδρις, ὃν Ἥφαιστος δέδαεν καὶ Παλλὰς Ἀθήνη
> τέχνην παντοίην, χαρίεντα δὲ ἔργα τελείει,
> 235 ὣς ἄρα τῷ κατέχευε χάριν κεφαλῇ τε καὶ ὤμοις.

Odyssey 6.229–235

> But Athena daughter of Zeus made him
> 230 Taller and broader to look at; and from his head
> She sent down curly locks, like the flower of the hyacinth.
> As when some man pours gold around silver,
> A skilled man, whom Hephaestus and Pallas Athena have
>   taught
> Every kind of craft—he achieves graceful works—
> 235 So she poured grace on his head and shoulders.

---

[40] Athena's subsequent actions prepare the ground for the seduction of Nausicaa. But they also correct expectations of a more disturbing encounter that are created by the description of Odysseus' emergence from the undergrowth. At that stage of the story the girls, like Korē and her companions in the *Hymn to Demeter*, are "playing" (*Hymn to Demeter* 5, 425; *Odyssey* 6.100) in a space far from human civilization (for the erotic connotations of such "play," see Rosenmeyer 2004 and the discussion above). The simile at *Odyssey* 6.130–134 compares Odysseus as he goes amongst the girls with a hungry lion attacking sheep. If Odysseus is hungry like this lion, then the following lines suggest that we should understand his hunger in erotic terms. The verb μίσγομαι (literally, "mingle"), which is frequently used of sexual intercourse in Homeric poetry, describes him as he prepares to go among the girls: ὣς Ὀδυσεὺς κούρῃσιν ἐϋπλοκάμοισιν ἔμελλε / μίξεσθαι, γυμνός περ ἐών ... ("thus Odysseus was about to mingle with the lovely-haired maidens, naked though he was ..." 6.135–136). The suggestion is that, like Hades in the *Hymn to Demeter*, Odysseus will threaten the girls with sexual violence. For the sexual connotations of μίσγομαι in this scene, see Ahl and Roisman 1996:51–52, Felson 1997:47, Glenn 1998:111–114; see also more generally LSJ s.v. μείγνυμι B.4, Snell 1955–2010 s.v. μίσγω I.2d, and specific instances from the Homeric poems, such as *Iliad* 2.232, *Odyssey* 1.73, and *Hymn to Aphrodite* 39. For the use of μίσγομαι later in Book 6, see n44 below.

This image suggests both the seductive and the deceptive qualities of Odysseus' appearance. But in order to see this, we need to take a careful look at the details of these lines. Firstly, the phrase "curly locks, like the flower of the hyacinth" (οὔλας ... κόμας, ὑακινθίνῳ ἄνθει ὁμοίας, 230–231) suggests an attractive young man, as opposed to the middle-aged, careworn Odysseus. The image of curly hair pouring down from Odysseus' head evokes the long hair of a Greek ephebe—that is, of a youth at the first moment of sexual maturity.[41]

The reference to the hyacinth would presumably have helped audiences to imagine Odysseus' youthful hair. According to the Byzantine commentator Eustathius (on *Odyssey* 6.230–231), the adjective ὑακίνθινος would have suggested either a dark coloration or curliness. And though Eustathius presents them as alternatives, both senses are possible here. If the term ὑάκινθος put audiences in mind of the *Hyacinthus orientalis*, which is native to the eastern Mediterranean, then the phrase ὑακινθίνῳ ἄνθει would have evoked a flower with dark, curly petals.[42] The notion of dark coloration is moreover supported by Sappho fr. 105b.2 Voigt, which refers to the "dark-red" flower (πόρφυρον ἄνθος) of the hyacinth.[43] And an evocation of curly petals is clearly consistent with the description of Odysseus' curly locks at 6.231.

These observations help us to understand how the image interacts with the erotic aspects of this scene. Odysseus has been granted the appearance of an attractive young man ready for marriage—precisely the sort of man that Nausicaa hopes to meet. In Book 6, then, Athena firstly puts Nausicaa in mind of a husband and then rouses her desires by presenting her with the sort of husband she might like.

[41] See Irwin 1990, Levaniouk 2011:67–68. In addition, if Anacreon fr. 1 Leo is anything to go by, the hyacinth may have had more general associations with eroticism: as we saw in Chapter 1, the poem associates "hyacinthine fields" (ὑακιν[θίνας ἀρ]ούρας, line 7) both with Aphrodite and with the attractive girl Herotima.

[42] Given that *H. orientalis* was not originally found in the Greek mainland, scholars have suggested other possibilities for the ancient Greek ὑάκινθος, including plants of the genera *Scilla*, *Delphinium*, *Iris*, and *Gladiolus*: cf. Irwin 1990n51, with bibliography. Nevertheless, it is perfectly possible that at *Odyssey* 6.231 and Sappho 105b.2 Voigt the term refers to the *H. orientalis*. Since it is native to the eastern Mediterranean (cf. Polunin 1980:496), it would have grown in areas of Asia Minor familiar to early audiences of Homeric and Sapphic verse. See also Amigues 1992, who identifies the ὑάκινθος at *Odyssey* 6.231 as *H. orientalis* and suggests that this plant was introduced to Greece as a whole at an early date.

[43] Moreover, when Athena gives Odysseus the appearance of a younger man at 16.172–176, a dark beard (κυάνεαι ... γενειάδες, 176) grows on his chin. As Irwin (1990) points out, such a description contrasts with the reference to the middle-aged Odysseus' blond hair at 13.431, which Athena "made him lose" (ὄλεσε) in order to create his beggar disguise. But perhaps, as Eustathius (on *Odyssey* 6.230–231) suggests, we should infer that Odysseus' hair became lighter with age. If that is the case, the three guises of Odysseus that we shall study below are distinguished by three different looks for his hair: the dark, flowing hair of the ephebe, the blond hair of the middle-aged man, and the patchy hair of the old beggar.

And the erotic charms that Athena has instilled into Odysseus work their effect immediately. Nausicaa wonders at (θηεῖτο, 237) Odysseus and his hyacinthine hair. Unlike Korē in her interaction with the narcissus, Nausicaa is alive to the possible presence of divinity: she tells her companions that the previously uncouth stranger now seems to her like the gods (242–243). Nevertheless his charms work their effect on her, in the manner that Athena has planned. She expresses a wish that Odysseus—or someone like him—should be her husband: αἲ γὰρ ἐμοὶ τοιόσδε πόσις κεκλημένος εἴη / ἐνθάδε ναιετάων, καί οἱ ἅδοι αὐτόθι μίμνειν ("I wish such a man might be called my husband, / dwelling here, and that it should please him to remain here," 244–245). A little later (276–284), she again betrays her desires. She tells Odysseus what might happen if they were to enter the city together: the Phaeacians might gossip and say that they are destined to be married.[44]

We have seen, then, that the suggestions of an attractive young man conveyed by the image of hyacinthine hair are fully in keeping with Nausicaa's reaction to Odysseus' new guise: the young girl is attracted to Odysseus as a potential husband. As with our passages from the *Hymn to Demeter* and the *Cypria*, then, flowers are here associated with the theme of seduction. The deceptive qualities of Odysseus' appearance are emphasized by other elements of the image from 6.229–235. Specifically, the allusions to metallurgy in the simile introduce the concepts of artistry, precious value, and concealment. A smith, taught by Athena and Hephaestus, pours gold around silver, much as Athena pours grace on the head and shoulders of Odysseus (232–235). Odysseus' regular characteristics, impressive in themselves, are thus concealed by Athena's artistry, endowing him with a more precious appearance. If he had simply washed off the brine and donned new clothes, he would not have been aesthetically appalling: his appearance would still have merited comparison with the precious metal silver. But the image of gold poured around silver suggests that something of great value is being concealed by something of still greater value.[45]

---

[44] Nausicaa's desires are moreover suggested by her use of the verb μίσγομαι in these lines, which is associated elsewhere in Homeric poetry with sexual intercourse (see n40 above). Earlier Nausicaa uses the verb μίσγομαι of strangers who come amongst the Phaeacians (205) but, once she has seen him in his enhanced state, she uses it also of Odysseus himself (241). At 286–288, she modestly distances herself from girls who would "mingle with" men before marriage: καὶ δ' ἄλλῃ νεμεσῶ, ἥ τις τοιαῦτά γε ῥέζοι, / ἥ τ' ἀέκητι φίλων πατρὸς καὶ μητρὸς ἐόντων / ἀνδράσι μίσγηται πρίν γ' ἀμφάδιον γάμον ἐλθεῖν. ("And I find blame with any other girl who would do such things, who mingles with men against the will of her father and mother while they are alive, before entering into a public marriage.") But seeing as she has just imagined how onlookers would gossip about Odysseus as a potential match for her (276–284), she appears to be intimating her desires to Odysseus in these lines: see de Jong 2001 on *Odyssey* 6.275–285, 286–288.

[45] Eustathius on *Odyssey* 6.231: the image of gold poured around silver suggests that Odysseus, "beautiful by nature" (φύσει καλὸς ὤν) is rendered still more beautiful (ἐξαλλάγη πρὸς τὸ

By presenting Nausicaa with this more attractive, more youthful version of Odysseus, Athena both offers her the kind of man she desires and conceals his more regular appearance. However impressive Odysseus may look without Athena's intervention, he is nevertheless a middle-aged man, who has been away at war for ten years and at sea for a further ten. But Odysseus' hyacinthine hair grants him the appearance of a younger man. And despite noticing divine aspects to his appearance, Nausicaa is nevertheless led to believe that Odysseus could be a suitable husband.[46]

We get a still clearer impression of the seductive, deceptive aspects of Odysseus' hyacinthine hair when we consider the other instance of the image. This second occurrence of the image is found in *Odyssey* 23, prior to the reunion of Odysseus and Penelope. Except for the first line, the description of Athena's enhancement of Odysseus is identical to lines 6.229–235:

αὐτὰρ κὰκ κεφαλῆς χεῦεν πολὺ κάλλος Ἀθήνη
μείζονά τ' εἰσιδέειν καὶ πάσσονα· κὰδ δὲ κάρητος
οὔλας ἧκε κόμας, ὑακινθίνῳ ἄνθει ὁμοίας.
ὡς δ' ὅτε τις χρυσὸν περιχεύεται ἀργύρῳ ἀνὴρ
160 ἴδρις, ὃν Ἥφαιστος δέδαεν καὶ Παλλὰς Ἀθήνη
τέχνην παντοίην, χαρίεντα δὲ ἔργα τελείει,
ὡς μὲν τῷ περίχευε χάριν κεφαλῇ τε καὶ ὤμοις.

Odyssey 23.156–162

But Athena poured much beauty from his head also,
[Making him] taller and broader to look at; and from his head
She sent down curly locks, like the flower of the hyacinth.
As when some man pours gold around silver,
160 A skilled man, whom Hephaestus and Pallas Athena have taught
Every kind of craft—he achieves graceful works—
So she poured grace on his head and shoulders.

We have already discussed the associations of this image of hyacinthine hair and metallurgy with youth, eroticism, and artistry, and considered how those themes play out in the Nausicaa episode. But in order to understand the precise implications of the similar image in Book 23 we need to bear in mind not only its immediate context—the meeting between Odysseus and Penelope—but also its interaction with other passages in the second half of the *Odyssey* and in the

---

κάλλιον). I quote Eustathius from Stallbaum 1825. Cf. Duigan 2004:81 on the themes of deception, concealment, and value in this image.

[46] Odysseus, by contrast, looks upon Nausicaa's beauty (e.g., *Odyssey* 6.160–169) but is not seduced: see Grethlein 2018:35–39.

Homeric corpus as a whole. If we compare the relevant lines with other Homeric accounts of heroes' transformations and consider allusions to Penelope's desires in the *Odyssey*, we gain clearer insights into the nature of Athena's intervention at 23.156–162 and into the impact of Odysseus' new appearance on his wife. The relevant passages confirm that Penelope is faced with an artificially rejuvenated version of her husband and show that Odysseus' enhanced appearance is in accordance with her desires: she longs for the man who left for Troy twenty years ago. Penelope is thus moved to accept Odysseus as her husband more readily than she might have done if presented with a world-weary, middle-aged Odysseus. As with Nausicaa, then, Penelope is both seduced and deceived by Odysseus' appearance.

As we have already seen, the image of hyacinthine hair and the elements of gilding in the images from Books 6 and 23 carry with them connotations of youth, eroticism, artistry and concealment, and we thereby understand that Odysseus' middle-aged appearance has been concealed behind an attractive, youthful veneer. But to understand the deceptive qualities of Odysseus' appearance in *Odyssey* 23, we should also bear in mind other descriptions of Odysseus' transformations in the second half of the *Odyssey*, some of which lend him a youthful appearance, while others give him the squalid appearance of an old beggar.

Odysseus' first such transformation occurs in Book 13, shortly after his arrival on Ithaca, and clearly carries deceptive connotations. Athena disguises Odysseus as a beggar with the explicit intention of rendering him "unrecognizable to all mortals" (ἄγνωστον ... πάντεσσι βρότοισι, 13.397).[47] To this end she withers his flesh, dims his eyes, and causes him to lose his blond hair.[48] And while the Graces and Seasons deck Aphrodite in beautiful clothes in preparation for her meeting with Paris, Athena dresses Odysseus in rags:

> Ὣς ἄρα μιν φαμένη ῥάβδῳ ἐπεμάσσατ' Ἀθήνη.
> 430 κάρψε μέν οἱ χρόα καλὸν ἐνὶ γναμπτοῖσι μέλεσσι,
> ξανθὰς δ' ἐκ κεφαλῆς ὄλεσε τρίχας, ἀμφὶ δὲ δέρμα
> πάντεσσιν μελέεσσι παλαιοῦ θῆκε γέροντος,
> κνύζωσεν δέ οἱ ὄσσε πάρος περικαλλέ' ἐόντε·
> ἀμφὶ δέ μιν ῥάκος ἄλλο κακὸν βάλεν ἠδὲ χιτῶνα,

---

[47] Cf. 13.192–193 (Athena plans that his wife, fellow citizens, and friends not recognize him before he has taken revenge on the suitors) and 16.455–459 (after his reunion with Telemachus in an enhanced form, Athena restores Odysseus' beggar disguise so that Eumaeus will not recognize him). For Odysseus' meeting with Telemachus, see below.

[48] On the apparent disjunction between Odysseus' blond hair in this passage, his dark hair at 16.176, and also the suggestions of dark coloration in the image of hyacinthine hair, see n43 above.

435 ῥωγαλέα ῥυπόωντα, κακῷ μεμορυγμένα καπνῷ·
    ἀμφὶ δέ μιν μέγα δέρμα ταχείης ἕσσ' ἐλάφοιο,
    ψιλόν· δῶκε δέ οἱ σκῆπτρον καὶ ἀεικέα πήρην,
    πυκνὰ ῥωγαλέην· ἐν δὲ στρόφος ἦεν ἀορτήρ.

Odyssey 13.429–438

Having spoken thus Athena touched him with her wand.
430 She withered the beautiful flesh on his flexible limbs,
    And made him lose the blond hairs from his head and placed
    Around all his limbs the skin of an old man,
    And she dimmed his eyes that had formerly been beautiful;
    And she cast around him new clothing—evil rags and a tunic,
435 Filthy, torn, and soiled badly with smoke;
    And clothed him all round with the great hide of a swift deer,
    Which was threadbare; and she gave him a staff and a shameful
        pouch,
    Full of holes; and on it was a twisted strap.

In this way, Odysseus takes on a false appearance that is designed to deceive viewers ("all mortals," 13.397): they will mistake the lord of Ithaca for a mere beggar.[49]

If this passage were our only guide to the implications of the image from *Odyssey* 23 we might assume that in granting Odysseus hyacinthine hair and thereby casting off his beggar disguise Athena is restoring him to his original appearance. But other evidence from the *Odyssey* shows that this is not the case and that, in fact, Odysseus' enhanced appearance in Book 23 is a disguise no less than his beggar costume.

We get a sense of this from the account of Odysseus' transformation from a beggar to a young man in Book 16. Shortly before Odysseus reveals to Telemachus that he has returned, Athena removes his beggar disguise and enhances his appearance. She grants him fine clothes, a dark complexion, and a dark beard:

Ἦ καὶ χρυσείη ῥάβδῳ ἐπεμάσσατ' Ἀθήνη.
φᾶρος μέν οἱ πρῶτον ἐϋπλυνὲς ἠδὲ χιτῶνα

---

[49] Deception is a major theme in the scene in which this transformation takes place. Athena takes on the appearance of a shepherd (13.222–325). She also renders the island unrecognizable to Odysseus by shrouding it in mist (189–197). She eventually reveals to him that he has indeed arrived on Ithaca; but even after hearing this, the wary Odysseus tells her a lying tale of his adventures (256–286). In response, Athena notes that he is "insatiable in his trickery" (δόλων ἆτ', 293) and that, while he is "best among all mortals for counsel and speeches" (βροτῶν ὄχ' ἄριστος ἁπάντων / βουλῇ καὶ μύθοισιν), she herself is "renowned for cunning and stratagems among all gods" (ἐν πᾶσι θεοῖσι / μήτι τε κλέομαι καὶ κέρδεσιν, 298–299).

θῆκ' ἀμφὶ στήθεσσι, δέμας δ' ὤφελλε καὶ ἥβην.
175 ἂψ δὲ μελαγχροιὴς γένετο, γναθμοὶ δὲ τάνυσθεν,
κυάνεαι δ' ἐγένοντο γενειάδες ἀμφὶ γένειον.

Odyssey 16.172–176

Athena spoke and touched him with her golden wand.
First she placed a well-washed cloak and a tunic
Around his chest, and she increased his body and youth.
175 He became dark of complexion again, and his jaw was stretched,
And a dark beard grew around his chin.

Telemachus has previously encountered the returned Odysseus only in his beggar disguise.[50] When he sees him in this new state, he protests that Odysseus must be a god: only a god could transform himself from an old to a young man (194–200). In reply, Odysseus assures Telemachus that his transformation is the work of Athena, who is able to make him "at one time like a beggar and at another time again like a young man with beautiful clothes around his flesh" (ἄλλοτε μὲν πτωχῷ ἐναλίγκιον, ἄλλοτε δ' αὖτε / ἀνδρὶ νέῳ καὶ καλὰ περὶ χροΐ εἵματ' ἔχοντι, 209–210). Odysseus, then, reveals two options for his appearance in the latter books of the *Odyssey*: either it is that of an old beggar or that of a young man.[51] Odysseus' hyacinthine hair is clearly a variant on the latter option: as with his transformation at 16.172–176, it replaces his beggar disguise in Book 23; moreover, as we have seen the image carries connotations of youthfulness.

Neither of these guises represents Odysseus' regular appearance, but of the two the appearance of a young man marks the greater departure from what we would expect him to look like at this stage in his life. As noted above, early audiences would have been aware that Odysseus has been away at war for ten years and has suffered toils on his travels for a further ten. They would have expected him, then, to bear a closer resemblance to the old man of the beggar disguise than to the young man who presents himself to Telemachus.[52] By "increas[ing]

---

[50] What is more, Telemachus was presumably too young to remember Odysseus' appearance when he left for Troy. Odysseus has been away twenty years, and in the narrative timeframe of the *Odyssey* Telemachus is just reaching manhood (see, for instance, 18.175–176).

[51] Levaniouk 2011:67, commenting on Odysseus' hyacinthine hair: "a remarkable sliding of age-markers characterizes Odysseus: he is represented alternatively as an ageing married man and as a youngster."

[52] Penelope herself acknowledges as much when, speaking of Odysseus in his beggar disguise, she tells Eurycleia to "wash your master's agemate" (νίψον σοῖο ἄνακτος ὁμήλικα, 19.358). She supposes that "Odysseus' hands and feet are similar now, since mortals age quickly in their misery" (καί που Ὀδυσσεὺς / ἤδη τοιόσδ' ἐστὶ πόδας τοιόσδε τε χεῖρας / αἶψα γὰρ ἐν κακότητι βροτοὶ καταγηράσκουσιν, 358–360). It is possible that Penelope suspects at this point that the beggar is Odysseus: see n70 below. Nevertheless, she finally accepts him as her husband in his guise as a young man (in Book 23).

his youth" (16.174), Athena reverses the ageing process and lends him the appearance of a much younger man. The beggar disguise by contrast exaggerates the careworn characteristics of a middle-aged man who has had his share of troubles.

As Athena makes clear in Book 13, the beggar disguise will deceive onlookers. But given the fact that his guise as a young man departs more clearly from his more regular appearance, the latter if anything carries a greater potential to deceive. We get our first glimpse of this potential in the meeting of Odysseus and Telemachus. In declaring that Odysseus must be a god, Telemachus makes a mistake about his father's identity (16.183–185, 194–200). His mistake is understandable: he no less than early audiences would expect Odysseus to have the appearance of a middle-aged man, not of the young man who stands before him.[53]

This is not, however, a case of a successful deception, which would require not merely that a character makes a mistake about Odysseus' appearance but also that s/he makes a mistake in the manner desired by the one who engineered the deception—in this case, Athena. In fact, her transformation of Odysseus fails to achieve what she is intending. She tells Odysseus at line 168 to "speak a word to your son nor conceal it" (σῷ παιδὶ ἔπος φάο μηδ᾽ ἐπίκευθε) so that they can then plot together against the suitors. Presumably she means for him to talk openly both about his identity and his plans. It seems, then, that by granting Odysseus a youthful appearance Athena is trying to support Odysseus in his efforts to reunite with his son. But Odysseus' transformation has the opposite and undesirable effect of causing Telemachus to doubt that Odysseus is his father.

The deceptive qualities of Odysseus' two guises are revealed more clearly when we read the relevant lines alongside other Homeric passages describing the alteration of a hero's appearance. In two such passages the change that is described correlates with certain aspects of Odysseus' transformation into a beggar. In both *Iliad* 18 and *Odyssey* 13, Athena exaggerates a hero's existing traits; earlier in the *Iliad*, Patroclus puts on Achilles' armor in order to play the role of his friend, much as Odysseus dons a beggar's rags. A third Iliadic scene offers a closer parallel for Athena's gift of hyacinthine hair, which returns Odysseus' appearance to that of a much younger man: Aphrodite intervenes to preserve Hector's body in *Iliad* 23, thus reversing the ageing process and lending it a potentially deceptive appearance.

The mechanics of Achilles' transformation in *Iliad* 18 offer a closer parallel for the beggar disguise than for the hyacinthine Odysseus of *Odyssey* 6 and 23. At *Iliad* 18.203–206, Athena places the aegis around Achilles' shoulders and causes

---

[53] See Ahl and Roisman 1996:194–195. In fact, Odysseus resembles the mature young man Telemachus has become. A key indication of Telemachus' maturity is his new beard (18.175–176, 269–270); Odysseus' beard is emphasized at 16.176.

fire to shine from his head; in addition, she adds her own voice to his as he bellows from the ditch (217–221). In this way, she greatly enhances Achilles' already fearsome characteristics. But unlike her gift of hyacinthine hair to Odysseus in *Odyssey* 6 and 23, which gives a middle-aged man the appearance of a young man, Athena does not reverse any of Achilles' existing traits. Rather, the exaggeration of Achilles' appearance in *Iliad* 18 parallels that of Odysseus in *Odyssey* 13: in the one case, Athena enhances the already impressive characteristics of the youthful Achilles; in the other, she exaggerates the characteristics of a careworn traveler.

We should however bear in mind the distinctions between these episodes, one of which gives us a further insight into the nature of the deception practiced by Odysseus' beggar disguise. Firstly, while in *Odyssey* 13 Athena lends Odysseus a foul and unimpressive appearance, in *Iliad* 18 she endows Achilles with terrifying characteristics designed to cause panic in the Trojan ranks. Secondly, when Achilles' enhanced appearance in *Iliad* 18.203–206 sows panic among the Trojans, they could not be said to have made a mistake about his appearance: rather, they are simply reacting to the flame around his head and to his bellowing, both of which they correctly perceive (225–229). They are aware, moreover, that this is Achilles standing before them—a man whose mere presence, if the hero's own words are accurate, used to keep Hector within the walls of Troy (9.351–355). There is no indication, then, that Achilles' appearance is deceptive, or even potentially so.[54]

In *Odyssey* 13, Athena likewise exaggerates the existing characteristics of a hero; but she also enables Odysseus to play a new role—that of a beggar—by dressing him in squalid rags. The deceptiveness of Odysseus' new guise depends on such role-play.[55] A closer parallel would exist between the two scenes if Achilles were to take on the role of another—say, the god Apollo—in addition

---

[54] The *Odyssey*'s descriptions of the transformations of Penelope and Telemachus seem to fall into this category: Athena enhances their existing traits, but unlike in the case of Odysseus' hyacinthine hair, her interventions do not reverse the ageing process; moreover, unlike Odysseus in Book 13 the characters in question do not take on new roles. At *Odyssey* 2.12–13 and 17.63–64, for instance, Athena pours grace on Telemachus; she does the same for Odysseus at 6.235 and 23.162. As a result of Athena's intervention, the Ithacans wonder at Telemachus (θηεῦντο, 2.13, 17.64); but they do not mistake him for someone else or for a younger man. Similarly, much as Athena makes Odysseus "larger and broader" at 6.230 and 23.157, she renders Penelope "taller and broader" at 18.195 "so that [the suitors] might wonder" (ἵνα ... θησαίατ', 191). And Penelope's appearance does, indeed, rouse their desires (211–212). But it is not deceptive: the suitors make no mistake about her identity. Any deceptive qualities in the scene center not on her appearance, but on her speech at 251–280. Penelope extracts gifts from the suitors with her possibly misleading suggestion that she is now ready to remarry (250–303); see Levine 1983 on deception in this scene.

[55] The clothes that Laertes wears as he tends his orchard, which are described at 24.227–231, might likewise have the potential to deceive (see Murnaghan 1987:26–30). Indeed, Odysseus pretends

to his enhanced appearance and if the Trojans had then mistaken him for this other character.

In fact, Odysseus' donning rags and playing the part of a beggar resembles an Iliadic scene where a hero's body is not transformed by a god. A little earlier in the *Iliad*, Patroclus goes out to battle wearing Achilles' armor and is thereby able to impersonate his friend on the battlefield. Patroclus hopes that the Trojans will mistake him for the more fearsome Achilles and thereby allow the Greeks some breathing space (16.40–43). And his plan has the desired effect: the Trojans take fright in the belief that Achilles has returned to the fighting (278–282). Audiences would have been able to compare Odysseus' beggar disguise with such scenes and thereby to understand its deceptive qualities. The disguise exaggerates existing physical characteristics and to that extent might not qualify as deceptive; but the fact that Odysseus dons a costume and plays a role explains his ability to mislead viewers in this guise.[56]

Other transformations of heroes offer more promising parallels for Athena's gift of hyacinthine hair in *Odyssey* 6 and 23, which reverses the ageing process rather than exaggerating existing traits.[57] And indeed audiences' knowledge of such scenes would have helped them to understand the deceptive potential of Odysseus' appearance in the relevant passages. For instance, Aphrodite's treatment of Hector's corpse in *Iliad* 23 halts the natural process of decay and lends it potentially deceptive qualities. Aphrodite preserves Hector's body with "rosy, ambrosial oil" (ῥοδόεντι ... ἐλαίῳ / ἀμβροσίῳ, 186–187); as a result, according to Hermes the corpse takes on a fresh, "dewy" (ἐερσήεις, 24.419) appearance, such that Hector's father Priam would wonder at it (θηοῖό κεν αὐτός, 418).[58] Hector's body, moreover, has the potential to mislead viewers. Hecuba notes that he now looks like one who has been slain by the arrows of Apollo—i.e., like someone who died a peaceful death (24.758–759). She knows that he died at the hands of Achilles; but someone else might not realize this if s/he happened on his body.[59]

Odysseus' transformations into a young man offer a closer parallel for Aphrodite's preservation of Hector's body at *Iliad* 23.186–187 than for Athena's enhancement of Achilles' body at *Iliad* 18.203–206. Odysseus' guise as a beggar

---

to mistake him for a slave, albeit one of impressive appearance (249–255). For the meeting of Odysseus and Laertes, see also Chapter 5 and n60 below.

[56] Patroclus' deception of the Trojans differs, however, from Odysseus' use of a beggar disguise to the extent that it imperils the deceiver himself. At *Iliad* 16.46–47 the narrator comments that, in asking Achilles for his armor, he was asking for his own death, and Patroclus is killed shortly after entering battle (786–857).

[57] Cf. *Iliad* 19.38–39, where Thetis drips the divine substances ambrosia and nectar into the nostrils of Patroclus' corpse to leave his flesh "unchanging or still better" (ἔμπεδος, ἢ καὶ ἀρείων, 19.33).

[58] The "dewy" appearance of Hector's corpse might also have carried floral connotations for audiences familiar with Homeric poetry: see Chapter 7 n16 below.

[59] For Aphrodite's rosy oil and the effect of Hector's body on viewers, see also Chapter 7 below.

and Achilles' appearance in *Iliad* 18 both exaggerate existing traits. Comparison of the two shows that the deceptiveness of Odysseus' appearance in this case inheres not so much in such exaggerations as in his adoption of a new role. But the preservation of Hector's body and the transformation of Odysseus into a young man both carry the potential to deceive. They hold in check or reverse natural processes. Aphrodite's intervention halts the process of decay; similarly, Odysseus' appearance as a young man constitutes a reversal of the ageing process.[60] Like the viewers imagined by Hecuba, who would think that Hector had passed away peacefully, viewers might well make a mistake about Odysseus in his new guise.[61]

As we shall see, in accordance with the deceptive potentials of Odysseus' guise as a young man the hyacinthine hair that Athena grants him at *Odyssey* 23.156–162 successfully deceives Penelope. But in order to gain a full understanding of Penelope's reaction to Odysseus' hyacinthine hair, it is necessary to consider also an earlier passage from the *Odyssey* that offers important insights into her desires. In the light of this passage, we see that the scene in *Odyssey* 23, as with the meeting of Odysseus and Nausicaa, incorporates not only a successful deception but also a successful seduction. Athena's actions at 6.229–235 lend Odysseus the appearance of the sort of young man that Nausicaa might want as a husband. Similarly, by presenting Odysseus to Penelope in the form of a young man Athena is giving her what she desires—namely, the Odysseus that she remembers from before the Trojan War.[62]

Penelope's desires are suggested at 20.79–90, where she both expresses a wish to be struck down by Artemis so that she might see Odysseus again in the

---

[60] Unlike other transformations of Odysseus' family members in the *Odyssey* (for which see n54 above), Athena's enhancement of Laertes' appearance at 24.367–369 could be understood as deceptive. In his new guise, he resembles a god (371), and Odysseus correctly surmises that a god has intervened to alter his appearance (373–374). What is more, at 24.376–382 Laertes expresses the wish that he were still the man he was when he took the city of Nericus. These lines might have led listeners to suspect that Athena has, in fact, given him the appearance of such a warrior and that therefore, as with Odysseus in Books 6, 16, and 23, she has rendered him more youthful. What is more, much as Athena dresses Odysseus in better clothing instead of his beggar's rags (16.173–174), Laertes dons a "beautiful cloak" (χλαῖναν καλήν, 24.367) in place of the squalid clothing that he had been wearing (227–231). For Laertes' clothing, see also n55 above.

[61] Moreover, in each case the goddess' actions benefit the object of her attentions. Odysseus' enhanced appearance helps him to secure a homecoming from the Phaeacians (*Odyssey* 6) and to achieve a reunion with Penelope (*Odyssey* 23). Aphrodite's ministrations in *Iliad* 23 help to preserve Hector's corpse (see 23.182–191).

[62] For the identification of the two episodes as seduction scenes, see Sowa 1984:67–73, Pucci 1987:91–92, Murnaghan 1987:92–103, Glenn 1998, Currie 2016:189–193; see also van Nortwick 1979, who observes that Nausicaa, more than any other female on Odysseus' travels, resembles his wife. For the parallels between the two scenes, see also Pucci 1987:91-92 and Arthur (Katz) 1991:114–115, 136–137.

Underworld (80–81) and also speaks of her joy at a vision she had of the young Odysseus:[63]

> τῇδε γὰρ αὖ μοι νυκτὶ παρέδραθεν εἴκελος αὐτῷ,
> τοῖος ἐὼν οἷος ᾖεν ἅμα στρατῷ· αὐτὰρ ἐμὸν κῆρ
> χαῖρ', ἐπεὶ οὐκ ἐφάμην ὄναρ ἔμμεναι, ἀλλ' ὕπαρ ἤδη.

Odyssey 20.88–90

On this night one like him lay beside me,
Such as he was when he went along with the expedition; but my
        heart
Rejoiced, since I thought it was no dream but now a waking vision.

In Penelope's vision, Odysseus returns to her as he was when he set sail for Troy.[64] Moreover, the language that Penelope uses suggests a vision not only of reunion but also of erotic fulfillment. The only other Homeric instance of the verb παραδαρθάνω, here in the aorist form παρέδραθεν (20.88), occurs in a clearly erotic context. At *Iliad* 14.163–164, the infinitive παραδραθέειν describes Hera's intentions in a scene of seduction that we shall discuss in the next chapter, the Διὸς ἀπάτη: εἴ πως ἱμείραιτο παραδραθέειν φιλότητι / ἦ χροίη ("if perhaps [Zeus] should desire to lie beside her flesh in love"). In *Iliad* 14, Hera manipulates Zeus' desires; Penelope's waking dream in *Odyssey* 20 is an expression of her desire for the Odysseus she lost twenty years ago.[65]

The evidence considered thus far suggests that Odysseus adopts two potentially deceptive guises in the second half of the *Odyssey*—that of an old beggar and that of a young man—and that Penelope desires the Odysseus she knew from

---

[63] Odysseus hears Penelope weeping as she recalls her vision and has a vision of his own, in which she recognizes him (20.92–94). The references to the younger Odysseus and to Penelope's recognition of Odysseus anticipate the events in Book 23 that we shall discuss below: Penelope eventually accepts Odysseus in his younger, hyacinthine form.

[64] Russo (1982:14) argues that the phrase εἴκελος αὐτῷ at 20.88 both refers to the Odysseus of twenty years ago and also suggests the beggar, whom Penelope likens to Odysseus as he would appear now at 19.358–360 (see n52 above). But such an allusion to the older Odysseus would create an awkward contrast with the clear reference in the next line to the Odysseus of twenty years ago.

[65] A second dream, which Penelope reports to Odysseus in his beggar disguise at 19.536–553, may offer a further indication of Penelope's desires. She mentions that she has twenty geese the sight of which warms her heart (536–537); an eagle arrives and kills them (538–540); Penelope remembers her distress at their deaths (541–543); the eagle explains clearly that he is Odysseus and that he will slay the suitors (546–550); but when she awoke the geese were still alive in her courtyard (552–553). Perhaps her distress at the apparent death of the geese and their actual survival reflects a certain tenderness that she has developed towards the suitors: see Rankin 1962 and Russo 1982 (cf. Marquardt 1985:43–45: the dream reflects her fear that she might be suspected of such desires). If this is the case, her tender feelings towards these younger men are consistent with her desire for the younger Odysseus and resistance to Odysseus in his guise as an old beggar.

before the expedition to Troy. Earlier we found that the image of hyacinthine hair evokes four themes in particular: youth, eroticisim, artistry, and concealment. With these findings in mind, we can now analyze the interaction of the image from *Odyssey* 23 with its immediate context.

Firstly, there are deceptive qualities to Odysseus' appearance at 23.156–162, and these qualities are closely connected with the themes of youth and concealment: Athena lends Odysseus the appearance of an attractive young man and thereby conceals the careworn appearance of a middle-aged traveler. As Odysseus himself makes clear at 16.208–210, Athena's interventions in the second half of the *Odyssey* lend him the form either of an old beggar or of a younger man. At 23.156–162, she transforms Odysseus from his beggar disguise: listeners would, then, have expected that she has given him the guise of a younger man, as she does in preparation for his meeting with Telemachus at 16.173–176. And such expectations would have been confirmed by the implications of the image of hyacinthine hair. As we have seen, the image evokes an attractive young man, not a middle-aged traveler. In addition, the references to craftsmanship and concealment in these lines suggest not only the beauty of Odysseus' appearance at this point in the *Odyssey* but also its artificial qualities. As noted above, his guise as a younger man reverses the ageing process: the (valuable) silver of his regular, middle-aged appearance is concealed behind the (more precious) gold of a youthful Odysseus.

By granting Odysseus an artificially rejuvenated appearance, Athena presents Penelope with an Odysseus more in keeping with her desires.[66] We can infer from 20.88–90 that Penelope desires not merely Odysseus but Odysseus as he was when he left for Troy. And such an inference is in keeping with the events of Book 23. At first, with Odysseus in his beggar disguise, Penelope fails to recognize him: ἀγνώσασκε κακὰ χροΐ εἵματ' ἔχοντα ("she did not recognize him with evil clothing on his flesh," 95).[67] Odysseus then retires to bathe, at which point Athena grants him hyacinthine hair (153–163), thereby giving him the appearance of a younger man.[68] Approaching her in his new guise, he asks that

---

[66] On this image as a reflection of Odysseus' artificial rejuvenation, see also Levaniouk 2011:67–68.

[67] Odysseus recognizes Penelope's state of mind at 23.115–116: "now because I am filthy and clothed in evil clothing on my flesh, / for that reason she dishonors and does not say that I am he" (νῦν δ' ὅττι ῥυπόω, κακὰ δὲ χροΐ εἵματα εἷμαι, / τούνεκ' ἀτιμάζει με καὶ οὔ πώ φησι τὸν εἶναι). For the connection of these lines with Penelope's desire for the younger Odysseus, see Felson 1997:62: "it is as if [Odysseus] had overheard her earlier fantasy, when she dreamed he lay beside her 'as he was when he went with the army' (20.89–90)."

[68] The themes introduced by Odysseus' instructions to Telemachus at 23.130–136 are in keeping with Odysseus' new guise. Telemachus should clean his clothes and tell the bard Phemius to play music for a wedding. In his hyacinthine guise, Odysseus resembles not only the young man who left for Troy, but also the youth who married her. She renews their marriage with Odysseus in this guise.

she now lay aside her stubbornness and accept him as her husband (166–172). In response she makes reference directly to the younger man who left her to go to Troy: μάλα δ᾽ εὖ οἶδ᾽ οἷος ἔησθα / ἐξ Ἰθάκης ἐπὶ νηὸς ἰὼν δολιχηρέτμοιο ("I know well how you were / when you left Ithaca on your long-oared ship," 175–176). Penelope has to judge whether the man standing before her really is Odysseus by comparing him with such memories.

Penelope hesitates before making her choice. In her caution she differs from Korē, who without hesitation seizes the narcissus, her own double, or indeed from Paris, who makes no attempt to resist the charms of Aphrodite.[69] But after testing his knowledge of the construction of their marriage bed (173–204), she accepts Odysseus in his artificially rejuvenated form (205–208).[70] Odysseus' demonstration of knowledge in lines 183–204 contributes to Penelope's recognition of her husband;[71] but his appearance must be acceptable to her if she is to make such a choice. Presumably, she compares the young man of her memories, to whom she refers in lines 175–176, with the Odysseus who stands before her and concludes that the two are sufficiently alike for her to welcome him back as her husband. But in fact, Athena has altered Odysseus' appearance. His hyacinthine hair elides the twenty years that they have spent apart and facilitates her comparison of the Odysseus of Book 23 with the Odysseus she once knew.[72] Odysseus' enhanced appearance, engineered by Athena, helps to overcome Penelope's resistance to reunion with her husband, circumspect though she is.

Athena has practiced a deception: Penelope does not notice that Odysseus' appearance has been enhanced, but these improvements nevertheless encourage her to accept him as her husband.[73] And indeed the reasons that she

---

[69] As Heitman (2005:89–95) points out, Penelope in her caution differs also from other characters in the *Odyssey* faced with Odysseus' enhanced appearance: Telemachus and Nausicaa, for instance, despite likening Odysseus to a god, soon accept his transformed appearance.

[70] It is possible, as some scholars have argued, that Penelope recognizes Odysseus or has her suspicions about his identity earlier than Book 23: Harsh 1950, Amory 1963, Winkler 1990:129–161, Ahl and Roisman 1996:229–272. If Penelope does have her suspicions, this would help to explain her decision to hold the archery contest shortly after meeting the disguised Odysseus (21.1–4) and her insistence that Odysseus be allowed a turn with the bow (21.111–142). Nevertheless, Penelope only accepts him as her husband when she has seen him in the guise of a younger man with hyacinthine hair. For Penelope's suspicions regarding Odysseus' identity, see also n52 above.

[71] See Chapter 5 below for discussion of imagery connected with Odysseus' bed.

[72] Cf. Murnaghan 1987:16: Athena's actions give Penelope the illusion that she is looking at the Odysseus who left her to fight at Troy.

[73] For the deceptive qualities of Odysseus' appearance, see Pucci 1987:92, who observes that Odysseus' seductive appearance in Book 23 is no truer than the beggar disguise it replaces, Ahl and Roisman 1996:264, who contend that "Athena recreates an image, a phantasm of the Odysseus Penelope loved," and Nooter 2019:49, who proposes that Athena's treatment of Odysseus "is framed not as an uncovering of the true Odysseus from under the cloak of his beggarly disguise, but rather as itself an act of artistic subterfuge on the part of a god." Dougherty (2015:134–140) argues that Odysseus' change of appearance at *Odyssey* 23.156–162 is part of a productive trial

goes on to give for her initial hesitation draw attention to the deception. At 216–217, Penelope explains the reason for her caution: she had always feared "that some mortal would come and trick her with words" (μή τίς με βροτῶν ἀπάφοιτο ἔπεσσιν / ἐλθών).[74] Given the dynamics of the scene in Book 23, there is a deep irony to what Penelope has to say: she has indeed been tricked, but by Odysseus' appearance rather than his words.[75]

The deception introduces a somewhat unsettling note to the episode, though Penelope does not suffer the sorts of unpleasant consequences described in the scenes from the *Hymn to Demeter* and the *Cypria* that we have discussed. Not only Penelope's ignorance of Athena's actions, but also the fact that Odysseus never takes off this disguise in Book 23 cast a slight shadow over the renewal of the marriage: we never hear that Odysseus is reunited with Penelope in his unenhanced state. Odysseus' speech to Penelope at 23.264–284 has a similarly unsettling effect. Odysseus anticipates a further journey that he will have to undertake in order to propitiate Poseidon, leaving her behind. And this calls into question the notion that their marriage has been re-established on a stable and permanent basis.[76] Nevertheless, in comparison with the other scenes that we have studied in this chapter, the deception practiced by Odysseus' artificially youthful appearance has relatively benign consequences for the viewer. Fortunately for Penelope, Odysseus' deceptive appearance does not place her in peril: Odysseus has in fact returned, and she has not been taken in by an impostor.

At the same time, Book 23 tells the story of a successful seduction. As Penelope embraces her husband and kisses his head in lines 205–206, she not only accepts that he is Odysseus but also welcomes him back as her lover, as is shown by subsequent events. She and the hyacinthine Odysseus retire to bed where in addition to conversation "they enjoyed desirous love" (φιλότητος ἐταρπήτην ἐρατεινῆς, 300). In *Odyssey* 23, then, a Homeric floral image is once

---

of different roles, as he and Penelope negotiate their new relationship with each other. But at this point Penelope is excluded from the game: her ignorance of the transformation that has occurred and its manipulation of her desires qualify Odysseus' appearance as deceptive.

[74] If Murnaghan (1987:141–142) is correct, Penelope's puzzling reference to Helen's adultery immediately afterwards (218–224) continues her explanation for her hesitancy. According to Murnaghan, Penelope hesitates precisely because she has always feared giving in to her desires (as Helen gave in to her desires) and accepting an impostor as Odysseus on the basis of his plausible speech (ἔπεσσιν).

[75] In a further irony, Penelope notes shortly beforehand that "the gods ... begrudged us the chance to enjoy youth, remaining with one another" (θεοί / ... νῶϊν ἀγάσαντο παρ' ἀλλήλοισι μένοντε / ἥβης ταρπῆναι, 23.210–212). Penelope herself will not enjoy a second youth, but, as we have seen, she is unaware that she has been presented with an artificially youthful Odysseus.

[76] For these and other unsettling elements in the denouement of the *Odyssey*, see Pucci 1987:83–97, Ahl and Roisman 1996:247–272, Purves 2006 and 2010:65–96. As we shall see in Chapter 5 below, such elements are balanced by arboreal images that suggest the endurance of Odysseus' and Penelope's marriage.

more associated with an erotic body that is both seductive and deceptive: the deceptive appearance of Odysseus' hyacinthine hair contributes to the (re-) seduction of his wife.

* * *

In Chapter 1, we discovered that poems from across the corpus of archaic Greek lyric show certain core similarities in their treatment of floral images of the erotic. Whether associated with girls or boys, with homosexual or hetero-sexual desire, whether found in the work of male or female lyric poets, erotic bodies associated with flowers are cast as the object of the speaker's gaze. In this chapter, we have encountered four instances of Homeric floral imagery that resemble one another in key respects. In all four cases, flowers are associated with an erotic body that both seduces and in some way deceives the one who encounters it.

As we have seen, the floral images of the two genres explore two different configurations of the relationship between subject and object, between viewer and viewed. The lyric poems that we have studied present similar dynamics of the gaze, whether the speaker or the object of the gaze happens to be male or female. In this way, they diverge from the films analyzed by Mulvey: according to her, the gaze in film is associated with the masculine gender. But in another respect the operations of the gaze in the relevant poems closely resemble those described by Mulvey. As in Mulvey's films, the viewer's subjectivity dominates the object of her/his gaze: in our poems the first-person speaker claims the right both to view and to evaluate the desirable bodies that are associated with flowers.[77]

By contrast, in the Homeric passages that we have studied the viewer does not exercise the same control over the object of her/his gaze. Erotic bodies associated with flowers both seduce and deceive the viewer. Korē misses the special enhancements of the narcissus that heighten her autoerotic desires for the flower, her own double. Moreover, the narcissus conceals hidden dangers: by plucking it, Korē exposes herself to abduction by Hades. Similarly, Aphrodite's flowery accoutrements facilitate her seduction of Paris, but unwelcome conse-quences hide behind the goddess' attractive appearance: audiences would have recognized that, in choosing Aphrodite and accepting her offer of Helen, Paris ensures the destruction of his city. Finally, Odysseus' hyacinthine hair conceals his middle-aged appearance and seduces both Nausicaa and Penelope; fortunately for both women, however, no unpleasant dangers lurk behind his appearance. Nausicaa's hopes that Odysseus might prove a suitable husband are

---

[77] Mulvey 1989b.

dashed, but she suffers no worse fate; and though Penelope accepts Odysseus in his enhanced form, she is nonetheless reunited with her husband.

And insofar as the erotic bodies in all these different episodes of Homeric poetry are both seductive and deceptive, they challenge the viewer's control over the scene. The dynamics of these interactions, then, resemble Lacan's account of the gaze: things in the visual field disturb the neat distinctions between subject and object that viewers might like to maintain.[78]

More specifically, while the viewer is able to judge erotic bodies that are associated with flowers in Greek lyric, the seductive and deceptive qualities of such bodies in Homeric poetry cause the viewer to *mis*judge their value. Sappho's girls or the boys and girls in Ibycus and Anacreon do not deceive the viewer; accordingly, the speaker/viewer is able to place a value on their beauty. In fr. 122 Voigt, for instance, Sappho (or her persona in the poem) judges a girl to be ἄγαν ἀπάλαν, "*too* attractive." By contrast the deceptive appearance of Homeric bodies misleads the viewer by concealing their true value. This is, for instance, suggested by the image of gold poured around silver in *Odyssey* 6 and 23: Nausicaa and Penelope behold an Odysseus artificially rejuvenated to stir their desires.

We have already observed some of the ways in which these images from Greek lyric and Homeric poetry interact with the characteristics of flowers in the Greek natural environment. I have suggested that associations of flowers with erotic bodies in Greek lyric drew on audiences' experiences of viewing flowers and judging them to be beautiful. We have also explored the relationship of particular flowers in Homeric poetry with the notions of seduction and deception: for instance, Korē's narcissus, with its hundred heads, represents an exaggeration of the sorts of narcissi that audiences would have encountered in the natural environment, and it rouses the autoerotic desires of this "flower-faced girl" with its special charms.

But given that different scenes focus on different plants—the narcissus in the *Hymn to Demeter*, the hyacinth in *Odyssey* 6 and 23—the Homeric corpus as a whole presents an association of seduction and deception with flowers *in general*. We should also, then, consider the bases for such associations in the natural phenomena familiar to these poets and their audiences. We should try to explain how the Homeric poets were able to draw on the characteristics of flowers in the Greek natural environment in order to illustrate the operations of seduction and deception in the relevant passages. The following chapter offers just such an explanation.

---

[78] Lacan 1977, e.g., pp. 95–96.

3

Shifting Surfaces of Art and Nature
Flowers, Deception, and the Ποικίλον

I WOULD NOW LIKE TO CONSIDER HOW HOMERIC ASSOCIATIONS of flowers, seduction, and deception interacted with the general characteristics of the Greek flora. As we shall see, we get a clearer sense of the origins of the relevant Homeric images when we consider them alongside a further set of Homeric images that associate seduction and deception with the concept of the ποικίλον. In wider Greek culture this concept is associated with objects with a many-colored, shifting appearance.[1] These objects are commonly the products of human manufacture; but they might also be elements of the natural environment.[2] The Homeric poems echo such associations of the ποικίλον; but they also present more specific associations of the root ποικιλ- with seductive, deceptive bodies, which closely parallel the associations of the floral images we discussed in the last chapter. Since flowers and ποικίλος objects are found in very similar circumstances in the Homeric poems, we can use one to aid our understanding of the other. In particular, we shall see that the qualities associated with the ποικίλον point us towards the particular characteristics of the Greek flora that form the basis for Homeric associations of flowers, seduction, and deception: the Homeric floral imagery of seduction and deception responded to the diverse, shifting surfaces of flowers in the Greek spring.

---

[1] By analogy, the term ποικίλος can also suggest quickly changing mental states. See Detienne and Vernant 1978:18–19: it is associated with the "shimmering, shifting movement" of both deceptive appearances and mental states; see also Winkler 1990:167: "[i]t designates the quality of having many internal contrasts whether perceived by the eye or the mind."

[2] For associations of the ποικίλον with manufactured products, see Bolling 1958, duBois 1995:183–184, Snyder 1997:91–95, Naiden 1999:181–182, Hamilton 2001, Jackson 2002, Rinaudo 2009:25–46; for its associations with items from the natural environment, see Frontisi-Ducroux 1975:71, Giannini 2009:65–72, and n4 below.

There are a number of parallels between the associations of flowers and those of the root ποικιλ- in Homeric poetry. Firstly, like flowers in the Homeric images that we have been discussing, the root ποικιλ- is associated with items derived from the natural environment.[3] But these ποικίλος items, as with the flowers in Aphrodite's robes at *Cypria* fr. 4 Bernabé, have often been translated from the realm of nature to that of culture. Aphrodite's robes are dipped in the sorts of flowers that would have been familiar to early audiences from the Greek natural environment, but those flowers, or at least their scents, are thereby incorporated into items of craftsmanship—the robes prepared by the Graces and Seasons. The root ποικιλ- carries similar associations, as we see from *Iliad* 10.30, where Menelaus dons a ποικίλος leopard's skin. The reference may well be to the animal's dappled coat—as at Euripides *Bacchae* 249, where Pentheus catches sight of Tiresias ἐν ποικίλαισι νεβρίσι ("in dappled fawnskins"), a costume that he has donned in honor of the god Dionysus.[4] But presumably, unlike the wild attire of a (would-be) bacchant Menelaus' garment has been prepared in some way and thus brought over from the realm of nature to the realm of culture: this is not an item directly sourced from the natural environment.[5]

In other passages the lexeme ποικίλος is associated with visually impressive objects crafted by human or divine hands. Such associations are for instance suggested by descriptions of the (παμ)ποίκιλοι robes woven by Athena (*Iliad* 5.735), Sidonian women (*Iliad* 6.289), or Helen (*Odyssey* 15.105).[6] In one such passage the adjective ποικίλος describes what appear to be floral motifs; and this would suggest the compatibility of the two concepts, flowers and the ποικίλον. If the ancient authorities are correct in their explanations of the rare lexeme θρόνα, it refers at *Iliad* 22.441 to floral motifs woven into a tapestry.[7] The

---

3   Frontisi-Ducroux 1975:71, Giannini 2009:65–70.

4   LSJ s.v. ποικίλος A.1: "*many-coloured, spotted, pied, dappled.*" LSJ cites this passage of the *Bacchae*, in addition to a number of other passages of archaic and classical poetry that describe the dappled hides or skins of animals. See also Snell 1955–2010 s.v. ποικίλος 1: "naturgegeben: *mehrfarbig gemustert*, von Fell/Schuppenzeichnung im Tierreich."

5   See also *Odyssey* 19.288, where the term ποικίλος is used of a fawn-skin on a brooch. In that passage the lexeme may refer to the object's workmanship but could also evoke the dappled skin of a real animal (cf. Morris 1992:28).

6   Duigan (2004) reads Athena's refusal to accept Hecuba's offering of Sidonian robes at *Iliad* 6.288–311 as an example of her cunning ability to see through beguiling appearances. On that reading, the παμποίκιλοι robes would be associated with an (unsuccessful) deception. For associations of the root ποικιλ- with deceptive appearances, see below.

7   For the floral associations of the lexeme θρόνα, see the scholium to Theocritus 2.59 (Ὅμηρος ... τὰ ῥόδα παρὰ τὸ ἄνω θορεῖν ἐκ τῆς γῆς, "Homer [uses] *thróna* for roses, from leaping [*thoreîn*] up from the ground": Wendel 1966:283) and Hesychius s.v. θρόνα and τρόνα, which Latte (1966) and Hansen and Cunningham (2009) understand as references to *Iliad* 22.441. Winkler (1990:172–174) is unusual among modern scholars in seeing *Iliad* 22.441 as a reference to "drugs." In interpreting the lexeme in this way, he responds to the meaning of θρόνα in its Theocritean context, to the

relevant passage describes Andromache's weaving θρόνα ποικίλ' (apparently, "elaborate flowers") as Hector faces death outside the walls of Troy:

ἀλλ' ἥ γ' ἱστὸν ὕφαινε μυχῷ δόμου ὑψηλοῖο
δίπλακα πορφυρέην, ἐν δὲ <u>θρόνα ποικίλ'</u> ἔπασσε.

Iliad 22.440–441

But she was weaving a tapestry in a nook of her high house,
Double and crimson, and she was scattering *elaborate flowers* on it.

In still other passages the root ποικιλ- denotes the finery that adorns seductive, deceptive bodies, thus creating a clear parallel with the floral imagery that we discussed in chapter 2. In the *Hymn to Aphrodite* Aphrodite sports both παμποίκιλοι necklaces (88–89) and flowery earrings (κάλυκας, 87), a fact that once more suggests the compatability of flowers with the concept of the ποικίλον.[8] The necklaces and earrings form part of the jewellery with which the Graces adorn her for the seduction of Anchises (cf. line 65), much as the Graces and Seasons prepare her for the seduction of Paris (*Cypria* fr. 4 Bernabé). And as with that scene from the *Cypria*, these adornments lure a mortal into danger. The seductive, deceptive charms of Aphrodite's appearance and speech induce Anchises to take the dangerous step of accepting a goddess as a sexual partner.

Firstly, Aphrodite's dazzling appearance rouses Anchises' desires. The narrator delays description of her robes and her jewelry, including her flowery earrings and παμποίκιλοι necklaces, until she comes face to face with the Trojan

---

association of Andromache's weaving at 22.441 with the verb πάσσω, and to the use of that same verb in connection with drugs elsewhere in the *Iliad* (4.219, 5.401, 900, 11.515, 830, and 15.394). He does not however take into account the explanations of the Homeric usage by the ancient authorities cited above. Nor is it clear how we could understand θρόνα at *Iliad* 22.441 in the context of Andromache's weaving without some reference to decorative motifs. Other scholars accept a floral meaning of θρόνα at *Iliad* 22.441 without arguing for allusions to drugs in that passage: Jouanna 1999:108 ("plantes à fleurs"), Chantraine 1984–1990 s.v. θρόνα ("ornements tissés d'une étoffe, fleurs"), Beekes 2010 s.v. θρόνα ("'flowers,' as a decoration in woven tissues and embroidery"). Bolling (1958) offers a way to reconcile Theocritus' usage of θρόνα to mean "drugs" and the translations of the lexeme by Hesychius and by the scholiast to Theocritus: Andromache's flowers are a protective charm (cf. magical drugs) for Hector; see Rissman 1983:4–5 (discussed in n14 below) for a similar reading of the term ποι⌉κιλόθρο⌊ν' at Sappho 1.1 Voigt, an epithet that may well have been inspired by the Homeric formula θρόνα ποικίλ'. For a second association of the root ποικιλ- with flowers in Sappho, see fr. 168c Voigt, where the verb ποικίλλω is used of the "many-wreathed earth": ποικίλλεται μὲν / γαῖα πολυστέφανος.

[8] For this interpretation of the term κάλυκας, see Faulkner 2008 ad loc., who suspects that the earrings resemble flower buds. Similar imagery is found in *Hymn* 6, where the Seasons decorate Aphrodite with flowery earrings "of yellow copper and precious gold" (ἄνθεμ' ὀρειχάλκου χρυσοῖό τε τιμήεντος, line 9). The hymn is a tale of seduction in miniature: after these preparations, the Seasons lead Aphrodite before the gods, each of whom instantly desires her as his wife (14–19).

prince (85–90). Listeners are thereby encouraged to imagine how he will react to these adornments.[9] In particular the adjective παμποίκιλοι, with its connotations of bright, shifting appearances and its intensifying prefix, suggests the dazzling, overwhelming impact of Aphrodite's jewelry on the young man. Line 91, which follows the description of her adornments, makes explicit the nature of Anchises' reaction. He is seduced by Aphrodite's charms: Ἀγχίσην δ' ἔρος εἷλεν ("desire seized Anchises," 91).[10]

Her appearance also contributes to a deception. She takes on the guise of "an untamed maiden" (παρθένῳ ἀδμήτῃ, 82) and thereby attempts to conceal her identity.[11] She does not at first succeed in convincing Anchises that she is a mortal: he surmises that she is one of the gods (92–106). But she backs up her disguise as a maiden with a lying tale to match: she describes her mortal upbringing and claims to have been abducted from the dance by Hermes to be his bride (108–142). The combination of her disguise and her words overcome Anchises' resistance. He proclaims her a "woman equal to the gods" (γύναι εἰκυῖα θεῇσι, 153), and immediately afterwards the two make love.

In accepting Aphrodite as a partner Anchises exposes himself to danger. Anchises explains these dangers immediately after they make love and Aphrodite reveals her identity: a man fears being left "without vigor" (ἀμενηνόν) from sex with a goddess (188).[12] But as Anchises explains in lines 186–187, he was deceived

---

[9] See Faulkner 2008 on *Hymn to Aphrodite* 81–90: the postponement of the description of the necklaces until the meeting with Anchises "allows the audience to join more actively in [his] reaction of amazement at seeing the goddess."

[10] Such effects may be reinforced by Aphrodite's speech (108–142), which we shall discuss below. Following the speech we hear that Ὣς εἰποῦσα θεὰ γλυκὺν ἵμερον ἔμβαλε θυμῷ / Ἀγχίσην δ' ἔρος εἷλεν (143–144). The phrase Ἀγχίσην δ' ἔρος εἷλεν, "and desire seized Anchises," is repeated from line 91. Two different translations are possible for lines 143–144, depending on the way in which we understand the aorist participle εἰποῦσα: either "by speaking thus the goddess cast sweet desire in his heart, / and desire seized Anchises" or "having spoken thus ..." If the former, her tale of abduction from the dance further rouses his desires; if the latter, she casts desire into his heart (γλυκὺν ἵμερον ἔμβαλε θυμῷ, 143) after finishing her speech, much as Zeus casts desire into *her* heart at line 53 (γλυκὺν ἵμερον ἔμβαλε θυμῷ). For Zeus' manipulation of Aphrodite in the hymn, see n13 below.

[11] The fact that Aphrodite has somehow concealed her appearance can be seen from Anchises' contrasting reactions to her before and after their lovemaking. Aphrodite takes on the form of a maiden "lest, perceiving her with his eyes, he should take fright" (μή μιν ταρβήσειεν ἐν ὀφθαλμοῖσι νοήσας, 83). And while Anchises does not at first accept her disguise, he does not take fright at her appearance. Rather, on first encountering her "he wondered" at her (θαύμαινεν, 84). But later in the poem, Aphrodite reveals her true form, and her new appearance elicits a different reaction: "he took fright when he saw the neck and beautiful eyes of Aphrodite" and had to look away (ὡς δὲ ἴδεν δειρήν τε καὶ ὄμματα κάλ' Ἀφροδίτης / τάρβησεν τε καὶ ὄσσε παρακλιδὸν ἔτραπεν ἄλλῃ, 181–182).

[12] On the dangers of sex with a goddess in the hymn, see also Giacomelli 1980, Segal 1986:43–44, and Clay 2006:183. In a Homeric context, the adjective ἀμενηνός suggests a threat not merely to

by Aphrodite: at first he believed that she was a goddess, but she "did not speak the truth": οὐ νημερτὲς ἔειπες, 187. As we have seen, as a consequence of her efforts at deception he was willing to accept her as a woman *equal* to the gods (153). If this were the case, there would be no danger from a sexual encounter with her: after all, the narrative describes Anchises himself as "like a god in his physique" (δέμας ἀθανάτοισιν ἐοικώς, 55) and as "possessing the beauty of the gods" (θεῶν ἄπο κάλλος ἔχοντα, 77). Aphrodite's godlike attractions would simply place her on a par with this Trojan prince. Aphrodite, then, has not only seduced Anchises but also succeeded in deceiving him.[13]

We have, then, one more instance where an erotic body is associated with flowers and with the seduction and deception of a mortal, but the erotic body in question is also associated with the concept of the ποικίλον: Aphrodite wears both flowery earrings and παμποίκιλοι necklaces. The term ποικίλος is likewise associated with a seductive, deceptive body in the Διὸς ἀπάτη from *Iliad* 14: the adjective describes Aphrodite's Girdle of Desire, the most important of the accoutrements that Hera dons in preparation for her encounter with Zeus.[14] With its help Hera succeeds not only in seducing her husband but also in deceiving him. When he makes love to her, he realizes neither that she is wearing Aphrodite's girdle nor that she has ulterior motives in seducing him: after their lovemaking, the god Sleep will incapacitate Zeus and thus allow Poseidon to aid the Greeks on the battlefield. In this way, while Aphrodite's flowery accoutrements in *Cypria* fr. 4 hide dangers that are planned by Zeus (namely, the destruction of Paris' city, Troy), Hera's charms imperil Zeus' own plans to favor the Trojans.

Unlike Aphrodite in the scenes that we have studied, Hera carries out most of her preparations without the help of fellow goddesses: lines 166–186 offer a detailed description of her scented unguents, robes, and jewelry as she carries

---

Anchises' manhood but also to his life: see Chapters 8 and 9 below on the "heads without vigor" (ἀμενηνὰ κάρηνα), as the dead are described at *Odyssey* 10.521, 536, 11.29, 49.

[13]   In addition, the seduction of Anchises is part of a plan of Zeus to deceive Aphrodite herself: irritated by her boasting that she has made gods sleep with mortals, Zeus decides to have his revenge by casting desire for a mortal in her heart (45–52). Aphrodite later acknowledges that she has been led astray (lines 253–255). For the plans of Zeus in the *Hymn to Aphrodite*, see Clay 2006:152–201; on the deception of Aphrodite in the hymn, see de Jong 1989. For further discussion of the *Hymn to Aphrodite*, see Chapter 5 below.

[14]   For the equivalence of the associations of the lexeme ποικίλος in this scene and those of flowers in other scenes that we have studied, see Rissman 1983:4–5. Rissman suggests that Sappho, in giving Aphrodite the epithet ποι]κιλόθρο[ν' (1.1 Voigt; cf. n7 above), alludes both to descriptions of the goddess' flowery clothing, such as *Cypria* fr. 4 Bernabé, and specifically to the ἱμάς ποικίλος of *Iliad* 14.219–220, which Rissman interprets as a "love charm" (p. 4). On that reading, Sappho, herself an archaic Greek recipient of the Homeric poems, treats the Homeric images of flowers and of the ποικίλον as belonging to the same system of imagery and as possessing similar connotations.

out her toilette behind closed doors. Nevertheless she appeals to Aphrodite for the Girdle of Desire, which is described as ποικίλος twice in six lines. Aphrodite takes it off...

> Ἦ, καὶ ἀπὸ στήθεσφιν ἐλύσατο κεστὸν ἱμάντα
> ποικίλον, ἔνθα τέ οἱ θελκτήρια πάντα τέτυκτο·
> ἔνθ' ἔνι μὲν φιλότης, ἐν δ' ἵμερος, ἐν δ' ὀαριστὺς
> πάρφασις, ἥ τ' ἔκλεψε νόον πύκα περ φρονεόντων.

Iliad 14.214–217

> She spoke and loosened from her chest *the embroidered,*
> *Elaborate girdle,* where all beguilements had been fashioned;
> On it there was love, desire, and lovers' words,
> Misleading speech, which steals the mind of even the wisest.[15]

... and instructs Hera in its use:

> "τῇ νῦν, τοῦτον ἱμάντα τεῷ ἐγκάτθεο κόλπῳ
> ποικίλον, ᾧ ἔνι πάντα τετεύχεται· οὐδὲ σέ φημι
> ἄπρηκτόν γε νέεσθαι, ὅ τι φρεσὶ σῇσι μενοινᾷς."

Iliad 14.219–221

> "There now, lay *this elaborate girdle* on your bosom,
> In which all things have been fashioned; I say that you
> Will not return without achieving that which you desire in your
> heart."

Decked out with this girdle and with her other accoutrements, Hera arouses Zeus' desires from the moment he sees her: ἴδε δὲ νεφεληγερέτα Ζεύς. / ὡς δ' ἴδεν, ὥς μιν ἔρως πυκινὰς φρένας ἀμφεκάλυψεν ("cloud-gathering Zeus saw her. / And as he saw her, just then desire covered his close wits," 294–295). But like the seductive bodies associated with flowers in Homeric poetry, Hera's body is also deceptive. The deceptive qualities of Hera's appearance in her meeting with Zeus are anticipated in line 217, where the girdle of desire is described. Its

---

[15] πάρφασις carries connotations both of "persuasion" and of "deception." This is clear from its context in *Iliad* 14 and from other usages of the lexeme. At 14.217, πάρφασις "steals" rather than simply "persuades," and it wins over "even the wisest": reason, then, is insufficient defense against its charms. At *Iliad* 11.793 and 15.404 a longer form of the lexeme, παραίφασις, is used of the "persuasion" that a comrade might bring to bear on Achilles (not necessarily through deceit). *Odyssey* 16.287 and 19.6 use the related verb πάρφημι of misleading words to the suitors: when they ask where the weapons from the hall have gone, Telemachus is to claim (falsely) that he has removed them for fear that they will be blackened with smoke or that the suitors will wound one another (16.288–294, 19.7–13).

ποικίλον appearance is strongly associated with deception: "it steals the mind of even the wisest" (ἔκλεψε νόον πύκα περ φρονεόντων). When she dons the girdle, Hera takes on its deceptive powers; accordingly, Zeus is deceived by her appearance. It is not that Zeus makes a mistake about who is before him: he is well aware that his visitor is Hera. Nevertheless he shows no awareness that she has prepared her body for seduction rather than for a long journey: as we shall see, in self-centered fashion he describes his own desires; and yet he makes no mention of Hera's appearance. Nor does he realize that Hera has donned a magical love-charm in preparation for their meeting. With this charm her appearance has deceptive qualities: she has the look of Hera, but she has, in fact, borrowed the seductive powers of Aphrodite.

Hera enhances the effect of her adornments with the help of deceptive words, which further enflame Zeus' desire. When Zeus asks her where she is heading, she replies with the intention of tricking him (δολοφρονέουσα, 300): she is going to reconcile Oceanus and Tethys, who have long stood apart from lovemaking; she has only stopped by to inform him of this fact (301–311). She makes no mention, of course, of her real plans: she hopes that Zeus will insist on having sex with her, thus allowing Sleep to lull him into a post-coital slumber. Suspecting nothing, but taking his cue from Hera's mention of lovemaking, Zeus makes a crass attempt to impress on her the urgency of his desire: he lists all the lovers that he has wanted less than he wants her at this moment (313–328). Again trying to trick him (δολοφρονέουσα, 329), Hera plays the coy lover and suggests that they retreat indoors (330–340). But Zeus can brook no delay: he promises to conceal their bodies in a golden cloud (342–345) so that they can make love there and then. As with Aphrodite in her *Homeric Hymn*, then, Hera's appearance and speeches both seduce and deceive a potential sexual partner.[16]

From the evidence presented thus far, we see that the concepts of flowers and the ποικίλον are compatible with one another. But more specifically we observe a parallelism in the role of floral imagery and the ποικίλον in Homeric descriptions of erotic encounters: both are associated with seductive, deceptive bodies. Given the similar function of flowers and the ποικίλον in these scenes, we would expect that they convey similar concepts.

And indeed the concepts associated with the ποικίλον resemble certain characteristics of flowers in the Greek natural environment. As we saw at the head of this chapter, the root ποικιλ- is often associated with many-colored, shifting appearance. And when we bear in mind the characteristics of the Greek flora set out in my Introduction, we see that flowers would have been well suited for conveying such notions. The Greek spring landscape is strewn

---

[16] For further discussion of the Διὸς ἀπάτη, see Chapter 4.

with many-colored carpets of flowers, which reflect the exceptional floral diversity of Greece.[17] Greek flowers also suggest the kind of shifting appearance that Detienne and Vernant associate with the adjective ποικίλος. The Greek spring is remarkable both for the sudden changes to the appearance of the landscape, caused by the brilliant blooming of its flowering plants, and for the equally sudden disappearance of those flowers.[18]

In addition to the characteristics of particular flowers, such as the *Narcissus tazetta* or *N. papyraceus* in the *Hymn to Demeter*, early audiences could draw on these more general characteristics of flowers to conceptualize the deceptive qualities of the erotic bodies described by the Homeric poets. It is not that Greek flowers are intrinsically deceptive.[19] But the many-colored, shifting qualities of spring landscapes offered a model for listeners to understand the mechanics of deception in the scenes that we have studied. The sudden, brilliant, short-lived blooms of Greek spring flowers provided a ready parallel for the cosmetically enhanced appearance of seductive bodies: that is, they would have helped audiences to envisage a particular kind of deception, based around attractive appearances. Like the Greek landscape, these bodies present attractive, short-lived surfaces.[20]

And like spring flowers on the Greek landscape, the attractive surfaces of these and other erotic bodies in the scenes that we have studied mask the more regular appearance of the gods and mortals in question. In spring, the arid landscape of Greece gives a fleeting impression of lush fertility.[21] Similarly, the erotic bodies of Homeric poetry mask their more regular appearance behind

---

[17] For the many-colored carpets of flowers in the Greek spring, see Strid and Tan 1997–2002 1:xx, Baumann 1993:10, Voliotis 1984. For the floral diversity of Greece, see Hughes 2014:17–18, Baumann 1993:10, Huxley and Taylor 1977:6. Some of our Homeric scenes indeed carry suggestions of floral diversity: the *Hymn to Demeter* lists elaborate catalogues of flowers that Korē and her companions are picking (6–8, 426–428); Aphrodite's robes are dipped in many kinds of spring flower (*Cypria* fr. 4 Bernabé).

[18] On the sudden bloom of Greek flowers, see Motte 1971:10, Braudel 1972:233, Huxley and Taylor 1977:21, 24, Polunin 1980:30–31, 37; see also Höhfeld 2008:39 on the Troad. For the brief duration of these blooms, see Polunin 1980:30-31, Voliotis 1984:135, and Baumann 1993:10.

[19] Such perceptions of flowers were nonetheless possible. For the idea that flowery surfaces could be perceived as deceptive, see Chirassi (1968:91) on flowery meadows. According to Chirassi, the attractive, seductive surfaces of meadows were believed to hide death and violence. He states that "L' ἱμερτὸς λειμών diventa l'ingannevole luogo del supplizio, l'obbligato passaggio al compimento di un atto finale di morte" ("The desirable meadow becomes the deceptive locus of torment, the necessary passageway to the completion of the final act of death."). For associations of flowery meadows with death in Homeric poetry, see Chapter 8 below.

[20] Duigan (2004:79) suggests that the manufacture of brilliant, attractive jewelry to adorn the bodies of women was inspired by "[t]he colourful flowers of Greece," which might also adorn the bodies of women.

[21] Baumann 1993:10: "The Greek region ... gives an impression of desert; only in spring does the ground become bedecked for a short period with a carpet of multicoloured flowers."

an attractive outer surface and thus beguile the viewer. Hyacinthine hair hides the regular appearance of the middle-aged Odysseus, much as a meadow of hyacinths spreads an attractive, colorful surface over the otherwise bland landscape. Hera or Aphrodite beautify themselves with a view to seducing a particular lover on a particular occasion. In this way, these erotic bodies possess the shifting qualities associated with the concept of the ποικίλον, which takes the place of floral imagery in episodes such as the Διὸς ἀπάτη.

Taking our cue from the concepts associated with the ποικίλον, then, we have come to understand how the Homeric poets were able to draw on the characteristics of flowers in the Greek natural environment to give their audiences a sense not only of the attractions of erotic bodies associated with flowers but also of their deceptive qualities. In accordance with the analyses of metaphor by George Lakoff et al., they thus used more concrete concepts drawn from the environment to help their audiences to understand more abstract concepts such as eroticism and deception. Listeners could picture the deceptiveness of erotic bodies in terms of the attractive, fleeting qualities of flowers in the world around them.

PART TWO

COSMIC AND CIVIC ORDER

Preamble

IN PART I, WE CONSIDERED A SET OF HOMERIC FLORAL IMAGES associated with erotic bodies, and we explored their interactions with the characteristics of flowers in the Greek natural environment. I would now like to focus on a rather different class of Homeric vegetal images. As we shall see, the Homeric poets developed both floral and arboreal images to illustrate the concepts of order and disorder, both as they relate to the cosmos as a whole and to human communities. Once again, I would like to set in relief the choices of the Homeric poets through comparison with another genre of archaic Greek poetry that treats similar themes. Of all such poetry the relevant Homeric images find their closest parallels in the Hesiodic poems. Nevertheless, the vegetal images of the two genres show significant differences in their treatments of order and disorder.

In making such distinctions, I diverge from other studies of order and disorder in the two genres, most notably those of Noriko Yasumura and Jenny Strauss Clay. Yasumura identifies a story-pattern of challenges to Zeus' supremacy that is present in the Homeric epics, the *Homeric Hymns* and the Hesiodic *Theogony*.[1] Clay situates the *Homeric Hymns* midway between the evolving cosmos of the Hesiodic *Theogony* and the more settled order of the major Homeric epics. Over the course of the *Theogony* and the *Homeric Hymns*, the physical structure of the cosmos is established and then refined; at the same time, the relations between the different divine beings and between gods and mortals settle into their current state. For Clay, the Hesiodic and Homeric poems form a continuum: they tell one overarching story of increasing order.[2] For Yasumura, some of the tales of order and disorder in the two genres are similar enough to be treated as instantiations of a single underlying archetype.

Yet when we focus on vegetal imagery of good order and its opposite, we notice distinctions between the two genres: at least in this respect, then, the two

---

[1] Yasumura 2011.
[2] See Clay 2003 on Hesiodic poetry and Clay 2006 on the *Homeric Hymns*.

sets of poets offered different treatments of such themes.[3] The Hesiodic poets did not develop vegetal imagery to illustrate forces of disorder, change, and revolution; such imagery does however accompany their descriptions of good order. The *Works and Days* associates the orderliness of just societies with flourishing vegetation. The *Theogony* by contrast associates the permanent structure of the cosmos with the structure of plants.

The Homeric poets developed a richer set of vegetal images to illustrate such cosmic and civic themes. While the Hesiodic poets associated the structure of the cosmos with the structure of plants, their Homeric counterparts associated images of trees and pillars with the stability and permanence of cosmic order. In the Homeric poems moreover images of managed vegetation accompany descriptions of civilized order. The *Iliad* employs both agricultural and arboricultural imagery for this purpose, while the *Odyssey*, in its images of civilized order, places particular emphasis on the management of trees. By contrast, the *Works and Days* associates orderly and just communities with flourishing vegetation in general, whether wild or domesticated—and this despite the fact that most of the poem focuses on agricultural labor.

What is more, unlike their Hesiodic counterparts the Homeric poets also developed vegetal images to accompany their descriptions of challenges and changes to good order, or of a simple lack of orderliness. While they associated trees and pillars with the stable order of the cosmos, they associated floral growths with changes or challenges to that order. And in their explorations of civic order and its opposite they contrasted their imagery of managed vegetation with descriptions of wild floral and arboreal growths untamed by human hands.

These Homeric and Hesiodic images represent two contrasting responses to the Greek natural environment. The Hesiodic images seem on the face of it easier to explain. The Hesiodic poets illustrated the more abstract concept of cosmic structure through the more readily observable structure of plants in the natural environment. And they helped their audiences to understand the notion of flourishing communities through reference to the more concrete concept of flourishing vegetation. But the Homeric associations require further explanation. As we shall discover, such images drew on early Greek perceptions of different types of vegetal growth. According to such conceptions, the sudden, apparently spontaneous growth of small flowering plants contrasted with the orderly growth of wild trees, and wild vegetation in general differed from the managed growths of fields and orchards.

---

[3] For general distinctions between the two genres and their treatments of order and disorder see my Conclusion.

And in these respects, the relevant Homeric images offered somewhat different treatments of good order and its opposite from their Hesiodic equivalents. Granted, the Hesiodic poems do not shy away from describing challenges to cosmic or civic order. In the *Theogony*, for instance, Zeus faces challenges from the Titans (*Theogony* 617–735) and the monstrous Typhoeus (820–850); the *Works and Days* explores the injustices present in human communities. And yet in their vegetal images the Hesiodic poets emphasized only the more stable structures of the cosmos or human societies. The equivalent Homeric imagery, by contrast, explores tensions between forces of order and disorder.

4

Stable Trees and Sudden Blooms
Images of Continuity and Change in the Cosmos

I N THIS CHAPTER, I WILL FOCUS ON THE SORTS OF IMAGES that the Homeric poets associated with the concepts of order in the cosmos and of changes and challenges to that order—or to put it another way, with changes put into effect or merely threatened. As we shall see, these poets drew on the sturdy trees and pillars that listeners would have known from their own natural and built environments to illustrate the stability and permanence of cosmic order. But they also manipulated the characteristics of particular flowers, such as the narcissus of the *Hymn to Demeter*, or more general characteristics of flowers in the natural environment, such as the sudden blooms of the Greek spring, to explore changes and challenges to cosmic order. The Homeric hymns and epics, then, present two contrasting sets of images that helped audiences to conceptualize tensions between forces of change and stability in the cosmos.

Descriptions of Cosmic Order and Disorder in the *Theogony*

In Part I, we were able to gain a clearer sense of the ways in which Homeric images of erotic bodies responded to the characteristics of flowers in the Greek natural environment by comparing them with equivalent images from the corpus of archaic Greek lyric. Similarly, we can set in relief the choices of the Homeric poets in forming their images of cosmic order and of changes and challenges to that order if we take into account imagery from the Hesiodic *Theogony* that treats similar themes. The *Theogony*, however, offers only partial parallels for the relevant Homeric images. The Hesiodic poets associated the structure of the cosmos with the structure of plants, and such imagery can readily be compared with Homeric arboreal images of cosmic order. But the *Theogony* does not employ vegetal imagery in its explorations of changes and challenges to cosmic order.

If Hesiodic parallels existed for the sorts of Homeric images of flowers and changes or challenges to cosmic order that we shall discuss below, we would expect most of all to find such imagery in the poem's succession myth, where a series of rulers of the cosmos is unseated by female guile and by the violence of the ruler's son. Cronus castrates his father Uranus with a sickle, from a hiding place provided by his mother Ge; he thus becomes ruler of the gods in his father's stead (*Theogony* 159–182). Cronus then swallows his own children in order to pre-empt potential challenges to his rule, but Rhea deceives him by substituting a stone for her last-born son, Zeus, who in this way survives to overpower his father (453–500). These two successions are reminiscent of two Homeric passages that, as we shall see, associate challenges to cosmic order with floral growths—the disabling of Zeus in the Διὸς ἀπάτη, which is achieved through Hera's guile, and the potential threat that Zeus faces from his own son in the *Hymn to Apollo*.[1] In neither Hesiodic passage, however, is there any hint of floral imagery;[2] nor have I been able to find secure parallels for Homeric associations of flowers and cosmic disruption elsewhere in archaic Greek literature.[3]

---

[1] *Catalogue of Women* frr. 51–54(c) MW offer another possible Hesiodic parallel for Apollo's threat to Zeus in the *Homeric Hymn to Apollo*. When Zeus kills Apollo's son Asclepius, Apollo slays the Cyclopes in retaliation. This insubordinate riposte realizes Apollo's potential for violence, which is suggested in the *Hymn to Apollo*; however, there is no floral imagery in what remains of the Hesiodic story. For discussion of this fragment, see also n38 below and my Conclusion. On similarities between Homeric and Hesiodic depictions of challenges to Zeus' supremacy, see Yasumura (2011).

[2] We do, in fact, find floral imagery following the final challenge to Zeus' rule in the *Theogony*: at line 878, winds from Typhoeus blow κατὰ γαῖαν ἀπείριτον ἀνθεμόεσσαν ("throughout the boundless, flowery earth"). By this stage, however, the monster has been defeated. If the Hesiodic episode echoed the Homeric associations of floral imagery with challenges to cosmic order, we would expect flowers to be associated not with Typhoeus' defeat but with his assault on Zeus. For further reflections on this image, see Chapter 5 n5 below.

[3] The earliest parallel that I have been able to identify for such Homeric imagery is offered by Pindar's *Seventh Olympian* from early in the classical period (464 BCE). As we shall see, at *Iliad* 15.187–193 Poseidon describes the division of the cosmos between himself, Zeus, and Hades. In Pindar's ode such a division of the world is shown to be problematic: Zeus realizes that Helios has been excluded from the sortition (*Olympian* 7.61). The problem is solved by the growth from the seabed of the island Rhodes, which will be assigned to Helios. This reorganization of the cosmos is accompanied by floral imagery: Rhodes is only ever referred to in oblique cases, where the word Ῥόδος has forms identical with the noun ῥόδον, "rose"; the island's emergence is described, moreover, in terms of a flower growing (αὐξομέναν, 62) and sprouting (βλάστε). Cf. Young 1968 on the vegetal imagery of the ode.

We do, however, find comparanda in the *Theogony* for the Homeric associations of trees and cosmic order that we shall discuss below. Two passages
from the poem describe the structure of the cosmos in terms of the structure of
plants. Firstly, in lines 727–728, the "roots of the earth and the sea" are said to
have grown above the "neck" of Tartarus:

αὐτὰρ ὕπερθε
γῆς ῥίζαι πεφύασι καὶ ἀτρυγέτοιο θαλάσσης.

Theogony 727–728

But above [the neck]
The roots of the earth and of the harvestless sea have grown.

This passage incorporates two images, both of which would have helped audiences to understand the structure of the cosmos. On the one hand the allusion to
a "neck" imagines Tartarus, the lowest region of the Hesiodic cosmos, in terms of
a jar or a body.[4] On the other hand, the image of roots explains the relationship of
the earth and the sea with what lies beneath them. Archaic audiences would have
been able to gain an appreciation of what is implied by the second image from
their observation of roots in the natural environment, particularly the knotted
roots of trees. As Martin West puts it, we should "perhaps imagin[e] the clear
division between land and sea gradually disappearing in the underworld, as the
two elements branch out in roots or veins that are inextricably intertwined with
one another."[5] Roots tangle with one another below ground but form distinct
plants above the ground, just as land and sea are distinct on the earth but (in the
Hesiodic conception) are confused with one another below it.[6]

At 811–813, we find another reference to roots, quite possibly the same
roots as those referred to in lines 727–728: the threshold of Tartarus is fixed on
"continuous roots." Apparently we are to suppose that they reach continuously
down (διηνεκέεσσιν), to the very bottom of Tartarus:

ἔνθα δὲ μαρμάρεαί τε πύλαι καὶ χάλκεος οὐδός,
ἀστεμφὲς ῥίζῃσι διηνεκέεσσιν ἀρηρώς,
αὐτοφυής·

Theogony 811–813

---

4   See West 1966 on *Theogony* 727 (δειρήν).
5   West 1966 on *Theogony* 728 (ῥίζα).
6   For the image of the "roots of the sea," cf. *Orphic Hymn* 23.1, where Nereus is described as the
     possessor of πόντου ῥίζας, or *Orphica* fr. 21a.6 Kern, where Zeus is identified as πόντου ῥίζα.
     Compare also the image of the "navel of the sea" at *Odyssey* 1.50, discussed below.

> And there are the marble gates and brazen threshold,
> Fixed unshakably on continuous roots,
> Self-generating.

The references in these lines to permanence and fixity (ἀστεμφὲς ... ἀρηρώς) suggest one reason for the evocation of roots in the two passages—audiences were to conceive of the compartments of the Hesiodic universe as set in place immovably like plants on a root-stock. That the parts of the cosmos are somehow rooted offers an explanation for their stability in terms of a readily observable fact: the existence of roots below the earth that anchor plants in place.[7]

And the roots of the Hesiodic earth appear to share a further quality with those of plants: they nurture growth, a concept suggested in both passages by the root φυ-. The brazen threshold of Tartarus, fixed on its roots, is "self-generating," αὐτοφυής. In the first passage, the roots "have grown," πεφύασι.[8] Without our modern understanding of photosynthesis, the ancient Greeks believed that all the food of a plant—all it needed for growth—was taken up through its roots. Theophrastus, for instance, notes that Ἔστι δὲ ῥίζα μὲν δι' οὗ τὴν τροφὴν ἐπάγεται ... ("The root is that through which [a plant] draws nourishment for itself," *Historia Plantarum* 1.1.9).[9] It appears, then, that these cosmic "roots" somehow nurture the development and continued growth of the cosmos.

---

[7] See Vernant 1965:148. The Presocratic philosophers likewise describe the structure of the cosmos in terms of the structure of plants. See, for instance, Xenophanes' statement that the earth is ἐπ' ἄπειρον ... ἐρριζῶσθαι (A47 Diels-Kranz 1954), perhaps "rooted up to boundlessness." (For the translation of ἐπί + accusative as "up to" cf. LSJ s.v. C.I.2.b.) With this phrase, like the Hesiodic poets at *Theogony* 727–728, Xenophanes offers an explanation for the stability of the earth (cf. Aristotle *De Caelo* 294a). By describing the earth as "rooted up to boundlessness," Xenophanes implies that there is no point below the earth's roots to which they could sink; hence, neither could the earth sink, since it rests on these infinite roots. See also Anaximander A10.33–36 DK, which describes the cosmos as surrounded by "a ball of flame ... like bark on a tree" (φλογὸς σφαῖραν ... ὡς τῶι δένδρωι φλοιόν). According to Hahn (2001, esp. 192–194), Anaximander's cosmos shows close structural similarities with a tree. It is cylindrical, and from an aerial view it would have the appearance of concentric circles, like the concentric rings of a tree trunk. On the use of metaphor by the Presocratics and later philosophers, see Lakoff and Johnson 1999.

[8] For further discussion of the lexical root φυ- in images of order and disorder, see Chapter 6 below.

[9] I quote *Historia Plantarum* from Amigues 1988–2006. Cf. Aristotle's comparisons of the root of a plant to the mouth of an animal, e.g., *De Vita et Morte* 468a.9–12.

Images of Trees, Pillars, and Cosmic Order in Homeric Poetry

With these images, then, the Hesiodic poets helped their audiences to imagine the permanent structure of the cosmos by describing it in terms of the plants that they were able to observe in their own environments. As we shall see, the Homeric poets likewise employed vegetal imagery in their descriptions of the cosmos; nevertheless, their use of such images clearly differs from that of their Hesiodic counterparts. In the Homeric poems, images of trees and pillars do not describe the actual structure of the cosmos, but rather evoke concepts associated with cosmic order, such as stability and permanence. Moreover, the Homeric poets associated challenges and changes to cosmic order with floral growths.

On the face of it, descriptions of Ogygia, island of Calypso, in *Odyssey* 1 and 5 offer the closest Homeric parallels for the Hesiodic images discussed above. Nevertheless, a careful study of the images in question reveals important differences from their Hesiodic equivalents that hold also for the other Homeric images of trees and pillars that we shall consider. Calypso's island is first described at *Odyssey* 1.50–54:

> νήσῳ ἐν ἀμφιρύτῃ, ὅθι τ' ὀμφαλός ἐστι θαλάσσης.
> νῆσος δενδρήεσσα, θεὰ δ' ἐν δώματα ναίει,
> Ἄτλαντος θυγάτηρ ὀλοόφρονος, ὅς τε θαλάσσης
> πάσης βένθεα οἶδεν, ἔχει δέ τε κίονας αὐτὸς
> μακράς, αἳ γαῖάν τε καὶ οὐρανὸν ἀμφὶς ἔχουσι.

> *Odyssey* 1.50–54

> ... on a sea-girt isle, where is the navel of the sea.
> It is a wooded isle, and a goddess dwells there,
> daughter of Atlas of the baleful mind, who knows
> the depths of all the sea, and he himself holds the long
> pillars, which keep apart the earth and heaven.

Some scholars have argued that this passage reflects claims in wider Greek culture about the way the cosmos is structured, which in turn echo descriptions of the cosmos in other cultures. As Mircea Eliade has shown, the world according to the belief systems of many preindustrial peoples is structured around a Cosmic Tree, Pillar, or Navel, representing an *axis mundi* that connects earth, heaven, and underworld and that allows communication between the three realms.[10] Such peoples, then, treat images of trees and pillars as equivalent. And this equivalence is readily explicable: pillars in buildings would originally have been formed from tree trunks, even if they were later replaced by stone cylinders.[11] The presence of such imagery in early Greek culture is suggested by references to the ὀμφαλός (navel) of Delphi, which was believed to be located at the center of the world.[12]

Michael Nagler and Egbert Bakker (the latter drawing directly on the work of Eliade) have identified echoes of such beliefs in our passage from the *Odyssey*, which likewise incorporates images of pillars, trees, and navels.[13] As we hear in lines 52–54, Calypso's father Atlas holds pillars that separate earth and heaven (γαῖάν τε καὶ οὐρανόν); the goddess herself lives ὅθι τ᾽ ὀμφαλός ἐστι θαλάσσης, "where is the navel of the sea" (50). According to these scholars, the ὀμφαλός at line 50 could be seen as "the umbilical cord between the various parts of the universe," while Atlas, whose body connects two compartments of the cosmos, is "the axial figure *par excellence*."[14] If this is the case, these different descriptions of navels, pillars, and trees would fulfill a similar function to that of the Hesiodic images discussed above: they would tell us something about the structure of the cosmos. These images from the *Odyssey* appear, moreover, to be echoed and reinforced by an arboreal image found in a later description of Calypso's island: a fir tree is described as οὐρανομήκης ("heaven-high," 5.239).[15] Like Atlas' body, this tree reaches from one distinct realm to another—from the earth to the heavens: perhaps, then, this image also suggests the *axis mundi*.[16]

But there is, in fact, a different way to construe the relationships between these images: rather than seeing them all as references to the *axis mundi* or,

---

[10] See Eliade 1963:265–300, 1988:269–274 (the Cosmic Tree), 1959:32–36, 53–54, 1988:259–266 (cosmic pillars), 1963:231–235, 374–379 (cosmic imagery of navels), 1963:367–385 (the *axis mundi*). For the interconnections between these four sets of images, see also Butterworth 1970.

[11] See Hahn 2001, esp. 192–194 on the equivalence of images of trees and pillars in Anaximander's descriptions of the cosmos: according to Hahn, this reflects the fact that in Anaximander's time stone columns had recently replaced trees in the construction of temples. For Anaximander's cosmic imagery, see also n7 above.

[12] For Delphi as the center of the world, see Eustathius on *Odyssey* 1.50. On the cosmic significance of the "navel" at Delphi, see Butterworth 1970:32–37.

[13] Nagler 1996, Bakker 2001.

[14] Bakker 2001:345, Nagler 1996:145.

[15] Relative to their treatments of Odyssean allusions to pillars and navels, Bakker and Nagler express less certainty over the axial associations of Calypso's tree. Nagler (1996:146n13) wonders whether "the fir tree on Calypso's island is 'heaven-reaching'... in more than a figurative sense." Bakker (2001:345) observes that "it might ... be repeating the axial nature of Calypso and her father [Atlas], with the trees acting as the symbol for the 'pillars of heaven' or the 'navel of the sea.'"

[16] We might also note that at 1.50–54 the trees of Calypso's island—it is a "wooded island" (νῆσος δενδρήεσσα, 51)—are juxtaposed with the imagery of Atlas' pillars and the navel of the sea.

indeed, to some other aspect of cosmic architecture, we can understand them as more general evocations of concepts associated with cosmic order, such as stability and permanence. Such a reading of these images would accord with the analysis of metaphor proposed by George Lakoff, Mark Johnson, and Mark Turner.[17] As Lakoff and his colleagues demonstrate, we draw on concrete constituents of our natural and built environments to help us grasp more abstract concepts. We might imagine rhetorical arguments in terms of architectural structures, or we might use the parts of plants to help us understand aspects of human lives: a plant's shedding its leaves or flowers could illustrate the loss of youth, as in the elegiac poems discussed in Chapter 7.[18] And the insights of Lakoff et al. are readily applicable to Homeric images of trees and pillars, whether in *Odyssey* 1 and 5 or in the passages that we shall discuss below. Early audiences would have been able to observe the stability of trees in the natural world, which contrast starkly with the sudden growths of Greek flowers. And they would also have been familiar with the stabilizing function of pillars in buildings. Accordingly, when the Homeric poets juxtaposed images of trees and pillars with allusions to cosmic stability, listeners would have been able to draw on the former, more concrete concepts to understand the latter.

Two considerations support the notion that these passages from the *Odyssey* do not offer literal depictions of cosmic architecture, but rather descriptions of cosmic stability in keeping with Lakoff's, Johnson's, and Turner's understanding of metaphor. Firstly, if the lines quoted above were giving a cosmic geography lesson, they would be doing a remarkably poor job at it. Those lines would offer a very vague account of cosmic structure. It is not at all clear how the different elements of the description at 1.50-54—Atlas, the navel, the pillars—relate to one another.[19] Nor is it clear how they relate to other descriptions of the cosmos that would have been familiar to early audiences. It is possible for instance that the unusual image of the "navel of the sea" would have reminded listeners of the "navel" at Delphi—and, indeed, the Byzantine commentator Eustathius associates these two "navels" in his discussion of *Odyssey* 1.50-51. But if the image in

---

[17] Lakoff and Johnson 2003; Lakoff and Turner 1989. For the work of Lakoff et al., see my Introduction.

[18] Lakoff and Johnson 2003:98–114 (arguments), Lakoff and Turner 1989:41 (parts of a plant).

[19] Equivalent imagery in the Hesiodic *Theogony* is somewhat more precise: at *Theogony* 517–519, Atlas is situated at the edges of the earth, near the Hesperides, and he supports heaven (οὐρανόν) with his shoulders. In another passage silver pillars reach to heaven from the home of Styx, likewise situated at the ends of the earth (777–779). A little later the water of the Styx, likewise situated at the end of the earth, receives the epithet ὠγύγιον, "primeval;" which is reminiscent of Ogygia, the name of Calypso's island (806). We are still left to figure out how the silver pillars of line 779 might relate to the labor of Atlas or, indeed, to the vegetal imagery explored above. But the individual passages are at least clear in their implications.

our passage of the *Odyssey* put early audiences in mind of Delphi and thereby of the center of the earth, it is not immediately obvious how they would have understood the relationship between the two images: it is not possible that both Delphi and Ogygia are situated at the earth's center.[20] It is more likely, then, that the image of the "navel of the sea" carries with it more general suggestions of cosmic order than that it offers a precise lesson in the structure of the cosmos.[21] At most, such imagery suggests the sorts of concepts associated with the axial images, such as cosmic stability.[22]

Secondly, early audiences would have construed the implications of the trees and pillars of *Odyssey* 1.50–54 not only on the basis of concepts from wider Greek culture, but also in the light of similar imagery from Homeric poetry, found in the sorts of passages we shall discuss below.[23] And such imagery would likewise have discouraged them from seeing the descriptions of Calypso's island as precise references to the structure of the cosmos. In none of the relevant passages could the images of trees and pillars represent elements of cosmic architecture. Nevertheless, all of the other passages that we shall consider in this chapter juxtapose such imagery with evocations of cosmic order. The *Hymn to Apollo*, for instance, offers no indication that the pillar in Zeus' house is part of the structure of the cosmos: we are not led to believe that it supports the heavens or acts as a conduit between the different levels of the cosmos. This stable feature of Zeus' home is, however, juxtaposed with a description of the union of Zeus and Apollo on Olympus. A reading of the hymn after the fashion of Lakoff, Johnson, and Turner offers an economical explanation for this juxtaposition: audiences are being invited to draw on their experience of pillars in their built environments to understand the cosmic stability that Apollo's alliance with Zeus guarantees. Similarly, it seems very unlikely that the tree on which Sleep comes to rest in *Iliad* 14 represents the *axis mundi* or, indeed, any other aspect of cosmic architecture. Nonetheless, the juxtaposition of this mighty tree with evocations of cosmic order in the relevant passage would have enabled audiences to use their knowledge of trees in the natural environment to understand

---

[20] Butterworth (1970:32–37) proposes that the two images both suggest "a navelstring between earth and heaven" (p. 37), rather than strictly the center of the earth. But if the phrase ὀμφαλός θαλάσσης carries such a significance, this is far from clear in our passage from *Odyssey* 1.

[21] Associations of the "navel of the sea" at *Odyssey* 1.50 with cosmic order would have particular salience from a divine perspective (see Chapter 5 below).

[22] Other Homeric usages of the lexeme ὀμφαλός, however, would have encouraged audiences to construe the phrase "the navel of the sea" not as an allusion to cosmic imagery but as a description of the geographical position of Calypso's island relative to the sea: it is like a nub surrounded by water on all sides: see chapter 5 n29 below. Such an interpretation of the phrase is particularly relevant to Odysseus' perspective on Ogygia.

[23] Cf. J. M. Foley's (1999, 2002) notion of "traditional referentiality" in oral poetics.

the more abstract concepts involved in the story. As we shall see, Sleep's settling on the tree would, in particular, have reminded listeners of the stable order that the god undermines by incapacitating Zeus, the ruler of the cosmos.

All this suggests that images of trees or pillars play very different roles in Homeric and Hesiodic poetry: the Hesiodic imagery studied above describes the actual structure of the cosmos, but the Homeric poets used images of trees and pillars to help their audiences understand the abstract concepts of cosmic order and stability. And as we shall see, we can apply a similar analysis also to the floral images in the relevant scenes. These latter images are juxtaposed with evocations of challenges and changes to cosmic order and would have helped audiences to understand those abstract concepts. Listeners would have been familiar with the sudden intrusions of flowers into Greek spring land-scapes, and this phenomenon offered them a way to conceptualize the disruption of orderly structures in the relevant scenes. And in this way a tension is generated between the associations of flowers and the associations of trees and pillars, both in the passages that we shall study and in the Homeric corpus as a whole.

Homeric Floral and Arboreal Imagery: Change and Continuity in the Cosmos

The *Hymn to Demeter* provides our first example of associations of flowers with cosmic change. We have already discussed the opening of the hymn as the story of the seduction and deception of Korē and considered the particular associa-tions of the narcissus with such themes. But the narcissus and the hymn's other floral images are also associated with changes in the order of the cosmos.[24] As will become clear, we can gain a full understanding of the treatment of such themes in the hymn only if we take into account the precise details of the poem's images and the interactions of such images with the characteristics of flowers in the Greek natural environment.

The hymn offers a clear picture of the way in which the cosmos was struc-tured prior to the events that it describes. The cosmos was neatly divided into three realms: Olympus, the earth and the Underworld. As we can infer from the final action of the poem (310–486), Zeus is the ruler of Olympus and, as Helios recalls in lines 85–87, Hades was allotted the world of the dead. What is more, Hades gained this privilege as part of a threefold division of the cosmos:

---

[24] For such changes in the hymn, see also Rudhardt 1994 and Clay 2006:202–266.

ἀμφὶ δὲ τιμὴν
ἔλλαχεν ὡς τὰ πρῶτα διάτριχα δασμὸς ἐτύχθη·
τοῖς μεταναιετάει τῶν ἔλλαχε κοίρανος εἶναι.

Hymn to Demeter 85–87

He was allotted
This honor when first the three-way division occurred;
He dwells with those whose king he is by lot.

Helios appears to be referring to the division of the world between Zeus, Hades, and Poseidon, to which the latter alludes in *Iliad* 15, as he asserts his claim to the sea and to honors equal to those of Zeus:[25]

τρεῖς γάρ τ' ἐκ Κρόνου εἰμὲν ἀδελφεοί, οὓς τέκετο Ῥέα,
Ζεὺς καὶ ἐγώ, τρίτατος δ' Ἀΐδης ἐνέροισιν ἀνάσσων·
τριχθὰ δὲ πάντα δέδασται, ἕκαστος δ' ἔμμορε τιμῆς·

Iliad 15.187–189

We are three brothers from Cronus, whom Rhea bore,
Zeus and I, and third Hades, lord of the dead;
All things have been divided in three, and each has a share of honor.

The events of *Iliad* 15 show that Poseidon's claim of equality is tendentious: it seems he ultimately has no choice but to accept Zeus' will. Yet his description of three realms and three broad spheres of influence is not challenged; and we can draw on it to understand Helios' statement at *Hymn to Demeter* 85–87.

But the hymn also adds one important detail that is not mentioned by Poseidon at *Iliad* 15.187–189. The relevant lines from the *Iliad* make no claim about the possibility or impossibility of communication between the three realms. The action of the *Hymn to Demeter*, however, only makes sense if in the narrative time of the hymn this threefold division includes a rigid boundary between the upper and lower worlds. If this strict division did not exist, the abduction of Korē would not represent such a problem for Demeter.[26] She searches for her daughter in the upper world (40–73), but as soon as she hears from Helios that Hades has taken her daughter (74–87), she abandons her search. Apparently Hermes alone is able to travel to and from the Underworld in his role of the guide of the mortal dead, who make a one-way journey from the upper to the

---

[25] Cf. Richardson 1974 and H. P. Foley 1994 on *Hymn to Demeter* 85–86; Clay 2006:220n66.
[26] Rudhardt 1994:203: "Unless we accept this impermeability, the myth of Demeter, Hades, and Persephone is incomprehensible."

lower world.[27] But Demeter is unable to pursue Korē to the Underworld; it must not be possible for her to pass through the boundary between the two worlds.

As we shall see, Demeter's problem is solved through changes to the existing order of the cosmos, and these changes are closely associated with descriptions of flowers. But Korē and Demeter are not the only ones to suffer from the rigid division between the upper and lower worlds:[28] it causes a problem also for another god, and the solution to that problem is likewise associated with floral imagery. If only Hermes is able to travel to and from the upper world at the start of the hymn, Hades, the god who separates mother and daughter in the first place, faces his own challenge: he is unable to visit the upper world to win a bride. The opening sequence describes the solution to Hades' problem: the narcissus punches a hole in the previously impassable barrier between the upper and lower worlds and thus allows Hades to leave the Underworld.

The importance of the growth of the narcissus to Hades' journey to the upper world is made clear in lines 15–17. The earth gapes immediately after Korē plucks the flower, and Hades leaps forth on the spot:

> ἡ δ' ἄρα θαμβήσασ' ὠρέξατο χερσὶν ἄμ' ἄμφω
> καλὸν ἄθυρμα λαβεῖν· χάνε δὲ χθὼν εὐρυάγυια
> Νύσιον ἄμ' πεδίον τῇ ὄρουσεν ἄναξ πολυδέγμων ...

> *Hymn to Demeter* 15–17

> Wondering at it she reached for it with both hands
> To seize the lovely toy; the earth of the wide ways gaped
> Along the Nysian Plain where the lord who welcomes many
> rose up ...

The speed with which these actions follow one another suggests that Korē's plucking the flower directly precipitates Hades' emergence from the land of the dead. The flower creates the necessary passageway for him to travel to the upper world.

But the narcissus' growth is of greater significance than is implied by its role in solving Hades' personal problem; crucially, it breaches the boundary between

---

[27] For Hermes' role as guide of the dead in Homeric poetry, see *Hymn to Hermes* 572 and *Odyssey* 24.1–14. See also Chapter 8 n54 below.

[28] If Rudhardt (1994) and Clay (2006:202–266) are correct, the strict division between the upper and lower world also causes a problem for mortals, who are condemned after death to a wretched existence below the earth. But Persephone's annual journeys to the Underworld (mentioned below) will allow her to intercede with Hades on behalf of those initiated into her Eleusinian cult and thereby to secure them a special status in the Underworld: they will be "blessed" after death (*Hymn to Demeter* 480–482). See also Chapter 9 n22 below.

the upper and lower worlds for the first time and thus creates the pattern for subsequent breaches. In this sense, the flower is a "miracle": it not only allows Hades to complete a previously impossible and impermissible journey but, more importantly, opens up the possibility of future journeys—whether for Hades or for other characters.[29] After the growth of the narcissus, the barrier between the upper and lower worlds can no longer be conceived as impassable: the question only remains for whom, when, and on what terms it may be crossed in the future.

Audiences' understanding of the importance of the narcissus to the ordering of the cosmos would have been enhanced by the description of the flower. The hymn's depiction of the narcissus evokes the three compartments of the Homeric cosmos—the heavens, the earth, and the Underworld—and suggests its effect on all three:

> τοῦ καὶ ἀπὸ ῥίζης ἑκατὸν κάρα ἐξεπεφύκει,
> κῶζ' ἥδιστ' ὀδμή, πᾶς δ' οὐρανὸς εὐρὺς ὕπερθε
> γαῖά τε πᾶσ' ἐγέλασσε καὶ ἁλμυρὸν οἶδμα θαλάσσης.
>
> *Hymn to Demeter 12–14*

And from its root a hundred heads had grown,
And the sweetest smell arose, and all wide heaven above,
And all the earth and the salt swell of the sea laughed.

The narcissus grows from a root (ἀπὸ ῥίζης), i.e., from the realm of Hades below the ground; it blooms above the ground with a hundred heads (ἑκατὸν κάρα ἐξεπεφύκει); its sweet scent (κῶζ' ἥδιστ' ὀδμή) causes all heaven, the earth, and the sea to smile. These details suggest the change that has occurred in the relationships between the three realms of the cosmos. The very structure of the flower, which connects roots below the ground to blooms above it, mirrors the new connections that it creates between the upper and lower worlds. And the flower's growth from beneath the ground suggests the new possibility of movement from the Underworld to the upper world.[30]

What is more, such suggestions of interconnections and movement between the different compartments of the cosmos are reinforced by the interactions of the description of the narcissus with the characteristics of narcissi in the Greek natural environment. Firstly, as Theophrastus informs us, the stem of the narcissus, like the suddenly growing plant of the hymn, emerges immediately,

---

[29] Rudhardt 1994:205.

[30] Cf. Chirassi (1968:102) on flowers in Greek culture more generally: "Il fiore affondando nella terra la sua parte essenziale, vitale (radice, rizoma o bulbo) appartiene fonadmentalmente al mondo ipogeo, rappresenta quasi un tramite, un passaggio dall'una all'altra sfera."

pushing up its flower-head.[31] It is, then, an excellent choice to convey the notion of a sudden growth that breaches the surface of the earth. Secondly, the appearance of the different species of *Narcissus* in nature echoes the clear division between flower and root described in the hymn, which suggests, in turn, the division between the upper and lower worlds: narcissi are comprised of a stem with no leaves that supports a single flower or inflorescence.[32]

The appearance of the flower in the hymn, however, represents an artistic development of the natural characteristics of narcissi, which would be impossible in nature. As explained in Chapter 2, the lines in question may well allude to many-headed narcissi such as the *Narcissus tazetta* or *N. papyraceus*, which grow multiple flower heads on a single stem. The Homeric poets have, however, exaggerated the profusion of the plant's inflorescence, from at most twenty flowers in nature to a hundred in the hymn.[33] This exaggeration serves further to emphasize the contrast between the head and root of the plant, and to give a still clearer impression of the distinction between the upper and lower worlds. Such manipulation of data from the natural environment would have given audiences an understanding of the disruptive function of the flower, as it breaks apart the existing divisions of the universe: its appearance encapsulates the contrasts between the different compartments of the cosmos, while its upward movement suggests the creation of a new pathway between them.

The growth of the narcissus not only causes the first breach in the boundary between the Underworld and the upper world but, as we see from floral imagery later in the hymn, is also reenacted in subsequent breaches. Such breaches are associated in the hymn with the annual returns of Korē, which solve the problem of Demeter described above. As a result of Demeter's actions in the second half of the hymn, Zeus grants Korē the ability to pass between the upper and lower worlds. In order to force Zeus' hand, Demeter starves mortals and animals of grain and thereby deprives the gods of sacrifices (305–332). And her plan succeeds: a compromise is eventually struck, whereby Persephone will spend two thirds of each year above ground but one third below it (398–400, 463–465). In every subsequent year, she will pass from the lower to the upper world and back again.

We saw in Chapter 2 that Korē is a double of the narcissus—a "flower-faced girl" who sees an image of herself in the flower.[34] When she re-appears from

---

[31] Theophrastus *Historia Plantarum* 7.13.6.

[32] Cf. Theophrastus *Historia Plantarum* 7.13.2.

[33] Cf. Huxley and Taylor 1977:153 and Polunin 1980:502 on narcissi in the Greek natural environment.

[34] As mentioned in Chapter 2, Korē is described as καλυκῶπις, "flower-faced," at the moment she picks the narcissus (line 8).

the Underworld every year, then, it is as if the narcissus blooms afresh. That we should interpret her re-emergence in this way is suggested by the following words of Demeter:

> ὁππότε δ' ἄνθεσι γαῖ' εὐώδε[σιν] ἠαρινο[ῖσι]
> παντοδαποῖς θάλλει, τότ' ἀπὸ ζόφου ἠερόεντος
> αὖτις ἄνει μέγα θαῦμα θεοῖς θνητοῖς τ' ἀνθρώποις.

Hymn to Demeter 401–403

When the earth blooms with all kinds of fragr[ant]
Spr[ing] flowers, then again you will rise up
A great wonder to the gods and mortal men.

Korē will rise up like a flower, along with the other blooms of the earth. With this prediction Demeter associates her daughter's annual re-birth with the annual re-appearance of flowers in the spring. Audiences were thus encouraged to imagine the puncturing of the barrier between the upper and lower worlds that is described in the hymn in terms of the blooming of spring flowers. The change to the cosmos was as great as the change from the winter landscape to that of the spring—a particularly sudden change in Greece.[35] Conversely, audiences would also have gained a new perspective on the blooms they saw every spring: these sudden irruptions into the Greek landscape reenacted and confirmed the original breach in the structure of the cosmos.

And it may, in fact, be the case that the spring growths of *Hymn to Demeter* 401–403 represent a still more marked change than these subsequent springs. The explicit reference to spring flowers at *Hymn to Demeter* 401 suggests a contrast with the flowery meadow at the start of the poem, which is not explicitly associated with the spring—even though it resembles the spring meadows that would have been familiar to early audiences. Korē's first re-birth may, then, precipitate the first spring—the first return of floral blooms after the darkness and barrenness of winter.[36] On this reading, before Demeter withers the plants

---

[35] On the suddenness of the Greek spring blooms, see Introduction; Motte 1971:10, Braudel 1972: 233, Huxley and Taylor 1977:21, 24, Polunin 1980:30–31. See also Höhfeld 2009:39 on the Troad.

[36] See Rudhardt 1994:207–208. Clay (2006:255–256), arguing against the idea that Korē's return coincides with the first spring, draws on two pieces of evidence from the hymn. She points out that Korē's mother Demeter is described as ὠρηφόρος, "bringer of seasons," not only after the description of Korē's annual returns (line 492), but also on two occasions earlier in the hymn (54, 192). And she argues that "[t]he presence of agriculture, upon which the hymn insists from its outset, presupposes the existence of seasons" (p. 255). But it is unclear whether the epithet ὠρηφόρος refers to Demeter's role before the narrative time of the hymn or in the present time of hymnic performance—that is, a time after the changes described in the hymn. Moreover, the concept of agricultural labor does not require seasonal change, any more than the flowery

of the earth in response to Korē's abduction (305–309), they had flourished constantly. Korē's return from the Underworld would thus act as an *aition* for the seasons that were observed by Homeric audiences and as an archetype for all subsequent disruptions of winter landscapes by spring blooms. If this is the case, the reordering of the cosmos as a whole is here illustrated by way of a reordering of time on earth.

We have seen, then, that the floral images of the *Hymn to Demeter* are associated with changes in the structure of the cosmos. Floral imagery in the Delian half of the *Hymn to Apollo* carries similar associations. The sudden growth of flowers on Delos suggests the changes to the cosmic order either threatened or actualized by the birth of Apollo. The arrival of Apollo carries with it a potential threat to Zeus' supremacy; nevertheless Apollo declares his allegiance to his father. Apollo claims new prerogatives and thus effects a change in cosmic order; but in so doing he strengthens rather than undermines Zeus' divine dispensation. Conversely, images of a pillar and a tree suggest the stability and endurance of the cosmic order guaranteed by Zeus and Apollo. In this way, the imagery of the hymn would have helped audiences to understand the tensions between forces of change and continuity in the poem.

Apollo demonstrates his ability to destabilize the cosmic order in the opening scene of the hymn; but an image of a pillar suggests the reconciliation of his power with that of Zeus. The potential threat posed by Apollo is made clear in the first four lines, which describe him as he makes an appearance among the Olympian gods, whether for the first time or on one of many occasions.[37] He draws his bow, and all the gods leap from their seats:

> Μνήσομαι οὐδὲ λάθωμαι Ἀπόλλωνος ἑκάτοιο,
> ὅν τε θεοὶ κατὰ δῶμα Διὸς τρομέουσιν ἰόντα·
> καί ῥά τ' ἀναΐσσουσιν ἐπὶ σχεδὸν ἐρχομένοιο
> πάντες ἀφ' ἑδράων, ὅτε φαίδιμα τόξα τιταίνει.
>
> *Hymn to Apollo* 1–4

> I will remember nor will I forget far-shooting Apollo,
> At whose entrance the gods tremble throughout the house of Zeus;
> And they all leap up from their seats
> As he comes close, when he draws his shining bow.

---

meadow of the opening lines has to be a spring meadow. Audiences were free to assume that the agricultural labor prior to the action of the hymn took place all year round.

[37] The mixture of tenses in the opening thirteen lines (present, aorist, imperfect) leaves it unclear whether the hymn is describing one particular occasion or Apollo's habitual actions on arriving at Zeus' house: see n39 below.

These opening lines set up the prospect of a violent challenge from the god. And since the action occurs specifically in "the house of Zeus," they suggest the possibility of a challenge to Zeus' authority.[38]

The following lines however create a more positive impression of Apollo's relationship with Zeus and with the other gods:

> 5 Λητὼ δ' οἴη μίμνε παραὶ Διὶ τερπικεραύνῳ,
> ἥ ῥα βιόν τ' ἐχάλασσε καὶ ἐκλήϊσε φαρέτρην,
> καί οἱ ἀπ' ἰφθίμων ὤμων χείρεσσιν ἑλοῦσα
> τόξον ἀνεκρέμασε πρὸς κίονα πατρὸς ἑοῖο
> πασσάλου ἐκ χρυσέου· τὸν δ' εἰς θρόνον εἷσεν ἄγουσα.
> 10 τῷ δ' ἄρα νέκταρ ἔδωκε πατὴρ δέπαϊ χρυσείῳ
> δεικνύμενος φίλον υἱόν, ἔπειτα δὲ δαίμονες ἄλλοι
> ἔνθα καθίζουσιν· χαίρει δέ τε πότνια Λητώ,
> οὕνεκα τοξοφόρον καὶ καρτερὸν υἱὸν ἔτικτεν.

Hymn to Apollo 5–13

> 5 Leto alone remained beside Zeus who delights in thunder;
> She slackened [Apollo's] bow and closed his quiver,
> And taking his weapon from his mighty shoulders
> With her hands she hung it on the pillar of his father
> From a golden peg; and leading him she sat him down on a chair.
> 10 Father Zeus gave Apollo nectar in a golden cup,
> And offered a pledge to his dear son; then the other gods
> Resume their seats; lady Leto rejoices,
> Because she bore a bow-wielding, mighty son.

While the other gods are alarmed and quite literally forced from their proper places, Zeus is unperturbed by Apollo's arrival. The calmness also of Leto, the only other god to keep her composure, associates her with Zeus and shows her confidence that her son does not, in fact, intend to attack Zeus and the other gods. And Apollo's menace is finally dissipated when Leto takes his bow and hangs it on a pillar of Zeus' house (8).

Audiences' familiarity with the stabilizing function of pillars in buildings would have helped them to understand the implications of this image. The

---

[38] And this suggestion might not have appeared far-fetched. Audiences acquainted with the Hesiodic *Catalogue of Women* would have heard how Apollo slew the Cyclopes after Zeus killed Apollo's son Asclepius (frr. 51–54(c) MW). Though this is not an all-out insurrection, it is at the very least a violent riposte to Zeus. See above on challenges to Zeus in Hesiodic poetry and n1 of this chapter on *Catalogue of Women* frr. 51–54(c) MW; see also my Conclusion. For Apollo's potential to challenge Zeus' rule in the hymn, see also Clay 2006:17–94 and Felson 2011:271–279. On the drama of this opening scene, cf. Martin 2000:422.

description of Apollo's disorderly arrival on Olympus in the opening lines has now given way to an image of stability associated with Zeus and Apollo and with the relationship between the two gods. Leto places Apollo's bow on the pillar of Zeus' house and at that moment Zeus is described as Apollo's father (line 8). Further emphasis is placed on their relationship in lines 10–11, which describe how "Father Zeus gave Apollo nectar in a golden cup, / And offered a pledge to his dear son." The demonstration of their bond serves as the signal for the other Olympians to resume their seats (11–12). While the opening lines depict a challenge to order on Olympus, the image of a pillar—a stable architectural element—associates the relationship between Zeus and Apollo with the concept of stability. As we shall see, these elements of the scene anticipate Apollo's adoption of positive roles within Zeus' Olympian regime later in the poem: father and son will work together in support of the same cosmic order.

But the mention of Leto's joy in lines 12–13 adds a somewhat discordant note to the opening scene: her joy (χαίρει, 12) is occasioned not by the reconciliation of Zeus and Apollo but by Apollo's might and archery (13), qualities that recall his violent entrance in the first four lines.[39] And this ambivalent ending sets the tone for the remainder of the Delian half of the hymn, which holds in balance suggestions of the young Apollo's potential for disorder with indications of the more positive contributions that he will eventually make.

Firstly, the account of Leto's search for a place to give birth to the new god echoes the description of Apollo's threatening behavior in the first four lines and gives a clearer indication of the threat that the new god poses. The pregnant Leto tours the Greek world, trying to find a land willing to host her son, but all the islands and cities take fright at the thought of the new god (30–47). Like the gods in the opening scene, who "tremble" at Apollo's fearsome appearance (τρομέουσιν, 2), these different places "were trembling" (ἐτρόμεον, 47) at the thought of Apollo's birth. And when Leto appeals last of all to Delos, the island likewise "tremble[s]" (τρομέω, 66). For it has heard that Apollo will be

---

[39] Cf. Clay 2006:22. What is more, the mixed verb tenses of these lines leave it unclear whether Apollo's threat has been contained once and for all. The first thirteen lines of the hymn mix present, imperfect, and aorist tenses, and thus leave open whether a single event (aorist) or a repeated event (present, imperfect) is being described. The aorist tenses that describe Leto's actions in lines 6–9—ἐχάλασσε, ἐκλήϊσε, ἀνεκρέμασε, εἷσεν ("slackened, closed, hung, sat ... down")—seem to describe a decisive resolution to the threat posed by Apollo. But the present tenses, particularly those in the first four lines (τρομέουσιν, ἀναΐσσουσιν, τιταίνει—"they tremble," "they leap up," "he draws"), suggest a repetition of Apollo's threatening arrival—this is what happens *whenever* Apollo appears on Olympus. Bakker's (2005:139–146) reading of these verbs, however, gives us more reason to be confident in the reconciliation of Zeus and Apollo. If he is correct, it is not so much the action of the god that is repeated but the performance of his action in the presence of the audience, once that action has been brought forth from memory by the poet.

"exceedingly reckless" (λίην ... ἀτάσθαλον, 67) and that "he will rule greatly over gods and mortals" (μέγα δὲ πρυτανευσέμεν ἀθανάτοισι / καὶ θνητοῖσι βροτοῖσιν, 68–69). Similarly, the unruly Typhoeus at *Theogony* 820–880 attempts to overthrow Zeus, "and would have ruled mortals and immortals" (καί κεν ὅ γε θνητοῖσι καὶ ἀθανάτοισιν ἄναξεν, 837). Delos, then, expects Apollo to seize power from his father in the same way that—as we learn from the *Theogony* and are reminded later in this hymn (*Hymn to Apollo* 339)—Zeus himself had displaced Cronus. If Delos' fears are in any way justified, the birth of Apollo brings with it the potential for an epochal shift in the rulership of the cosmos.

Other factors in the hymn, however, counteract the impression made by Delos' speech. As we have already heard, Zeus is unperturbed by Apollo's arrival on Olympus (line 5): it does not seem that he shares Delos' concerns about his son. But we are nowhere given reason to believe that Apollo is simply too weak to mount a challenge to his father. Presumably, then, Zeus is confident that Apollo will not *choose* to challenge him. If this is the case, the hymn offers Apollo a double compliment: he possesses the kind of dangerous power that would make him a worthy adversary for his father, but he elects to use it to more constructive ends. And as we shall see, Apollo answers Delos' fears of revolutionary change in the cosmos when, shortly after his birth, he declares his allegiance to Zeus' will: "I shall prophesy the unfailing will of Zeus to mankind" (χρήσω δ' ἀνθρώποισι Διὸς νημερτέα βουλήν, 132). The hymn, then, explores themes of change and continuity in the cosmos, but finds a way to reconcile the two: a new god claims new powers, but he will use these powers in a manner consonant with the order established by Zeus.[40]

With these considerations in mind, we can approach the vegetal imagery of the Delian half of the hymn and explore the ways in which it helps audiences to understand the themes of cosmic change and continuity. In order to get a full sense of the implications of the relevant images, it is necessary to consider their interactions with natural environments that would have been familiar to archaic Greek audiences. Early performances of the hymn may well have taken place on Delos itself. Walter Burkert, for instance, proposes that the syncretized Delian and Pythian hymn preserved in our texts—with its descriptions of Apollo's birth on Delos and subsequent career at Delphi—was performed for the first time at Polycrates of Samos' "Pythian and Delian Festival" on Delos in 523 or 522 BCE.[41] If, however, as many scholars believe, our version of the

---

[40] And it is not just Apollo's power of prophecy that benefits Zeus' cosmic regime. Despite the threat suggested in the opening scene, Apollo employs his bow to positive ends in the Pythian half of the hymn, when he slays the Pytho (see below). For Apollo's use of his powers in support of Zeus, see in general Clay 2006:17–94.

[41] Burkert 1979.

hymn combines two originally separate compositions, earlier performances of the Delian half of the hymn would nevertheless in all probability have taken place on Delos.[42] Audiences on Delos would have appreciated references to the appearance of the island and would have noticed the ways in which the Homeric poets responded to it.

We should bear this in mind when we consider references to a date-palm at lines 18 and 117 of the hymn. Firstly, Leto is described "leaning against the tall mountain and the Cynthian mound, / very close to the date-palm under the flows of the Inopus" (κεκλιμένη πρὸς μακρὸν ὄρος καὶ Κύνθιον ὄχθον, / ἀγχοτάτω φοίνικος ὑπ' Ἰνωποῖο ῥεέθροις, 17–18). Later, the hymn describes more clearly the role of the date-palm in Apollo's birth. As Leto gives birth, she kneels and braces herself against the tree: ἀμφὶ δὲ φοίνικι βάλε πήχεε ("she threw her arms around a date-palm," 117). Allen, Halliday, and Sikes explain that Greek women might adopt a kneeling position during parturition;[43] that being the case, it is reasonable that Leto would want to brace herself against a solid object of some kind. But we might ask why, in particular, a date-palm should carry out this role, rather than, for instance, the mountain that is mentioned in line 17.

In order to understand the tree's significance, we need to consider its relationship to the other vegetation described in the hymn and to the sort of Delian landscapes that would have been familiar to early audiences. Firstly, palm-trees sacred to Apollo were a notable feature of the Delian landscape.[44] They had been present on the island from an early date, as is suggested by the reference to such a tree at *Odyssey* 6.161–163: Odysseus recalls the awe he felt on seeing a date-palm by the altar of Delian Apollo. It is likely that early audiences listening to performances of the hymn on Delos would likewise have seen a tree by Apollo's altar.[45]

The hymn indeed places special emphasis on the antiquity of Delian palm-trees in contrast with the other vegetation of Delos. When the island is left uncultivated, as is the case nowadays, it reverts to a rocky and relatively infertile landscape (Plate 5).[46] The hymn's description of the island prior to the birth of Apollo responds to and, indeed, exaggerates the natural sparseness of the

---

[42] For the *Hymn to Apollo* as a composite of two originally separate compositions, see Janko 1982:99–115, who dates the Delian hymn to ca. 650 BCE.

[43] Allen, Halliday, and Sikes 1963 on *Hymn to Apollo* 117.

[44] Deonna 1946:156–157.

[45] See Stehle 1997:180–181 on the interaction of the hymn with such a tree and with other elements of its performance setting on Delos. On the antiquity of palm-trees in Delian cult, see Gallet de Santerre 1958, esp. 193–195.

[46] See Deonna's (1946:154) description of modern Delos: "Elle est resolument hostile à la végétation." This is a little extreme but does capture the barrenness of the island relative to other Greek landscapes.

vegetation on the island. Delos is portrayed as rugged and apparently barren; only the date-palm is mentioned as growing there. Early in the poem, Delos is craggy (16, 26), as the island itself admits (72), and every other land visited by Leto is more fertile (48). Leto threatens that, if Delos does not accept Apollo, it will remain infertile and will never bear animals and plants (54–55). Audiences were thus encouraged to believe that the island was at first almost lifeless. They would have gotten the impression that no vegetation other than the date-palm linked pre-Apolline and Apolline Delos, but that this one element of the island's flora had endured to their own day.[47]

Through its role in the story of Apollo's birth and its relation to the other vegetation of Delos—both that described in the hymn and that which would have been familiar to early audiences on the island, the date-palm is associated with two concepts. On one level, it is an image of stability: it is the object against which Leto braces herself as she give birth.[48] On another level, it is an image of continuity: it is the only element of the Delian vegetation that is said to have endured from pre-Apolline to Apolline Delos. And such notions would have been reinforced in early performances by audiences' knowledge of the characteristics of the palm-trees of Delos, which as noted above were an enduring feature of the island.

In this way, the arboreal image in line 117 interacts with important themes of the hymn. The Delian hymn as a whole explores notions of change and stability, of (potential) insurrection and maintenance of order: Apollo's violent intrusion at the start of the hymn is balanced by Zeus' and Leto's calm reactions; Delos' alarm at the thought of the new god is answered by Apollo's declaration of allegiance to Zeus' will (line 132). The date-palm contributes to the poem's explorations of stability and counteracts the impression that Apollo will be a source of disorder. And as with the pillar in the opening scene, this stable object is closely associated with Leto and Apollo: she places his bow on the pillar; at line 117–119 he "leaps forth" as she braces herself against the tree. Unlike the pillar, the date-palm is not explicitly associated with Zeus. Rather, given its importance to Delian cult it suggests the stability that Apollo's presence on Delos will bring. But with both images, the Homeric poets helped their audiences to understand the abstract concept of stability through concrete concepts drawn from their environments—the pillars that they would have seen in buildings and the trees of Delos and elsewhere.

---

[47] Similarly, the Pythian half of the hymn alludes to groves that would presumably have been present at Delphi in archaic times (lines 221 and 384).

[48] In its immediate context, the firm date-palm contrasts with an image of softness from the natural environment: Leto throws her arms around the tree, but presses her knees into a soft meadow (γοῦνα δ' ἔρεισε / λειμῶνι μαλακῷ, 107–108).

By contrast, floral imagery in lines 135–139 emphasizes the changes wrought by the coming of the god.[49] The relevant lines mark the moment when, shortly after his birth, Apollo first strides onto Delos. As he does so, golden blooms cover the island:

χρυσῷ δ' ἄρα Δῆλος ἅπασα

C βεβρίθει καθορῶσα Διὸς Λητοῦς τε γενέθλην,

C γηθοσύνῃ ὅτι μιν θεὸς εἵλετο οἰκία θέσθαι

C νήσων ἠπείρου τε, φίλησε δὲ κηρόθι μᾶλλον.

• ἤνθησ' ὡς ὅτε τε ῥίον οὔρεος ἄνθεσιν ὕλης.[50]

Hymn to Apollo 135–139

With gold all Delos

Was burgeoning as it saw the offspring of Zeus and Leto,
In its joy that the god chose it of the islands and mainland
To make his home, and that in his heart he liked it more.
It bloomed as a mountain headland blooms with flowers of the forest.

As scholars have noted, the description of these golden blooms marks the island's response to Apollo's divine presence—much as, for instance, the floral growths of *Odyssey* 5 or the *Hymn to Pan* respond to the presence of Calypso and Pan (see Chapters 5 and 6 below).[51] But more remains to be said about this floral image. In particular, we need to take into account its interactions with the natural environments familiar to early audiences and with the hymn's depiction of change

---

[49] Other vegetal images reflect an awareness of actual changes to the Delian flora wrought by the coming of the cult of Apollo. As mentioned above, Delos, when not subject to cultivation, presents a relatively barren terrain. In ancient times, however, extensive plantations of fruit trees and vines along with sacred groves and gardens were cultivated in honor of the god, both on Delos and on nearby islands: see Deonna 1946. And such plantations are recognized explicitly in the hymn. At line 55, Leto alludes to the vines that will grow on Delos if it accepts Apollo, and the island itself, expressing its fear that the god will establish them on another island, anticipates the planting of sacred groves (76).

[50] Lines 136–138 are preserved in the margins of manuscripts. Some critics have concluded that they belong alongside lines 135 and 139 in the main text, whether in the order that we find them in our manuscripts or in an alternative order. Other critics have regarded them as interpolations. With the exception of Càssola (1975), however, all retain line 139 and thereby the floral elements of these lines. And given that 136–138 are preserved as marginalia and 139 in the main text, the retention of line 139 is, indeed, reasonable. For the scholarly debate over the text of *Hymn to Apollo* 135–139, see also Clay 2006:45n88 with bibliography. I have printed the lines as they appear in Allen's 1912–1920 vol. V—that is, with symbols indicating main text and marginalia, but with 136–138 and 139 printed as a continuous text.

[51] For the flowers of *Hymn to Apollo* 134–139 as a response to Apollo's divine presence, see Richardson 2010 *ad loc.* Richardson compares this imagery to responses to divine epiphanies elsewhere in Homeric poetry—as for instance in *Hymn* 7, where a vine grows under the influence of Dionysus.

and continuity. We have already seen how the hymn's descriptions of the date-palm respond to characteristics of the Delian natural environment and interact with allusions in the hymn to the barrenness of Delos. Likewise, in order to get a full understanding of the floral imagery from lines 135–139 we need to consider its relationship with the other vegetation of the hymn and with the Delian landscapes that would have been familiar to early audiences. Unlike the descriptions of flowers in *Odyssey* 5 and *Hymn to Pan*, which portray them as constant features of the landscapes inhabited by Calypso and Pan (Chapter 5 below), *Hymn to Apollo* 135–139 places emphasis on the change that has occurred in the Delian flora. What is more, when we consider the relationship of the golden flowers with their immediate context and with the wider themes of the Delian half of the hymn, it becomes clear that this floral image echoes and reinforces the idea of the significant changes to the Olympian order threatened or actualized by the coming of Apollo.

The description of the golden flowers at lines 135–139 of the hymn responds to annual changes in the Delian natural environment. In spring and at the beginning of summer Delos, like other islands and coastlands of the Aegean, is lit up by a "short-lived burst of colour."[52] But the description of the flowers in the hymn departs from such natural phenomena. By describing the flowers that bloom on Apollo's arrival in terms that recall the spring blooms of the island, the Homeric poets transferred the characteristics of an annual, impermanent phenomenon to a single, transformative event, which renders the previously barren island lush with vegetation. Every subsequent spring on the previously barren island would repeat this first, miraculous bloom.[53] Similarly, as we saw above, the *Hymn to Demeter* suggests that Persephone's first re-birth from the Underworld does not merely accompany the growth of spring flowers but may also herald the world's first spring. In both instances, a repeated phenomenon from the natural environment is concentrated into a one-off, supernatural event that provides the origin for that phenomenon.

The floral imagery in lines 135–139, then, associates Apollo's presence on Delos with a significant change in the natural environment. And this depiction of a significant change in the natural world accompanies a change in the cosmic order, as we see from its immediate context and from the wider narrative of the Delian half of the hymn.

---

[52] Polunin 1980:65n4 on the spring flowers of Delos, and Bruneau 1970:89: "chaque année le printemps répand des millions de fleurs sur Délos et la Grèce entière ... ." See also Allen, Halliday, and Sikes 1963 on *Hymn to Apollo* 135: "the island is suddenly covered with golden scrub, i.e. the natural scrub burst into flower."

[53] Bruneau 1970:89 suggests that the description of flowers at *Hymn to Apollo* 135–139 anticipates the spring blooms that would accompany festivals of Apollo every year.

To understand the sort of change that has occurred we should consider, in particular, Apollo's claim of new prerogatives, which he makes immediately before the description of golden flowers. The first line of Apollo's speech has mixed connotations: "May I possess the dear cithara and the bent bow" (εἴη μοι κίθαρίς τε φίλη καὶ καμπύλα τόξα, 131). Apollo's patronage of music will benefit both gods and men. Shortly afterwards the hymn describes the music-making of the Delian maidens, who sing of the gods and of men and women of the past (157–161). In lines 182–206 Apollo himself is depicted as he makes music with the other gods. And this new association of Apollo with the sphere of music represents a change to the benefit of gods and men: both will delight in musical performances; and the gods will derive additional pleasure from the hymns of mankind.

The reference in line 131 to Apollo's "bent bow," however, would have reminded audiences of his violent entrance into the house of Zeus in the first four lines of the hymn. The description of Leto's joy at her "mighty, bow-wielding son" (125–126) also recalls the opening scene. The relevant phrases echo the language of lines 12–13, which as we have seen strike a discordant note at the end of the opening sequence: χαίρει δὲ πότνια Λητὼ / οὕνεκα τοξοφόρον καὶ καρτερὸν υἱὸν ἔτικτεν, 12–13; χαῖρε δὲ Λητώ, οὕνεκα τοξοφόρον καὶ καρτερὸν υἱὸν ἔτικτεν, 125–126 ("lady Leto rejoices [Leto was rejoicing, 125] because she bore a mighty, bow-wielding son"). As is clear by this point in the hymn, Apollo will not challenge Zeus' rule. And in fact, he later uses his bow in service of Zeus: he slays the Pytho, the foster-mother of Typhaon (357–358), whom Hera brings into the world in defiance of Zeus. But the echo of the opening scene in line 131 reminds us that Apollo had to choose not to use his potentially dangerous power against the Olympian order. In the light of these later events, we understand the significance of Leto's actions in lines 6–9: by hanging his bow on the stable pillar of his father's house, Leto suggests the stability that the alliance between Apollo and Zeus brings to the cosmos.

Moreover, the second line of Apollo's declaration carries clearly positive connotations. As mentioned above, Apollo states that he will reveal Zeus' will to mankind (132). A change to the better has thus occurred in the relationship between gods and mortals. In the absence of indications to the contrary in the hymn, it may be that this moment marks the birth of prophecy—of the communication of divine purposes to mortals.[54] At the very least, Apollo's words anticipate the establishment of the most important oracle of the Greek world, that of Delphi, which is the subject of the second half of the hymn. The coming of the oracle improves communications between the different levels of the cosmos, though in a manner distinct from the growth of the narcissus in the *Hymn to*

---

[54] See Clay 2006:43–44.

Demeter: while the narcissus opens up a physical breach between the upper and lower worlds and enables Hades to journey between them, Apollo's oracle conveys Zeus' will from Olympus to the earth.

The floral imagery of *Hymn to Apollo* 135–139 works in tandem with the surrounding lines to give a sense of the changes that have occurred, or that might have occurred, if Apollo had chosen to use his strength against the Olympian order. Apollo's words at 132–133 describe two kinds of change, one threatened and one actualized. The references to his archery in lines 125–126 and 132 remind us of his potentially dangerous power, with which he might have chosen to challenge the existing order of things. But greater emphasis is placed on the positive change that, in fact, takes place: he claims new prerogatives that support rather than undermine Zeus' Olympian order. And the floral images of lines 135–139, which describe a significant change in the natural environment, underline the significance of the change that has occurred in the cosmic order as Apollo assumes his new roles. In this way, concrete concepts of floral growth drawn from the sorts of natural environments familiar to early audiences would have helped them to understand the more abstract notion of changes to cosmic order and the part played by such concepts in this scene.

Our final set of images is taken from the Διὸς ἀπάτη in *Iliad* 14, which we studied in Chapter 3 as a story of seduction and deception. But as in the other passages that we have considered, the relevant lines also employ arboreal and floral imagery to explore the themes of cosmic order and of challenges to that order.[55] The cosmic change described in the Διὸς ἀπάτη differs, however, from the other changes that we have studied in this chapter. In the *Hymn to Demeter*, the narcissus initiates a change to the structure of the cosmos that is in accordance with Zeus' plans. In the *Hymn to Apollo*, flowers suggest the change brought about by the new god. But he chooses not to use his might in defiance of Zeus; ultimately his arrival marks an alteration of the Olympian system, not

---

[55] Since we find (a) common floral associations in these poems but (b) considerable differences in the details of their floral imagery, these passages would seem to draw on an underlying archetype of traditional Homeric poetics rather than on one another. If, for instance, the Iliadic poets were drawing directly on the hymns, we would expect the floral imagery of the Διὸς ἀπάτη to resemble more closely the imagery from one or more of the hymns. For this reason, I would agree with Schein's rather than Clay's assessment of the similarities between these passages. Clay (2011:248–249) sees thematic parallels between the stories of the hymns and the Διὸς ἀπάτη as "an instance of the epic's appropriation of hymnic material." Schein however (2012:300) regards such similarities as reflections of a common poetic system. Yasumura (2011) for her part observes that a story-pattern of challenges to Zeus' supremacy is to be found in both Homeric and Hesiodic poetry. Nevertheless, the lack of floral imagery in the relevant Hesiodic passages suggests that the challenges depicted in Homeric poetry form a class of their own. See Chapter 5 below, the opening pages of this chapter, the Preamble to Part II, and my Conclusion for comparisons of Homeric and Hesiodic explorations of order and disorder.

its overthrow. In the Διὸς ἀπάτη, by contrast, flowers are associated with a challenge to Zeus that is put into effect—though the eventual impact on the cosmic order is not nearly as great as that which is threatened by the arrival of Apollo.

As we saw in Chapter 3, Book 14 tells the story of Hera's seduction of Zeus in order to further her own aims in the Trojan War. Hera is angry at her husband for favoring the Trojans; she therefore plots to divert his attention from the battlefield so that their brother, Poseidon, can rally the Greeks. She decides to seduce her husband and therefore asks Aphrodite for the Girdle of Desire. She also appeals to the god Sleep, who is to lull Zeus into a post-coital slumber (232–279). As a result, Zeus is overcome with sleep and Hera's seductive wiles: he acknowledges that desire has conquered his mind (ἔρος ... ἐδάμασσεν, 315–316), and at lines 352–353 he lies prostrate, "conquered by love and sleep" (ὕπνῳ καὶ φιλότητι δαμείς, 353).

If we focused on these details alone, we would read this purely as a seduction scene. But a second theme that we have not yet explored runs through the whole episode alongside these erotic elements: there are a number of allusions to order and disorder in the cosmos. In Book 14, the most striking of these allusions are found in the speeches of Hera. She is obliged to explain her actions both to Aphrodite and to Zeus; and she gives pretty much the same excuse in both cases (14.200–202, 205–207 ≈ 301–306). And the justifications that she presents mingle the theme of seduction with broader cosmic themes.

At first sight, Hera's excuses seem to focus only on the theme of eroticism and to have purely innocent implications: she plans to reconcile two divine lovers, Oceanus and Tethys, who have fallen into strife. And she has a ready explanation for why she would want to help the couple: she owes them a debt of gratitude, since they raised her (14.202, 303). In this way she justifies her request for "affection and desire" (φιλότητα καὶ ἵμερον, 14.198), which Aphrodite honors by lending her the Girdle of Desire. Presumably, Hera wants Aphrodite to believe that she will use the girdle's powers to renew the divine couple's affections for one another (φιλότητος, φιλότητι, 207, 209). Hera's story also helps allay Zeus' suspicions regarding her presence on Mount Ida: she is on the way from Olympus to visit the home of Oceanus and Tethys.

Other elements of Hera's speeches, however, allude to cosmic structure and to cosmic disruption and thereby hint at the more subversive intentions that she harbors in her interactions with Zeus. In conversation with Aphrodite, she mentions the reason why she was cared for by Oceanus and Tethys: they received her from her mother Rhea "when wide-seeing Zeus / settled Cronus beneath the earth and the harvestless sea" (ὅτε τε Κρόνον εὐρύοπα Ζεὺς / γαίης νέρθε καθεῖσε καὶ ἀτρυγέτοιο θαλάσσης, 203–204). She thus refers to the structure of the cosmos (the earth and sea, the realm below) and also to a significant change in the cosmic order—Zeus' overthrow of his father Cronus. As mentioned above, this is one of the major upheavals that occur in the cosmos of the Hesiodic *Theogony* (492–500).

Hera prudently omits this last detail from her speech to Zeus. But in her speeches both to Aphrodite and to Zeus, the language that she uses to describe Oceanus and Tethys introduces further allusions to cosmic structure and disruption. She claims that she is planning to visit the ends of the earth (πείρατα γαίης, 200), a second reference to the structure of the cosmos. There she will visit "Oceanus, origin of the gods, and mother Tethys" (Ὠκεανόν τε, θεῶν γένεσιν, καὶ μητέρα Τηθύν, 201) and "resolve their indiscriminate quarrels" (σφ' ἄκριτα νείκεα λύσω, 205, 304). The two gods are described in terms reminiscent of the kinds of theogonic poetry that would have been familiar to at least some early listeners. The description of Oceanus as the "origin of the gods" departs from the Hesiodic tradition, which traces the genealogy of the gods back to Earth and Heaven. But it is reminiscent of an Orphic fragment, which Socrates cites at Plato *Cratylus* 402B, shortly after quoting *Iliad* 14.201:[56]

> Ὠκεανὸς πρῶτος καλλίρροος ἦρξε γάμοιο,
> ὅς ῥα κασιγνήτην ὁμομήτορα Τηθὺν ὄπυιεν.
>
> Plato *Cratylus* 402B = *Orphica* fr. 15 Kern

> Beautifully flowing Oceanus first began marriage,
> He who wedded Tethys, offspring of the same mother.

What is more, as Richard Janko points out, the reference at *Iliad* 14.205 and 305 to the "indiscriminate quarrels" (ἄκριτα νείκεα) of these primordial gods suggests a first stage in a theogony. Such a theogony imagines the original chaotic state of the cosmos in anthropomorphic terms, as a quarrel between two lovers. The introduction of order to the cosmos is then conceptualized as the separation of the squabbling lovers. Perhaps, then, if Hera were somehow able to reconcile these primordial parents, she would return the cosmos to its primeval, undifferentiated state.[57]

---

[56] For intersections between the Orphic and Homeric traditions, see Martin 2001 and Nagy 2010.

[57] Janko 1994 on *Iliad* 14.200–207. For the use of the term ἄκριτος to suggest disorder, see *Hymn to Pan* 26, discussed in Chapter 5 below. The description of Hera's interaction with Sleep explores similar themes to those that we have identified in her speeches to Aphrodite and to Zeus. Hera, by this stage not only decked out in her finery (14.170–186) but also wearing the Girdle of Desire, offers Sleep one of the Graces as his wife (267–268). Her tactics are, then, similar to those of Aphrodite in *Cypria* fr. 4 Bernabé, which we discussed in Chapter 2: like Aphrodite, Hera appears in her finery and wins over her interlocutor with the offer of another's hand. It is this offer that convinces Sleep to aid Hera: he asks her to swear that she will grant him the particular object of his desire, the Grace Pasithea (271–276). But the language of his speech recalls our theme of the

Hera's words would have invited ancient audiences to view the events of Book 14 in terms not only of seduction but also of cosmic disruption. Granted, it is not likely that they would have expected a complete overthrow of cosmic order of the sort hinted at by Hera's talk of reconciling Oceanus and Tethys. As with audiences of the *Hymn to Apollo*, who were aware that Apollo would not, in fact, overthrow his father, they would have known that Hera's actions would not reconstitute primal chaos, since the cosmos retained its good order in their own day. Nevertheless, Hera's allusions to Oceanus and Tethys cast her actions against her husband in *Iliad* 14 as a challenge to cosmic order. And indeed, her disabling Zeus will undermine his control of the cosmos.

Listeners would have understood the vegetal imagery of Book 14 in the light of such themes. As in the *Hymn to Apollo*, we encounter both an arboreal image that evokes the concept of stability in the cosmos and a floral image suggestive of change. After arriving on Mount Ida, where he will shortly disable the king of the gods, Sleep withdraws to a tree:

> ἔνθ' Ὕπνος μὲν ἔμεινε πάρος Διὸς ὄσσε ἰδέσθαι,
> εἰς ἐλάτην ἀναβὰς περιμήκετον, ἣ τότ' ἐν Ἴδῃ
> μακροτάτη πεφυυῖα δι' ἠέρος αἰθέρ' ἵκανεν·
> ἔνθ' ἧστ' ὄζοισιν πεπυκασμένος εἰλατίνοισιν ...

> *Iliad* 14.286–289

> There Sleep waited before the eyes of Zeus could see him,
> Having climbed onto an exceedingly high pine, which then on Ida
> Had grown very tall and reached the clear air through the mists;[58]
> There he sat, hidden by the pine branches ...

The tree on Ida could not be mistaken for the axis of the world. It is an exceptionally tall tree (περιμήκετον, μακροτάτη), which soars above the mists on the mountain; but unlike the tree on Calypso's island at *Odyssey* 5.239, it does not reach οὐρανός, the highest point of the Homeric cosmos.[59] Nevertheless, in

---

structure of the cosmos: he asks Hera to lay her hands on the earth and the sea, and to swear by the river Styx, with the Titans and Cronus beneath the earth as witnesses. He thus refers both to the upper and to the lower worlds as the basis for her oath. Cf. Hera's oath to Zeus by Earth, Heaven, and the Styx at 15.36–38, as she tries to deny responsibility for Poseidon's actions on the battlefield—that is, precisely those actions that she facilitated by disabling Zeus (14.153–165).

[58] For this interpretation of ἀήρ and αἰθήρ in *Iliad* 14.288, see Schmidt 1976:75–81 and Janko 1994 on *Iliad* 14.286–288.

[59] For the positioning of Sleep's tree, see Janko 1994 on *Iliad* 14.286–288. *Pace* Vermeule, who appears to imagine the tree as a kind of *axis mundi*, connecting two compartments of the cosmos: "The tree's branches stick through the skin of air into heaven, joining the two worlds" (1979:147).

the context of *Iliad* 14 and 15 the growth of this tree into the clear air (αἰθήρ) associates it with Zeus' cosmic governance. Such associations become evident in the following book. After Zeus has awoken and re-established his supremacy on earth, Poseidon not only lays claim to the sea (as mentioned above) but also specifies that αἰθήρ and οὐρανός are under the sway of his brother: Ζεὺς δ' ἔλαχ' οὐρανὸν εὐρὺν ἐν αἰθέρι καὶ νεφέλῃσι ("Zeus was allotted the wide heaven in the air and the clouds," *Iliad* 15.192). Sleep's tree, then, is associated with the realm of Zeus, as it is defined in this part of the *Iliad*.

The tree of 14.287–289 is also, like the date-palm and pillar of the *Hymn to Apollo*, suggestive of the stability of Zeus' rulership, which Hera hopes to undermine. As we have noted, trees were strong and stable constituents of the natural environments familiar to early audiences; the Homeric poets were therefore able to use arboreal images to help their audiences to conceptualize more abstract kinds of stability. Given the association of Sleep's tree with Zeus' realm, our passage from *Iliad* 14 suggests specifically the stability guaranteed by Zeus' rule. But when Sleep settles on this tree that reaches the clear air, his action prefigures his conquest of Zeus at 14.352–353, which offers a challenge to such stability. The image of Sleep settling on this tree would, then, have suggested to archaic audiences the potential significance of Hera's betrayal: her disabling of Zeus will (albeit temporarily) neutralize his control of the cosmos.

The floral imagery that we find later in the scene likewise suggests the cosmic implications of the events of the Διὸς ἀπάτη. At the moment when Zeus takes Hera in his arms, flowers begin to bloom beneath the divine lovers:

ἦ ῥα, καὶ ἀγκὰς ἔμαρπτε Κρόνου παῖς ἣν παράκοιτιν·
τοῖσι δ' ὑπὸ χθὼν δῖα φύεν νεοθηλέα ποίην,
λωτόν θ' ἑρσήεντα ἰδὲ κρόκον ἠδ' ὑάκινθον
πυκνὸν καὶ μαλακόν, ὃς ἀπὸ χθονὸς ὑψόσ' ἔεργε.

Iliad 14.346–349

He spoke, and the son of Cronus seized his wife in his arms;
And the bright earth was sending up fresh grass under them,
Dewy lotus, saffron and hyacinth,
Thick and soft, which kept them on high, away from the ground.

On one level, this floral imagery reflects the erotic themes explored in *Iliad* 14. While the floral images that we discussed in Chapter 2 are associated with erotic bodies prepared for seduction and deception, the imagery of *Iliad* 14.346–349 marks the climax of a story of seduction and deception. And it does so with suitably striking imagery: the floral term ὑάκινθος is found nowhere else in the *Iliad*, and the formula χθὼν δῖα, which evokes the gleam of the fecund earth, is not attested in the nominative in any other passage of Homeric poetry. But these lines also interact with the sorts of cosmic themes introduced by Hera's speeches. As in the *Hymn to Apollo*, we have an image of change in the natural environment that helps to illustrate a cosmic change. As in the hymn, an annual phenomenon—the blooming of spring flowers on Mount Ida—is here imagined not as a recurring event but as a unique response to the events of the Διὸς ἀπάτη. The bloom is sudden and miraculous: flowers appear where previously there were none.[60] This remarkable effusion of flowers suggests the potentially serious implications of the disabling of Zeus at *Iliad* 14.346–353. At line 353, he lies prostrate, conquered by love and sleep; and his governorship of the cosmos sleeps with him.[61]

When he awakes, Zeus acknowledges that Hera's insubordination could have had serious consequences. By allowing Poseidon to aid the Greeks in defiance of Zeus' will, she might have caused conflict between the two brothers. Such a conflict would have shaken the cosmos: even Cronus and the Titans would have known of it (15.225). Zeus' words echo 14.203–204, where Hera refers to Zeus' placement of Cronus below the earth.[62] Moreover, Poseidon's own words challenge Zeus' vision of cosmic order. Zeus orders Poseidon to leave the battlefield, citing his earlier birth and greater might (15.157–183). In response, Poseidon alludes to the equal apportionment of the cosmos between Zeus, Hades, and himself, quoted earlier in this chapter. He also explains that the earth was left as common ground (187–199). Poseidon thus suggests that Zeus' command to him to leave the battlefield is an affront to the proper ordering of the cosmos: he should by right enjoy freedom of action on the earth.[63]

But despite this contest of words Zeus is able quickly to reassert his control over the battlefield and over his fellow gods: the disruption caused by Hera's

---

[60] Motte 1971:218: this is a "prairie miraculeuse."

[61] As we shall see in Chapter 5, the flowers that bloom at *Hymn to Aphrodite* 169 carry similar associations: they mark both the climax of Aphrodite's seduction of Anchises and the disruption of his control over the spaces of Mount Ida.

[62] In addition, the language used by Zeus at 15.225 (οἵ περ ἐνέρτεροί εἰσι θεοί, Κρόνον ἀμφὶς ἐόντες) closely resembles that of Sleep at 14.274 (οἱ ἔνερθε θεοὶ Κρόνον ἀμφὶς ἐόντες), when he requests that Hera swears to grant him the hand of Pasithea. With these phrases, Sleep and Zeus allude to the structure of the cosmos. For Sleep's speech, see n57 above.

[63] For themes of cosmic order and disruption in the Διὸς ἀπάτη, see Fenno 2005:495–497. See also Enright and Papalas 2002, who explore the implications of the punishment with which Zeus threatens Hera early in Book 15. When Zeus wakes up he reminds Hera of the last time she disabled him with sleep, in order to disrupt Heracles' return from Troy. He punished her by hanging her from heaven on a golden chain with anvils at her feet (*Iliad* 15.16–28). Enright and Papalas argue that Zeus is describing a plumb line, a cosmic symbol of truth. With Hera suspended in this way, Zeus would have been able to use her own body to measure her deviation from justice. His threat to repeat this punishment casts her actions in Book 14 as a challenge to the just ordering of the cosmos.

disabling of Zeus does not, then, turn out to be as serious as it might have been. Poseidon chooses not to defy his brother and, at Iris' suggestion, tones down his response to Zeus (200–217): he threatens only that if Zeus chooses to spare Troy against the will of his fellow gods, he will hold "incurable anger" (ἀνήκεστος χόλος, 217) against him. Zeus' assertion of superiority over his brother, then, wins out over Poseidon's claim of equality between them, and the conflict imagined by Zeus at 224–225 does not materialize; nor, *a fortiori*, do the more serious consequences hinted at by Hera in Book 14. Zeus is also able to reverse the damage done to the Trojans by Poseidon's interference in the battle. Most importantly, he sends Apollo to revive Hector, whom during the Greeks' brief ascendancy Aias had incapacitated with a stone (14.409–420, 15.220–270).[64] The change indicated by the sudden growth of flowers at 14.346–349 is shown to be only temporary.

In this and the other Homeric passages that we have studied, the Homeric poets drew on vegetal imagery to help their audiences understand the abstract notion of order in the cosmos. Cosmic order and in particular the order guaranteed by Zeus' divine dispensation was as strong and enduring as great trees. The Homeric poets also employed floral imagery to illustrate the challenges and changes to the established order of the cosmos—whether the revolutionary challenge imagined by Hera or changes in accordance with Zeus' plans. In so doing, they drew on the changes that occurred in landscapes every year with the blooming of spring flowers but concentrated them into one-off, miraculous events.

There is more to be said about these images and about their interactions with the natural environments familiar to the Homeric poets and their audiences. In particular, we need to explain not only why flowers and trees carried *different* associations from one another, but also why they should be associated with *antithetical* notions of the established order of the cosmos and of changes and challenges to that order. As we shall see in Chapter 6, such an antithesis can be explained if we bear in mind Greek perceptions of contrasting modes of vegetal reproduction.

But before doing so we need to explore other Homeric vegetal images that form a complement to the sorts of cosmic images that we have considered in this chapter, and which will aid in our study of the modes of vegetal reproduction in Chapter 6. As will become clear, the depiction of an ongoing tension between

---

[64] Zeus moreover asserts control over mortal affairs in a manner unprecedented in the *Iliad*. He describes his plan for the remainder of the Trojan War: the Achaeans will retreat to the ships; Achilles will send Patroclus; Hector will kill Patroclus; Achilles will kill Hector; the Achaeans will take Troy (15.61–71).

the established order of the cosmos and forces of change is echoed in Homeric representations of civilization and wilderness—of good order and its opposite as those concepts relate to humankind. And again, the Homeric poets employed arboreal and floral imagery to illustrate these abstract concepts.

5

Anchises' Pastures, Laertes' Orchards
Images of Civilization and Its Opposite

Having explored Homeric vegetal imagery that describes order and threats to that order at the cosmic level, we turn now to a set of images that explores similar concepts on the human scale. We found in Chapter 4 that the Homeric poets associated trees and pillars with stability in the cosmos and flowers with challenges to that order, and thereby offered their audiences insights into these abstract concepts. As we shall see, floral and arboreal images also accompany Homeric descriptions of civic order and its opposite.

But there are important distinctions to be drawn between the two sets of images. Firstly, the images of uncivilized wildernesses that we shall study do not, in fact, distinguish between floral and arboreal growths. Both kinds of growth are associated with the wild lands haunted by Pan or with the exotic locations visited by Odysseus. Secondly, Homeric images of cosmic and civic order differ in their treatment of wild and cultivated plants. The sorts of images of cosmic order that we considered in Chapter 4 all describe wild growths. There is no indication in any of these images that the growths in question were the result of human tendance: the heaven-high fir of *Odyssey* 5, the date-palm of the *Hymn to Apollo*, and the fir tree of the Διὸς ἀπάτη are all natural growths, no less than the flowers in the relevant passages. But as we shall see, the Homeric poems associate good order in human societies not simply with images of trees but more specifically with managed growths of trees, particularly those found in orchards. In the *Odyssey*, the labor required to maintain such plantations is associated with the work of kings, which upholds the good order of their communities.[1]

In this way, the Homeric poets suggested the comparative difficulty of maintaining order on earth. Only through the constant labor of kings can the good order of human societies be preserved; appropriately, the Homeric poets associate the maintenance of that order with the careful management of arboreal growths. By contrast, the images of wild arboreal growths that we studied above do not suggest that careful labor is needed to maintain order in the cosmos. And this is in keeping with the depictions of potential threats to Zeus' supremacy that we discussed in the last chapter. Either these threats are not carried through or, if they are, they are not of a very serious nature. We might think, for instance, of the potential threat from Apollo in his Homeric hymn, which is never actualized, or of Hera's brief challenge to Zeus' rule in the Διὸς ἀπάτη, which he is able to face down with relative ease. Zeus' power and might is much greater than that of kings; accordingly, his cosmic order is much more strongly established than the order of human communities.

Arboreal and Floral Imagery of Flourishing Cities in Hesiodic Poetry

We can set in relief the particular choices made by the Homeric poets in fashioning such imagery if again we consider equivalent images from the Hesiodic tradition. In Chapter 4, we studied comparanda from the *Theogony* for Homeric vegetal imagery of cosmic order. This time we shall focus on the *Works and Days*, which not only provides advice on farming but also depicts just and unjust human societies. Like their Homeric counterparts, the Hesiodic poets use vegetal imagery to explore the notion of the well-functioning polity. There is, however, an important difference between the uses of such imagery in the two poetic traditions. The Hesiodic poets associate both wild and cultivated growths with well-ordered societies, but as we shall see the Homeric images of flourishing polities focus on managed growths.

The Hesiodic poets, for instance, illustrated the notion of flourishing communities with the verbal root ἀνθε-, which is associated with wild vegetation and particularly with flowers. At *Works and Days* 227, the verb ἀνθέω describes the flourishing of the Just city and of its people: τοῖσι τέθηλε πόλις,

---

[1] Previous studies have tended to note only similarities between these two sets of Homeric arboreal images. Nagler (1996), for instance, argues for an equivalence between the bedpost and pillar in Odysseus' house and the images of pillars and trees associated with goddesses such as Calypso (for the latter see Chapter 4 above), which in his opinion are associated with the structure of the cosmos. For such equivalences, see also Evans 1901 and Bakker 2001.

λαοὶ δ' ἀνθέουσιν ἐν αὐτῇ. In Homeric poetry, the verbal root ἀνθε- possesses either general vegetal or specifically floral meanings (see Appendix). Much the same can be said of the usages of that root in Hesiodic poetry. At *Works and Days* 582, for example, the phrase σκόλυμος ἀνθεῖ refers not to general vegetal flourishing but specifically to the blooming time of the thistle.[2] On the basis of such usages, we could interpret the phrase λαοὶ δ' ἀνθέουσιν ἐν αὐτῇ at *Works and Days* 227 either as a general reference to vegetal flourishing or more specifically as a floral metaphor. The second meaning is certainly possible here: Glenn Most renders the line, "their city blooms and the people in it flower."[3] Similarly, the Hesiodic *Shield* refers to the cities Ἄνθεια and Ἄνθην (381, 474). These names would presumably have suggested to early audiences thriving rather than disorderly communities. And again, the terms Ἄνθεια and Ἄνθην could allude to wild floral growths or to wild vegetation more generally.

The Hesiodic poets thus helped their audiences to understand the concept of the flourishing city. If the passages mentioned above were seen as floral images, they would have drawn on the time of flowering and fertility as the peak of the functioning and health of a plant in order to illustrate the vigor of these cities.[4] Alternatively, such uses of the ἀνθο/ε- root may have carried general vegetal associations and may thus have helped audiences to understand the more abstract notion of the flourishing of a city through the more concrete notion of the flourshing of plants.

The Homeric poets provide only partial parallels for such Hesiodic usages. There are some echoes of the Hesiodic associations of cities and flourishing in Homeric poetry: Ἄνθεια is the name of a city that Agamemnon offers to Achilles (*Iliad* 9.151, 293), and the Catalogue of Ships refers to an Ἀνθηδὼν ἐσχατόωσα (2.508). As with the places from the Hesiodic *Shield* discussed above, these lexemes evoke either wild growths in general or specifically wild flowers. But with the exception of these place-names, wild growths carry very different connotations in Homeric poetry. In the Homeric images of cities and civilization that we shall discuss below, wild flowers and trees are associated with an absence of civilized order.[5]

---

[2]   West 1978 *ad loc.*

[3]   Most 2006:107.

[4]   Theophrastus develops such ideas in combination with the Aristotelian notions of the teleological development and division into parts of living animals. When plants grow, bloom, and bear fruit, they have reached the peak of excellence and beauty: Βλαστάνοντα γὰρ καὶ θάλλοντα καὶ καρπὸν ἔχοντα πάντα καλλίω καὶ τελειότερα καὶ δοκεῖ καὶ ἔστιν ("When sprouting, flourishing and in possession of fruit all things appear and are more beautiful and more perfect," *Historia Plantarum* 1.1.2).

[5]   The only possible parallel for associations of flowers and civic disorder in extant Hesiodic poetry is offered by the description of the winds that blow from the prone Typhoeus "throughout the

The differences between the treatments of wild growths in the Homeric and Hesiodic corpora become still more apparent when we compare further details from the Hesiodic description of the Just City with a Homeric image that at first sight appears closely to resemble the relevant lines from the *Works and Days*. At *Works and Days* 232–237, we learn that the city whose rulers give straight judgements to citizen and foreigner alike will be blessed with fertility of soil and womb:

> τοῖσι φέρει μὲν γαῖα πολὺν βίον, οὔρεσι δὲ δρῦς
> ἄκρη μέν τε φέρει βαλάνους, μέσση δὲ μελίσσας·
> εἰροπόκοι δ' ὄιες μαλλοῖς καταβεβρίθασιν·
> 235 τίκτουσιν δὲ γυναῖκες ἐοικότα τέκνα γονεῦσιν·
> θάλλουσιν δ' ἀγαθοῖσι διαμπερές· οὐδ' ἐπὶ νηῶν
> νίσονται, καρπὸν δὲ φέρει ζείδωρος ἄρουρα.

> *Works and Days* 232–237

> To them the earth bears much livelihood; in the mountains the oak
> Bears acorns on high and bees in its middle;
> The woolly sheep are weighed down by their fleeces;
> 235 Women bear children that are like their parents;
> They flourish with good things continually; nor do they journey
> On ships, but the grain-giving plow-land bears fruit.

This passage alludes to numerous kinds of human, animal, and vegetal flourishing, including that of trees: children are born, resembling their parents;[6] sheep are heavy with wool; the fields abound with fruit; oaks bear both acorns and bees.

At first glance, Odysseus' description of the blessings brought by a just king at *Odyssey* 19.108–114 would seem to offer a close parallel for this Hesiodic passage:

---

boundless, flowery earth": κατὰ γαῖαν ἀπείριτον ἀνθεμόεσσαν (*Theogony* 878). These winds throw agricultural lands into confusion: ἔργ' ἐρατὰ φθείρουσι χαμαιγενέων ἀνθρώπων, / πιμπλεῖσαι κόνιός τε καὶ ἀργαλέου κολοσυρτοῦ ("they destroy the lovely fields of earth-dwelling men, / filling them with dust and grievous tumult," *Theogony* 879–880). If we take the adjective ἀνθεμόεσσαν proleptically, it would be an indication of the disordered state of the earth after Typhoeus' winds have passed over it. Alternatively, however, these lines could refer simply to the fertility of the earth, without any suggestion of disorder. For this image, see also Chapter 4 n2. A clearer parallel for Homeric associations of flowers and civic disorder is offered by Solon's description of Εὐνομία, Good Order in the city, that "withers the flowers of delusion [ἄτη]" (fr. 3.35–36 West²). In marked contrast with the Hesiodic image of the Just City, which "flourishes" (ἀνθεῖ) as a result of righteous judgements, Solon here associates the root ἀνθο/ε- with those who pervert justice and thus threaten the functioning of the political community.

6   As West (1978 *ad loc.*) points out, the reference may be to children who resemble their fathers and are hence legitimate, or to children without deformities.

ἦ γάρ σευ κλέος οὐρανὸν εὐρὺν ἱκάνει,
ὥς τέ τευ ἢ βασιλῆος ἀμύμονος, ὅς τε θεουδὴς
110 ἀνδράσιν ἐν πολλοῖσιν καὶ ἰφθίμοισιν ἀνάσσων
εὐδικίας ἀνέχῃσι, φέρῃσι δὲ γαῖα μέλαινα
πυροὺς καὶ κριθάς, βρίθῃσι δὲ δένδρεα καρπῷ,
τίκτῃ δ' ἔμπεδα μῆλα, θάλασσα δὲ παρέχῃ ἰχθῦς
ἐξ εὐηγεσίης, ἀρετῶσι δὲ λαοὶ ὑπ' αὐτοῦ.

Odyssey 19.108–114

Your fame reaches the wide heaven,
As that of some excellent, god-fearing king,
110 Who among many men upholds justice,
Ruling mighty subjects, and the black earth bears
Wheat and barley, and the trees burgeon with fruit,
And the flocks constantly bear young; through his good leadership
The sea provides fish, and the people excel under him.

As with *Works and Days* 232–237, these lines associate just rulership with a flourishing realm. Due to the king's good leadership (ἐξ εὐηγεσίης, 19.114) and to the justice he upholds (εὐδικίας ἀνέχῃσι, 109), not only do his people flourish—they are many, strong, and excellent (110, 114)—but the earth and its waters burgeon with life. The land bears cereal crops; trees are weighed down with fruit (111-112). Sheep moreover increase constantly, and the sea provides the king's people with fish (113).

There are differences however between the vegetal images of the two passages and, indeed, between this passage of the *Works and Days* and the imagery of the *Odyssey* more generally. Odysseus' allusion to trees heavy with fruit at *Odyssey* 19.112 might suggest an orchard—that is, a plantation within the spaces belonging to a human community. Note that it follows a reference to wheat and barley, the sorts of species that we would expect to find in agricultural fields (111–112). In any case, these trees are not explicitly associated with wild spaces. Our passage from the *Works and Days*, however, not only describes "grain-giving plow-land" but also oaks growing in the mountains—that is, in wild places beyond the control of the city. The flourishing of the Just City is associated, then, with both wild and domesticated spaces.

And we can observe a further distinction between the Hesiodic description of the image of the Just City and other images from the Homeric corpus: unlike the equivalent passages from Homeric poetry, *Works and Days* 232–237 associate a flourishing polity with both cultivated and uncultivated vegetal growths. The plow-land of *Works and Days* 237 would be tended by human hands—and indeed the remainder of the Hesiodic poem focuses on such agricultural labor. But the oaks in the image of the Just City fall beyond the remit of cultivators. People might step outside the boundaries of the land tamed by agriculture to gather the bounty of the oaks; yet their acorns are not the product of human labor. The Homeric image of the Just King is ambiguous in this respect: while it refers to agricultural fields, the fruit trees of *Odyssey* 19.112 might be growing in orchards or in the wild. Other images from the Homeric corpus, however, associate civic order both with agricultural crops and with trees managed by human hands.[7]

Wild Growths and Uncivilized Lands: The Hymns to Aphrodite and Pan, and *Odyssey* 5

In the passages from Homeric poetry that we shall discuss below, wild growths—both floral and arboreal—are associated with challenges to civilized order or with uncivilized spaces. Our first example of such imagery derives from the *Hymn to Aphrodite*, which we have already discussed as the tale of Aphrodite's seduction of Anchises.[8] But the hymn also tells the story of a clash between the forces of the wild and the civilized.[9] The themes of the wild and the civilized in the hymn are closely linked to its characterizations of Aphrodite and Anchises and of their interactions with the world of nature. Anchises, as a prince of Troy, is a man of breeding and culture, and he has introduced some measure of civilization to the wild spaces of Ida. Along with other shepherds he has attempted to assert control over the environment of Ida by establishing a settlement: he and his companions have constructed "well-built huts" (κλίσιας εὐποιήτους, 75). When Aphrodite first encounters him she finds him in this civilized setting, engaged in the refined activity of lyre-playing (80). The landscape of Ida outside the settlement is a "mother of wild beasts" (μητέρα θηρῶν), but Anchises has exercised control over these animals by hunting them: on the mountain's slopes he has slain bears and lions to line the floor of his hut (159–160).[10]

Aphrodite takes on the outward appearance of a civilized human being, but this masks her affiliation with wild nature. We have already explored intersections of Aphrodite's costume and speech with the themes of seduction and deception. But these elements of the hymn also interact with the theme of civilization. In order to seduce Anchises, Aphrodite dons the sorts of accoutrements that he might associate with a civilized maiden: she is decked in perfumes, oils,

---

[7] For further reflections on the similarities and differences between the Homeric image of the Just King and the Hesiodic description of the Just City, see Slatkin 1986:265–266.

[8] See Chapter 3 above.

[9] Cf. Segal 1974, Ory 1984, and Olson 2012 on *Hymn to Aphrodite* 68 and 122–124.

[10] According to Faulkner (2008 on *Hymn to Aphrodite* 158–160), mention of the pelts at this point in the scene suggests Anchises' momentary ascendancy over Aphrodite. See below for Anchises' loss of control over the encounter when he sleeps with her.

beautiful clothes, and dazzling jewelry (61–65, 85–90). In her lying speech at lines 108–142, she complements her refined appearance with allusions to civilized life, mentioning such details as a Trojan nurse and illustrious parents. And most importantly, she raises the prospect of marriage with Anchises—that is, the prospect of a union within the bounds of civilized mortal institutions.

But such promises are not borne out in her encounter with the Trojan prince, which turns out to be a brief erotic dalliance rather than the prelude to a marriage. What is more, events earlier in the hymn reveal Aphrodite to be not so much a civilized maiden as a goddess of wild nature. She has power over all creatures (lines 3–5), and while Anchises hunts wild animals and thus asserts dominance over them, Aphrodite encourages their natural proclivities: she causes them to mate as she journeys from Olympus to Ida (69–74). Under her influence, "they all at once / lay down two-by-two in their shady haunts" (οἱ δ' ἄμα πάντες / σύνδυο κοιμήσαντο κατὰ σκιόεντας ἐναύλους, 73–74). The latter detail is echoed in her lying speech, despite its general focus on civilized themes. She describes how Hermes led her not only over environments controlled by mankind—their "many fields" (πολλὰ ... ἔργα, 122)—but also over undefined spaces: she witnessed "unapportioned and unsettled land through which wild / flesh-eating beasts wander in their shady haunts" (ἄκληρόν τε καὶ ἄκτιτον ἦν διὰ θῆρες / ὠμοφάγοι φοιτῶσι κατὰ σκιόεντας ἐναύλους, 123–124). The phrase κατὰ σκιόεντας ἐναύλους thus appears both in Aphrodite's speech (74) and in the narrator's description of the wild places that she visits on her real journey to Ida (124) and gives emphasis to the goddess' associations with wild nature. Anchises' efforts to control the landscape of Ida, then, contrast with the wild forces associated with Aphrodite.

The pastureland where Anchises and his fellow shepherds graze their cows is however a space between the wild or civilized.[11] The work of shepherds takes place in apparently wild spaces outside the bounds of human settlements. Nevertheless, their activities represent the exploitation of such spaces to the benefit of humans: they use these lands to raise cows, sheep, and goats, whose flesh and milk will eventually feed human communities. The tension between these two facets of pastureland, the wild and the civilized, is suggested in lines 54–55, our very first description of Anchises in the hymn: "he used to herd cows in the high mountains of Ida of the many dales" (ἐν ἀκροπόλοις ὄρεσιν πολυπιδάκου Ἴδης / βουκολέεσκεν βοῦς). His task of herding cows, which would benefit his community, is set against an allusion to the wild spaces of Ida.[12]

---

[11] For such liminal spaces and for their associations with herdsmen in Homeric poetry, see Redfield 1994:189–192.

[12] Cf. the description of oaks in the mountains (οὔρεσι) at *Works and Days* 232, discussed above.

These pastures are, then, at once the haunt of wild animals and spaces that are exploited by herdsmen for civilized purposes: this is a landscape contested by forces of the wild and the civilized—the forces represented in the hymn by Aphrodite and Anchises. And such a contest is reflected in the descriptions of vegetation in these pastures. This vegetation is described in different ways before and after the lovemaking of Aphrodite and Anchises: the pastures are "grassy" ποιήεντας (78) on Aphrodite's arrival, but "flowery" ἀνθεμοέντων (169) immediately after their lovemaking. The first phrase, νομοὺς κατὰ ποιήεντας, defines the lands of Ida in terms of their use by Anchises and his fellow pastoralists: they provide grassy fodder for their cows. It reflects the civilized purpose for which these lands are being exploited by the herdsmen. But the second phrase, νομῶν ἐξ ἀνθεμοέντων, describes these lands in terms of wild flowers.

This subtle change in the description of the pastures draws on concrete aspects of the natural environments that would have been familiar to early audiences and would thus have helped them to understand the change that has taken place in the narrative: the power relations between the Trojan prince, the goddess and the world of nature have altered. Before their lovemaking, Anchises had exercised a degree of control over his environment. He also seemed to have the upper hand in his encounter with Aphrodite: she appeared before him in the meek guise of a maiden (82) and sued for his hand with the promise of influential connections and bridal gifts (131–142). But Aphrodite's seduction of Anchises turns the tables. Like Zeus in *Iliad* 14, Anchises is overcome by a goddess' seductive wiles and lies prostrate in sleep (170–171). And as in the Διὸς ἀπάτη, this development is marked by floral imagery.[13] The allusion to wild flowers in ordered spaces at *Hymn to Aphrodite* 169 casts light on the events of the wider narrative: the wild power of Aphrodite has insinuated itself into the civilized spaces created by Anchises and his fellow shepherds. Her conquest of the Trojan prince in his hut is reflected in the spaces that the shepherds have attempted to tame outside their settlement.[14]

Flowers, then, mark Aphrodite's conquest of civilized order in the hymn and the irruption of the forces of the wild with which she is associated. We find

[13] Manuscript M preserves another possible reference to flowers at line 175: the goddess is given the epithet ἰοστεφάνου, "violet crowned." This adjective would contrast with her more regular epithet, ἐϋστέφανος, found both at the beginning of the hymn (line 6) and at the end (line 287). Faulkner (2008 *ad loc.*) tentatively adopts the reading of M on the principle of *lectio difficilior*, as do Càssola (1975) and van Eck (1978:63). If this reading is accepted, the change in the goddess' epithets mirrors the change in Anchises' pastures and thereby associates the goddess more directly with the new description of the pastures. For the Διὸς ἀπάτη, see Chapters 3 and 4 above.

[14] Smith 1981:37: "Aphrodite is nature's most powerful agent in the invasion of the settlements of men."

further examples of such imagery in the *Hymn to Pan*.[15] But this second hymn offers a more straightforward celebration of wild forces, which are associated with the figure of Pan himself and with the landscapes that he roams. Like Anchises, Pan is associated with herding, hunting, and music; but these apparently civilized qualities are greatly outweighed by the disorderly characteristics of the god and of his landscapes.

At first sight, we might notice intersections between the characterization of Pan in the hymn and that of Anchises in the *Hymn to Aphrodite*. Not only does Pan haunt mountainous regions (6–7), but he is also somehow connected with pastoralism, even though he is not himself depicted as a herdsman: he is νόμιον θεόν, either "the god of herdsmen [νομῆες]" or "the god of pasture [νομός]" (5).[16] And like Anchises he is a hunter. He slays wild beasts in the hills (13–14) and collects their pelts: presumably, the lynx hide that he is wearing in lines 23–24 is the product of such a hunt.[17] Similarly, as we have seen, Anchises lines his hut with the hides of beasts that he has slain. Pan is also a musician, though of a rather different sort from Anchises. Aphrodite finds Anchises playing the lyre (κιθαρίζων, *Hymn to Aphrodite* 80), an instrument associated with the cultured activity of epic poetry.[18] But Pan plays a reed-pipe, an instrument derived from his natural surroundings, and whose music competes with the song of the nightingale, a denizen of the natural world (*Hymn to Pan* 16–18).[19]

Other characteristics of Pan distinguish him still more clearly from the Trojan prince. We might think in particular of the descriptions of the god's birth and physique, which are closely associated with the notion of mingling. The

---

[15] The hymn survives in a version usually assigned to late archaic or early classical times: see Janko 1982:184–186, Borgeaud 1988:54. But scholars have shown that the hymn contains elements typical of Homeric poetry of the archaic period: Villarrubia 1997, Germany 2005, Thomas 2011:166–172. The similarities that we shall observe between the metaphorical systems of the hymn and those of *Hymn to Aphrodite* and the *Odyssey* support such arguments. This would not necessarily imply an early date for our version of the *Hymn to Pan*. But it would indicate that the hymn was composed by and prepared for people familiar with traditional Homeric diction, perhaps as part of an ongoing tradition of composition-in-performance: see Thomas 2011:169–170.

[16] Likewise a phrase from the description of Pan's haunts, ἀκροτάτην κορυφὴν μηλοσκόπον ("a very high peak, a lookout for sheep," 11) alludes to pastoralism (Borgeaud 1988:61). But Pan is not said to look out for flocks; rather, he glares (δερκόμενος, 14) at the wild beasts that he hunts. Unlike Pan himself, his father Hermes engages in pastoralism: "he pastured flocks / beside a mortal man" (μῆλ' ἐνόμευεν / ἀνδρὶ πάρα θνητῷ, 33).

[17] Note also the hare's pelt in which Hermes wraps the young Pan at line 43. For associations of Pan with civilized activities, see Cardete del Olmo 2016.

[18] We see this, for instance, at *Odyssey* 1.153, where a herald hands a κίθαρις to the bard Phemius.

[19] Moreover, if Borgeaud's analysis (1988:74–89) is correct, Pan's music is associated with a wild eroticism. Such an eroticism is more reminiscent of the depiction of Aphrodite than that of her lover Anchises in her *Homeric Hymn*.

nymphs who sing of his conception and birth in the second half of the hymn (29–47) use the verbal root μιγ- to describe the mingling in love of his parents: μιγῆναι, line 34. Hermes, an Olympian god, mingled with a wood-nymph, a spirit of the natural world (33–35). For this reason, we may assume, Pan's body is a monstrous mixture of anthropomorphic god and wild goat: he is "monstrous ... goat-footed, two-horned" (τερατωπόν ... αἰγιπόδην δικέρωτα, 36–37).[20]

Pan's landscapes are likewise characterized by disorderliness, in contrast with the civilized order that Anchises and his companions have attempted to impose on the wild spaces of Ida. The first half of the hymn describes the untamed wilderness through which the god wanders. He visits snowy peaks (λόφον νιφόεντα, 6), rocky paths (πετρήεντα κέλευθα, 7), soft streams (ῥείθροισιν ... μαλακοῖσιν, 9), and sheer rocks (πέτρῃσιν ἐν ἠλιβάτοισι, 10). The hymn mentions also the wild vegetation of Pan's haunts, which include wooded groves (πίσῃ / δενδρήεντ᾽, 2–3) and dense thickets (ῥωπήϊα πυκνά, 8). When the description of Pan's haunts resumes in lines 25–26, we are once more offered an image of wild disorder. The god is depicted cavorting with nymphs in a disorderly meadow of saffron and hyacinth flowers. Pan's saffron and hyacinth flowers are said to mingle "indiscriminately" (ἄκριτα, 26) with grass—in contrast with the discriminate (κριτά) spaces of civilization.[21] As in the case of Pan's body, then, the root μι(σ)γ- describes a disorderly mingling. The description of disorderly mingling in the natural environment would have helped audiences to imagine the disorderly nature of Pan himself:

> ἐν μαλακῷ λειμῶνι τόθι κρόκος ἠδ᾽ ὑάκινθος
> εὐώδης θαλέθων καταμίσγεται ἄκριτα ποίη.

Hymn to Pan 25–26

---

[20] On Pan's associations both with disorder and with wild places, see Borgeaud 1988. See also Elliger 1975:162 on the correspondence in the hymn between Pan's directionless wanderings and the "diffuseness" ("Diffusität") of the elements that make up his landscape.

[21] Such associations of the lexeme ἄκριτος are also operative on a cosmic level: as we saw in Chapter 4 above, Hera's promise to resolve the "indiscriminate quarrels" (ἄκριτα νείκεα, *Iliad* 14.205, 304) of Oceanus and Tethys suggests a fantasy of returning the cosmos to a primal chaos. For the association of κρίνω with civilized order in early hexameter, cf. *Theogony* 535–536: ἐκρίνοντο θεοὶ θνητοί τ᾽ ἄνθρωποι / Μηκώνῃ ("gods and men were being distinguished / at Meconē"). According to the scholium to *Theogony* 535, this statement, which introduces the description of Prometheus' encounter with Zeus, alludes to the distinctions drawn between gods and men in the relevant episode: ἐκρίνετο τί θεὸς καὶ τί ἄνθρωπος ἐν τῇ Μηκώνῃ ("it was judged what was a god and what was a man at Meconē"; text from di Gregorio 1975:83). If Vernant (1974, 1989) and Clay (2003:100–118) are correct, the scholiast thus refers to the definitions of mortals and immortals that Prometheus establishes with his invention of sacrifice: men are allotted perishable meat, but the gods receive imperishable smoke.

> ... in a soft meadow where saffron and fragrant
> Flourishing hyacinth mingle indiscriminately with the grass.

The indiscriminate mingling of this vegetation recalls the allusions to wild spaces and wild growths in the *Hymn to Aphrodite*, rather than the order that Anchises and other humans have tried to introduce to such spaces. As with the description of the "unapportioned and unsettled" (ἀκλήρόν τε καὶ ἄκτιτον) haunts of wild beasts at *Hymn to Aphrodite* 123–124, lines 25–26 of the *Hymn to Pan* emphasize the lack of differentiation in Pan's meadows; and as with the "flowery pastures" of *Hymn to Aphrodite* 169, which suggest the invasion of Aphrodite's wild powers, these lines focus on the wild growths of flowers in the landscapes of Pan. Despite their occupying similar mountainous landscapes, then, Pan's association with the disorder of wild nature contrasts sharply with Anchises' attempts to impose order on such wildernesses.

The contrasts between Pan's landscapes and the more civilized spaces of mankind are borne out further when we refer to other *Homeric Hymns*. In the *Hymn to Aphrodite*, the wild slopes of Ida have been settled by shepherds. But the uninhabited landscapes described in other hymns are, in fact, more reminiscent of Pan's haunts. *Homeric Hymn* 1 describes the birth of Dionysus, a god of wild nature who in the *Hymn to Pan* is particularly pleased at the birth of the new god (*Hymn to Pan* 45–46). *Hymn* 1 identifies Dionysus' birthplace as Nysa and depicts it as a land of untended vegetal growth. If we accept Martin West's reconstruction of the poem, Nysa is described as growing μενοεικέα πολλά, "many means of sustenance" (line 14).[22] But no human hand is responsible for such growth. Nysa is situated "far from humans" (πολλὸν ἀπ' ἀνθρώπων, 8). It is enclosed by a cliff and has no harbor; it is therefore unvisited by ships (11-14).[23] Likewise Pan's haunts, described in the first half of his hymn, are wild, craggy landscapes frequented only by the god and his retinue of nymphs. The flowers at lines 25–26 form the climax to this description and encapsulate the wildness of Pan's landscape.

The flower-gathering of Korē and her companions, which we discussed in Chapters 2 and 4, is set in a similar location—or perhaps even in the very same place as is described in *Hymn* 1. Her flowers grow on the Nysian Plain (line 17). Listeners familiar with Orphic traditions might have located this landscape at

---

[22] West 2001, 2003. Flowers are not mentioned directly in the surviving fragments of the hymn, but at line 9 forests are described with the verb ἀνθέω, which is used to refer to wild floral growths elsewhere, as at *Hymn to Apollo* 139. For the semantics of ἀνθέω and for other Homeric instances of the verb, see the Appendix.

[23] West 2001:2. For allusions to Orphic traditions in Homeric poetry, see the discussion of the Διὸς ἀπάτη in Chapter 4 above.

the ends of the earth, the very furthest point from the civilized lands of Greece: an Orphic account of the abduction of Korē (fr. 43 Kern) situated it by the streams of Oceanus, i.e., at the edge of the world.[24] The identification of Korē's companions as "the daughters of Oceanus" (*Hymn to Demeter* 5) would have supported such associations. Alternatively, audiences might have equated the Nysian Plain with the Nysa of *Hymn 1*, which is set "far off in Phoenicia, near the flows of the Nile" (τηλοῦ Φοινίκης, σχεδὸν Αἰγύπτοιο ῥοάων, *Hymn* 1.10). But in either case, the reference to the Nysian Plain would have suggested a land far from human civilization.

Moreover, the descriptions of the flowery meadows in the *Hymn to Demeter* bear a close resemblance to those of the meadows at *Hymn to Pan* 25–26. In particular, Korē's depiction of the flowers that she and her companions were gathering echoes the language of *Hymn to Pan* 25–26: μίγδα κρόκον τ' ἀγανὸν καὶ ἀγαλλίδας ἠδ' ὑάκινθον / καὶ ῥοδέας κάλυκας καὶ λείρια ... ("mixedly, gentle saffron, irises, hyacinth, / rose-cups, and lilies ..." *Hymn to Demeter* 426–427).[25] Among these flowers Persephone mentions saffron and hyacinth, the two flowers described in our passage from the *Hymn to Pan*. And as at *Hymn to Pan* 26 the root μι(σ)γ- suggests the disordered mingling of such flowers. In both hymns, then, disordered flowery growths are associated with lands untamed by human hands.

The passages considered thus far draw on the wild floral and arboreal growths of the Greek natural environment to illustrate the notion of a lack of civilization: in the *Hymn to Aphrodite*, the description of flowery pastures accompanies the irruption of Aphrodite's wild power into the spaces that Anchises and his fellow shepherds have attempted to control. The indiscriminate mingling of flowers in the meadow of *Hymn to Pan* 25–26 echoes the disorderly nature of the god himself and encapsulates the wild disorder of his favorite haunts.

We turn now to the vegetation that the *Odyssey* depicts in its account of Odysseus' return home to Ithaca. The descriptions of the lands of Odysseus' travels, both those of the main narrator and those of Odysseus, are remarkable for their sensitive portrayals of vegetation. As with the descriptions of Pan's haunts in the *Hymn to Pan*, the relevant passages from the *Odyssey* focus on wild growths, particularly those of flowers and trees, and on the absence of cultivation. And as in the *Hymn to Pan*, such features reflect the lack of civilized order in the places that are being described. The Lotus-Eaters, for instance, consume what Odysseus calls a "flowery food" (ἄνθινον εἶδαρ, 9.84) and a "honey-sweet fruit" (μελιηδέα καρπόν, 94), rather than the diet of an agricultural people. It

---

[24] See Richardson 1974 on *Hymn to Demeter* 17.
[25] On parallels between the meadows of *Hymn to Pan* and *Hymn to Demeter*, see Thomas 2011:158.

is ironic that on arrival in their land Odysseus sends out scouts to determine "which men they are eating grain on the earth" (οἵ τινες ἀνέρες εἶεν ἐπὶ χθονὶ σῖτον ἔδοντες, 89). The Cyclopes for their part have neither laws nor assemblies; in keeping with their general avoidance of civilized institutions, they do not engage in the civilized practices of agriculture (108-115).[26] Nevertheless wheat, barley, and vines grow for them with the help of rain from Zeus (108-111).[27] An island facing their territory (often called Goat Island by critics) hosts abundant growths of wild plants: Odysseus observes poplars, vines, and well-watered meadows (132–133, 141). When he arrives on Aeaea, he spies Circe's dwelling "through thick brush and woodland" (διὰ δρυμὰ πυκνὰ καὶ ὕλην, 10.150). And there are no agricultural fields on Circe's island.[28]

Of all the wild lands of Odysseus' travels the vegetation of Ogygia, the island of Calypso, is described in the most detail. And as with the other lands that he visits, the wild vegetation of Ogygia is indicative of an absence of civilization. But in order to see this, we need to distinguish between mortal and immortal perspectives on the island. While a god might associate the island with cosmic order and experience simple joy at the island's vegetal abundance, for Odysseus it is an isolated land far from the civilized environment of Ithaca.

Such distinctions in perspective are first introduced at 1.45–62. We have already noted that the image of "the navel of the sea" (ὀμφαλός ... θαλάσσης, 1.50) associates Ogygia with cosmic order. But this image, in fact, derives from a speech of Athena at a council of the gods, and the possibility arises that such an interpretation is valid only from their perspective; from Odysseus' point of view the notion of "the navel of the sea" might have altogether different associations. And indeed Athena herself is at pains also to advertise Odysseus' particular perspective to her divine addressees. Immediately before she mentions "the navel of the sea" she describes the pain that Odysseus is experiencing "far from his friends" (δηθὰ φίλων ἄπο, 49); soon afterwards (57–59) she describes his longing for home. The image of "the navel of the sea" would normally suggest the notion of cosmic stability to the gods, but Athena invites them also to see it from Odysseus' perspective, as an image of isolation: for him the island is surrounded by the sea like a boss (ὀμφαλός) in the middle of

---

[26] Cf. 9.191–192: Odysseus likens the Cyclops himself to "a wooded peak" (ῥίῳ ὑλήεντι), rather than to a "grain-eating man" (ἀνδρί ... σιτοφάγῳ).

[27] See also 9.357–358, where Polyphemus explains that "the grain-giving plow-land bears wine with many grapes for the Cyclopes, and Zeus' rain increases it for them" (Κυκλώπεσσι φέρει ζείδωρος ἄρουρα / οἶνον ἐριστάφυλον, καί σφιν Διὸς ὄμβρος ἀέξει).

[28] We shall study other uncivilized lands in Chapter 8 below, together with their vegetation: both the island of the Sirens and, surprisingly, the lightless land of the dead possess flowery meadows (11.539, 12.159); the Underworld also boasts fruit trees (10.509–510, 11.588–560).

a shield.[29] Stranded on Ogygia, the wretched Odysseus is as far from home as he will ever be.

Similarly, Hermes' reaction to Calypso's island in Book 5 contrasts with the feelings attributed to Odysseus soon afterwards. Upon Hermes' arrival on Ogygia, considerable emphasis is placed on the island's wild vegetation, which is allotted eleven lines in the narrative (63–73). A flourishing forest (ὕλη ... τηλεθόωσα, 63) of alder, poplar, and cypress (64) surrounds the goddess' cave;[30] a young vine burgeoning with grapes stretches around it (ἡμερὶς ἡβώωσα, τεθήλει δὲ σταφυλῆσι, 69). And as in the description of Pan's haunts in the *Hymn to Pan*, the passage concludes with an allusion to flowery meadows: ἀμφὶ δὲ λειμῶνες μαλακοὶ ἴου ἠδὲ σελίνου / θήλεον· ("all around soft meadows of violet and celery / were flourishing," *Odyssey* 5.72–73). With the exception of the vine, none of the plants in this description would have been found in the orderly plantations familiar to early audiences from their own settlements or from the fields surrounding them. The trees, like the oaks in the Hesiodic image of the Just City, are not the kinds of species that ancient listeners would have seen in the managed spaces of orchards. And the abundant flowers would have called to mind the meadows of the Greek world—wild spaces whose luxuriant growth required no human tendance.

Hermes wonders at this flourishing vegetation (θηεῖτο, 75), and such a reaction appears to have purely positive connotations in this context. In other passages of Homeric poetry, the experience of wonderment, θαῦμα, encompasses feelings of awe or even trepidation: it is the sort of awed wonder that mortals feel before the divine.[31] But here it is associated with the feelings of a god and with simple joy: "even an immortal, if he came and saw it, would wonder and rejoice in his mind" (ἔνθα κ' ἔπειτα καὶ ἀθάνατός περ ἐπελθὼν / θηήσαιτο ἰδὼν καὶ τερφθείη φρεσὶν ᾗσιν, 73–74).[32]

The description of Odysseus soon afterwards creates a clear contrast with this depiction of Hermes' positive reaction to Calypso's vegetation: Odysseus

---

[29] Indeed, elsewhere in Homeric poetry the lexeme ὀμφαλός describes a nub in the middle of an object, whether a shield boss, a human navel, or a knob on a carriage (cf. *Iliad* 4.525, 11.34, 13.192, 568, 21.180, 24.273). On the basis of such usages, audiences would have imagined Calypso's island as having the appearance of a nub of land surrounded by the sea (cf. νήσῳ ἐν ἀμφιρύτῃ, "on a sea-girt isle," *Odyssey* 1.50)—much as a boss is a nub in the middle of a shield.

[30] Cf. 1.51, where Athena describes Ogygia as νῆσος δενδρήεσσα ("a wooded island," 1.51).

[31] For associations of this lexeme with dread and the divine, see also Prier's analysis (1989:84–97) of θαῦμα and related terms, and my discussion of reactions of wonder in the Phaeacian episode below.

[32] The phrase "there, *even* an immortal if he came would wonder" (73–74) seems to anticipate the same reaction from both mortal and immortal visitors. Perhaps, then, a casual mortal visitor, who was not trapped on the island like Odysseus, might share Hermes' joy. But there is no indication that any other mortal has ever visited Ogygia.

sits on the seashore, weeping and looking out at the sea (82–84). His grief is said to arise from two sources—his disenchantment with Calypso and his longing for Ithaca. As we learn from line 153, where Odysseus' emotions are once more described, his life was wasting away "as he mourned for his return, since the nymph was no longer pleasing to him" (νόστον ὀδυρομένῳ, ἐπεὶ οὐκέτι ἥνδανε νύμφῳ, 153).

But audiences would have seen that Odysseus is also disillusioned with Calypso's wondrous surroundings. The narrative of *Odyssey* 5 offers a number of reasons to arrive at such a conclusion. Firstly, it associates Calypso, the nymph who "no longer pleased" Odysseus, with her environs. The long description of her island (53–73) positions her in the midst of her vegetation: she sings in her cave, and her cave is surrounded by forests and meadows (ἀμφί, 63, 72).[33] Secondly, on the basis of passages such as *Hymn* 7.38–42, where Dionysus inspires the growth of vines and ivy, listeners are likely to have inferred a still closer connection between Calypso and her vegetation: her divine presence inspires its growth.[34] Thirdly, there is a clear contrast not only between the emotions of Hermes and Odysseus, but also between the positioning of their bodies relative to Calypso and her surroundings. While Hermes gazes at Calypso's vegetation, Odysseus, by settling himself on the shore and looking out to sea, turns away both from Calypso and from the abundant flowers and trees that grow around her cave.[35]

Fourthly, audiences familiar with Homeric descriptions of heroes' homelands would have sensed a connection between Odysseus' pining for Ithaca and his rejection of Calypso and of her island: Ogygia is an uncivilized land, unfit to be the home of a civilized individual such as Odysseus. It is not that Calypso utterly lacks the trappings of civilization. She is, for instance, described as singing and weaving when Hermes arrives on the island. She is also able to offer Odysseus mortal food (196–197), and when he leaves she provides clothing and provisions (264–267).[36] Nevertheless her living in a cave is hardly indicative of civilization. As *Hymn* 20 makes clear, such was the state of mankind before the

---

[33] Calypso is once more associated with her surroundings at line 155: unwillingly, Odysseus lies with her at night "in her hollow caves" (ἐν σπέεσσι γλαφυροῖσι).

[34] See Elliger 1975:128–131 and the discussion of Calypso's vegetation in Chapter 6 below.

[35] As de Jong puts it (2001 on *Odyssey* 5.76–91), "he literally turns his back on [Calypso] and her idyllic surroundings." Moreover, if Odysseus is indeed disenchanted with Calypso's vegetation, this would explain his choice of environs. He sits "on rocks and sand" (ἄμ πέτρῃσι καὶ ἠϊόνεσσι, 156), looking out "at the harvestless sea" (πόντον ἐπ' ἀτρύγετον, 158; also 84). This standard epithet for the sea gains particular salience when juxtaposed with allusions to rocks and sand. Odysseus seems to have chosen the only infertile place on this wondrously fertile island. For the distinction between divine and mortal perspectives in these lines, see also Rinon 2008:51.

[36] Calypso also supplies an ax and an adze, with which Odysseus fashions his raft (234–237).

kindly teachings of Hephaestus god of craftsmanship: they lived in mountain caves "like beasts" (ἠΰτε θῆρες, 4).[37]

Other aspects of her island likewise point to a lack of civilization and to its undesirability from the perspective of a mortal such as Odysseus. As we learn from Hermes at 5.100–102, it is far from the cities of mankind. Hermes expresses this notion from a god's point of view: Calypso's island is distant from "mortals who perform sacrifices and choice hecatombs for the gods" (βροτῶν ... οἵ τε θεοῖσιν / ἱερά τε ῥέζουσι καὶ ἐξαίτους ἑκατόμβας, 5.101–102). Hermes thus explains his own reluctance to travel to Ogygia—a god can derive no benefits from visiting, since there is no one there who might offer a sacrifice.[38] But Hermes' words also remind us of the undesirability of Ogygia from the point of view of a mortal such as Odysseus: it is far from the rites of civilization, from the sorts of practices that are important to the self-definition of mortals (cf. βροτῶν, 101). The implications of Hermes' words, then, echo those of Athena's speech in Book 1, where she emphasizes the isolation of Ogygia: this is a land cut off from civilization and is hence no sort of homeland for Odysseus.[39]

What is more, the flowery meadows and wild, super-abundant vegetal growths of Calypso's island would in no way have reminded Odysseus of his homeland.[40] As we shall see, Ithaca is a land of ordered plantations of domesticated trees, whose vegetation forms a clear contrast with that of Ogygia. In fact, the wild, superabundant growths of Calypso's island represent the furthest point—in both spatial and qualitative terms—from the civilized plantations of Ithaca. A land that represents a kind of Golden Age paradise from the perspective of a god such as Hermes would carry much less pleasant connotations for Odysseus.[41]

---

[37] The Cyclops' cave (e.g., *Odyssey* 9.216) is likewise indicative of a lack of civilization.

[38] We can contrast Hermes' reluctance to visit Ogygia with Poseidon's journey to the distant but fully inhabited land of Ethiopia, where he receives hecatombs (*Odyssey* 1.22–26).

[39] For the remoteness of Calypso's island, see also *Odyssey* 5.55 and 80.

[40] The description of Calypso's meadow of violets and celery at *Odyssey* 5.72 may also suggest that Odysseus' stay on Ogygia, cut off from civilization, is a kind of death for him. In particular, celery was closely associated with death in wider Greek culture. It was used as a floral offering to the dead, and it also marked the houses of the recently deceased: see Erasmo 2012:6 and Garland 1985:116, 171. See also, in general, Zusanek 1996:114: celery was "eine allgemein verwendete Totenpflanze" in Greek lands. For further associations of flowery meadows and death in the *Odyssey*, see Chapter 8 below.

[41] In fact, the Golden Age itself may have carried ambiguous connotations for a Greek audience. It is a time both of unstinting vegetal abundance, as on Calypso's island, and of barbarous behavior: Cronus, who was then king of the gods, swallowed his own children; see Nieto Hernández 2000.

Homeric Vegetal Imagery and Descriptions of Civilized Spaces

We turn now to Homeric vegetal imagery that, in clear contrast with the wild flowers and trees discussed above, is associated with civilized order and, in particular, with the good order ensured by patriarchal social structures. Most of these images fall into one of two categories: they either describe cereal crops and the labor required to maintain them, or they focus on managed arboreal growths. As we shall see, both of these kinds of image are present in the *Iliad*, which does not associate one more closely than the other with civilized order. The *Odyssey*, however, does in fact distinguish between them. While some passages of the *Odyssey* associate agriculture with civilization, the poem places particular emphasis on managed growths of trees, especially on those associated with the orderly spaces of orchards.

The *Iliad* associates both agricultural and arboricultural labor with patriarchal social structures and patriarchal authority.[42] At 11.67–71, for instance, the Trojans and Achaeans, as they attack one another, are compared with reapers who work opposite one another "in the field of a blessed man" (ἀνδρὸς μάκαρος κατ' ἄρουραν, 68). This brief phrase evokes both the orderly spaces of agriculture and a hierarchical, patriarchal society—a peacetime equivalent of the hierarchical social structures depicted on the Iliadic battlefield and in Iliadic assembly scenes. A rich man owns the field and has sufficient resources to hire reapers to work it for him. The description of agricultural labor in this simile appears consonant with its allusions to a patriarchal societal order: in the context of the Homeric poems, both agriculture and patriarchy are redolent of civilization.

Such associations of societal order with agricultural labor are echoed on the shield of Achilles, crafted by Hephaestus at *Iliad* 18.478–608.[43] At 541–572 Hephaestus creates a series of agricultural scenes, including one that is set in the allotment of a king (τέμενος βασιλήϊον, 550). The relevant lines (550–560) offer a more extended description of the kinds of tasks and societal structures depicted in the simile that we have just discussed. There is a clear division of labor between the several workers. Reapers cut down the wheat; boys collect the wheat that they cut; other men bind it into sheaves. Meanwhile food is prepared for the laborers; but once more, different tasks have been assigned. Heralds have slaughtered an ox and are now preparing it; women are scattering barley. The

---

[42] For the importance of agriculture to the value systems of the Homeric poems, see Redfield 1994:189–192, 2009:275–276; Vidal-Naquet 1996; H. P. Foley 2009:197–198.

[43] Most other Iliadic similes that describe agricultural labor—of which there are many—do not explicitly allude to structured societies. For such similes, see also Chapter 8 n1.

king presides over the entire scene: βασιλεὺς δ' ἐν τοῖσι σιωπῇ / σκῆπτρον ἔχων ἑστήκει ἐπ' ὄγμου γηθόσυνος κῆρ ("the king, holding his scepter, was standing among them with a happy heart," 556–557). These lines suggest both the hierarchical, patriarchal nature of the society that Hephaestus has depicted and its peaceful functioning. The king holds the scepter, a symbol of royal authority in the Homeric poems. He stands in silence, there being no need to give instructions, and feels joy at the good work that is being carried out on his behalf.[44]

The *Iliad* also associates royal authority with a second kind of managed vegetal growth—the managed trees found in orchards, which the epic mentions alongside agricultural fields on a number of occcasions. When Diomedes wishes to claim the authority to speak among the Achaean lords, he evokes his late father's wheat-fields and orchards: ἅλις δέ οἱ ἦσαν ἄρουραι / πυροφόροι, πολλοὶ δὲ φυτῶν ἔσαν ὄρχατοι ἀμφίς ("he had sufficient wheat-bearing fields, and many were the orchards of trees all around," *Iliad* 14.122-123). Elsewhere in the epic, orchards as well as agricultural fields are bestowed on kings and princes in recognition of their royal authority. Three times this concept is conveyed with the formula φυταλιῆς καὶ ἀρούρης, "of orchards and plowland": the king of the Lycians grants Bellerophon his daughter's hand, half his kingdom, and a fine allotment of orchards and plow-land (6.192-195); the same sorts of lands are granted to Sarpedon and to Glaucus (12.313–314), and might have been given to Aeneas, had he killed Achilles (20.184-186).[45]

Only one passage from the *Iliad* focuses on royal orchards without also mentioning agricultural fields. Achilles abducts Lycaon, son of Priam, from his father's orchard (ἐκ πατρὸς ἀλωῆς, 21.36), where he was exploiting these growths of trees for a particular purpose: "he was cutting new branches from a fig tree with the sharp bronze, so that they might form the rails of a chariot" (ὁ δ' ἐρινεὸν ὀξέϊ χαλκῷ / τάμνε νέους ὄρπηκας, ἵν' ἅρματος ἄντυγες εἶεν, 37–38). The association of these orchards with Lycaon's homeland and with the royal estate of Priam is highly reminiscent of the description of Laertes' orchards in the *Odyssey*, which as we shall see are associated with Odysseus' homecoming and with his patriarchal inheritance on Ithaca.

From this Iliadic evidence it would not be possible to conclude that agricultural fields or managed allotments of trees were associated more closely with civilized order and with the royal authority that guarantees such order—the *Iliad*

---

[44] The societies of *Iliad* 11.67–71 and 18.541–572, however, represent an ideal from which the incompetent leadership of Agamemnon departs: his quarrelling with a subordinate (Book 1), his unwise attempt to test his troops (Book 2), and his readiness to despair (Books 9 and 14) contrast with the orderly, patriarchal governance depicted in the simile and in the scene from the shield.

[45] For the associations of the roots φυτο/ε- and ἀρο- in these and other passages, see Chapter 6 below.

does not rank these two kinds of vegetal growth in its allusions to orderly societies. The *Odyssey*, however, places greater emphasis on associations of orchards and arboricultural labor with civilized order than on equivalent associations of agricultural fields and agricultural labor: a series of images of managed trees accompanies Odysseus' reintegration into the patriarchal society of Ithaca. We shall discuss the relevant evidence below, before considering in Chapter 6 what characteristics of agricultural and arboricultural growths in the environments familiar to early poets and audiences might have justified such differentiation in the *Odyssey*.

We get a first sense of the relative importance of agriculture in the *Odyssey* from the epic's depictions of the uncivilized and civilized lands that Odysseus visits. There are few allusions to agriculture in the relevant passages. Of the descriptions of uncivilized lands mentioned above, only Odysseus' narrative of the Cyclops episode bucks this trend. Odysseus notes that the Cyclopes do not engage in the civilized practices of agriculture—they neither plow nor sow (108-115). The nearby Goat Island is likewise "unsown and unplowed" (ἄσπαρτος καὶ ἀνήρατος, 123) and possesses flat land that could be ploughed (ἄροσις λείη, 134). The island, then, possesses resources that have not been exploited by the Cyclopes but that could be harnessed by a civilized individual such as Odysseus, who is familiar with the techniques of agriculture.[46] Otherwise, as we have seen, the uncivilized lands of Odysseus' travels are defined in terms of their wild floral and arboreal growths, rather than the presence or absence of agriculture.

The *Odyssey*'s depictions of more civilized lands—Ithaca and Scheria, land of the Phaeacians—allude to agriculture, but place greater emphasis on orderly plantations of trees. In three out of four cases, these plantations are defined by enclosures, and in two out of four cases they are associated with human labor. We should firstly consider the descriptions of Scheria, since it is not only Odysseus' last stopping-off point before reaching Ithaca, but also forms a thematic point of transition between the uncivilized lands mentioned above and the Ithacan environments that we shall discuss below. Scheria is a land with many of the trappings of civilization—a royal court, athletic games, religious rites, fine clothes, guest-gifts, feasting, and epic song. Nevertheless, aspects of Phaeacian culture mark a clear departure from the characteristics of civilized lands such as Ithaca. For instance, while the Phaeacians are known for their seamanship, their ships have no helmsmen or rudders: they are able simply to read the minds of the sailors (8.555–562).

---

[46] Critics have associated Goat Island with the colonization of new lands in Ionia: see, for instance, Elliger 1975:143. Clay (1980), however, suggests that it used to be the home of the more civilized Phaeacians, who were the neighbors of the Cyclopes (*Odyssey* 6.4–6).

In its descriptions of Scheria, the poem dwells to a considerable extent on the vegetation near the city and the royal palace, and this vegetation, like the Phaeacian homeland more generally, carries both civilized and less civilized connotations. When the land of the Phaeacians is introduced at the start of Book 6, the poem mentions how Nausithous led them to this new homeland and there "divided agricultural fields" among his subjects (ἐδάσσατ' ἀρούρας, 6.10). Later Nausicaa explains that she will lead Odysseus through "the fields and the works of mankind" (ἀγροὺς ἴομεν καὶ ἔργ' ἀνθρώπων, 7.259).[47] As with the descriptions of Ithaca that we shall consider, then, some mention is made of the civilized practice of agriculture.

More emphasis is given, however, to the plantations near the Phaeacian palace. In the course of the descriptions of these plantations, clear contrasts are drawn between their more civilized and their less civilized characteristics.[48] They are bounded by a wall (ἕρκος) and hence occupy a space defined by human planners, unlike the wildernesses described in the *Hymn to Pan* or in *Odyssey* 5: περὶ δ' ἕρκος ἐλήλαται ἀμφοτέρωθεν ("a wall has been driven around it on both sides," 7.113). We shall observe similar references to enclosures in the descriptions of Ithaca later in the *Odyssey*. There are also a few allusions in this passage to the sorts of human labor needed to maintain civilized plots of land. People gather and tread grapes (7.124-125). Perhaps workers are also employed to keep the plantations tidy: the vegetable beds are κοσμηταί, "ordered" (127). In these respects the Phaeacian plantations suggest a greater degree of civilization than the wild lands of Odysseus' travels. These are not merely wild growths but have been tamed to some degree by human hands.

And yet in other ways these plantations depart markedly both from the managed growths of Ithaca, which we shall discuss below, and from the managed growths with which audiences would have been familiar from their own communities. No human tendance is required to nurture these plants, since they grow automatically and throughout the year. The garden beds, for instance, "burgeon unfailingly" (ἐπηετανὸν γανόωσαι, 128). In the description of the orchards, which forms the greater part of the depiction of the Phaeacian plantations (112-121), particular emphasis is placed on such impressive qualities. Rather than following the cycles of nature, the fruit ripens all year round (117-118);

---

[47] See also 7.26, where Odysseus professes ignorance of the men who "exploit the fields" (ἔργα νέμονται) of Scheria.

[48] We find further indications of the ambiguous status of the vegetation of Scheria on Odysseus' arrival. At line 5.463, the wild growths of reeds around the river are juxtaposed with the "grain-giving plowland" (ζείδωρον ἄρουραν) that Odysseus kisses on his arrival. See also Ahl and Roisman (1996:97, 100), who argue that the "half-wild and half-cultivated" olive under which Odysseus sleeps when he first arrives in Scheria (5.477) reflects the Phaeacians' and (at that moment) Odysseus' ambiguous status, caught between civilization and its opposite.

and this is not the result of any human tendance but of the West Wind (118-119):

> ἔκτοσθεν δ' αὐλῆς μέγας ὄρχατος ἄγχι θυράων
> τετράγυος· περὶ δ' ἕρκος ἐλήλαται ἀμφοτέρωθεν.
> ἔνθα δὲ δένδρεα μακρὰ πεφύκασι τηλεθόωντα,
> 115 ὄγχναι καὶ ῥοιαὶ καὶ μηλέαι ἀγλαόκαρποι
> συκέαι τε γλυκεραὶ καὶ ἐλαῖαι τηλεθόωσαι.
> τάων οὔ ποτε καρπὸς ἀπόλλυται οὐδ' ἀπολείπει
> χείματος οὐδὲ θέρευς, ἐπετήσιος· ἀλλὰ μάλ' αἰεί
> Ζεφυρίη πνείουσα τὰ μὲν φύει, ἄλλα δὲ πέσσει.
> 120 ὄγχνη ἐπ' ὄγχνη γηράσκει, μῆλον δ' ἐπὶ μήλῳ,
> αὐτὰρ ἐπὶ σταφυλῇ σταφυλή, σῦκον δ' ἐπὶ σύκῳ.

Odyssey 7.112-121

> Outside the courtyard and near the gates was a great orchard
> Of four guai; a wall has been driven around it on both sides;
> There tall, flourishing trees have grown,
> 115 Pears and pomegranates and apples with shining fruit,
> Sweet figs and flourishing olives.
> Of these the fruit never perishes nor fails,
> Neither in winter nor summer—it is there throughout the year; but
>   the West Wind
> Always blows, growing some and ripening others.
> 120 Pear on pear matures, apple on apple,
> And grape on grape, fig on fig.

At first sight Odysseus seems to have encountered a kind of paradise—an allotment that gives of its bounty whether or not it is managed by human hands. And his reaction in lines 133–134 appears entirely positive, in clear contrast with his distress on Calypso's island: he wonders at these plantations.[49] In fact, his emotions echo those of Hermes on Ogygia, with the same phrases used of both characters: "standing there [Hermes, Odysseus] wondered. / But when he had wondered at all these things in his heart ..." (ἔνθα στὰς θηεῖτο ... / αὐτὰρ ἐπεὶ δὴ πάντα ἑῷ θηήσατο θυμῷ, 5.75–76, 7.133–134).

Nevertheless, Odysseus chooses not to stay in Scheria. And we can start to understand why the sight of these plantations might be less than satisfying to him when we compare them with the orchards of *Odyssey* 24, which we shall consider below. True, the pears, pomegranates, apples, figs, and olives

---

49 According to de Jong (2001:176), the scene as a whole is focalized by Odysseus.

of 7.112–121 anticipate Laertes' own pear-, apple-, and fig-trees (24.340–341). But while Laertes tends his orchards, the Phaeacian plantations are not subject to human tendance in the same way and to the same degree.[50] The fact that the Phaeacian orchards bear fruit automatically and unceasingly differentiates them from the orderly plantations of Ithaca.[51]

In this respect, they bear a closer resemblance to landscapes that the *Odyssey* associates with the divine. Indeed, the lack of influence of the seasons in these plantations reminds us of a description of Olympus early in the Phaeacian episode: "it is neither shaken by winds nor ever wet with rain, nor does snow come near it" (οὔτ' ἀνέμοισι τινάσσεται οὔτε ποτ' ὄμβρῳ / δεύεται οὔτε χιὼν ἐπιπίλναται, 6.43–44). There is a still greater resemblance between the Phaeacian orchard and the Islands of the Blessed, described at 4.565–569. On these islands, the West Wind is likewise a beneficial influence and, while there are seasons, they have little impact on the inhabitants. The wind cools the fortunate mortals who live there, and there is "neither snow nor much winter nor ever rain" (οὐ νιφετός, οὔτ' ἄρ χειμὼν πολὺς οὔτε ποτ' ὄμβρος). Menelaus is to enjoy "the easiest life for mortals" because he is the son-in-law of Zeus. The Phaeacian orchards, with their lack of human management and their growth under the influence of the West Wind, likewise carry associations with the divine: they are said to be the "glorious gifts of the gods" (θεῶν ... ἀγλαὰ δῶρα, 132).[52]

Odysseus' reaction of wonder at 7.133–134 is entirely appropriate to plantations that resemble such divine landscapes: as mentioned above, it is the sort of reaction that humans experience in the face of the divine. But while for a god such as Hermes feelings of wonder would have purely positive connotations, for a mortal they carry with them a sense of awe or even dread at the more-than-human.[53] Odysseus' wonderment at these semi-divine growths is, then, quite consistent with his decision not to stay in Scheria. Given their automatic

[50] Presumably human labor is required to collect all this produce; and perhaps workers would need to keep pests off the ever-ripening fruit. But such activities are mentioned nowhere in this passage. And the fact remains that the Phaeacian trees, unlike the plantations described in *Odyssey* 24, would produce fruit whether tended or not. By contrast, the description of orchards on Ithaca in Book 24 focuses on the hard work of Laertes.

[51] For the contrasts between Laertes' orchard and that of the Phaeacians, see Vidal-Naquet 1996:48.

[52] On the themes of the human and the divine in the descriptions of the Phaeacian plantations and Laertes' orchards, see also de Romilly 1993 and Bonnafé 1984–1987, 1:153–155. For the Phaeacians' closeness to the gods, see also *Odyssey* 6.203 and 7.201–203.

[53] Cf. Prier 1989:84–97 and *Iliad* 18.466–467, where Hephaestus predicts that mortals will feel wonderment before the Shield of Achilles, which is the product of his divine craftsmanship: οἱ τεύχεα καλὰ παρέσσεται, οἷά τις αὖτε / ἀνθρώπων πολέων θαυμάσσεται ... ("he will have beautiful armor, such that any one / of the many mortals will wonder ..."). The negative connotations of this wonderment are made clear at *Iliad* 19.14–15, when none of the Myrmidons can summon the courage to look at the shield.

flourishing, there is something *unheimlich* about these plantations. The vegetation of Phaeacia, then, represents a greater degree of civilization than the wild lands of Odysseus' travels; but it falls short of the carefully managed growths of his homeland.

As with the depiction of Scheria, greater emphasis is placed on orchards than on agricultural fields in the descriptions of Ithaca in the second half of the *Odyssey*. Granted, the relevant passages make some mention of agriculture. At 13.244–247, for instance, Athena lists the natural resources of Ithaca, the civilized land to which Odysseus has been striving to return. Among other things she mentions its "wondrous grain" (σῖτος ἀθέσφατος, 244). And at 18.366–375, the disguised Odysseus boasts to Eurymachus of his own excellence at reaping and plowing. But in the final part of the epic, during the course of which Odysseus regains his place in Ithacan society, considerable emphasis is placed on arboreal imagery.[54]

In the last five books of the *Odyssey* we find a series of images of orderly, flourishing trees, culminating with the managed growths of Laertes' orchards. The images in question not only distinguish Odysseus' homeland from the lands of his travels but also accompany his resumption of his place at the head of Ithacan society—as in the *Iliad*, good order in society is closely associated with the patriarchal rule of kings such as Odysseus. We can, then, observe a development in the *Odyssey* from images of wild growths to images of ordered trees and from an absence of civilization to the good order of Ithaca. While the wild floral and arboreal growths of Ogygia or of the lands described in Books 9-12 suggest the lack of civilization in such places, and the orderly but automatic growths found in the Phaeacian plantations place Scheria between civilization and its opposite, the flourishing trees of *Odyssey* 19–24 provide an image for the civilized, patriarchal society of Ithaca, re-established or soon to be re-established by Odysseus' return.[55]

We have already mentioned one of the arboreal images from the latter books of the *Odyssey*. At 19.108-114, Odysseus, still in his beggar disguise, compares

---

[54] Furthermore, in Books 23–24 Ithaca with its managed trees is set against an agricultural civilization that Odysseus will visit after the events of the *Odyssey*. At 11.121–128, Tiresias describes the journey that Odysseus must undertake in order to propitiate Poseidon, a prophecy that is repeated by Odysseus himself at 23.266–275, shortly before the description of Laertes' orchards in Book 24. Odysseus will travel inland, carrying an oar, until he comes to a place where the inhabitants have no knowledge of the sea. They are, however, an agricultural people: they know of the use of winnowing-fans, for which the oar will be mistaken (274–275). This land forms the opposite pole to Ithaca in Odysseus' second journey, and in Books 23–24 its association with agriculture creates a contrast with the ordered trees of Odysseus' homeland.

[55] On the importance of arboreal imagery to Odysseus' νόστος, see in general Thalmann 1992:74 and Henderson 1997.

Penelope's fame to that of a Just King who inspires flourishing in trees, crops, and animals alike, and whose people excel. I quote the passage for the second time, for ease of reference:

> ἦ γάρ σευ κλέος οὐρανὸν εὐρὺν ἱκάνει,
> ὥς τέ τευ ἢ βασιλῆος ἀμύμονος, ὅς τε θεουδὴς
> 110 ἀνδράσιν ἐν πολλοῖσιν καὶ ἰφθίμοισιν ἀνάσσων
> εὐδικίας ἀνέχῃσι, φέρῃσι δὲ γαῖα μέλαινα
> πυροὺς καὶ κριθάς, βρίθῃσι δὲ δένδρεα καρπῷ,
> τίκτῃ δ᾽ ἔμπεδα μῆλα, θάλασσα δὲ παρέχῃ ἰχθῦς
> ἐξ εὐηγεσίης, ἀρετῶσι δὲ λαοὶ ὑπ᾽ αὐτοῦ.

Odyssey 19.108-114

> Your fame reaches the wide heaven,
> As that of some excellent, god-fearing king,
> 110 Who among many men upholds justice,
> Ruling mighty subjects, and the black earth bears
> Wheat and barley, and the trees burgeon with fruit,
> And the flocks constantly bear young; through his good
>   leadership
> The sea provides fish, and the people excel under him.

The allusions to animal and vegetal flourishing in these lines would have helped audiences to imagine the human well-being that results from the beneficial rule of a just king. The king's citizens will abound in excellences like plants at the peak of health. The Homeric poets thus referenced more concrete concepts associated with the natural environment—the flourishing of animals and plants—to aid their audiences' understanding of a more abstract kind of well-being.

Odysseus' simile refers not only to flourishing but also to patriarchal rule. The association of this image with a woman might seem at first sight to run counter to the notion of patriarchal rule embodied by the Just King. Penelope, however, in her reply to her disguised husband distances herself from the figure of the Just King and emphasizes the need for Odysseus' presence on Ithaca. She describes the withering of her body and of her beauty in the absence of her husband (124-126) and states that "if he came and cared for my life, / my fame would thus be greater and more beautiful" (εἰ κεῖνος γ᾽ ἐλθὼν τὸν ἐμὸν βίον ἀμφιπολεύοι, / μεῖζον κε κλέος εἴη ἐμὸν καὶ κάλλιον οὕτω, 127-128).[56] Odysseus has just compared her with a ruler who causes his people, animals, and plants to

---

[56] As we learn from *Odyssey* 20.88–90, Penelope imagines Odysseus returning as he was when he left for Troy as a younger man: see Chapter 2 and the discussion below.

flourish, but she claims in these lines that she would be more deserving of such fame if he were present.

And one can see her point. The depredations of the suitors have had a severe impact on the livestock of the island: the flocks (μῆλα) of Ithaca are not flourishing like those of the Just King (19.113), but will have to be restored by Odysseus (23.356–358). Penelope has succeeded, as we shall see, in maintaining the rootedness of their marriage, symbolized by the olive-tree bed in their bedchamber. But while the trees of Ithaca do, indeed, "burgeon with fruit" (19.112), this, as explained below, is the result of Laertes' labor, not Penelope's. Penelope, then, quite reasonably points out that she is unable on her own, in the absence of Odysseus, to ensure that the kingdom will flourish in the manner described in the simile. That sort of flourishing can only be actualized if Odysseus' rule is re-established on Ithaca.[57]

But there is one thing about this passage that remains unclear, and it is of relevance to our analysis of the associations of trees in the *Odyssey*. As noted above, the trees described in line 112 are the sort of fruit trees we would find in orchards—civilized spaces under the control of human societies. Audiences, however, when they heard Odysseus' image of flourishing fruit trees, had the choice of imagining two different kinds of planatation. They might have remembered the descriptions of the anomalous, automatic growths of Scheria from Book 7 (or from other, similar passages of Homeric poetry), which bear fruit without the need for human labor. Alternatively, they might have associated the fruit trees of 19.112 with the carefully managed growths that they would have known from their own homelands. But the lines quoted above refer explicitly neither to the management of trees nor to automatic growths. In this way, the image of the Just King helps to form a bridge between the preternatural orchards of Scheria, which produce fruit without the need for human intervention, and the trees of Ithaca, which must be carefully managed by human hands: the trees in our passage from Book 19 represent a neutral term between these two extremes, and they could be assimilated to either in the minds of listeners.

The two most important stages in Odysseus' bid to regain his place in Ithacan society, the recognitions of him by his wife and his father, are both associated with images of managed trees. The first of the relevant passages is found in Book 23, where the marriage of Penelope and Odysseus is re-established. We noted in Chapter 2 that Penelope accepts Odysseus in the enhanced form that Athena has granted him, but that she hesitates before doing so. Odysseus overcomes her initial hesitation by describing the origins of their marital bed.

---

[57] See H. P. Foley 2009.

Penelope has set him a test. She asks Eurycleia to set up their marriage bed outside the bedchamber, so that she may see if he is able to relate the secret of its construction (23.177-181). If this is truly Odysseus, he will be aware that the bed cannot be moved, since he himself built it around an olive-tree, still rooted in the ground.

Odysseus passes the test: he is able to describe both the tree itself and his own handiwork in fashioning the bed. Odysseus remembers that, before he made the bed, the olive-tree was growing "within a wall" (ἕρκος ἐντός, 23.190). It had been set off, then, within space demarcated for civilized usages. In this respect, it resembles the trees in the Phaeacian orchard, which are likewise surrounded by a wall (ἕρκος, 7.113). Next, Odysseus focuses on the olive's healthful growth and strength: "a leafy thicket of olive grew ... at its peak and flourishing; it was thick like a pillar" (θάμνος ἔφυ τανύφυλλος ἐλαίης ... / ἀκμηνὸς θαλέθων· πάχετος δ' ἦν ἠΰτε κίων, 23.190-191; cf. 195, 204).[58] He goes on to describe how he manipulated the tree as he constructed the bed. He cut off its leaves and prepared the trunk: he trimmed it, bored it and made it straight (23.195–201). This tree, rooted in the ground, formed the post (ἑρμῖν', 198) of the bed as a whole. For this reason, Odysseus explains, it is impossible to move it (203–204).

We can work out some of the implications of this arresting image from its context in *Odyssey* 23 and from the fact that these lines are voiced by Odysseus: the description of the bed would have helped audiences to understand Odysseus' hopes for his marriage with Penelope. As scholars have noted, Odysseus' emphasis on the bed's rootedness in the ground suggests his wish that their marriage has remained stable despite their twenty years apart. He wonders whether the bed is "still in place" (ἔτ' ἔμπεδον, 203) and whether any man has moved it (203–204). Similarly, audiences could have inferred, he hopes that no man has intruded on their marriage. Such hopes are fulfilled by Penelope's reaction in the subsequent lines, as she acknowledges the σήματ' ... ἔμπεδα ("constant signs," 206) provided by Odysseus' description of the bed: she embraces her husband (207–208) and makes clear that no other mortal, except for a single female attendant, knows the "clear signs ... of our bed" (σήματ' ἀριφραδέα ... εὐνῆς ἡμετέρης, 23.225–226).[59]

---

[58] As we have seen, trees and pillars carry similar associations in Homeric poetry. The description of an olive tree "thick like a pillar" reinforces this sense of an equivalence between the two kinds of image. But in its immediate context the phrase also suggests the dual status of the tree: it is both a natural growth and an architectural feature, like a pillar.

[59] Cf. 23.110, where Penelope refers to the hidden σήματα known only to her and Odysseus; also 19.250, where Penelope recognizes the "constant signs" (σήματ' ... ἔμπεδα) that seem to prove that "the beggar" once met Odysseus. On the bed as an image of the stability of Odysseus' and Penelope's marriage, see Murnaghan 1987:116, Arthur (Katz) 1991:178, Zeitlin 1995.

And these allusions to stability in Odysseus' and Penelope's speeches also carry important implications for our understanding of Book 23 as a whole. Specifically, they counterbalance the unsettling notes introduced by the description of Odysseus' appearance in lines 156-162. As noted in Chapter 2, Odysseus' hyacinthine hair has deceptive qualities: Athena lends him the appearance of a young man in his prime. Moreover, we never hear that Odysseus is reunited with his wife in his regular, unenhanced form. But the allusions to stability in this scene emphasize the fact that their marriage has endured, even if Odysseus' appearance is not quite what it seems.

We can also deduce the significance of references to labor in Odysseus' speech, which have not tended to be the focus of scholarship on this scene.[60] If the bed represents Odysseus' marriage with Penelope, then his work in fashioning it suggests the efforts on his part to craft their marriage (presumably matched by Penelope's own efforts). Nevertheless, Odysseus has been absent these past twenty years. During that time, Penelope's fidelity has forestalled a second, deleterious action on the part of another man, who might have "cut from under the stock of the olive" (ταμὼν ὕπο πυθμέν' ἐλαίης, 204). While she may not have been able to inspire increase in the kingdom in the manner of the Just King, her fidelity to Odysseus has allowed their marriage to endure in his absence. She has ensured that the olive-tree bed and the marriage that it represented remained rooted in the ground.

The olive tree thus provides an image for Penelope's preservation of their marriage, which is a prerequisite for Odysseus' successful homecoming. And his recall of its construction marks an important stage in his re-assumption of his position in Ithacan society—the reconstitution of the marriage. The importance of the olive tree to Odysseus' homecoming is reinforced when we observe its relationship with a passage in the following book. This second passage echoes elements of Odysseus' description of the tree and is likewise associated with an important stage in his homecoming. The relevant lines depict managed trees growing within a plot defined by a wall, ἕρκος: at *Odyssey* 24.224 Dolius, his sons and some slaves are off collecting stones to form the "wall" ἕρκος, 24.224 of the orchard that is worked by Laertes. And Laertes' orchard provides the setting for Odysseus' reunion with his father and for the reconstitution of the patriarchal line on Ithaca.[61]

---

60 Minchin (2007:268–269) comments on this theme but not in connection with Odysseus' and Penelope's marriage: according to her, Odysseus' description of his own labor suggests a man's interest in technical details.

61 For the association of the olive-tree bed with Laertes' orchards, see Henderson 1997:94, and Vernant and Frontisi-Ducroux 1997:284.

Just as Odysseus emphasizes the labor required to fashion his bed, the narrative of Book 24 dwells to a considerable extent on Laertes' management of his orchard. His labor is emphasized the very first time that the orchard is mentioned: "Laertes himself had once gained possession [of it], since he had toiled greatly" (ὅν ῥά ποτ' αὐτὸς / Λαέρτης κτεάτισσεν, ἐπεὶ μάλα πόλλ' ἐμόγησεν, 24.206–207). Shortly afterwards Odysseus finds Laertes "digging around a tree" (λιστρεύοντα φυτόν, 227; φυτὸν ἀμφελάχαινε, 242).[62] And when Odysseus addresses him, he stresses the care that Laertes is taking in looking after his plants:

> "ὦ γέρον, οὐκ ἀδαημονίη σ' ἔχει ἀμφιπολεύειν
> ὄρχατον, ἀλλ' εὖ τοι κομιδὴ ἔχει, οὐδέ τι πάμπαν,
> οὐ φυτόν, οὐ συκέη, οὐκ ἄμπελος, οὐ μὲν ἐλαίη,
> οὐκ ὄγχνη, οὐ πρασιή τοι ἄνευ κομιδῆς κατὰ κῆπον..."

Odyssey 24.244–247

"Old man, you do not care for this plot
In ignorance, but your care for it is good, and not anything,
No tree, no fig, no vine, no olive,
No pear-tree, no garden-bed goes without care throughout the plantation ..."

The importance of managed orchards (as opposed to any other type of vegetal growth) in this passage is underlined when we contrast it with descriptions of vegetation and/or agriculture elsewhere in the *Odyssey*. Firstly, the wild floral and arboreal growths of lands such as Ogygia provide a clear contrast with the ordered orchards of Ithaca: there are no flourishing fruit trees amid Calypso's meadows.[63] What is more, even when Odysseus encounters orchards in Scheria, they lack a key characteristic of Laertes' plantation: tendance by human hands. The figs, pears, and apples of Scheria (7.120–121) are matched by similar varieties in Laertes' orchard. But while the trees of Scheria grow automatically, under the influence of the West Wind, the trees of Laertes' orchard require the assiduous attention of their owner.

Nevertheless, there is something not quite right about the scene before Odysseus' eyes, which can only be remedied by his reunion with Laertes. Odysseus continues:

> "ἄλλο δέ τοι ἐρέω, σὺ δὲ μὴ χόλον ἔνθεο θυμῷ·
> αὐτόν σ' οὐκ ἀγαθὴ κομιδὴ ἔχει, ἀλλ' ἅμα γῆρας

---

[62] For the implications of the lexeme φυτόν, see Chapter 6 below.
[63] See Zusanek 1996:108–109.

250 λυγρὸν ἔχεις αὐχμεῖς τε κακῶς καὶ ἀεικέα ἕσσαι.
οὐ μὲν ἀεργίης γε ἄναξ ἕνεκ' οὔ σε κομίζει,
οὐδέ τί τοι δούλειον ἐπιπρέπει εἰσοράασθαι
εἶδος καὶ μέγεθος· βασιλῆι γὰρ ἀνδρὶ ἔοικας.
τοιούτῳ δὲ ἔοικας, ἐπεὶ λούσαιτο φάγοι τε,
255 εὑδέμεναι μαλακῶς· ἡ γὰρ δίκη ἐστὶ γερόντων ... "

Odyssey 24.248–255

"But I will tell you this, and place no anger in your heart:
No good care attends your own person, but you possess a grievous
250 Old age; and at the same time you are dirty and dressed in an
unseemly fashion.
Not for the sake of your idleness does your lord not care for you,
And your appearance and size are impressive to look at,
Not at all those of a slave; you seem like a king.
You seem like the sort of man who should sleep softly,
255 Once he has washed and eaten; such is the right of old men ... "

Properly, then, Laertes' care for the trees (κομιδή, 245, 247) should be matched by the care of his lord for Laertes' own person (κομιδή, 249; κομίζει, 251). And in the context of this meeting of Odysseus and Laertes—that is, of the king of Ithaca and of his aging father—these references to a lord and to proper care in old age take on a particular relevance: Laertes' care for the orchards should have been matched by Odysseus' care of his father. Odysseus is the ἄναξ, "lord," whose duty it was to care for Laertes. He owes this care for two reasons: Laertes has grown old (255) and he is a man of the royal family (253). In his absence, Odysseus has been unable to fulfill his duties; accordingly, Laertes has suffered neglect.[64] The problem caused by Odysseus' absence is solved soon afterwards, when Odysseus reveals his identity to Laertes and the royal line of Ithaca is thereby restored. Presumably, Odysseus will now be able to ensure his father does not suffer neglect: Laertes' labor will now be matched by Odysseus' own care of Laertes.

The trees in Laertes' orchards are crucial to the restoration of ties between royal father and royal son: Odysseus proves his identity not only by showing Laertes the scar that he sustained in a boar hunt (24.331–335; cf. 19.428–466), but also by demonstrating his knowledge of the trees. Odysseus describes how,

---

[64] Achilles acknowledges a similar duty and similar regrets towards the end of the *Iliad*. At *Iliad* 24.540–541 he recognizes that he is unable to care for Peleus in his old age (οὐδέ νυ τόν γε / γηράσκοντα κομίζω, "nor may I care for him as he grows old"). Achilles, then, employs the lexeme κομίζω to refer to his duty of care to his father. Odysseus uses the same lexeme of the care that Laertes should have enjoyed (cf. *Odyssey* 24.249, 251).

as a child, Laertes led him through the orchard, naming and numbering the trees that were to be his:

> εἰ δ' ἄγε τοι καὶ δένδρε' ἐϋκτιμένην κατ' ἀλωὴν
> εἴπω, ἅ μοί ποτ' ἔδωκας, ἐγὼ δ' ᾔτεόν σε ἕκαστα
> παιδνὸς ἐών, κατὰ κῆπον ἐπισπόμενος· διὰ δ' αὐτῶν
> ἱκνεύμεσθα, σὺ δ' ὠνόμοσας καὶ ἔειπες ἕκαστα.
> 340 ὄγχνας μοι δῶκας τρισκαίδεκα καὶ δέκα μηλέας,
> συκέας τεσσαράκοντ'·

Odyssey 24.336–341

> Come on, let me also tell you the trees throughout the well-built
> Orchard, which you once gave to me; still a child, I was asking you
> For each type, following you through the plantation; we were
>   walking
> Through them, and you named and told me each kind.
> 340 You gave me thirteen pear-trees and ten apple-trees,
> Forty fig-trees.

These trees offer an image for the flourishing and endurance of the patriarchal line of Ithaca. As a gift from the old king to the young prince (cf. ποτ' ἔδωκας ... δῶκας, "you once gave ... you gave," 337–340), they constitute a part of the royal inheritance of Ithaca. This inheritance is reactivated through Odysseus' remembrance of the conversation he once had with his father.[65] Moreover the fact that the trees have endured in this spot and continued to flourish suggests that, thanks to Laertes' labor, the patriarchal line of Ithaca has remained stable and viable in Odysseus' absence—even if Laertes lacked the resources (or the will) to care for his own person.[66] It is appropriate, then, that Laertes should regard the trees as σήματ' ... ἔμπεδα, "constant signs" (346).[67] Like the olive-tree bed, which likewise provides "constant signs" (σήματ' ... ἔμπεδα, 206), they provide an image for important constituents of Odysseus' identity—his

---

[65] See Arthur (Katz) 1991:178–179, who argues that Odysseus here reenacts the speech with which Laertes passed his inheritance to him many years previously and thus accepted him into the patriarchal lineage of Ithaca. Arthur links this speech of Odysseus with his description of the bed—both are performances of Odysseus' identity. On the re-establishment of Odysseus as Laertes' heir through his description of the trees, see also Whitman 1958:304–305.

[66] Cf. Pucci 1996 and Henderson 1997. Pucci sees Laertes as hoping that Odysseus, fixed in the soil, will flourish along with his people, like the subjects of the Just King in *Odyssey* 19. Henderson argues that Laertes' planting and tendance of trees is as one with his planting and tendance of the young Odysseus, and that his gift of trees to his son constitutes an attempt to anchor the boy in the Ithacan soil and in his paternal inheritance.

[67] For these trees as "constant signs" (σήματ ... ἔμπεδα), see Henderson 1997. According to him, the adjective suggests signs that are "well-grounded" like the trees themselves (p. 89).

marriage with Penelope and his place in the royal line of Ithaca—and for their endurance in his absence. Much as Penelope's efforts have ensured that their marriage remains rooted in the soil, Laertes' labor has preserved the patriarchal inheritance of Ithaca.

And now that Odysseus has returned and the patriarchal line of Ithaca has been restored, his labor as king can ensure the well-being not only of family members such as Laertes and Penelope, but of the Ithacan people as a whole. The Just King in Odysseus' own image in Book 19 ensures the flourishing of his people through his good leadership (εὐηγεσίη, 114): ἀρετῶσι δὲ λαοὶ ὑπ' αὐτοῦ ("the people excel under him," 114). But we saw that Penelope disclaims the ability to inspire such flourishing in Odysseus' absence. Now that he has returned and his rulership has been re-established, his labor can bring about such happy states of affairs.[68] As Tiresias predicts at 11.136-137 and as Odysseus recalls in conversation with Penelope at 23.283–284, Odysseus' people will be blessed (ὄλβιοι).

We have, then, observed a progression from the wild lands of Odysseus' travels to the managed vegetation of Ithaca, which is associated with his journey back to the civilization of Ithaca and his re-assumption of his place at the head of Ithacan soceity. Much as the lack of civilization on Ogygia contrasts with the good order of Scheria and Ithaca, the wild flowers and trees of Calypso's island contrast with the orderly plantations of those more civilized lands. And we have traced a progression through three descriptions of trees in an enclosure (ἕρκος)—from the orchard of the Phaeacians, which requires no human tendance, through the managed olive tree of Book 23 to the orchards managed by Laertes in Book 24. In each case, Odysseus comes closer to the completion of his homecoming. The Phaeacian orchards more closely resemble the orderly allotments of Ithaca than any other vegetation that Odysseus encounters on his travels; Odysseus' description of the olive-tree bed leads to his reunion with Penelope; and the royal orchard hosts his reunion with Laertes.

In this way, the Homeric poets offered images drawn from the natural environment to help their audiences understand the abstract concepts of civilization and its opposite. Uncivilized places were like the wild growths that they would have seen beyond the bounds of settlements, fields, and plantations. The orderliness of civilized societies could be imagined in terms of the orderly vegetation that they would have seen in orchards. As in those plantations, however, constant labor was required to maintain their good order.

[68] Some versions of *Odyssey* 19.114 have ἐξ εὐεργεσίης ("through his good works") in place of ἐξ εὐηγεσίης ("through his good leadership"): see Allen 1912-20 *ad loc.* Such versions associate the flourishing of the Just King's realm directly with his labor; cf. 24.250, where Odysseus notes that Laertes' squalid state is not the result of his idleness (ἀεργεσίη).

But there are still aspects of such vegetal imagery and, indeed, of the cosmic imagery discussed in Chapter 4 that we have yet to explain. As noted above, the *Odyssey* makes comparatively little mention of fields of cereal crops in its definitions of civilized and uncivilized spaces. We need to consider why the *Odyssey* poets might have focused on the managed growths of trees to convey the notion of civilized spaces, rather than on the agricultural fields that would also have been familiar to early audiences. And we have yet to explain why, in the Homeric imagery of cosmic order, flowers should be imagined as antithetical to the growth of trees. I shall address these questions in the following chapter, where I consider the relationship of such images with beliefs about the modes of reproduction of flowers, trees, and cereal crops.

6

The Modes of Generation of
Flowers and Trees
Homeric Poetry and Theophrastus

IN CHAPTERS 4 AND 5, WE SURVEYED TWO SETS of Homeric vegetal images. The one set associates arboreal images with the established order of the cosmos and floral images with changes or challenges to that order. In the other set, the wild growths both of flowers and of trees are associated with uncivilized lands, in contrast with the managed growths of agricultural fields and orchards, which are in turn associated with the good order of civilized societies.

The two sets of images do not map perfectly onto one another: wild growths of flowers and trees are differentiated in images of cosmic order and of changes and challenges to that order, but not in the equivalent civic images. Nevertheless, if we consider these two sets of images alongside one another, it is possible to distinguish four different kinds of vegetal growth, together with their respective conceptual associations. Wild floral growths are associated both with challenges or changes to cosmic order and with an absence of civic order. Wild growths of trees, by contrast, are associated with uncivilized lands, but not with changes or challenges to cosmic order. At the other end of the scale, two kinds of vegetal growth managed by human hands—cereal crops and fruit trees—are associated with good order in the city; and as we have seen, the *Odyssey* places special emphasis on the orderly connotations of orchards.

I have already suggested that the associations of crops and orchards with civic and not with cosmic order reflects a belief that civilized societies could only be maintained through the careful efforts of their rulers. But we have yet to gain a sense of the reasons why the poets of the *Odyssey* might have seen fit to differentiate between agricultural and arboricultural labor; nor, *a fortiori*, can we yet intuit why the Homeric poets might have distinguished between the four different kinds of vegetal growth outlined above. But as we shall see, it is possible to explain why they associated these four kinds of vegetal growth with different degrees of order and disorder, if we read our Homeric evidence alongside the descriptions of plants in the botanical treatises of Theophrastus.[1] Theophrastus' treatment of vegetal generation draws on an intellectual tradition dating back to the Presocratics and hence to the archaic age, the focus of our study.[2] But of all archaic and classical Greek authors, Theophrastus gives us our clearest exposition of the various types of vegetal growth.

When we compare Homeric vegetal imagery with Theophrastus' treatises, we can see why the Homeric poets might have associated flowers and trees with cosmic order and with challenges to that order: such associations relied on Greek perceptions of distinctions between spontaneous and non-spontaneous growths. Reflecting such beliefs, Theophrastus explains that small flowering plants were capable of spontaneous generation, outside the bounds of regular causality, but that wild trees are more likely to arise from more regular origins, such as seeds. In Homeric poetry, this contrast is echoed in a distinction between the perfect and pluperfect tenses of φύω (regular arboreal growths) and the verb's present, future, and aorist tenses (spontaneous floral growths).

A combination of Theophrastus' treatises with the linguistic choices of the Homeric poets also helps us to understand why orchards might carry particularly close associations with civic order in the *Odyssey*. Theophrastus distinguishes between the modes of propagation of domesticated trees and crops: while agriculture depended on modes of generation found also in the natural world, trees in orchards were propagated through techniques not paralleled in the wild, such as grafting: these were, then, modes of propagation associated only with civilized spaces. The Homeric poets reflected this distinction in their

---

[1] For such a comparison, see Nagy 2013:345–364, esp. 350–351. Nagy reads the associations of good kingship with flourishing vegetation in the Just King simile (*Odyssey* 19.108–114) and in the description of Laertes' orchards (*Odyssey* 24) alongside Theophrastus' references to the taming of "overweening" vegetation, to be discussed below. He notes associations of justice with orderly vegetation and of injustice with uncontrolled vegetal growth.

[2] See Quinn 1964, Amigues 2002b:22–23, and Theophrastus' own discussion of spontaneous generation at *Historia Plantarum* 3.1.4, where he cites Anaxagoras, Diogenes, and Cleidemus. Like the Homeric poems, the work of the Presocratic philosophers arises from a tradition of oral performance active in the archaic period and continuing into classical times. For instance, a notice of Theophrastus (*apud* Simplicius *Commentary on Aristotle's* Physics p. 23 lines 29–33 Diels = Thales B1 DK), regarding the first named figure in the tradition, Thales, records both that there were many earlier thinkers who studied nature (φύσις) and that Thales himself left only one written work. Diogenes Laertius refers to the opinions of some who go further in saying that Thales left no written works at all (1.23 = Thales A1 DK). Anaximander, moreover, received oral instruction from Thales: he was a "listener of Thales" (Θαλοῦ/Θαλέω ἀκουστής, Anaximander A4, 6 DK). Likewise, in the fifth century BCE oral performance was important to the activities of the successors of these archaic Greek thinkers, such as the sophists and Socrates. For further discussion of the Presocratics, see Chapter 4 n7.

use of the root ἀρο- to describe agricultural labor and agricultural fields, and of φυτο/ε- to describe arboricultural labor and orchards.

Spontaneous and Non-Spontaneous Growths of Wild Plants: Homeric Poetry and Theophrastus

In preparation for my comparison of Homeric and Theophrastan depictions of vegetal generation, I would like to focus firstly on *Historia Plantarum* 2.1.1, where Theophrastus categorizes the different modes of vegetal generation:

> Αἱ γενέσεις τῶν δένδρων καὶ ὅλως τῶν φυτῶν ἢ αὐτόματοι ἢ ἀπὸ σπέρματος ἢ ἀπὸ ῥίζης ἢ ἀπὸ παρασπάδος ἢ ἀπὸ ἀκρεμόνος ἢ ἀπὸ κλωνὸς ἢ ἀπ' αὐτοῦ τοῦ στελέχους εἰσίν... Τούτων δὲ ἡ μὲν αὐτόματος πρώτη τις, αἱ δὲ ἀπὸ σπέρματος καὶ ῥίζης φυσικώταται δόξαιεν ἄν· ὥσπερ γὰρ αὐτόματοι καὶ αὐταί, διὸ καὶ τοῖς ἀγρίοις ὑπάρχουσιν· αἱ δὲ ἄλλαι τέχνης ἢ δὴ προαιρέσεως.

Theophrastus *Historia Plantarum* 2.1.1

The modes of generation of trees and plants in general are either spontaneous or from a seed or from a root or from a shoot or from a branch or from a slip or from the trunk itself... Of these the spontaneous is first, but those from seed and root might seem the most natural; they are themselves also, as it were, spontaneous in that they are found in wild plants; the others are matters of skill or deliberate choice.

In this passage, Theophrastus establishes two contrasts which, when supplemented with other statements of his, suggest four modes of generation. On the one hand, he sets spontaneous (αὐτόματος) generation against generation from some part of a parent plant (seed, root, shoot, branch, slip, or trunk). On the other, he distinguishes the generation of wild plants in general from those modes of generation requiring human input, i.e., generation from shoot, branch, slip, or trunk. As he explains, the propagation of wild plants might also be called αὐτόματος, but only by analogy (ὥσπερ, "as if") with αὐτόματος generation *sensu stricto*: presumably, such generation is spontaneous in the sense that it occurs of its own accord, without the need for human management.[3] As for genera-

---

[3] See also *De Causis Plantarum* 3.1.1, where Theophrastus distinguishes between two objects of botanical study: μίαν μὲν τὴν ἐν τοῖς αὐτομάτοις γινομένην ... ἑτέραν δὲ τὴν ἐκ τῆς ἐπινοίας καὶ παρασκευῆς ... ("one, in the case of spontaneous things ... the other that is from planning and preparation"). The second grouping is concerned with the human management of plants, such as the techniques of arboriculture. Quotations from *De Causis Plantarum* are taken from Amigues 2012–2017.

tion from shoot, branch, slip, or trunk, Theophrastus elsewhere makes it clear that these practices belong not to the cultivation of agricultural crops, but to arboriculture: cereals and legumes grow only from seed or (weakly) from root-stock.[4] He implies, then, that there are four modes of generation: spontaneous (*sensu stricto*) generation deriving from no part of a parent plant; wild generation from seed or root-stock (which might be called spontaneous by analogy); agricultural generation from seed or root-stock; and generation using techniques specific to arboriculture—from shoot, branch, slip or trunk. As we shall see, these four modes of generation offer a parallel for the four kinds of vegetal growth in our Homeric passages and help us to understand the origins of the relevant Homeric images in perceptions of vegetal growth in the natural environment.

I would like to start with the Homeric associations of flowers with challenges or changes to cosmic order. As we shall see, the growths in the relevant passages broadly resemble descriptions of spontaneous (*sensu stricto*) generation in the work of Theophrastus and his predecessors in the Presocratic tradition. This suggests that in their descriptions of flowers the Homeric poets were, like Theophrastus and his archaic predecessors, describing a mode of propagation outside the bounds of regular vegetal reproduction. Such generation, which did not follow the rules for regular propagation, would have provided a ready model for Homeric poets to explore actions and events that undermined the established order of the cosmos.

In keeping with the tendencies of their respective genres, the Homeric poets trace these irregular growths to divine influence, but Theophrastus and his predecessors employ purely physical explanations for such processes. Personified gods are a strong presence not only in the *Homeric Hymns* but also in the *Iliad* and the *Odyssey*; and in all of the Homeric poems such characters help to bring about events that are beyond the control of human agents. Their interventions include manipulations of the world of nature: at *Odyssey* 23.241–246, for instance, Athena holds back the dawn so that Odysseus and Penelope can enjoy the first night together after their reunion. Similarly, the actions or simply the presence of gods in our descriptions of changes or challenges to cosmic order appear to cause wild growths of flowers. Gaia for instance "sends up" the narcissus in the *Hymn to Demeter*. The flowers of *Hymn to Apollo* 135–139 sprout automatically the moment that Apollo first strides onto Delos. Likewise, flowers grow in the Διὸς ἀπάτη as Zeus takes Hera in his arms (*Iliad* 14.346–349).

By contrast, the models of spontaneous generation developed by the Presocratics and by Theophrastus attribute such processes to physical causes alone. Theophrastus and his predecessors tend to explain spontaneous

---

[4] Cf. *Historia Plantarum* 8.1.2 (cereals and legumes) and below on the techniques of arboriculture.

generation as the result of the sun's warming mixtures of earth and water. Anaximander for instance is of the opinion that *ex aqua terraque calefactis exortos esse siue pisces seu piscibus simillima animalia* ("from heated water and earth arose either fish or animals very similar to fish," A30 DK).[5] Theophrastus explains spontaneous generation in similar terms: it occurs when the sun warms a mixture of earth and water (*De Causis Plantarum* 1.5.5).[6] At 1.1.2, he adds the element of decomposition: spontaneous generation arises ἐκ συρροῆς καὶ σήψεως ("from flowing together and rotting," *De Causis Plantarum* 1.1.2; cf. 5.4.6).[7]

In other respects, however, the descriptions of wild floral growths in our Homeric passages bear a close resemblance to Theophrastus' descriptions of spontaneous generation. Firstly, the kinds of plants that Theophrastus associates with spontaneous generation match those that are described in our Homeric passages. Theophrastus believes that spontaneous generation is typical of smaller plants, especially annuals (ἐπετείων) and herbaceous (πωδῶν) species: αἱ δ' αὐτόματοι γίνονται μέν ... τῶν ἐλαττόνων καὶ μάλιστα τῶν ἐπετείων καὶ πωδῶν ("spontaneous modes of generation pertain to smaller plants, especially annuals and herbs," *De Causis Plantarum* 1.5.1). The descriptions of flowers in Homeric images of cosmic change accord with Theophrastus' statements: Theophrastus' annual and herbaceous plants are precisely the sort of small, flowering plants that we have encountered in the relevant Homeric passages.

Secondly, Theophrastus and his predecessors describe spontaneous generation as unparented growth—in the case of plants, growth that did not originate from a part of a parent plant, such as a root or a seed.[8] Our Homeric passages are consistent with this notion: in none of the passages that we have studied is

---

[5] See also Theophrastus' accounts of Diogenes' and Anaxagoras' statements on spontaneous generation at *Historia Plantarum* 3.1.4. For spontaneous generation in Anaximander, see Gregory 2016:38–41. For the Presocratics more generally, see Lowe 2015:47.

[6] Spontaneous generation happens διαθερμαινομένης τῆς γῆς καὶ ἀλλοιουμένης τῆς ἀθροισθείσης μίξεως ὑπὸ τοῦ ἡλίου ("when the earth is warmed and the collected mixture is altered by the sun," *De Causis Plantarum* 1.5.5). Theophrastus does not explicitly mention water, but the phrase τῆς ἀθροισθείσης μίξεως ("the collected mixture") suggests more than just earth: cf. Einarson and Link 1976–1990 1:41 n. d.

[7] In Chapter 4 n3 above, I note intersections between Pindar *Seventh Olympian* and the Homeric floral images of cosmic change. But the description of the emergence of Rhodes/the rose in Pindar's poem more closely resembles scientific accounts of spontaneous generation than those Homeric images (see Quinn 1964:53–54). Lines 69–71 associate the growth of the new land with the wet sea and with Helios' rays: βλάστε μὲν ἐξ ἁλὸς ὑγρᾶς / νᾶσος, ἔχει τέ νιν ὀξειᾶν γενέθλιος ἀκτίνων πατήρ, / πῦρ πνεόντων ἀρχὸς ἵππων ... ("There sprouted from the wet sea / An island, and the generative father of the sharp rays holds it, / Leader of the fire-breathing horses ..."). Like plants in Theophrastus and the Presocratics, the rose grows out of a heated mixture of earth and water: the seabed, from which it originates, is a meeting place of earth and water, and the flower/island sprouts up under the sun's rays.

[8] See Quinn 1964. For spontaneous generation in Theophrastus, see also Balme 1962.

there any mention of a seed or a bulb whence the flower might have originated. This omission is particularly striking in the case of the narcissus in the *Hymn to Demeter*. As we saw in Chapter 4 above, lines 12–14 of the hymn describe in detail the parts of the narcissus. But there is no mention of a bulb: the plant emerges only as a result of Gaia's actions. As in Theophrastus' treatises, then, these Homeric flowers emerge suddenly and without obvious botanical cause. We can observe a correlation between Theophrastus' descriptions of irregular vegetal growths and Homeric descriptions of floral growths associated with changes or challenges to cosmic order: both the Homeric poets and Theophrastus describe irregular growths that do not require seeds or bulbs.

There is also a correlation between the sorts of plants that are associated with more regular vegetal growths in Theophrastus' treatises and in the Homeric poems. The trees that the Homeric poets associate with the more permanent order of the cosmos are the sorts of wild plants that, according to Theophrastus, do not typically follow spontaneous modes of generation. Theophrastus explains that spontaneous generation only occurs in larger plants under special conditions: where there is heavy rain, or some other peculiar configuration of the air or the ground (οὐ μὴν ἀλλὰ καὶ τῶν μειζόνων ἔστιν ὅτε συμβαίνουσιν, ὅταν ἢ ἐπομβρίαι κατάσχωσιν ἢ ἄλλη τις ἰδιότης γένηται περὶ τὸν ἀέρα καὶ τὴν γῆν, *De Causis Plantarum*, 1.5.1). These larger plants, which would include the trees of the Greek natural environment, reproduce instead from seeds or root-stock, as can be seen from the extract quoted at the top of this section (*Historia Plantarum* 2.1.1).

The relevant Homeric passages place emphasis on mature arboreal growths rather than on the generation of trees. Nevertheless, like the trees that reproduce from seeds or root-stock in Theophrastus' treatises these arboreal growths form a clear contrast with the spontaneous growths of flowers. In Theophrastus' treatises the non-spontaneous generation of larger plants, which arise from identifiable botanical causes, contrast with the spontaneous generation of smaller plants and with their origins in warmed earth and water. In Homeric poetry, arboreal growths such as Sleep's tree in the Διὸς ἀπάτη or the date-palm in the *Hymn to Apollo* are stable and enduring features of the landscape, quite unlike the sudden growths of flowers in those passages.

Such a contrast between stable arboreal growths and sudden growths of flowers is reinforced in our Homeric passages through the use of different forms of the verb φύω.[9] Growths of flowers in Homeric descriptions of challenges to

---

[9] This distinction is not paralleled in Theophrastus' treatises: Theophrastus uses the present tense of the verb's middle voice (φύομαι) of any sort of growth, spontaneous or non-spontaneous. At *Historia Plantarum* 7.7.3, for instance, he uses the form φύεται of growth from roots, seeds, and spontaneous generation.

cosmic order are marked by the present, future, imperfect, or aorist tenses of the verb or, to speak more technically, by its continuous or perfective aspects.[10] The aorist (perfective aspect) draws attention to the suddenness of the growth. It is used of the growth of the narcissus in the *Homeric Hymn to Demeter*, once by the external narrator and once by Persephone: φῦσε (8), ἔφυσ' (428).[11] By contrast, the present and imperfect tenses (continuous aspect) dramatize the process of growth. For the duration of Zeus and Hera's lovemaking, the earth "was sending up" (φύεν, *Iliad* 14.347) flowers beneath the divine couple.[12]

The *Hymn to Apollo* associates the future tense of φύω with floral growths. The future may describe either duration or punctuality and may therefore emphasize either the suddenness of the emergence of flowers or the process of their growth. Leto's threat to Delos that she will never bring forth plants, which is answered by the flowers that bloom as Apollo steps onto the island, is couched in the future tense: οὔτ' ἄρ φυτὰ μυρία φύσεις ("you will not grow [nor continue to grow?] countless plants/trees," *Hymn to Apollo* 55).[13] The use of this tense anticipates either the continuous process implied by the present participle in the phrase χρυσῷ ... βεβρίθει καθορῶσα ("as [Delos] looked [at him], she was weighed down with gold," 135–136), or the perfective ἤνθησ' ("flowered," 139), which emphasizes the moment when the golden flowers first bloomed on the island.

The perfect stem of φύω, a stative form of the verb, describes stable arboreal growths that are associated with the established order of the cosmos. While the flowers that bloom beneath the divine lovers in *Iliad* 14 are linked to the imperfect of φύω, the sky-high tree on which Sleep sits, foreshadowing his challenge to Zeus' control of the cosmos, is described with the perfect participle of φύω as "having grown very tall" (μακροτάτη πεφυυῖα, 288). The "heaven-high" fir of Calypso's island (*Odyssey* 5.239) is twice associated with the pluperfect of φύω: it is one of the "tall trees" (δένδρεα μακρά, 238, 241) that "had grown" (πεφύκει, 238, 241) at the edge of the island. Unlike the verb βεβρίθει at *Hymn to Apollo* 136, the pluperfect seems here to have a stative rather than continuous force.

---

[10] On Greek aspect, see Comrie 1976:16–22, 52–58.

[11] Note however that the heads of the narcissus are also described with the pluperfect of φύω, which may have either stative or continuous meaning (see below): ἐξεπεφύκει, line 12 ("had grown" or "were growing").

[12] This is not to say that the growth of the narcissus is an intrinsically punctual action, while that of the flowers in *Iliad* 14 is intrinsically durative. As Comrie (1976:3–40) observes, the same situation may be described either with perfective or imperfective verbs, according to whether it is treated as a "single whole" or emphasis is placed on its "internal structure" (p. 16). On the spontaneity of vegetation at *Iliad* 14.346–349, see Irwin 1984:155 and Bonnafé 1984–1987 1:78–79.

[13] On the spontaneity of vegetation in the *Hymn to Apollo*, see Irwin 1997:384–385 and Bonnafé 1984–1987 2:125. See below for the semantics of φυτά, which refers either to cultivated plants in general or to cultivated trees in particular.

While Delos becomes weighed down with golden flowers during the course of the *Hymn to Apollo*, the trees of Calypso's island are in a full state of growth in the historic past of the hymn. This difference is signaled by the use of a present participle along with the pluperfect in the first passage but not the second.[14]

Such Homeric uses of the perfect and pluperfect tenses suggest endurance and stability, in keeping with the evocations of cosmic stability and orderliness in the passages cited above. While the imperfect describes processes and the aorist is associated with punctual actions, the perfect tense denotes a state that is an enduring, non-momentary achievement of the subject. Likewise, the pluperfect frequently describes an enduring state in the past.[15] And when coupled in Homeric poetry with prepositions or adverbs of place, the perfect and pluperfect of φύω also suggest fixity, i.e., permanence of location.[16] Described with such verb forms, the growths of trees in the relevant passages would have provided a ready image for ancient audiences to understand the stability of cosmic order, which could likewise be associated with stative verbs. The perfect tense is, for instance, used by Poseidon at 15.189 in his description of the division of the cosmos, which we discussed in Chapter 4: τριχθὰ δὲ πάντα δέδασται, ἕκαστος δ' ἔμμορε τιμῆς ("all things *have been divided* in three, and each *has received a share* of honor.")[17]

From this evidence, then, we can infer that Homeric images of order and disorder are based on a distinction between stable and spontaneous growths of wild plants that parallels Theophrastus' distinction between spontaneous and non-spontaneous modes of generation. And in both cases such distinctions

---

[14] On the association of the perfect stem of φύω with arboreal growth in Homeric poetry, see Heinemann 2005:20. See also the examples from Homeric images of civic order and its opposite that are given below.

[15] Cf. *Hymn to Demeter* 100: an olive that shades Demeter is described with the pluperfect tense of the verb—it "had grown above" (ὕπερθε πεφύκει). The use of this tense at *Hymn to Demeter* 100 suggests the permanence of the olive: if we follow Richardson (1974 *ad loc.*), this description of an olive by the Maiden Well probably alludes to a feature of the Eleusinian landscape familiar to early audiences.

[16] See Patzer 1993:24–26. See, for instance, *Iliad* 21.352, where the location of trees and other vegetation is specified with the preposition περί and with the verb πεφύκει, and *Odyssey* 7.114, from the description of the Phaeacian orchards: ἔνθα ... δένδρεα μακρὰ πεφύκασι ("there ... tall trees have grown"). For the latter passage, see also below.

[17] See Adkins 1983:214–217 on the use of the perfect tense in this passage of Homeric poetry and in Greek thought more generally. The perfect tense "express[es] states of affairs as states of affairs, and ... distinguish[es] them sharply from momentary or continuous *actions*" (p. 214; his italics). See also the use of the perfect tense in the Hesiodic passages that describe the structure of the cosmos, discussed in Chapter 4 above. The brazen threshold is "fixed unshakably" (ἀστεμφές ... ἀρηρώς, *Theogony* 812); the roots of the world "have grown" (πεφύασι, 728) above the neck of Tartarus. For the use of the perfect of φύω to describe roots, see *Iliad* 4.482–484, where the roots of a poplar "have grown" (πεφύασι, 484). The tree as a whole is described with the pluperfect of φύω (πεφύκει, 483).

are readily explicable in terms of the natural phenomena that would have been familiar to the Homeric poets, Theophrastus, and their respective listeners and readers. In my Introduction, I noted the remarkable suddenness of Greek spring blooms. These sudden growths of flowers, appearing as if from nowhere to cover the barren winter landscape, would have created the impression of generation outside the confines of regular causality.[18] And such irregular floral growths would have offered a contrast with the more regular growths of trees in the Greek landscape.

It appears, then, that the Homeric images of cosmic order and its opposite respond to a contrast between sudden growths of flowers, perceived as spontaneous, and the more enduring growths of trees in the Greek landscape. Such imagery draws on concepts that would have been familiar to early audiences: the Homeric poets created images that linked the apparently more concrete dichotomy of regular and irregular modes of vegetal growth to the abstract concepts of cosmic order and of challenges to that order and thus enhanced listeners' understanding of the relevant concepts. Order in the cosmos possessed the kind of stability and endurance of trees in the natural environment; but changes or challenges to that order arrived as suddenly as the Greek spring flowers.

Managed and Unmanaged Growths

Theophrastus' distinctions between regular and irregular growths of wild plants, together with the linguistic distinctions presented by the use of φύω in our Homeric passages have helped us to understand the basis for Homeric images of order in the cosmos and of changes and challenges to that order. And if again we bear in mind not only the linguistic choices of the Homeric poets but also Theophrastus' work on vegetal growth, we can gain new insights into the bases for Homeric images of civic order and its opposite. As demonstrated in Chapter 5, the relevant passages of Homeric poetry contrast wild growths in general—both flowers and trees—with managed growths. But at times the Homeric poets also distinguished between agricultural and arboricultural growths, the latter having a particularly close association with civilized order in the latter books of the *Odyssey*. Such distinctions are reflected in the language of the passages that we have studied. Wild growths are again associated with the verb φύω; but we do not find the clear distinctions between associations of spontaneous (*sensu stricto*) growth with the present, future, and aorist, and of non-spontaneous growth with the perfect and pluperfect tenses that we observed above. Rather,

---

[18]   On the suddenness of the Greek spring, see Introduction above; Motte 1971:10, Braudel 1972:233, Huxley and Taylor 1977:21, 24, Polunin 1980:30–31. See also Höhfeld 2009:39 on the Troad.

the Homeric poets contrasted agricultural and arboricultural growths with wild growths and with each other through use of the root ἀρο- ("plow") and of the stem φυτο/ε- ("plant [trees]"). And such Homeric contrasts are mirrored in Theophrastus' descriptions of wild as opposed to cultivated growth, and of arboricultural as opposed to agricultural techniques.

The differences between the kinds of plants that the Homeric poets associate with challenges and changes to cosmic and civic order can readily be explained if we bear in mind Theophrastus' discussions of wild and cultivated growths at *Historia Plantarum* 2.1.1. Theophrastus presents two different perspectives on modes of propagation, which are reflected in alternative classifications of those modes. As we have already seen, Theophrastus distinguishes not only between spontaneous (αὐτόματος *sensu stricto*) and non-spontaneous generation in the wild, but also between wild growth and cultivated growth. Since wild growths arise not from deliberate management but of their own accord, they are "as it were, spontaneous" (ὥσπερ ... αὐτόμαται). Theophrastus, then, describes two different conceptions of vegetal generation, which are reflected in the literal (*sensu stricto*) and metaphorical uses of the term αὐτόματος. If his readers focused only on plants in the wild, they could distinguish between those that reproduced without botanical cause, following spontaneous (*sensu stricto*) modes of generation, and those that reproduced from seeds or root-stock. But they could also contrast these different kinds of wild growth, which were all "as it were, spontaneous," with the kinds of generation that occurred in cultivated plants.

Such differences in perspective are suggested also in our Homeric passages. On the one hand we have observed associations of the regular growths of trees in the wild with cosmic order and associations of irregular growths of flowers with challenges to that order. Such a contrast mirrors Theophrastus' distinction between the spontaneous (*sensu stricto*) generation of smaller plants in the wild and the non-spontaneous generation of larger plants in similar settings. On the other hand, the Homeric poets associate cultivated plants with civic order and wild growths *in general* with uncivilized lands. This second contrast echoes Theophrastus' distinction between the modes of generation of cultivated plants and of wild plants in general, which might be thought of as spontaneous, but only by analogy. This evidence from Theophrastus, then, draws our attention to the different viewpoints embodied in the two sets of Homeric images studied in Part II: images of cosmic order and of challenges and changes to that order distinguish between different kinds of wild growths, while images of civic order and its opposite treat wild growths as a single category and contrast them with cultivated growths.

Theophrastus' treatises also help us to understand the particular emphasis on arboriculture in our Odyssean descriptions of civilized order. As we have already seen, Theophrastus distinguishes between the techniques used to propagate agricultural crops (cereals and legumes) and those used in arboriculture. Cereals and legumes are usually grown from seed: that is, they follow a mode of generation also found in the wild. But arboriculture employs modes of propagation not found in the wild, such as the use of a slip from the parent plant. These modes are the result "of skill or deliberate choice" (τέχνης ἢ δὴ προαιρέσεως, *Historia Plantarum* 2.1.1): that is, they require the labor and decision-making capabilities of a gardener. Such observations are in keeping with the contrasts that we have observed in Homeric poetry. Although the *Odyssey* does not list the various techniques of arboriculture, it places emphasis on the work required to manage arboreal growths.

What is more, like the final books of the *Odyssey*, Theophrastus' treatises associate civilized order more closely with arboriculture than with agriculture. Only once in his treatises does Theophrastus associate the cultivation of cereals with the act of civilizing: at *De Causis Plantarum* 3.20.6, he describes land that has been worked in preparation for sowing as "tamed"—διημερωθείσης τῆς γῆς. But in several other passages Theophrastus and the other authors whom he cites associate arboriculture with civilization or, more specifically, with the act of civilizing the recalcitrant. Propagation from shoot, branch, or slip, as mentioned at *Historia Plantarum* 2.1.1, would often be carried out by grafting the torn-off piece onto a new plant. At 2.7.6–7, Theophrastus cites some who refer to such techniques as the punishment of an overweening host tree (κολάζειν ὡς ὑβρίζον τὸ δένδρον, "to punish the tree as if it were overweening"),[19] or others who imagine it as an act of correction (εὐθύνειν).

Theophrastus' treatises have given us a sense, then, of the reasons for some of the choices of the Homeric poets. We have come to see why, in forming their imagery of civic order and its opposite, they might have chosen to distinguish between wild growths and managed growths and at times also between agricultural and arboricultural growths. While cultivated growths are managed by human hands, wild growths might be considered "spontaneous" (αὐτόματος) in the sense that they grow of their own accord. And owing to the techniques of arboriculture, managed growths of trees are more clearly separated from wild growths than agricultural crops.

We can moreover see how Homeric images of the civilized and the uncivilized drew on audiences' perceptions of their environments to help them understand these abstract concepts. They could conceive of the distinction between

---

[19] For the "punishment" of trees, see also *De Causis Plantarum* 1.17.9, 2.4.1, 3.18.2, 5.9.11, and 16.3. For the association of the verb ὑβρίζω in classical texts with superabundant vegetal growth requiring "punishment," see Michelini 1978.

civic order and its opposite through the rather more tangible contrast between the orderly plantations of the civilized world and the wild lands beyond it.[20] These plantations are set off from the wild lands beyond the community—with the sorts of walls (ἕρκος) that surround the orchards of Scheria and Ithaca—and managed by farmers and gardeners. From their observations of those at work in orchards and fields, at least some listeners would also have been aware of distinctions between the techniques of agriculture and arboriculture.

And these distinctions between managed and unmanaged growths, and between agricultural and arboricultural labor are reflected in the language found in our Homeric images of civic order and its opposite. Wild growths in the relevant passages are described with the verb φύω. The managed growths of agricultural lands and orchards are, however, associated with different linguistic markers. The root ἀρο- most commonly describes agricultural fields and agricultural labor; but the substantival stem φυτο/ε-, built on the root φυ-, is frequently associated with arboricultural labor.

Earlier in this chapter, we noted a distinction between the different parts of φύω used to designate the sudden emergence of flowers and the stable growth of wild trees in the Homeric images of cosmic order and of challenges to that order. The passages that describe civic order and its opposite present evidence of similar distinctions; however, in keeping with the greater importance of contrasts between managed and unmanaged growths in the relevant passages, such distinctions are not drawn as precisely as in the first set of images that we discussed. The present tense of φύω is associated with spontaneous growths, but not with spontaneous growths of flowers; arboreal growths are described with the perfect and pluperfect of φύω, but can also be associated with other parts of that verb.

Some of the relevant passages suggest a general distinction between spontaneous growths and more orderly arboreal growths, marked with different forms of the verb φύω. The first *Hymn to Dionysus*, for instance, uses the present tense of φύω to describe superabundant vegetation that is also associated with a lack of civilized order. Dionysus' uncivilized birthplace sends up beautiful, nourishing plants (φύει, *Hymn* 1.14).[21] As with the descriptions of flowers considered above, these plants appear to grow spontaneously under the influence of the god. The present tense of φύω also describes the spontaneous vegetation of the

---

[20] On the importance of the distinction between agricultural lands and the land beyond them in Homeric poetry, the former being associated with culture and the latter with nature, see Redfield 1994:189–192.

[21] I quote the first *Hymn to Dionysus* from West 2003. The present tense of φύω is also employed by Solon in his image of the "flowers of ἄτη" (ἄτης ἄνθεα φυόμενα, fr. 3.35), for which see Chapter 5 n5.

land of the Cyclopes, in a passage that we shall discuss in more detail below. These growths are likewise inspired by the gods: "trusting in the immortal gods, / [the Cyclopes] neither plant nor sow ..." (*Odyssey* 9.107–108); nevertheless, rain from Zeus swells their cereals and vines (110–111). Apparently, these plants grow without the need for seeds (ἄσπαρτα, 109), like the small plants described by Theophrastus.

In other passages, the perfect tense of φύω describes wild growths of trees. For instance, the wild poplars on Goat Island "have grown" (πεφύασιν, 9.141).[22] As we might expect, the Phaeacian orchards, which combine more regular growths with spontaneous effusions of fruit, are associated both with stative and with non-stative aspects of φύω. On the one hand, the present tense of the verb refers to the *unheimlich*, superabundant fruit that grows in the orchards (φύει, *Odyssey* 7.119). This fruit is nurtured by the West Wind: again, spontaneous growth is associated with divine influence.[23] On the other hand, the perfect tense of the verb describes the trees and garden-beds of the Phaeacian plantations (πεφύκασι, 7.114; πεφύασι 128).

But still other Homeric passages that explore the concepts of civilized order and its opposite associate arboreal growths with non-stative tenses of φύω: these passages, then, do not distinguish between arboreal and non-arboreal growths as clearly as those that we considered above. In contrast with Homeric descriptions of cosmic order, the relevant images emphasize the process of growth of these trees, rather than the stable states that they eventually achieve. The two olive trees that shelter Odysseus on his arrival in Scheria are described not only with the perfect, but also with the aorist of φύω (πεφυῶτας, 5.477; ἔφυν, 481). This use of the aorist dramatizes the process by which they came to be interwoven: πυκνοὶ / ἀλλήλοισι ἔφυν ἐπαμοιβαδίς, "they grew thick and intertwined." The aorist of the verb likewise describes the olive tree around which Odysseus constructs his bed (23.190). In this way, the description of the olive on Ithaca echoes that of the olives of Scheria, the land that of all those visited by Odysseus most closely resembles Ithaca. The use of the aorist at 23.190 would also have encouraged audiences to imagine the natural growth that took place before Odysseus carried out his work on the olive and thus drew it fully into the realm of culture: θάμνος ἔφυ τανύφυλλος ἐλαίης ... / ... ἀπέκοψα κόμην

---

[22] Cf. the use of the pluperfect of φύω to describe trees and other vegetation on the banks of the Xanthus (*Iliad* 21.352).

[23] On spontaneous growth in the Phaeacian orchard, see Ahl and Roisman 1996:119. For the use of the continuous aspect of φύω to describe the non-permanent parts of trees, see also the descriptions of leaves at *Iliad* 1.235 and 6.148–149. In the latter passage, Glaucus uses the present tense of φύω both of leaves and of human generations. For discussion of Glaucus' simile, see Chapter 7 below.

τανυφύλλου ἐλαίης, "a leafy thicket of olive grew ... / I cut off the foliage of the long-leafed olive" (190, 195).[24]

What is more, although the allusions to flowers in the Homeric imagery of uncivilized lands accord with the descriptions of spontaneous, divinely inspired growths in the passages that we considered above, they are not marked by the present, aorist, or future tenses of φύω: this, then, marks a further departure from the Homeric descriptions of challenges to cosmic order. As we have seen, the "flowery meadows" of *Hymn to Aphrodite* 169 suggest the wild power of Aphrodite that undermines Anchises' efforts to tame the wild spaces of Mount Ida. Similarly, as we have observed, the disorderly nature of the god Pan receives its complement in the wild floral growths of *Hymn to Pan* 25–26. And in *Odyssey* 5, Calypso's divine power appears to inspire violets to grow in her meadows: as we noted in Chapter 5, this demi-goddess is closely associated both with her cave and with the luxuriant vegetation surrounding it.[25] But in none of these passages are floral growths described with the verb φύω.

The managed growths associated with civilized order in the relevant passages are, however, clearly marked with the root ἀρο- or with the stem φυτο/ε-. The former root occurs in a number of the Homeric passages that associate agricultural labor with civilized order. At *Iliad* 11.67–71, for instance, the Trojans and Achaeans are compared with reapers working ἀνδρὸς μάκαρος κατ' ἄρουραν, "in the field of a blessed man" (68). In Scheria, Nausithous "divided agricultural fields" (ἐδάσσατ' ἀρούρας) among the Phaeacians (*Odyssey* 6.10). At 9.134, Odysseus sees the potential in the "flat plowland" (ἄροσις λείη) of Goat Island.[26]

Our passages associate the management of trees with the stem φυτο/ε-. We have seen how in Homeric images of cosmic order and its opposite spontaneous and non-spontaneous wild growths are described by different aspects of the verb φύω. By contrast, the stem φυτο/ε-, a substantival stem from the same verb, denotes managed growth, plants that have been grown by someone rather than simply left to grow. It is associated, in particular, with the managed trees

---

[24] The aorist of φύω is also used to describe trees at *Hymn to Aphrodite* 265. Aphrodite places emphasis on the long but ultimately circumscribed lives of trees and of the nymphs who dwell within them. It would have been less appropriate, then, if she had used the perfect of φύω, with its suggestions of permanence.

[25] The descriptions of divinely inspired vegetation in *Odyssey* 5 and the *Hymn to Pan* lead Thalmann (1992:48) and Elliger (1975:128-31) to state explicitly that these are spontaneous growths. What is more, if we follow Zanetto (1996:304) the associations of Dionysus and Pan at the end of the *Hymn to Pan* suggest their shared power of inspiring spontaneous growth: "sono divinità della vegetazione spontanea, connesse con la forza generativa della natura."

[26] Goat Island may in fact have been the former home of the Phaeacians: see Clay 1980. For associations of the root ἀρο- with civilized order see also *Odyssey* 18.374, where Odysseus boasts to Eurymachus of his skill "with the plow" (ἀρότρῳ).

found in orchards: according to LSJ, φυτόν denotes a *"plant ... esp. garden plant or tree"*; φυταλιά suggests a *"planted place, esp. orchard or vineyard, opp. to corn-land"*; and φυτεύω means to *"plant trees, esp. fruit trees."*[27]

In a number of our Homeric images, the substantival stem φυτο/ε- forms a contrast not only with the bare verbal root φυ- but also with the root ἀρο-, which as we have seen is connected with the growth of cereal crops. We can observe this in some of the passages that we explored in Chapter 5. The techniques and types of landscape denoted by φυτο/ε- and ἀρο- form a pair of complementary but distinct terms, as in the Iliadic formula φυταλιῆς καὶ ἀρούρης, "of orchard and plow-land" (*Iliad* 6.195, 12.134, 20.185). In these passages, the paired stems φυτο/ε- and ἀρο- describe the two chief kinds of cultivated lands. Similarly, in a passage mentioned above, Odysseus emphasizes the Cyclopes' complete igno-rance of the techniques of cultivation by pairing the stem φυτο/ε- with the root ἀρο- (*Odyssey* 9.108–109). He contrasts such techniques with the spontaneous generation of plants in the Cyclopes' land, which he designates with the present tense of the verb φύω and again associates with an absence of agricultural labor: "they grow" (φύονται, 109) "unsown" (ἀνήροτα, a negativized adjective from the root ἀρο-):

> οὔτε <u>φυτεύουσιν</u> χερσὶν <u>φυτὸν</u> οὔτ' <u>ἀρόωσιν</u>,
> ἀλλὰ τά γ' ἄσπαρτα καὶ <u>ἀνήροτα</u> πάντα <u>φύονται</u> ...

Odyssey 9.108–109

> They neither *plant plants/trees* with their hands nor *sow*,
> But all these things *grow* unseeded and un*sown*.

In other passages of Homeric poetry the stem φυτο/ε- is used in isolation of arboricultural labor. We have encountered one instance where the noun φυτόν may refer to plants in general (Leto's threat of barrenness to Delos at *Hymn to Apollo* 55).[28] But in other cases it clearly refers to trees grown in orchards. The noun is associated with Laertes' manual labor in *Odyssey* 24: Odysseus observes him "digging around a tree," λιστρεύοντα φυτόν (227; cf. φυτὸν ἀμφελάχαινε, 242), and praises his knowledge of every tree (φυτόν, 246). φυτόν is likewise used of trees in an orchard at *Iliad* 14.123, where Diomedes describes his father's wealth: πολλοὶ δὲ φυτῶν ἔσαν ὄρχατοι ἀμφίς ("there are many orchards of

---

[27] See Heinemann 2005:20: citing only Homeric examples, he notes that φυτόν is used of that which has been planted. See also Snell 1955–2010 s.v. φυτόν: "cultivated ... *plant*; of fruit-tree(s) and/or vine(s) as ag. sown crops."

[28] For instances where φυτόν refers to plants in general, see *Iliad* 21.258 and perhaps also *Odyssey* 9.108, quoted above. For *Hymn to Apollo* 55, however, see also West's translation (2003 *ad loc.*): "nor will you bring forth a harvest or grow abundant fruit trees" (οὐδὲ τρύγην οἴσεις, οὔτ' ἂρ φυτὰ μυρία φύσεις).

trees all around"). The noun φυτόν, again with the meaning "tree," is most famously associated with a character's homeland at *Iliad* 18.57 and 438, where Thetis remembers how she raised Achilles φυτὸν ὣς ... ἀλωῆς, "like a tree in an orchard."[29] In other passages, the verb φυτεύω is used to describe arboricultural labor. At *Iliad* 6.419, nymphs are said to have tended elms around the tomb of Eetion: πτελέας ἐφύτευσαν. At *Odyssey* 18.359, Eurymachus makes a demeaning offer to his disguised king: he might make a living tending his long trees, δένδρεα μακρὰ φυτεύων.[30]

We have already seen that Odysseus' attempts to reclaim his place in Ithacan society are closely associated with the management of trees. It is noteworthy, then, that one key aspect of his efforts—his plots against the suitors—is described with the verb φυτεύω, suggesting an arboricultural metaphor. Odysseus does not "plan" their deaths but rather "plants" or perhaps (to convey the specifically arboricultural sense of φυτεύω) "grafts" them.[31] For instance, as Halitherses predicts, φόνον καὶ κῆρα φυτεύει πάντεσσιν: "he plants/grafts murder and death for all," *Odyssey* 2.165–166.[32] By contrast, the suitors' plots against Odysseus and his family are most often described with the verb μηχανάω ("contrive").[33] Odysseus' description of the creation of the olive-tree bed, which enables him to be re-establish his marriage with Penelope, and Laertes' tendance of his orchard, where Odysseus' reintegration into the royal house of Ithaca is completed, are thus prefigured by Odysseus' tendance of plots against the suitors' lives, the first stage in that process.

The Homeric vegetal images of civilized order and of its opposite were based, then, on contrasts between the managed growths of agriculture or arboriculture and the untamed growths of the natural environment, contrasts which are reflected both in the treatises of Theophrastus and in the language of the relevant Homeric passages. By drawing on elements of the natural and tamed environments familiar to their audiences, the Homeric poets would have clarified their understanding of the antithetical relationship between disorder and civilization: while disorder in human communities resembled a return to the

---

[29] For φυτόν and the cultivation of non-cereal crops, see *Hymn to Hermes* 90, where the god observes that an old man is digging around his vines (φυτὰ σκάπτεις).

[30] Odysseus answers Eurymachus' insult with a boast about his prowess in agricultural labor (18.366–374). For this passage, see Chapter 5 above.

[31] Bonnafé 1984–1987 1:121: this use of φυτεύω suggests the sense of "« planter », c'est-à-dire préparer de longue date, « le malheur » de quelqu'un."

[32] The metaphor is used of Odysseus' plots against the suitors throughout the *Odyssey*: see also *Odyssey* 2.165, 14.110, 15.178, 17.27, 82, 159. Cf. 14.218, where Odysseus uses φυτεύω in a lying tale to describe his plots against his enemies, and 5.340, where Leucothea uses the verb to describe Poseidon's plots against Odysseus. In the *Iliad* φυτεύω is used in this sense only at 15.134: Hera asks if Ares wishes to "plant a great evil" (κακὸν μέγα ... φυτεῦσαι) for his fellow gods.

[33] *Odyssey* 3.207, 213, 4.822, 16.93, 134, 17.499, 588, 18.143, 20.170, 370, 394, 21.375.

lawlessness of nature, the well-administered state was the result of careful management, like a tree governed by grafting and pollarding.

And if we combine these observations with our findings concerning the Homeric imagery of cosmic order and of challenges to that order, we detect a similar four-fold categorization of different kinds of vegetal growth in Theophrastus and Homeric poetry, though with verbal distinctions in the latter that are not found in the former: the spontaneous (*sensu stricto*) generation associated with small, flowering plants by Theophrastus and marked by the present, future, and aorist of φύω in Homeric poetry; the more regular growths of trees, marked by the perfect or pluperfect of φύω; the cultivation of cereals, associated with the root ἀρο-; and the techniques of arboriculture, connected with the substantival stem φυτο/ε-. My observations are summarized in Table 1 (next page).

The Homeric vegetal images of order and disorder were grounded, then, in perceived contrasts between spontaneous and more regular growths in the wild environment, between cultivated and non-cultivated growths, and between the techniques of agriculture and arboriculture. Cosmic order was strong and stable like the regular, enduring growths of trees in the natural environment; by contrast, the sudden emergence of flowers offered an image for challenges and changes to such established order. Civic order required the careful attention of a king, who managed his kingdom like the good gardener in his orchard. Uncivilized lands were like the wild growths beyond the boundaries of a community.

	WILD PLANTS		CULTIVATED PLANTS	
	Irregular growth-patterns	*Regular growth-patterns*	*Harnessing processes found in the wild*	*Using techniques not found in the wild*
Theophrastus	Spontaneous (*sensu stricto*)	Non-spontaneous (*sensu stricto*)		
	Harnessing processes found in the wild	Reproduction from seeds or root-stock.	Reproduction from seeds (or root-stock).	Reproduction incl. grafting. (="punishment")
	Common in smaller plants, rare in trees.	Common in larger plants.	Cereal crops.	Trees in orchards.
Homeric Poetry	φύω, continuous and perfective aspects.	φύω, stative aspect.	ἀρο-	φυτο/ε-
	Spontaneous growths of flowers.	Enduring growths of trees.	Cereal crops.	Trees in orchards.
	Cosmic disorder *and* civic disorder.	Cosmic order *but also* civic disorder.	Civic order.	Civic order.

Table 1: Regular, Irregular, and Managed Growths in
Theophrastus and Homeric Poetry

PART THREE

YOUTH AND DEATH

Preamble

THE THIRD AND FINAL PART OF THIS MONOGRAPH focuses on Homeric vegetal images of death and, in particular, on Homeric associations of death with flowers, which provide some of the most striking examples of such imagery. We might feel intuitively that such floral images will capture the brevity of life—its brief bloom—an idea that is common in the modern west, as for instance in Shakespeare's image of the "darling buds of May." And such a reading seems to gain justification when we consider the floral imagery of Greek elegiac poetry, which carries connotations similar to those of its western equivalents. We should however be wary of applying modern ideas to ancient texts, even when we find support for our conceptions from some elements of ancient culture. When we carefully consider the Homeric floral imagery of death, both from the *Iliad* and elsewhere, we see that it focuses on a concept altogether different from the brevity of life: namely, the monstrous otherness of death.

We get a first glimpse of the conception of death suggested by Homeric floral imagery and of its place in wider Greek culture when we consider Christiane Sourvinou-Inwood's seminal study *"Reading" Greek Death*, Ian Morris' response to her work, and Jean-Pierre Vernant's separate explorations of death in Greek culture. Sourvinou-Inwood argues that the passage from the Dark Age to the archaic age witnessed a change in attitudes to death. In the Dark Age, death was hated but not feared; its incorporation into notions of generational continuity and into the structures of the family and of the wider community made it somewhat more acceptable. The archaic age, by contrast, saw the development of a more individualistic conception of death; death came to be feared as the dissolution of an individual's identity. These attitudes were expressed in part through depictions of monstrous figures such as the Sphinx or the Gorgons. Sourvinou-Inwood associates Homeric conceptions of death primarily with the Dark Age and with its acceptance of death, but identifies occasional intrusions of archaic sensibilities into the Homeric poems: for instance, according to her the notion of punishments and rewards for the dead in *Odyssey* 11 or Hermes' function as the conveyer of souls to the Underworld in *Odyssey* 24 reflect archaic Greek attempts to assuage fears of death.[1]

Sourvinou-Inwood's findings (at least as they are presented in earlier articles) have come under attack from Ian Morris.[2] In a review both of her literary and of her archaeological evidence, Morris argues that no clear progression can be traced from Dark-Age to archaic Greek conceptions of death: a particular set of early Greek poets might place greater emphasis on one or other aspect of death in response to different social milieux or to changing political circumstances; nevertheless, a relatively consistent attitude towards death unites the output of poets from this period. Morris accepts that depictions of death in pre-classical poetry to some extent reflect contemporary political developments. The Homeric poems focus on the glory of the noble individual, which would have been celebrated in traditional, aristocratic societies. Poets such as Tyrtaeus and Callinus responded to the development of the archaic Greek *polis*: their poems place emphasis on the warrior-as-citizen, as a representative and defender of his community. Morris also acknowledges that poets might have emphasized particular aspects of death in response to particular social contexts, such as the symposium. For instance, the elegiac poetry of Mimnermus, which "stress[es] youthful sympotic pleasures," carries different emphases from the Homeric poems, or indeed from the elegiac poetry of Tyrtaeus and Callinus.[3] But Morris argues that a consistent conception of death underlies all of these depictions: they reflect a general acceptance of death—whether through the winning of glory on the battlefield or through dying on behalf of the *polis*, or in the course of old age—rather than the individualistic fear of death described by Sourvinou-Inwood.

Vernant, for his part, argues that both early epic and Greek culture as a whole explore contrasting perspectives on death. And unlike Morris, he does not suggest that such perspectives reflect a single underlying conception of death. For Vernant, death in Homeric epic presents two "faces": the one, glorious and beautiful; the other, horrific and monstrous.[4] And such elements of Homeric poetry reflect attitudes to death in wider Greek culture. Myths of terrifying female deities such as the Gorgon and Medusa explore the notion of the monstrousness of death.[5] And poets such as Tyrtaeus offered their own depictions of the beautiful death.[6]

---

[1] Sourvinou-Inwood 1995. See pp. 66–70 on justice for the Homeric dead and pp. 103–107, 303–356 on Hermes Psychopompus.

[2] Morris 1989.

[3] Morris 1989:307. I discuss Mimnermus' poetry alongside that of Tyrtaeus in Chapter 7 below.

[4] Vernant 1996.

[5] Vernant 1991a, c.

[6] Vernant 2001.

Space does not allow for an extensive review of all the evidence explored by these scholars. However, the vegetal imagery to be considered in the following chapters gives us reasons to endorse elements of all three scholars' arguments. Given the continuation of the Homeric performance tradition throughout the archaic age alongside other poetic traditions, we have reason to question Sourvinou-Inwood's attribution of the Homeric poems to the Dark Age and her arguments for their anteriority to archaic Greek conceptions of death.[7] In this respect, then, Morris is right to resist the idea of a neat progression from one conception of death to another in early Greece.

In addition, floral images from the elegiac and Homeric corpora support Morris' notion of distinctions between different Greek genres; however, the distinctions that we shall observe suggest not to much the sort of unified picture of archaic Greek culture offered by Morris as the clear contrasts identified by Vernant. As will become clear, a comparison of the floral imagery of archaic Greek elegy with that of Homeric poetry (which I treat as products of contemporaneous performance traditions) reveals a dialogue between two different conceptions of death.

These conceptions, moreover, recall aspects of death explored by all three scholars. As Morris points out, the elegiac image of the "flower of youth" suggests that death is a part (albeit an unwelcome part) of life: it succeeds the brief pleasures of youth all too quickly. But in the images that we shall consider the Homeric poems reflect the kind of terror of death that Sourvinou-Inwood attributes to the archaic age. And when we supplement her work with Vernant's observations, we come to see that these Homeric floral images treat death itself as something monstrous.[8]

---

[7] See my Introduction for the different poetic traditions of archaic Greece. With particular relevance to the poems that I shall discuss below, see Nagy 1985:46–50 on Greek elegy.
[8] Vernant 1991a, 1991b, 1996.

7

Beauty and Transience?
Flowers and Death in Greek Elegy and Homeric Poetry

G IVEN THE PREOCCUPATION OF MANY POEMS in the Greek elegiac tradition with death, the floral imagery of that tradition offers the most obvious
comparandum for the Homeric floral images of death that we shall discuss
below.[1] We can get a first sense of the particular associations of the relevant
Homeric floral images, if we compare treatments of the "flower of youth" (ἄνθος
ἥβης) in the two genres. In Greek elegy, this image often conveys the notion of
the brevity of life and hence suggests that death will come all too soon; less
frequently, it evokes a beauty that is preserved after death. The Homeric treatments of the image, however, focus only on the prime of life. As will become
clear in Chapters 8 and 9 below, we have to look elsewhere for the Homeric floral
imagery of death and to radically different concepts.

---

[1] We might expect that the genre of women's lament, which was likewise closely connected with
death, would offer useful comparanda for the passages from Homeric poetry to be discussed in
Part III. And indeed, it is likely that the vegetal images of the two genres interacted with one
another: scholars have argued that the poetry of lament influenced Homeric images, such as the
Euphorbus simile (*Iliad* 17.50–60) or Thetis' comparison of Achilles with "a tree in an orchard"
(18.57)—see Holst-Warhaft 1992:109, Alexiou 2002:198, Dué 2006:65–67. For the influence of
lament on Homeric poetry, see more generally, Martin 1989:86–88, Holst-Warhaft 1992:108–113,
Nagy 1999:170–177, Murnaghan 1999, Alexiou 2002:11–13, Dué 2002, 2006:30–56. But while elegiac
poems incorporating vegetal images survive from the seventh century BCE onwards (see below
on Tyrtaeus), we lack direct evidence of women's lament from early Greece: in fact, the Homeric
poems themselves present some of our best indications of what archaic Greek lament might have
been like (e.g., Thetis' lament at *Iliad* 18.52–64). This being the case, it is not possible (in keeping
with the methodology of this volume) to set the images of archaic lament against their Homeric
equivalents and to determine how the two bodies of imagery differed from one another.

The Greek elegiac poets frequently associated the phrase ἄνθος ἥβης (the "flower of youth") with brevity, old age, and death.[2] A prime example of the elegiac use of ἄνθος ἥβης is offered by Mimnermus fr. 2 West², which couples the phrase (this time in the plural) with highly developed imagery, both of vegetation and of death. Like the generalizing statements from Greek elegy mentioned above, Mimnermus' poem establishes a general, pessimistic contrast between the brief joys of youth and the trials of old age. I quote the first ten lines:

> ἡμεῖς δ' οἷά τε <u>φύλλα φύει πολυάνθεμος ὥρη</u>
>   ἔαρος, ὅτ' <u>αἶψ'</u> αὐγῇς αὔξεται ἠελίου,
> τοῖς ἴκελοι πήχυιον ἐπὶ χρόνον <u>ἄνθεσιν ἥβης</u>
>   τερπόμεθα, πρὸς θεῶν εἰδότες οὔτε κακὸν
> 5 οὔτ' ἀγαθόν· Κῆρες δὲ παρεστήκασι μέλαιναι,
>   ἡ μὲν ἔχουσα τέλος γήραος ἀργαλέου,
> ἡ δ' ἑτέρη θανάτοιο· <u>μίνυνθα δὲ γίνεται ἥβης</u>
>   <u>καρπός</u>, ὅσον τ' ἐπὶ γῆν κίδναται ἠέλιος.
> αὐτὰρ ἐπὴν δὴ τοῦτο τέλος παραμείψεται ὥρης,
> 10 αὐτίκα δὴ τεθνάναι βέλτιον ἢ βίοτος·

Mimnermus fr. 2.1–10 West²

> We are like <u>the leaves that the many-flowered season of spring</u>
>   Sends forth [*phúei*], when <u>immediately</u> they are increased by
>   the rays of the sun,
> Like them we enjoy <u>the flowers of youth</u> for a cubit's
>   Span, knowing from the gods neither evil
> 5 Nor good; but the black Fates stand beside us,
>   One having the fulfillment of grievous old age,
> The other of death; <u>the fruit of youth is</u>
>   <u>As brief</u> as the time the sun spreads over the earth.
> But when this end of the season passes,
> 10 Straightway dying is better than life.

<hr/>

[2] Cf. Theognis 1007–1012 (youth will not come twice, and death is inevitable for mortals; we should therefore enjoy ourselves while we still have the ἄνθος ἥβης); Theognis 1069–1070 West² (we should mourn the passing not of death, but of the ἄνθος ἥβης); Mimnermus fr. 1 West² (the speaker claims to prefer death to an old age excluded from the joys of Aphrodite, which are the "flowers of youth [ἥβης ἄνθεα] to be seized by men and women," lines 4–5). See also Mimnermus fr. 5.2–5 West² (= Theognis 1018–1021 West²), which employs the similar phrase ἄνθος ὁμηλικίης. The speaker describes his desire for others, but regrets the brevity of their youth: "I am aflutter as I look on the flower of my coevals [ἄνθος ὁμηλικίης], / At the same time pleasurable and beautiful; would that it were more; / But prized youth ... / like a dream lasts a short time." Early audiences would also have been familiar with the phrase ἄνθος ἥβης and related imagery from epitaphs: see Lattimore 1962:195.

Mimnermus' poem incorporates traits peculiar to Greek spring vegetation. The phrase πολυάνθεμος ὥρη / ἔαρος ("the many-flowered season of spring") suggests the abundance of Greek spring flowers, and the use of the plural ἄνθεσιν ἥβης in line 3, as opposed to the singular ἄνθος ἥβης that we find in many other elegiac poems, is in keeping with this notion: we imagine a plurality of flowers. But Mimnermus places greater emphasis on the notion of the brevity of flowers and of other vegetal growths, which he associates with the brevity of youth and of life itself. We pass quickly to old age and then to death (lines 5–7). Leaves grow suddenly (αἶψ') under the rays of the spring sun (ἔαρος, ὅτ' ... αὐγῇς αὔξεται ἠελίου, line 2). Mimnermus thus captures the suddenness of vegetal growth in the early Greek spring. In the first line, the present tense of the verb φύω, describing the bursting forth both of leaves (φύλλα), may reinforce this notion of sudden growth: as we saw at the end of Part II, the Homeric poets associate the non-stative tenses of φύω with the sudden, apparently spontaneous floral growths of the Greek spring. The brevity of the blooming period of Greek flowers is then suggested in lines 3–4 with the association of "the flowers of youth" with "a cubit's span," presumably to be understood as a brief period of time.[3] We find a further image of brevity in lines 7–10, which associate the passing of the brief "fruit of youth" (ἥβης / καρπός, 7–8) with the departure of the sun at "this end of the season" (τοῦτο τέλος ... ὥρης, 9)—presumably a reference to the passage from autumn to winter. In this poem, then, the notion of the "flowers of youth" forms part of a rich set of vegetal images that suggest the brevity of human and vegetal flourishing.

Given how widespread such imagery was in archaic Greek elegy, we might expect to find that Homeric floral imagery likewise evokes the brevity of youth and life; we would, however, be disappointed in this expectation. The theme of the brevity of life is relatively rare in Homeric poetry, and in the passages that do indeed allude to the concept, it is not associated with flowers.[4] The Homeric image that most closely resembles Mimnermus fr. 2—indeed, the two appear to be related in some way—is Glaucus' simile of the leaves (*Iliad* 6.146–149).[5] Like Mimnermus' poem, the relevant lines describe the growth of

---

[3] On flowers and the brevity of life in Greek elegiac poetry, see also Irwin 1984:152–154. For the brevity of the blooming period of Greek spring flowers, see Polunin 1980:30–31, Braudel 1972:233, and my Introduction.

[4] Where this theme is found, it is associated most prominently with Achilles: see Thetis' plaints over her son's short life at *Iliad* 1.414–418. Thetis, however, is unusual for her knowledge that Achilles will soon die, so long as he remains at Troy; other characters, ignorant of their fate, do not tend to express such sentiments.

[5] The precise nature of the relationship between the two sets of imagery is unclear. Griffith (1975) believes that Mimnermus is reacting against the Homeric passage, providing a more personalized, pessimistic depiction of death; see also Sourvinou-Inwood 1995:393–394, 426–427. Martin

leaves (φύλλα) in the "season of spring" (ἔαρος ... ὥρη), with the present tense of the verb φύω:

οἵη περ φύλλων γενεή, τοίη δὲ καὶ ἀνδρῶν.
φύλλα τὰ μέν τ' ἄνεμος χαμάδις χέει, ἄλλα δέ θ' ὕλη
τηλεθόωσα φύει, ἔαρος δ' ἐπιγίγνεται ὥρη·
ὣς ἀνδρῶν γενεὴ ἡ μὲν φύει ἡ δ' ἀπολήγει.

Iliad 6.146–149

Like a generation of <u>leaves</u>, just so is a generation of men.
The wind scatters some <u>leaves</u> on the ground, but the flourishing
　　forest
<u>Grows</u> [*phúei*] others, and the <u>season of spring</u> comes;
Just so one generation of men <u>grows</u> [*phúei*] and another ceases.

It is possible to read Glaucus' image as an evocation not just of the succession of flourishing generations, but also of the brevity of life: our generation will pass quickly, like the leaves that scatter in a forest. And indeed the elegist Simonides appears to offer such a reading of this Homeric passage. In fr. 19 West², which quotes the first line of Glaucus' simile in its entirety, Simonides interprets the image as a warning that is all too often ignored, especially by the young:

ἓν δὲ τὸ κάλλιστον Χῖος ἔειπεν ἀνήρ·
"οἵη περ φύλλων γενεή, τοίη δὲ καὶ ἀνδρῶν"·
παῦροί μιν θνητῶν οὔασι δεξάμενοι
στέρνοις ἐγκατέθεντο· πάρεστι γὰρ ἐλπὶς ἑκάστωι
ἀνδρῶν, ἥ τε νέων στήθεσιν ἐμφύεται.

Simonides fr. 19 West²

The Chian man [i.e. Homer] said this one most beautiful
　　thing:
"Like a generation of leaves, just so is a generation of men";
Few mortals, receiving this with their ears
Have placed it in their breasts; for hope, which grows
　　In the chests of youths, accompanies each man.

Presumably, the hope referrered to in the fourth line is a kind of blind hope that youth and life will last; in Simonides' opinion, Glaucus' image challenges such delusions.

(1989:128), however, reads Glaucus' image as an intrusion of elegiac sensibilities into epic. Allen (1993:41) is uncertain whether a direct relationship exists between the two texts: they may both have been "formed from traditional, common stock."

What is more, if West's reconstruction is correct, Simonides believed that the Homeric passage and its themes were fully compatible with the elegiac notion of the ἄνθος ἥβης. West prints Simonides fr. 19 separately in his edition of Greek elegy; but subsequent to its publication, he has argued that fr. 19 followed the admonition in Simonides fr. 20 West[2] concerning the blindness of mortals, who have no expectation of death, so long as they have ἄνθος ... πολυήρατον ἥβης ("the much-beloved flower of youth," line 5). And as in Mimnermus fr. 2, Simonides in fr. 20 associates the concept of flowers and youth with the notion of the brevity of life (lines 9–10):[6]

5   θνητῶ|ν δ' ὄ|φρα τις| ἄνθος ἔχη|ι πολυήρατον ἥβης,
        κοῦφο|ν ἔχω|ν θυμ|ὸν πόλλ' ἀτέλεσ|τα νοεῖ·
        οὔ|τε γὰρ ἐλπ|ίδ' ἔχ|ει γηρασέμεν |οὔτε θανεῖσθαι,
        οὐδ', ὑ|γιὴς ὅτα|ν ἦι, φ|ροντίδ' ἔχει κ|αμάτου.
        νή|πιοι, οἷς ταύ|τηι| κεῖται νόος, ο|ὐδὲ ἴσασιν
10   ὡς χρό|νος ἔ|σθ' ἥβη|ς καὶ βιότου ὀλ|ίγος
        θνη|τοῖς. ἀλλὰ |σὺ| ταῦτα μαθὼν |βιότου ποτὶ τέρμα
        ψυχῆι τῶν| ἀγαθῶν τλῆθι χα|ριζόμενος.

                                  Simonides fr. 20.5–12 West[2]

5   As long as any mortal possesses the much-beloved flower of
        youth
        With a light heart he thinks of many things that will have no
        end;
    Nor does he have any expectation that he will grow old and die;
        Nor, while he is healthy, does he worry about sickness;
    The fools, whose minds are thus disposed, do not even know
10   That the time of youth and life is short
    For mortals. But you—learn these things and endure to the end of life
        Rejoicing at good things in your soul!

If these lines did indeed precede fr. 19 West[2], then in the combined poem Simonides contrasted the reasonable expectation (ἐλπ[ίδ' fr. 20.7) that we shall grow old and die with the blind hope that we shall live and thrive forever (ἐλπίς, fr. 19.4). Youths are seduced by the false promise of the latter.[7]

But there is one important difference between Glaucus' simile as it is presented in *Iliad* 6 and the explorations of the ἄνθος ἥβης in elegiac poems

---

[6]   West 1993:10–11.

[7]   For the ambiguity of the term ἐλπίς, "hope," see Clay 2003:103 on the presence of Ἐλπίς among the evils of Pandora's jar (*Works and Days* 94–98): "Hope promises and seduces, but all too rarely delivers."

such as Simonides fr. 20(/19) West[2]: Glaucus makes no mention of flowers. We cannot, then, assume that Homeric instances of the phrase ἄνθος ἥβης will carry connotations similar to those of their elegiac instantiations.

And indeed in the two passages where the phrase ἄνθος ἥβης occurs in Homeric poetry, we find that it does not carry the sorts of associations with brevity, old age, and death that are typical of its elegiac instantiations. In fact, the relevant passages offer a rather different response to the Greek natural environment from the equivalent elegiac images. While poems such as Mimnermus fr. 2 and Simonides fr. 20(/19) West[2] associate the brevity of youth with the brevity of flowers in the Greek spring, the relevant Homeric passages associate the prime of life with vegetal flourishing. At *Iliad* 13.484, for instance, Idomeneus uses the phrase ἄνθος ἥβης to allude to Aeneas' youthful vigor: καὶ δ' ἔχει ἥβης ἄνθος, ὅ τε κράτος ἐστὶ μέγιστον ("and he has the flower of youth, which is the greatest power"). Idomeneus is clearly the older man: he points out that he and Aeneas are not of the same age (*Iliad* 13.485); a little earlier, our texts describe Idomeneus as graying (μεσαιπόλιος, 361). But there is no suggestion in these lines that Aeneas himself, who possesses the "flower of youth," is soon to grow old. A second Homeric passage that employs the phrase ἄνθος ἥβης likewise associates it with flourishing youth but not with the brevity of life. At lines 375–376 of his *Homeric Hymn*, Hermes contrasts his own infancy with Apollo's youthful flourishing: ὁ μὲν τέρεν ἄνθος ἔχει φιλοκυδέος ἥβης, / αὐτὰρ ἐγὼ χθιζὸς γενόμην ("he has the tender flower of glorious youth, / but I was born yesterday"). In Apollo's case, there is not even the possibility of old age and decay: the flower of his youth may be tender (τέρεν), but as an immortal he will always possess it.[8]

It would seem, then, that while elegists such as Mimnermus or Simonides employed "the flower of youth" as a symbol for the inevitability of aging, the Homeric poets associated it with the prime of life. Further differences emerge between Homeric and elegiac treatments of the phrase ἄνθος ἥβης when we consider elegiac depictions of death in battle, which offer a closer parallel than Mimnermus' or Simonides' poems for the events described in the Homeric epics. The elegist Tyrtaeus associates the flower of youth not just with the brevity of life and the inevitability of death, but also with the preservation of a young warrior's beauty after death. The Homeric poets do on occasion associate

---

8   For another association of youthful vigor with flowers in Homeric poetry, see the hyacinthine hair that Athena grants Odysseus (*Odyssey* 6.229–235 ≈ 23.156–162), discussed in Chapter 2 above. Odysseus is decked with the curly locks of an archaic κοῦρος statue, an image of youth (see Irwin 1990). Again, there is no suggestion in Odysseus' appearance of youthful vitality that will soon wither into old age: rather, we get a sense of old age artificially reversed. As noted in Chapter 2, this use of floral imagery is reminiscent of Aphrodite's preservation of Hector's body with "rosy oil" (*Iliad* 23.186–187), which is also discussed below.

flowers with such miraculous preservation, but much more often they focus on the inevitable decay of corpses.

Tyrtaeus fr. 10 West², for instance, contrasts the ugly death in battle of an older man who lies, breathing his last in the dust and clutching his genitals, with that of a young man, who has the ἥβης ... ἄνθος (line 28) and whose beautiful body is admired both in life and death:

αἰσχρὸν γὰρ δὴ τοῦτο, μετὰ προμάχοισι πεσόντα
   κεῖσθαι πρόσθε νέων ἄνδρα παλαιότερον,
ἤδη λευκὸν ἔχοντα κάρη πολιόν τε γένειον,
   θυμὸν ἀποπνείοντ᾽ ἄλκιμον ἐν κονίηι,
25 αἱματόεντ᾽ αἰδοῖα φίλαις ἐν χερσὶν ἔχοντα—
   αἰσχρὰ τά γ᾽ ὀφθαλμοῖς καὶ νεμεσητὸν ἰδεῖν,
καὶ χρόα γυμνωθέντα· <u>νέοισι δὲ πάντ᾽ ἐπέοικεν,</u>
   <u>ὄφρ᾽ ἐρατῆς ἥβης ἀγλαὸν ἄνθος ἔχηι,</u>
ἀνδράσι μὲν θηητὸς ἰδεῖν, ἐρατὸς δὲ γυναιξὶ
30 ζωὸς ἐών, <u>καλὸς δ᾽ ἐν προμάχοισι πεσών.</u>
ἀλλά τις εὖ διαβὰς μενέτω ποσὶν ἀμφοτέροισι
   στηριχθεὶς ἐπὶ γῆς, χεῖλος ὀδοῦσι δακών.

                    Tyrtaeus fr. 10. 21–32 West²

For this is a shameful thing, that an older man lie
   Having fallen among the first fighters before the youths,
Already with a white head and gray chin,
   Breathing out his bold spirit in the dust,
25 Holding his bloody genitals in his own hands—
   These are shameful things for eyes to see and a source of
      blame,
And his flesh is also naked; <u>for young men everything is fitting,</u>
   <u>So long as the glorious flower of lovely youth holds them;</u>
[A youth] is admirable for men to see, desirable for women
  30 While he is alive, <u>and beautiful/fine having fallen among the</u>
      <u>first fighters.</u>
But let any man remain in place, standing with both feet well apart,
   Fixed on the earth, biting his lip with his teeth.

At the start of the poem, in a phrase that offers a clear contrast with the first two lines quoted above, Tyrtaeus states that "it is <u>beautiful/fine</u> for a noble man fighting for his fatherland to die having fallen among the first fighters" (τεθνάμεναι γὰρ <u>καλὸν</u> ἐνὶ προμάχοισι πεσόντα / ἄνδρ᾽ ἀγαθὸν περὶ ἧι πατρίδι μαρνάμενον). This usage of καλόν in the neuter ("it is beautiful/fine") in line 1 is then echoed by the use of the καλός in the masculine near the end of the poem ("[he is] beautiful/fine," 30). In this way, Tyrtaeus' poem, strikingly, conflates the ethical fineness (καλόν, 1) of the young man's death for his country with the esthetic fineness or beauty of his dead body (καλός, 30).

As we seek to understand the relation of this passage to Homeric treatments of death, we can bear in mind Jean-Pierre Vernant's reading of the poem. But while other insights from Vernant will prove important to our understanding of Homeric floral imagery (Chapter 9 below), in this instance I depart from his analysis and, in particular, from his tendency to assimilate Tyrtaean, Homeric, and wider Greek conceptions of death. Vernant cites Tyrtaeus' poem as a classic example of a Greek ideal of the beautiful death of the warrior, which he claims also to find in the *Iliad*. According to him, the corpse of the Iliadic hero, like that of Tyrtaeus' young man, exemplifies both physical and ethical beauty. Vernant points out that the companions and kinsmen of heroes such as Sarpedon, Patroclus, and Hector take great pains to ensure that the bodies of those men suffer no degradation when they die. What is more, the brief, mortal flower of their youth is miraculously preserved after death by the ministrations of the gods or by the Homeric poets' commemoration of their exploits.[9]

In particular, Vernant points up similarities between Tyrtaeus' poem and a passage of Homeric poetry, *Iliad* 22.71–76, where Priam appeals to Hector to come within the walls, lest in dying he expose his father to a still worse fate.[10] Like Tyrtaeus, Priam contrasts the shameful death of an old man, whose genitals are befouled by dogs, with the fine death of a young man in battle. The first line is an almost exact verbal echo of Tyrtaeus' twenty-seventh line:

> "... <u>νέῳ δέ τε πάντ' ἐπέοικεν</u>,
> ἀρηϊκταμένῳ, δεδαϊγμένῳ ὀξέϊ χαλκῷ,
> κεῖσθαι· <u>πάντα δὲ καλὰ θανόντι περ, ὅττι φανήῃ·</u>
> ἀλλ' ὅτε δὴ πολιόν τε κάρη πολιόν τε γένειον
> 75 αἰδῶ τ' αἰσχύνωσι κύνες κταμένοιο γέροντος,
> τοῦτο δὲ οἴκιστον πέλεται δειλοῖσι βροτοῖσιν."
>
> *Iliad* 22.71–76

> "... <u>For a young man all things are fitting</u>,
> To lie slain in war, rent by the sharp
> Bronze; <u>all things are beautiful for the dead youth, whatever appears</u>;
> But when the dogs befoul the gray head
> 75 And gray chin and genitals of a dead old man,
> This is a most pitiable thing for wretched mortals."

9   Vernant 2001:328–331, on Tyrtaeus fr. 10 West[2].
10 Vernant 2001:327–330.

Vernant fails, however, to note certain dissimilarities between the two passages, which are indicative of important distinctions between the Homeric and Tyrtaean treatments of death.[11] While Tyrtaeus states explicitly that the dying youth is himself καλός ("beautiful/fine"), the Iliadic passage is somewhat vaguer: πάντα δὲ καλὰ θανόντι περ, ὅττι φανήῃ, "all things are fine for the dead [youth], whatever appears" or "all things are fine for the [youth], though he be dead, whatever appears." The phrase might refer to the youth's body, but it could also allude to the ethical fineness of his actions.[12] Tyrtaeus, however, focuses boldly and unequivocally on the physical beauty of the young warrior's body. He asserts not only that the young man while alive is admirable to men and sexually attractive to women (ἀνδράσι μὲν θηητὸς ἰδεῖν, ἐρατὸς δὲ γυναιξί, 29), but also that he retains such beauty when he has fallen among the first ranks (καλὸς δ' ἐν προμάχοισι πεσών, 30). Tyrtaeus' poem eroticizes and makes a spectacle of the young warrior's corpse. Tyrtaeus may be drawing on a traditional image that contrasted the deaths of a young man and an old man in battle, or more directly on a Homeric instantiation of such imagery; but whichever is the case, he has recast his model in a strikingly innovative manner. His Spartan addressees might well have been spurred more readily to martial boldness and to stand their ground in battle (cf. lines 31–32) by the remarkable attribution of beauty to the corpses of youths slain in battle.

Further differences between Homeric and Tyrtaean treatments of death emerge if we compare their respective manipulations of the image of the flower of youth. Vernant adduces Idomeneus' use of the phrase ἄνθος ἥβης (*Iliad* 13.484), discussed above, as an example of an Iliadic ideal of youthful beauty that is preserved after death.[13] However, as we have already seen, this Homeric instantiation of the phrase differs markedly from the treatments of it in the work of Greek elegists such as Mimnermus or Simonides; it is also distinct from Tyrtaeus' image. Idomeneus' reference to the ἄνθος ἥβης, though it occurs in a martial context, carries no suggestion that the young Aeneas might make

[11] For reasons to question Vernant's attribution to Homeric poetry of the Tyrtaean notion of the beautiful death, other than those that I set out below, see Mirto 2012:126–139.

[12] The words ὅττι φανήῃ, for instance, could refer either to visible things (cf. LSJ s.v. φαίνομαι, B.I) or to facts that are manifestly the case (B.II), such as the dead youth's moral excellence. Vernant (1991d:84) points out that the dead body of Priam's addressee, Hector, is the object of wonder on the part of the Achaeans (*Iliad* 22.370). It should be noted, however, that the relevant line refers to the stature and general appearance of Hector (φυὴ καὶ εἶδος) not, as Vernant would have it, to his beauty ("beauté"). What is more, the surrounding lines make clear that Hector's body has been defiled: Achilles lifts "bloody spoils" from his opponent's shoulders (368–369) after drawing his spear out from the body; the Achaean onlookers join in, each dealing a fresh wound to the corpse (371).

[13] Vernant 2001:322–328. On the preservation of youthful beauty after death, see Loraux 1982:32: "La belle mort réalise d'un coup la valeur ... d'un combattant: elle fixe la jeunesse des guerriers homériques, éternisés dans la fleur de leur âge ... ."

a beautiful corpse: if anything, Aeneas' flower of youthful vigor threatens Idomeneus himself with death. And the Tyrtaean and Homeric passages represent contrasting engagements with the natural environment. Idomeneus' image associates the flourishing of a living flower with that of a living warrior; Tyrtaeus however associates floral beauty with the remarkable beauty of a corpse.[14]

Vernant appears at first sight to be on stronger ground when he adduces the "rosy oil" with which Aphrodite preserves Hector's body at *Iliad* 23.186–187:[15] ῥοδόεντι δὲ χρῖεν ἐλαίῳ / ἀμβροσίῳ, ἵνα μή μιν ἀποδρύφοι ἑλκυστάζων ("she kept anointing [his body] with ambrosial, rosy oil, lest [Achilles] lacerate it as he dragged it"). This passage does not employ the phrase ἄνθος ἥβης. Nevertheless, it does associate flowers both with death and with a youthful beauty retained after death: thanks to Aphrodite's actions, Hector's body has not lost the beauty it possessed when he died.[16] In both Tyrtaeus' poem and this passage of the *Iliad*, then, flowers are associated with the preservation of beauty after death.

But when we consider the respective contexts of these floral images, we find further differences between the Tyrtaean and Homeric treatments of death. For Tyrtaeus, the beauty of the brave young warrior's corpse is a given, a fact of the world, but the beauty of Hector's corpse is the result of special cleansing and preservation by the gods. Had Aphrodite not intervened, Hector's body would have been destroyed by Achilles' maltreatment; Hermes makes it clear to Priam that the corpse's preservation results from divine favor (*Iliad* 24.422–423). Aphrodite's intervention, then, does not suggest a Homeric belief in the esthetic beauty of dead warriors, but rather the opposite: in the normal course of things, their bodies will be mangled by enemies, eaten by dogs and birds, or infested with worms.[17] Hector's death may be ethically fine, but without Aphrodite's

---

[14] Tyrtaeus' image also departs from the elegiac treatments of the "flower of youth" that we considered above: while flowers in poems such as Mimnermus fr. 2 West[2] are associated with the brevity of floral blooms, the flower of youth possessed by the dead warrior will endure.

[15] Vernant 2001:339.

[16] Descriptions of Hector's corpse in the following book may, moreover, associate the preserved body with flowers for a second time. In an image of "extraordinary boldness" (Garland 1985:41), both Hermes and Hecuba describe his body as ἐερσήεις/ἐρσήεις ("dewy," *Iliad* 24.419 and 757), an epithet used elsewhere in Homeric poetry only of flowering plants: the galingale (*Hymn to Hermes* 107) and the lotus (*Iliad* 14.348—at *Odyssey* 9.84 the lotus is the "flowery food" of the Lotus-Eaters). Hector's flesh, it would seem, has the look of a flower in the morning dew. On the floral resonances of this image, see Segal 1971:70, who sees a possible connection between these passages and the description of Aphrodite's "rosy oil." For further discussion of Aphrodite's "rosy oil," see Chapter 2 above.

[17] Cf. *Iliad* 24.411, where Hermes tells Priam that birds and dogs have been kept from Hector's corpse. Likewise, in the proem the narrator anticipates that many heroes will become food for dogs and birds (*Iliad* 1.4–5). And at *Iliad* 19.23–27, Achilles expresses fears that worms will burrow into Patroclus' corpse. Responding to her son's concerns, Thetis drips ruddy nectar into Patroclus' nostrils (38–39), an action that is reminiscent of Aphrodite's preservation of Hector's body with "ambrosial, rosy oil."

ministrations Achilles would have rendered his body as esthetically appalling as those of the slain old men evoked by Priam and Tyrtaeus.[18]

These passages, then, together with the other evidence that we have considered in this chapter, suggest differences between the floral images of death in Greek elegy and Homeric poetry. The Homeric poets might, at times, set the transient beauty of flowers against the preservation of a corpse's beauty; but such notions cannot be said to lie behind the entire class of Homeric floral images of death. They do not, for instance, explain the attribution of the ἄνθος ἥβης to Aeneas, who is far from being a corpse in need of preservation. Moreover, the Homeric uses of the phrase ἄνθος ἥβης do not share in the focus on the brevity of life that we find in elegiac treatments of the same phrase.

In subsequent chapters, I shall build on these observations as I study other Homeric floral images of death. As we shall see, while the floral imagery of elegiac poetry dwells on the brevity of youth (Mimnermus, Simonides) or on the preservation of beauty after death (Tyrtaeus), rather different concerns unite the equivalent Homeric images: they focus on notions such as fertility and the dissolution of form.

Such associations demand explanation. It is clear that poems such as Mimnermus fr. 2 West² associate the brevity of spring flowers with the brevity of youth and life, and that the floral imagery of poems such as Tyrtaeus fr. 10 West² or *Iliad* 23.186–187 associates the beauty of flowers with the beauty of dead warriors. But it is not immediately obvious which aspects of death would be evoked by the concepts of fertility and formlessness, nor precisely how such imagery would interact with the characteristics of flowers in the natural environment. Accordingly, it is on such imagery that I shall focus in the remainder of Part III, in order to lay bare its conceptual associations and to explore its relationships with the concepts of death and flowers.

---

[18] For the theme of mistreatment of the corpse in the *Iliad*, see Segal 1971. While heroes' bodies are threatened with physical degradation in the *Iliad* and, in the absence of special intervention, lose the "flower of youth" after death, the poem associates the memory of those same heroes with unwithering vegetation. See especially the phrase κλέος ἄφθιτον, "unwithering fame" (*Iliad* 9.413), which anticipates Achilles' future glory, if he should stay and die at Troy. Given the associations of κλέος with Homeric poetry (cf. *Iliad* 2.486, 9.189; *Odyssey* 8.73–74, 24.196–198), this allusion to "unwithering fame" suggests the preservation of Achilles' memory in epic song: see Nagy 1974:229–261, 1999:175–189. Nagy also (e.g., 2013:314–364) associates this and other Homeric vegetal images with the preservation of a warrior's memory in hero cult. See too Nagy 2013:406–410 on the cult of Achilles, described at Philostratus *Heroicus* 53.8–13: Achilles receives offerings of στεφάνους ἀμαραντίνους (53.9)—either "garlands of amaranth" or "unwilting garlands" (cf. LSJ s.v. ἀμαράντινος)—a phrase that Nagy connects with the "unwithering fame" of *Iliad* 9.413.

8

Fertility and Formlessness
Images of Death in the *Iliad* and the *Odyssey*

IN THE LAST CHAPTER, WE COMPARED Homeric and elegiac treatments of the "flower of youth" and found that, while the elegiac poets associated the phrase with the brevity of life, their Homeric counterparts employed it only in evocations of the prime of life. In order to study the Homeric floral imagery of death, we need, in fact, to look to different passages from the Homeric corpus. The relevant passages associate fallen warriors with flowers, or flowery meadows with the concept of death. As we shall see, these passages consistently evoke the concept of fertility; some also allude to the notions of insubstantiality or the dissolution of form.

Trees, Flowers, and the Deaths of Warriors in the *Iliad*

Many of the Homeric floral images of death that we have yet to consider are found in the Homeric epic of war, the *Iliad*. That being the case, it is reasonable to continue our investigation of such imagery with a focus on its Iliadic instantiations. As in the previous chapter, it is possible to set such imagery in relief by comparing it with other vegetal imagery. But whereas in Chapter 7 we compared Homeric floral images with images from a different genre (that of elegiac poetry), I would now like to draw on comparanda from the Homeric corpus itself. As we shall see, we can gain a clearer understanding of the relevant floral images if we compare them with Iliadic arboreal images that are likewise associated with individual warriors, though not always with their deaths.[1]

In the light of existing scholarship, such a treatment of these two bodies of Homeric imagery may seem surprising. Critics, given the apparent contrast between the grisly deaths endured by many Iliadic warriors and the visually appealing images of plants that often accompany them, have tended to lump Homeric arboreal and floral similes together into a single category of images of vegetation, or images of the natural world. If we follow the readings of these scholars, such images would serve to heighten the pathos of a warrior's demise, setting his death in ugly relief and suggesting a peaceful world beyond the battlefield.[2]

But when we survey the full range of arboreal and floral similes that are associated with individual warriors in the *Iliad*, we come to suspect that neither set of images is primarily associated with beauty or with peace. It will become clear moreover that Iliadic arboreal and floral images differ from one another in their respective associations. Even in similes that critics have read as evocations of weakness or beauty, arboreal elements attribute some degree of strength and steadfastness to the warrior.[3] Floral elements in these Homeric images carry very different associations: they consistently evoke the concept of fertility.[4]

Perhaps the clearest example of a simile that associates trees and warriors' strength is found at *Iliad* 12.131–136. As Polypoetes and Leonteus take their stand against Asius' assault on the Achaean wall, their strong resistance is likened to that of oaks enduring the wind and the rain:

---

[1] Similarly, though agricultural similes in the *Iliad* may be associated with the deaths of warriors, they do not all carry such associations. For instance, the comparison of the Trojans and Achaeans with reapers at 11.67–71, which we considered in Chapter 5, suggests that they will mow down their opponents like the wheat and barley in the simile. But at 2.147–149, another simile describing a wheat-field focuses not on mowing but on motion: following Agamemnon's proposal that the Greek troops return home, their movements at the assembly are like that of a wheat field stirred by the West Wind.

[2] See Griffin 1976 (esp. 179–181), Kauffman 2016, Scheijnen 2017:4–5, and my Conclusion.

[3] This conclusion is somewhat similar to that of Bonnafé (1984–1987 1:19–22). She, however, sees the arboreal elements in Iliadic similes as evocations of a resistance that is insufficient in the face of death. As will become clear, I do not believe that such imagery carries any connotations of inadequacy on the part of the warrior. For readings of Iliadic arboreal images in terms of beauty or weakness, see for instance Schein 1976 on the Simoeisius simile from Book 4 and Scott 2009:147, 152, on the Euphorbus simile from Book 17, both of which are discussed below.

[4] Wofford (1992:51, 61, 62) notes the elements of fertility in a number of the images that I shall discuss, including the Simoeisius and Gorgythion similes. She argues that this fertility creates a contrast with the violent finality of death on the battlefield; but as we shall see in Chapter 9, it in fact reveals something about death itself—its monstrous otherness.

τὼ μὲν ἄρα προπάροιθε πυλάων ὑψηλάων
ἕστασαν ὡς ὅτε τε δρύες οὔρεσιν ὑψικάρηνοι,
αἵ τ' ἄνεμον μίμνουσι καὶ ὑετὸν ἤματα πάντα,
ῥίζῃσιν μεγάλῃσι διηνεκέεσσ' ἀραρυῖαι·
135 ὣς ἄρα τὼ χείρεσσι πεποιθότες ἠδὲ βίηφι
μίμνον ἐπερχόμενον μέγαν Ἄσιον οὐδὲ φέβοντο.

Iliad 12.131–136

The two men were standing before the high
Gates, as high-headed oaks in the mountains,
Which wait out wind and rain all their days,
Fixed on great, continuous roots;
135 So they, trusting in their hands and force,
Were awaiting great Asius' attack, nor did they flee.

This simile accesses the botanical characteristics of oaks to emphasize the warriors' steadfastness. In choosing oaks the Homeric poets focused their audiences' minds on some of the strongest and most enduring elements of the Greek flora.[5] Early audiences would have been able to imagine gnarled old oaks standing alone at a vantage point in the landscape (οὔρεσιν, 12.132), resisting the assaults of wind and rain, much as Leonteus and Polypoetes endure all that Asius can throw at them. The allusion to the trees' "great continuous roots" (ῥίζῃσιν μεγάλῃσιν διηνεκέεσσ', 134) places further emphasis on the warriors' firm resistance.[6] The simile, then, focuses not on peacefulness but on the concept of strength: the steadfastness that Leonteus and Polypoetes share with oak trees enables them to excel at their martial task.

If we consider arboreal similes that are associated with injured or dying warriors, we find—alongside comparisons of tree-felling with the slaying of men—similar associations of trees, sturdiness, and strength. For instance, when a little later Asius meets his end, he is compared with an oak, poplar or pine cut down by craftsmen to form a ship's timber:

---

[5]   See Theophrastus' comments on the strength and endurance of oak wood (*Historia Plantarum* 5.3.3, 4.1, 4.2).

[6]   In fact, the oaks in the simile are fixed in place as firmly as the Hesiodic cosmos, which is described in very similar terms at *Theogony* 812. Like the trees at *Iliad* 12.134, the threshold of the Hesiodic Tartarus is fixed (ἀρηρώς/ἀραρυῖαι) on continuous roots (ῥίζῃσι(ν) … διηνεκέεσσ(ιν)). For the importance of roots to the Leonteus and Polypoetes image, see Ready 2011:188. He studies Vergil's rendering of the simile at *Aeneid* 9.679–682, where Bitias and Pandarus are compared with trees. But he notes that Vergil's lines make no mention of roots and that Bitias, unlike Leonteus or Polypoetes, is killed. Ready therefore associates the description of roots in the Iliadic image with Leonteus' and Polypoetes' successful resistance.

ἤριπε δ' ὡς ὅτε τις δρῦς ἤριπεν ἢ ἀχερωΐς,
ἠὲ πίτυς βλωθρή, τήν τ' οὔρεσι τέκτονες ἄνδρες
ἐξέταμον πελέκεσσι νεήκεσι νήϊον εἶναι·
ὣς ὁ πρόσθ' ἵππων καὶ δίφρου κεῖτο τανυσθείς,
βεβρυχώς, κόνιος δεδραγμένος αἱματοέσσης.

Iliad 13.389–393

He fell as when an oak or poplar or tall pine
Falls, which craftsmen cut in the mountains
With newly sharpened axes, to be a ship's timber;
So he lay stretched out before the horses and chariot,
Groaning, clutching the bloodied dust.

The same simile is used for the death of one of the foremost Trojan allies, Sarpedon (*Iliad* 16.482–486). On the basis that Asius is a lesser warrior than Sarpedon and on the assumption that similes of the natural world better suit the pathetic deaths of minor characters, Wolf-Hartmut Friedrich proposes that the image was originally employed only for Asius.[7] However, when we consider the details of the image in combination with Asius' actions, we come to suspect that the simile does not consign him to a subordinate status. Asius is no weak fighter, as we gather from the main narrative, which describes his single-handed attack on the Achaean wall. The simile likewise carries no suggestion of a warrior too weak to resist. The montane setting, similar to that of the Polypoetes and Leonteus image, would draw on archaic audiences' experience of the natural environment to suggest "a tree that has grown independently and developed its own strength."[8] Early listeners—or at least those with knowledge of tree-felling and shipbuilding—would have imagined that the craftsmen selected a tall, strong tree, suitable for a ship's timber.[9]

---

[7] Friedrich 2003:88–91.

[8] Scott 2009:179.

[9] See Minchin 2001:147 on the height of the tree and its suggestion of Asius' impressive stature. At 17.742–746, a similar image of a sturdy beam describes the corpse of Sarpedon's killer, Patroclus—though here the tree from which the beam is fashioned is not mentioned. The passage in question develops the narrative of the Sarpedon simile a stage further. Mules are now employed to "drag a supporting beam or great ship's timber from the mountain, down a rugged path" (ἕλκωσ' ἐξ ὄρεος κατὰ παιπαλόεσσαν ἀταρπὸν / ἢ δοκὸν ἠὲ δόρυ μέγα νήϊον, 17.743–744). The mules are likened to the two Aiantes, as they strain to carry away the mighty form of Patroclus over the battlefield. The possibility that the timber in the simile will serve as a supporting beam, δόκος, suggests the significance of the loss of Patroclus' powerful support to the Achaeans. The progression between these two similes echoes that of the main narrative. These are the first two in the chain of three deaths, Sarpedon-Patroclus-Hector, that will complete Zeus' plan to honor Achilles (see Scott 2009:243n104). On the progression between these images, see also Rood 2008.

When Hector (albeit temporarily) is laid low with a stone, even he, the greatest of the Trojans, is likened to a tree. The relevant lines compare the impact of the stone hurled by Aias with that of Zeus' thunderbolt:

> ὡς δ' ὅθ' ὑπὸ πληγῆς πατρὸς Διὸς ἐξερίπῃ δρῦς
> πρόρριζος· δεινὴ δὲ θεείου γίγνεται ὀδμὴ
> ἐξ αὐτῆς, τὸν δ' οὔ περ ἔχει θράσος, ὅς κεν ἴδηται
> ἐγγὺς ἐών, χαλεπὸς δὲ Διὸς μεγάλοιο κεραυνός,
> ὣς ἔπεσ' Ἕκτορος ὦκα χαμαὶ μένος ἐν κονίῃσι.
>
> *Iliad* 14.414–418

As when under the blow of father Zeus an oak falls,
Uprooted; and a terrible smell of sulfur arises
From it; and he is not possessed by boldness, whoever is close
And sees it, but the thunderbolt of great Zeus is a difficult thing;
So the might of Hector fell swiftly onto the ground in the dust.

As with the Leonteus and Polypoetes simile, this image evokes the roots of the oak. But unlike the oaks that are "fixed on great, continuous roots" at 12.134, the tree in the image from Book 14 is "uprooted" (πρόρριζος, 14.415). Audiences would have recognized that no weak blow could have done this: as noted above, oaks are among the sturdiest trees of the Greek world. And indeed, the simile draws attention to the power of Zeus' thunderbolt, which is a "difficult thing" and terrifies onlookers (416–417). These lines, then, give an impression not of Hector's weakness, but rather of the great power of Aias' assault, which overcomes such a steadfast warrior, much as Zeus' thunderbolt is able to uproot even an oak tree.

Our findings thus far suggest that Iliadic arboreal similes focus not on weakness or on the peaceful world the warrior has left behind but on his strength and steadfastness. In this way, they are suitable for describing major heroes no less than minor warriors. With them, the Homeric poets encouraged their audiences to draw on their knowledge of trees in the natural environment; they could thereby imagine steadfast warriors in terms of strong roots, great height, and sturdy trunks.

We turn now to arboreal similes that incorporate floral elements or which are otherwise closely connected with flowers in order to consider what particular associations such elements introduce. Our first such passage comes from an account of a warrior's death early in the *Iliad*. When Simoeisius dies at *Iliad* 4.473–489, he is likened to a poplar that grows in a meadow, is cut down by a chariot-maker, and dries by a riverbank. But the narrative surrounding the simile also introduces floral elements to the description of Simoeisius' death. As we shall see, the comparison of the warrior with a tree in these lines once more suggests strength, even if his strength is not as great as that of the warriors discussed above; but the floral elements in this passage are associated with the notion of fertility:

> ἔνθ᾽ ἔβαλ᾽ Ἀνθεμίωνος υἱὸν Τελαμώνιος Αἴας,
> ἠΐθεον θαλερὸν Σιμοείσιον, ὅν ποτε μήτηρ
> 475 Ἴδηθεν κατιοῦσα παρ᾽ ὄχθῃσιν Σιμόεντος
> γείνατ᾽, ἐπεὶ ῥα τοκεῦσιν ἅμ᾽ ἕσπετο μῆλα ἰδέσθαι.
> τοὔνεκά μιν κάλεον Σιμοείσιον· οὐ δὲ τοκεῦσι
> θρέπτρα φίλοις ἀπέδωκε, μινυνθάδιος δέ οἱ αἰὼν
> ἔπλεθ᾽ ὑπ᾽ Αἴαντος μεγαθύμου δουρὶ δαμέντι.
> 480 πρῶτον γάρ μιν ἰόντα βάλε στῆθος παρὰ μαζὸν
> δεξιόν· ἀντικρὺ δὲ δι᾽ ὤμου χάλκεον ἔγχος
> ἦλθεν· ὁ δ᾽ ἐν κονίῃσι χαμαὶ πέσεν, αἴγειρος ὥς,
> ἥ ῥά τ᾽ ἐν εἰαμενῇ ἕλεος μεγάλοιο πεφύκει
> λείη, ἀτάρ τέ οἱ ὄζοι ἐπ᾽ ἀκροτάτῃ πεφύασι·
> 485 τὴν μὲν θ᾽ ἁρματοπηγὸς ἀνὴρ αἴθωνι σιδήρῳ
> ἐξέταμ᾽, ὄφρα ἴτυν κάμψῃ περικαλλέϊ δίφρῳ·
> ἡ μὲν τ᾽ ἀζομένη κεῖται ποταμοῖο παρ᾽ ὄχθας.
> τοῖον ἄρ᾽ Ἀνθεμίδην Σιμοείσιον ἐξενάριξεν
> Αἴας διογενής.

Iliad 4.473–489

> Then Telamonian Aias hit the son of Anthemion,
> The burgeoning youth Simoeisius, whom once
> 475 His mother bore, coming down from Ida by the banks
> Of the Simoeis, when she followed her parents to see their flocks.
> For that reason they used to call him Simoeisius; but he did not compensate
> His dear parents for his rearing: short was his life
> When he was conquered by the spear of great-hearted Aias.
> 480 First he struck him in the chest by the right nipple
> As he approached; the bronze spear went straight on
> Through his shoulder; and he lay on the ground in the dust like a poplar,
> Which had grown in the meadow of a great marsh;
> It is smooth, but branches have grown at its very top;
> 485 A chariot-maker cut it down with gleaming

Iron, so that he might bend a wheel-rim for a very beautiful
> double-car;
It lies drying by the banks of a river.
Simoeisius the son of Anthemion was like that when god-born
> Aias slew him.

This simile includes notes of pathos that are not paralleled in the Iliadic arboreal images discussed so far. The reference to the smoothness of the tree (λείη, 484) and the focus on Simoeisius' right nipple and shoulder just before the simile (480–482) combine to suggest the smooth, hairless torso of a young warrior, which is pierced by Aias' spear. Simoeisius has the appearance of a poplar whose lower branches have been pollarded:[10] listeners were invited to imagine Simoeisius' arms atop a smooth trunk, like the branches that are left at the top of the tree in the simile. The poplar possesses softer wood than the oaks that we find in two of the similes studied above, a fact that is in keeping with suggestions of the tenderness of the young man's body.[11] The tree will not form a ship's timber or supporting beam, but will be bent (κάμψῃ, 486) into the shape required by the craftsman.

The image, however, also carries connotations of strength, suggesting that Simoeisius, though young and tender, is no weakling. As we saw in Chapter 6, in Homeric poetry the perfect and pluperfect tenses of φύω evoke the stability and endurance of trees. Here such forms describe the tree itself (πεφύκει) and its branches (πεφύασι) at the end of successive lines (483–484). Moreover, as with the craftsmen at 13.389–393, who choose a tree to be a ship's timber, we would expect the chariot-maker of line 485 to have selected a piece of wood strong enough for his wheel-rim. It must be pliable enough to be bent, but also resistant to the harsh terrain of the battlefield.[12] The comparison of Simoeisius with a tree suitable for the construction of a war-chariot suggests a youth strong enough to serve on the battlefield.

The arboreal elements of the simile, then, focus as much on Simoeisius' strength and suitability for warfare as on his youth. Floral elements in the narrative that surrounds the simile, however, are associated not with strength, but with the concept of fertility. Modern readers might not expect to find

---

[10] See Kirk 1985 on *Iliad* 4.484.

[11] Cf. Friedrich's (2003:54–58) comparison of the Simoeisius simile with the arboreal image for the death of Imbrius (*Iliad* 13.177–181). He notes that while Simoeisius' death is associated with the poplar, Imbrius is associated with a stronger tree, the ash (13.178). On these grounds, he concludes that Simoeisius' death is the more pathetic.

[12] We should not assume that ancient audiences would see the soft wood of the poplar as unsuitable for a chariot-wheel: see Kirk 1985 on *Iliad* 4.485–486 on the use of soft woods for wheels in Mycenaean times.

such a concept associated with flowers. As we have seen, both Greek elegiac and modern Anglophone poets associate flowers with the brevity of life (Chapter 7). And indeed the concept of the brevity of life is introduced in lines 477–479: Simoeisius lived too short a time to repay his parents for raising him. Nonetheless, the floral lexemes Ἀνθεμίωνος (473) and Ἀνθεμίδην (488) are not juxtaposed with such details.[13]

Floral elements are introduced to the narrative through the name of Simoeisius' father: before and after the simile, Simoeisius is described with the patronymic "son of Anthemion"—Ἀνθεμίωνος υἱόν (473) and Ἀνθεμίδην (488). As explained in the Appendix, the adjective ἀνθεμόεις in Homeric poetry is best translated "flowery"; the name Anthemion, from the same lexical root as this adjective, would therefore have suggested the notion of flowers to early audiences. And lines 473–474, where Anthemion is first mentioned, focus on the concepts of human generations and of vegetal fertility. The lexeme Ἀνθεμίωνος is associated in this passage with two generations of Simoeisius' family: the father Anthemion and his son, Simoeisius. The warrior himself is described with a metaphor evoking vegetal fertility: he is ἠΐθεον θαλερόν (474), "a burgeoning youth."[14]

The following lines reinforce such notions: they likewise evoke both vegetal fertility and human fecundity, and indeed associate them with one another. Lines 474–477 describe Simoeisius' birth on the banks of the river Simoeis, a minor river of the Troad, for which he was named. For early audiences, the description of such a landscape would have carried connotations of vegetal fertility. They would have been familiar with the fertile soil around the rivers of the Greek world, which is still in evidence today: for instance, the banks of the Scamander, the major river of the Troad, are notable for their rich vegetal life, as we see from Plate 6.[15] Audiences would also have been familiar with Homeric descriptions of the lush vegetation growing in such places. A little earlier in *Iliad* 4, we hear of the deep rushes and grassy banks of the river Asopus (Ἀσωπόν ... βαθύσχοινον λεχεποίην, 383); at 5.777 the river Simoeis itself sends up ambrosia for Hera's horses; at *Iliad* 21.350–351, trees and other vegetation crowd the banks

---

[13] Comparison with a similar passage from Book 17 confirms the distinction between the references to a short life at 4.477–479 and the allusions to flowers and fertility elsewhere in the passage. Hippothous' brief life and inability to repay his parents is described in terms identical to Simoeisius' (4.478–479 = 17.303–4), but the account of his death lacks both the floral elements and the references to fertility that we find in the passage from Book 4. Moreover, the other Iliadic passages that use the adjective μινυνθάδιος to describe the short lives of warriors— Achilles at 1.352, Hector at 15.612, and Lycaon at 21.84—do not include floral imagery.

[14] The use of this root in the patronymic Ἀνθεμίωνος may in this instance color the general vegetal implications of θαλερός with floral overtones. It is in this sense that Bakker (2002:25) takes these lines: "Simoeisios the 'blossoming' [θαλερόν] son of 'Flowerman' [Ἀνθεμίωνος υἱόν]."

[15] See also Höhfeld 2009:112 (from an essay by R. Aslan).

of the Scamander; *Odyssey* 5.463 mentions rushes around a river in Scheria; and *Hymn* 9.3 alludes to the deep rushes of the river Meles (βαθυσχοίνοιο Μέλητος). Moreover, the description of the tree in the simile that accompanies the death of Simoeisius in *Iliad* 4 would have reminded audiences of such fertile landscapes. The tree is cut down and left to dry by a river (487); presumably the marsh in which it grew (483) is near this river. Audiences would, then, have imagined the banks of the river Simoeis, which are described in the main narrative, as fertile terrain.

Lines 474–479 juxtapose descriptions of this fertile landscape with allusions to the notion of human fertility. When Simoeisius' mother gives birth on the banks of the Simoeis, the fertility of her body is assimilated to the fertility of the landscape.[16] Her fecundity is, moreover, situated within a succession of fertile human generations, of grandparents (τοκεῦσιν, 476) begetting parents (τοκεῦσι, 477). This succession is interrupted when Simoeisius is killed: he might have sired a new generation, but his "flourishing" (θαλερός, 474) body was cut down by Aias.[17]

The description of Simoeisius' death, then, resembles the other passages that we have studied in this chapter, insofar as it uses an arboreal image to illustrate a warrior's strength; but the Homeric poets chose in this case to introduce floral lexemes. The references to human and vegetal fertility in these lines suggest the significance of such elements. As we have observed, the rich blooming of flowers in the Greek spring gives the impression of a lush fertility, in contrast with the arid Greek summer or the much less colorful winter season.[18] For audiences familiar with these phenomena, the floral lexeme Ἀνθεμίωνος (473) would have suggested the concept of fertility, and these suggestions would have been supported by the allusions to human and vegetal fertility in the remainder of the passage.

Other Iliadic descriptions of the death of warriors that likewise allude to flowers support this interpretation of the floral lexemes in the Simoeisius simile. In the passages that we shall study, we find references to human and vegetal fertility alongside explicit evocations of floral fertility. We might, for

---

[16] See Motte 1971 on Greek meadows: like riverbanks, meadows were well-watered lands that would have differed markedly from the dry terrain that dominated the Greek world. According to Motte, meadows were imagined as fertile female bodies. See also the next section for Homeric associations of flowers, meadows, fertility, and death.

[17] See Bakker 2002:25 and Schein 1976:3. Schein argues that the tragedy of Simoeisius is condensed in the phrase ἠίθεον θαλερόν, which carries the associations not-married/ready-for-marriage: elsewhere in the *Iliad* (6.430, 8.156, 190), θαλερός describes husbands.

[18] See Introduction and Chapter 3 above. As emphasized in Chapter 9, however, the depiction of flowers in Homeric poetry suggests more specifically a disorderly fertility, and this concept helps us to understand the associations of Homeric floral images with the monstrous disorder of death.

instance, consider the description of Euphorbus' death at 17.50–60. As with the other Iliadic images that we have discussed, the relevant lines associate trees with strength; but they also emphasize the notion of fertility. Euphorbus falls like an olive-sapling, brimming with blossoms, that is thrown from a ditch by a storm-wind:

50 δούπησεν δὲ πεσών, ἀράβησε δὲ τεύχε᾽ ἐπ᾽ αὐτῷ·
αἵματί οἱ δεύοντο κόμαι Χαρίτεσσιν ὁμοῖαι,
πλοχμοί θ᾽, οἳ χρυσῷ τε καὶ ἀργύρῳ ἐσφήκωντο.
οἷον δὲ τρέφει ἔρνος ἀνὴρ ἐριθηλὲς ἐλαίης
χώρῳ ἐν οἰοπόλῳ, ὅθ᾽ ἅλις ἀναβέβρυχεν ὕδωρ,
55 καλὸν, τηλεθάον· τὸ δέ τε πνοιαὶ δονέουσι
παντοίων ἀνέμων, καί τε βρύει ἄνθεϊ λευκῷ·
ἐλθὼν δ᾽ ἐξαπίνης ἄνεμος σὺν λαίλαπι πολλῇ
βόθρου τ᾽ ἐξέστρεψε καὶ ἐξετάνυσσ᾽ ἐπὶ γαίῃ·
τοῖον Πάνθου υἱόν, ἐϋμμελίην Εὔφορβον,
60 Ἀτρεΐδης Μενέλαος, ἐπεὶ κτάνε, τεύχε᾽ ἐσύλα.

Iliad 17.50–60

50 He fell with a thud and his armor clattered about him;
His hair like the Graces and the locks that he used to bind
With gold and silver, wasp-style, were wet with blood,
Like a vigorous olive-sapling, beautiful, burgeoning,
That a man rears in a lonely spot
55 Where enough water has bubbled up; the breaths of every sort of
        wind
Twist it, and it overflows with white blossom;
The wind coming suddenly with a great gale
Turns it out of its ditch and stretches it on the ground;
Just so was Panthous' son, Euphorbus of the good ash spear,
60 When Menelaus son of Atreus killed him and stripped his armor.

There is less emphasis here on the strength of the tree than in the arboreal images discussed above. Nonetheless, when we focus on the details of this passage, we see that its arboreal elements once more suggest a doughty warrior. The term ἔρνος, which is here associated with Euphorbus' upbringing, evokes strong, healthful growth. We should not be deceived by the regular English translation "sapling," whose first syllable alludes to one of the least sturdy attributes of a tree, its sap, and whose diminutive suffix suggests puny size. In fact, the word ἔρνος derives from the root ὀρ-/ἐρ-, found in the verbs ὄρνυμι, "stir to action" and ἐρέθω, "stir to anger."[19] As is suggested by these verbs, the noun ἔρνος focuses on vigorous action rather than weak passivity.[20] In line 53, such connotations are echoed by the term ἐριθηλὲς, "flourishing exceedingly"; this adjective, though etymologically unrelated to ἔρνος, forms a rhyme with the first syllable of that noun and reinforces its associations with strong growth.

When we compare this passage with the only other Iliadic instance of an ἔρνος image, we find that it suggests specifically the strong growth that results from careful nurture early in a warrior's life. The term is used by Thetis of the pre-eminent Greek warrior Achilles at 18.55–57 and 436–438: she describes him as a mighty son (κρατερόν, 55) and the best of heroes (ἔξοχον ἡρώων, 56, 437), who shot up like a sapling (ὃ δ' ἀνέδραμεν ἔρνεϊ ἶσος, 56, 437). Thetis' choice of a young tree in her image is determined by her wish to emphasize not Achilles' current appearance, but her tendance of him as a youth (τὸν μὲν ἐγὼ θρέψασα ... , 57, 438), which is rendered futile by his impending death (59–62, 440–443). Similarly, the Euphorbus simile places emphasis on the rearing of the warrior/tree. Within the simile, a man tends the sapling. Before and after the image, several references are made to Euphorbus' mother and father: Menelaus reminds Euphorbus that he allowed his brother Hyperenor no happy return to his parents (τοκῆας, 17.28), but Euphorbus boasts that he will give them Menelaus' head and armor (38–40); and at the end of our passage, the narrator calls Euphorbus Πάνθου υἱόν, "the son of Panthous" (59).[21] It appears, then, that the ἔρνος in the image is a symbol of Euphorbus' upbringing and vigorous growth as a boy, rendered vain now that he has come of age by Menelaus' blows. And if we bear in mind Thetis' words, we would assume that Euphorbus is now a strong warrior—even if he is not of the same caliber as Achilles.

Other elements of the tree's description are likewise consonant with the notion of Euphorbus' strength on the battlefield. We might, for instance, see in the winds that the tree was strong enough to endure (55–56) a suggestion of Euphorbus' having overcome previous physical challenges.[22] There is, indeed, an allusion to his earlier triumphs at the end of the previous book, when he is

---

[19] Chantraine 1984–1990 s.v. ἔρνος.

[20] In this reading of Homeric sapling imagery, I depart to some extent from Scott (2009:229–230n67), who states that "there seems to be a scaling in the relative strength/weakness of trees within the tree simileme: oak trees are consistently strong ... vs. saplings that are vulnerable." (For Scott, a "simileme" is the oral-poetic template underlying a given class of Homeric similes.) As I explain above, I do not regard Iliadic sapling images as evocations of vulnerability. I would, however, endorse Scott's view that the various Iliadic arboreal similes suggest different *degrees* of strength: the Simoeisius image suggests that the young warrior is strong but also tender; but there is no hint of tenderness in comparisons of warriors with oaks or ship's timbers.

[21] For Menelaus' killing of Hyperenor, see *Iliad* 14.516–519.

[22] See Edwards 1991 on *Iliad* 17.53–60.

introduced as the first mortal to strike the mighty Patroclus (16.806–808). We hear that he surpasses his agemates in his speed of foot, in his skill with the spear and in horsemanship (16.808–809), and that he once "removed twenty men from their chariots" (φῶτας ἐείκοσι βῆσεν ἀφ' ἵππων, 16.810). Possibly, the men that he threw from the chariots were the losers in war-games rather than victims on the battlefield.[23] But even if that were the case, these would still constitute notable feats and indicate Euphorbus' martial capabilities. Such capabilities are then proven in his assault on Patroclus.

The blast that uproots the tree in the simile suggests, of course, the fatal blow that Menelaus delivers to Euphorbus. But such elements of the simile and the narrative cast neither the tree nor the warrior in a negative light. As we have seen, the tree has already endured "the breaths / of every sort of wind" (πνοιαί / ... παντοίων ἀνέμων, 55–56); therefore only a particularly strong blast would be able to uproot it. Line 57 stresses the power of this blast: it "com[es] suddenly with a great gale" (ἐλθὼν δ' ἐξαπίνης... σὺν λαίλαπι πολλῇ). Similarly, Euphorbus' defeat at the hands of Menelaus does nothing to counter the impression of his martial prowess. In our passage from Book 17, Euphorbus faces Menelaus in his aristeia. At that time, when no other Trojan is willing to face the Greek champion (17.68–69), Euphorbus takes the initiative in challenging Menelaus, much as he had earlier been the first to strike Patroclus: he orders Menelaus to retreat and to leave Patroclus' corpse (12–17). But his valor is in vain. As our simile indicates, at this moment Menelaus is irresistible as the storm-wind that fells a tree (57–58).

The arboreal elements of this simile, then, suggest a strong and capable warrior who is overcome by a still mightier adversary. But the description of the ἔρνος reared in a lonely plot also introduces themes of generational succession and fertility. Such associations are reinforced and made more explicit by the floral elements of the Euphorbus simile. The description of the tree's blossom (17.56) and the specification that it is an olive (54) suggest that the fallen tree was shortly to bear fruit. We might then recall that the uprooting of an olive tree in blossom destroys not only this year's fruit but also that of future years. Similarly Menelaus, who denied Euphorbus' brother Hyperenor a return to his family, may have put an end to Panthous' hopes of grandchildren, if Euphorbus

---

[23] See Janko 1994 on *Iliad* 16.808–811.

was the one remaining child.[24] The simile's floral elements, then, focus on the fertility of a young warrior and on its interruption by death.[25]

But we should also note a distinction between the descriptions of human and vegetal fertility in this passage. While the allusions to Panthous and his son in lines 59–60 evoke the regular fertility of human generations, the floral elements of the simile suggest a vegetal fertility that exceeds such human fecundity. In particular, the verb βρύω, which is associated with the blossom in line 56, evokes exuberant growth.[26] It is, for instance, the term used to describe the wild growth inspired by Dionysus in Euripides' *Bacchae* (line 107).[27] As we shall see, some of the other Homeric floral images of death likewise evoke an exceptional fertility.

We turn lastly to an image for the death of an individual warrior which, uniquely for Iliadic similes of death, incorporates floral but not arboreal elements. As we might expect, then, there is little emphasis on the warrior's strength, a concept that is associated with trees in the other Iliadic images that we have studied. But once more flowers are associated with the theme of fertility; and as in the Euphorbus simile there is a suggestion of an exceptional fertility. When Gorgythion is killed by Teucer in Book 8, he hangs his neck to one side like a poppy in a garden, whose head is weighed down by seeds and spring rains:

> ὁ δ' ἀμύμονα Γοργυθίωνα,
> υἱὸν ἐῢν Πριάμοιο, κατὰ στῆθος βάλεν ἰῷ·
> τὸν ῥ' ἐξ Αἰσύμηθεν ὀπυιομένη τέκε μήτηρ
> 305 καλὴ Καστιάνειρα, δέμας εἰκυῖα θεῇσιν.
> μήκων δ' ὡς ἑτέρωσε κάρη βάλεν, ἥ τ' ἐνὶ κήπῳ,
> καρπῷ βριθομένη νοτίῃσί τε εἰαρινῇσιν·

---

[24] Cf. Irwin 1997:377–378. The occurrence of reflexes of the root θαλ- twice in three lines (ἐριθηλές, 17.53; τηλεθάον, 55) is reminiscent of the term θαλερόν (4.474), which, as noted above (n17), suggests Simoeisius' readiness for marriage. Here, similarly, Euphorbus is a youth killed at the time he should have wed.

[25] Audiences acquainted with Homeric poetics might perceive further associations with flowers in this passage, given that it echoes a floral image that we discussed in Chapter 2 above. If the olive's blossom is to be associated with any particular part of Euphorbus' body, it would be his hair (Griffin 1976:181, Edwards 1991 on *Iliad* 17.53–60), and the comparison of Euphorbus' hair, bound in gold and silver, to the Graces (Χαρίτεσσιν, 51–52) is reminiscent of Odysseus' hyacinthine hair: Athena pours grace (χάρις) on his hair, like a craftsman mixing gold and silver (*Odyssey* 6.229–235 ≈ 23.156–162; and see Edwards on *Iliad* 17.51–52).

[26] LSJ s.v. βρύω: "to be full to bursting."

[27] The verb βρύω may also have been a striking lexeme in a Homeric context. Beyond the Euphorbus episode there are no other occurrences of this verb in our versions of the Homeric poems. It would seem, then, that exceptional language is here used to evoke an exceptional vegetal fertility.

ὡς ἑτέρωσ' ἤμυσε κάρη πήληκι βαρυνθέν.

Iliad 8.302–308

But he hit the blameless Gorgythion,
A noble son of Priam, through the chest with an arrow;
His mother, the beautiful Castianeira, with a body like a goddess,
305   Bore him when she came from Aisymē for marriage;
He threw his head to one side like a poppy, which is in a garden,
Weighed down by fruit and spring rains;
So his head bent to one side, weighed down by his helmet.

Some of the details of the opening lines might lead us to expect an impressive warrior, perhaps the equal of Euphorbus: Gorgythion is "blameless," "noble," and a scion of the Trojan royal house. But other elements of the narrative in Book 8 and of the Gorgythion simile run counter to such expectations, as can be seen if we compare the relevant lines with the descriptions of Euphorbus in Books 16 and 17. Euphorbus is active on the battlefield: he is the first mortal to strike Patroclus (16.806–808) and he takes the fight to Menelaus (17.12–17). But the poem attributes no prior accomplishments to Gorgythion; in fact, he is not even mentioned before the passage quoted above. And while Euphorbus falls victim to a man that he himself has confronted, Gorgythion is killed by accident: Teucer actually intended to hit Hector (8.300–303).

Moreover, our passage from *Iliad* 8 describes Gorgythion's body as a locus of passivity rather than as a source of action. Teucer hits him in the chest with an arrow (303); in response Gorgythion's head droops to one side, weighed down by his helmet (308). Nor are the details of the simile suggestive of strength. Warriors such as Asius, Simoeisius, and Euphorbus are compared with trees that have been cut down and now lie dead. Gorgythion by contrast is likened to a poppy too weak to stand tall under the spring rains, even when it is still alive (306–307).[28] Given the allusion to a living plant in the simile, listeners might have wondered whether Gorgythion was also weak while he was alive. At the very least, the simile does not suggest a mighty warrior.

But while the concept of strength is not emphasized in these lines, the description of Gorgythion's demise, like the floral images we studied above, evokes the notions of death and fertility. This time the particular flower described in the simile—a poppy—would have carried associations with death

---

[28]   We might also compare the description of Gorgythion's death with that of Lycon at 16.335–341. Lycon takes an active part in the fighting: he and Peneleos encounter one another (συνέδραμον, 335) and engage one another with swords and spears. Peneleos, the victorious warrior, shears through Lycon's neck, leaving his head hanging only by a flap of skin. But there is no suggestion of Lycon's weakness prior to his death.

for at least some members of archaic Greek audiences. Those familiar with its use in medicine would have been aware of the power of opium to induce sleep or death.[29] And such associations with death might have been reinforced by the characteristics of poppies in the natural environment: their red flowers resemble the spilled blood of a fallen warrior.[30]

The passage also alludes to regular human fertility and to the nurturing of human generations, and certain elements of the simile reinforce these allusions. Lines 304–305 introduce the fertile body of Gorgythion's mother (δέμας, 305), who bore the warrior when she united with Priam in marriage. And the description of the poppy in line 306 suggests a parallel between the tendance of the flower and Gorgythion's relationship with his mother: the placement of the poppy in a garden implies that it was cultivated; we assume that, likewise, Gorgythion was nurtured by Castianeira. The half-rhymes μητ-, μηκ-, κηπ-, and καρπ- ("mother," "poppy," "garden," "fruit"), all occurring at the beginning or end of lines, support these associations of maternal and horticultural nurture.[31]

In other respects, however, the description of Gorgythion and his mother contrasts with the vegetal elements of the simile. As with the description of Euphorbus' death, allusions to the regular fertility of human generations (304–305) are juxtaposed with a description of an exceptional floral fertility (306–308). The choice of a poppy helps to evoke this latter concept.[32] Ancient botanists note the remarkable yield of poppies: according to Theophrastus, the cumin and the poppy have the greatest yield of all plants (they are πολυχούστατα, *De Causis Plantarum* 4.15.2).[33] The notion of vegetal fertility is given special emphasis in this passage: the poppy in the simile has produced so many seeds that it can no longer hold up its head, even under the gentlest of showers (*Iliad* 8.306–307).

But the relationship between these two kinds of fertility—human and vegetal—differs from that of the equivalent elements of the Euphorbus simile. The Euphorbus passage describes the destruction of both human and vegetal fertility: the tree and its blossom are cut down just like the warrior himself.

---

[29] No variety of poppy is specified, but given the focus on the head and seeds of the plant (lines 306–307), archaic audiences might well have been put in mind of *Papaver somniferum*. This species is the source of opium, whose narcotic and potentially fatal properties were well known to ancient writers. Theophrastus observes that opium can be mixed with hemlock to bring about a painless death (*Historia Plantarum* 9.16.8); Dioscorides notes that in smaller doses it induces sleep but that in larger doses it is fatal (4.64).

[30] See Maggiuli 1989:194, Lazzeri 2008:259, and Curtis 2011:150. Lazzeri and Curtis are commenting on a Stesichoran image very similar to that of *Iliad* 8.302–308, for which see Chapter 9 below.

[31] For the wordplay in this passage, see Salvador Castillo 1994:228.

[32] See Murr (1969:184), who notes that there are typically 30,000 seeds in each head of *P. somniferum*.

[33] The poppy was also connected with fertility in Greek religion: Porphyry notes that it was associated with Demeter as a symbol both of vegetal fertility and of her own fecundity in giving birth to Korē (τῆς πολυγονίας σύμβολον, fr. 357aF Smith).

In the Gorgythion simile, however, there is a stark contrast between the burgeoning fertility of the flower and the state of the warrior.[34] The poppy, nourished by spring rains, is weighed down by its fruit—καρπῷ βριθομένη νοτίῃσί τε εἰαρινῇσιν (307)—but the only gift Gorgythion receives from the sky is Teucer's arrow.[35] The poppy is ready to engender many new plants; Gorgythion will never sire a grandchild for Castianeira.[36]

In contrast with many previous studies, then, we have found that the floral and arboreal elements in Iliadic similes of death carry two contrasting sets of associations. Trees suggest sturdiness and strength; only when no arboreal element is present, as in the Gorgythion image, does a vegetal image of death fail to emphasize such concepts. Flowers, however, evoke fertility and, at times, an exceptional fertility. As we shall see in Chapter 9, this concept is important to our understanding of the particular conception of death evoked by such Homeric imagery.

Meadows of Death in the *Odyssey*

We find associations of flowers and death also in Odyssean descriptions of flowery meadows.[37] And given the characteristics of meadows in the Greek natural environment, these floral images, like their Iliadic counterparts, evoke the concept of fertility. But the relevant passages also explore two further concepts—insubstantiality and the dissolution of form. The flowery meadow of the Sirens episode is associated with the decay of corpses—and therefore

---

[34] Cf. Silk 1974:5, who cites this simile as a prime example of the effect of "unlikeness" in comparisons.

[35] On the contrast between the fertility of the rains and Gorgythion's death, see also Irwin 1997:378. For the notion of fertility in the reference to rain, see Kelly 2007:31 and 290–291, who places the passage in the context of other Iliadic similes that allude to the season of spring. He argues that such details evoke "vitality."

[36] See also Taplin 2007:188: "the tipping flower will have profuse progeny, while the beautiful young man Gorgythion will have none."

[37] Audiences may also have perceived allusions to death and fertility in an Iliadic image of a flowery meadow, which describes the Greek army as it musters for battle: ἔσταν δ' ἐν λειμῶνι Σκαμανδρίῳ ἀνθεμόεντι / μυρίοι, ὅσσα τε φύλλα καὶ ἄνθεα γίγνεται ὥρῃ ("they were standing on the flowery meadow of the Scamander / numberless, as many as the leaves and flowers that grow in due season," *Iliad* 2.467–468). By comparing these warriors with flowers (ἄνθεα), the Homeric poets assimilated them also to the flowery (ἀνθεμόεντι) meadow on which they are standing. On the basis of their familiarity with the sorts of Iliadic floral images that we discussed above, audiences might well have associated this image with the deaths of these warriors in the coming battles. The floral image of *Iliad* 2 is, moreover, followed by a comparison of the soldiers to flies, which are associated with corpses in other Iliadic passages: at 16.641–646 for instance the warriors who crowd around the corpse of Sarpedon are like flies buzzing around milk-pails (see also 17.570–573, 19.24–26, 30–31 for associations of flies and dead bodies).

also with the loss of bodily form. The Odyssean descriptions of the Underworld allude to the related concept of formlessness.

The juxtaposition of flowers with such concepts is far from coincidental. The particular flowers mentioned in our second set of passages from the *Odyssey* were themselves suggestive of formlessness: the meadows of gray asphodel in the Underworld would have helped audiences to imagine the insubstantiality of the dead souls. And as noted in Chapter 9, the general associations of flowers in Homeric poetry would have complemented allusions to formlessness and the dissolution of form in the scenes that we shall study. The descriptions of moldering bodies or of insubstantial shades in our Odyssean passages suggest the breakdown of the order on which an individual's living identity depends. And the Homeric associations of flowers with disorder (Part II) would have supported the allusions to such concepts in the relevant passages.

The Sirens' meadow is first introduced at *Odyssey* 12.37–54, where Circe describes the singers as the first in a line of deadly threats that Odysseus and his men must face:

Σειρῆνας μὲν πρῶτον ἀφίξεαι, αἵ ῥά τε πάντας
40 ἀνθρώπους θέλγουσιν, ὅτις σφεας εἰσαφίκηται.
ὅς τις ἀϊδρείῃ πελάσῃ καὶ φθόγγον ἀκούσῃ
Σειρήνων, τῷ δ' οὔ τι γυνὴ καὶ νήπια τέκνα
οἴκαδε νοστήσαντι παρίσταται οὐδὲ γάνυνται,
ἀλλά τε Σειρῆνες λιγυρῇ θέλγουσιν ἀοιδῇ,
45 ἥμεναι ἐν λειμῶνι· πολὺς δ' ἀμφ' ὀστεόφιν θὶς
ἀνδρῶν πυθομένων, περὶ δὲ ῥινοὶ μινύθουσι.

Odyssey 12.39–46

You will firstly approach the Sirens, who beguile
40 All men, whoever arrives in their land.
Whoever approaches them in ignorance and hears the voices
Of the Sirens, for that man neither wife nor infant children
Stand beside him and rejoice when he returns home,
But the Sirens charm with their clear song,
45 Sitting in a meadow; on every side is a great heap of bones
Of rotting men; and skin withers around them.

Circe does not make the connections between the different elements of her speech explicit, but the logic seems to run like this: any man who approaches the Sirens in ignorance (ἀϊδρείῃ, 41) of their powers will be lured in by their beguiling song (θέλγουσιν, 40, 44); he will want to stay forever, forgoing the chance to return home to his wife and children (42–43) and eventually dying on the Sirens' island; accordingly, he will join the rotting bodies of their previous victims (45–46). In this very first mention of the Sirens' meadow, then, it is closely associated with the danger of death and specifically with the rotting corpses of those who tarry on the island.[38] We are offered an image of the dissolution of form. In place of distinct bodies, one would see only a confused mass of bones (ὀστεόφιν, 45) and skin (ῥινοί, 46). And in the place of living individuals, there is only a "heap" (θίς, 45) of what used to be men (ἀνδρῶν, 46).

But for ancient audiences the reference to a meadow (λειμών) at line 45 would also have suggested the concept of fertility: meadows are particularly fertile elements of the Greek landscape. They play host to an abundance of vegetal and animal life;[39] and while the rest of the archaic Greek world would quickly have become arid in the heat of summer, its meadows would have retained their moisture.[40] The Greek term λειμών, which is found at *Odyssey* 12.45 and also in the other passages that we shall consider, picks up on this characteristic: the root λειμ-/λιμ- is associated with other watery words such as λίμνη, "marsh," and perhaps also λείβω, "drip."[41] Lines 45–46, then, juxtapose an evocation of the dissolution of dead bodies with a reference to a fertile landscape.

When Odysseus repeats Circe's warnings to his men at 12.154–164, his speech serves once more to associate the Sirens' deadly threat with their fertile environment; but he also introduces the concept of flowers into his description of those surroundings. Odysseus' choice of words, moreover, associates the three themes of death, fertility, and flowers with one another: he uses the verb ἀλέομαι ("avoid") twice in three lines, firstly in connection with the

---

[38] See Ford 1992:83–84. For the Sirens' associations with death, see in general Buschor 1944. Circe's allusions to death, however, contrast with the attractive promises of the Sirens themselves at 12.184–191: they claim that, after hearing their song, travellers will "return home, having rejoiced and knowing more" (τερψάμενος νεῖται καὶ πλείονα εἰδώς, 188). We are offered no clear way to adjudicate between their claims and the warnings of Circe. See Doherty 1995a:138: "the confirmation of [the Sirens'] hostility that might have been provided by Odysseus or the epic narrator is lacking"; see also Doherty 1995b:87. For discussions of the implications of the contrast between Circe's description of decaying corpses and the Sirens' promises, see also Ford 1982:83–84 and Pucci 1979.

[39] Motte 1971:11–15, 161–162 and Chirassi 1968:91–95.

[40] Motte 1971:5–9.

[41] See Motte 1971:7–9 and Beekes 2009 s.v. λειμών. Early audiences' beliefs about meadows would moreover have supported their association of the concept of death with Odyssean descriptions of flowery meadows. As Motte explains (1971:233–279), the three-dimensional structure of meadows motivated associations with death in wider Greek culture. Their attractive surfaces hid deep fissures and unstable, watery soil into which, it was believed, the unwary might sink. They were thought to be places of decay or gateways to the Underworld—as in the *Hymn to Demeter*, where Hades emerges from a flowery meadow to seize Korē. For ancient Greek associations of meadows with death, see also Chirassi 1968:113–124.

threat of death (157) and then with reference to the Sirens' voices and their flowery meadow (159). In lines 156–157, he warns of the Sirens' threat to sailors but implies that he and his men have a chance of avoiding death (ἀλευάμενοι θάνατον) if they heed Circe's advice: "I shall tell you [what Circe said], so that knowing it either we may die / or we may flee, avoiding death and fate" (ἐρέω μὲν ἐγών, ἵνα εἰδότες ἤ κε θάνωμεν / ἤ κεν ἀλευάμενοι θάνατον καὶ κῆρα φύγοιμεν). Odysseus also makes clear that they should avoid (ἀλεύασθαι) the Sirens' voices and their meadow, which he describes specifically as "flowery": "she orders us first to avoid the voice of the divine Sirens and their flowery meadow" (Σειρήνων μὲν πρῶτον ἀνώγει θεσπεσιάων / φθόγγον ἀλεύασθαι καὶ λειμῶν' ἀνθεμόεντα, 159).[42]

Circe's and Odysseus' descriptions of the Sirens' meadows, then, evoke the concepts of flowers, fertility, death, and the dissolution of form, and associate them with one another. The Odyssean descriptions of meadows in the Underworld likewise associate such fertile, flowery locales with the concept of death. But the relevant passages focus on slightly different aspects of death from their equivalents in the Sirens episode. Circe associates the Sirens' meadows with the dissolution of form through her description of moldering bodies; but the gray meadows of asphodel mentioned in the *Nekyiai* offer an image for the insubstantiality of the shades and hence for their lack of distinct forms.

We find the first allusions to vegetation in the land of the dead towards the end of Book 10, and these are followed by more extensive descriptions in Books 11 and 24. Passages from all three books associate the Underworld with fertile landscapes. And such suggestions of fertility are striking in this context: the Underworld is a land devoid of light. As the companions leave Circe's island on their way to the land of the dead, the sun sets and the ways grow dark (*Odyssey* 11.12). Sailing on, Odysseus and his men pass the land of the Cimmerians, which is shrouded in endless night (13–19). It appears, then, that they have journeyed beyond the reach of the sun's rays and that the Underworld, the next stop on Odysseus' travels, would fully deserve its formulaic description ζόφον ἠερόεντα, "misty darkness" (57, 155).[43] It seems unlikely that the populations of archaic Greece, whose economies were based on agriculture, were unaware that plants

---

[42] Ancient listeners appear to have been struck by the usage of the epithet ἀνθεμόεις at this point in the *Odyssey* or in similar Homeric descriptions of the Sirens' island. In other Greek poems, this adjective serves as the name of the island, Ἀνθεμόεσσα: see Hesiod fr. 27 MW and Apollonius Rhodius 4.892.

[43] Cf. *Odyssey* 10.498 (on hearing from Circe that he must travel to the land of the dead, Odysseus fears that he will never again see the light of the sun); 11.93–94 (the soul of Tiresias asks Odysseus why he has left the light of the sun); 11.498 and 619 (the soul of Achilles and the shade of Heracles refer to their former lives "under the sun's rays").

needed light to grow. It would, then, have appeared just as striking to early audiences as to us that plants should flourish in this dark place.[44]

We first hear of vegetation growing in the Underworld at the end of Book 10, when Circe describes the place to Odysseus. According to her, the first landmark of the Underworld is the Grove of Persephone, where tall poplars and willow trees grow (10.509–510). The description of "willows whose fruit dies" (ἰτέαι ὠλεσίκαρποι, 10.510) suggests vegetation appropriate to the land of the dead: presumably, the epithet ὠλεσίκαρποι reflects the fact that willows drop their fruit before it matures.[45] Perhaps, then, as with the images for the deaths of Euphorbus and Simoeisius, this phrase suggests the interruption of human fertility through early death.[46]

But other details of Circe's description simply draw attention to the fertility of the grove, without alluding also to the interruption of fertility. In fact, the relevant phrases remind us of the abundant vegetation found in other lands visited by Odysseus, which we discussed in Chapter 5. The poplars in the grove are reminiscent of the poplars both of Goat Island and of Ogygia (5.64, 9.141, 10.510). And as with Odysseus' depiction of Goat Island, Circe describes the grove with the adjective λάχεια (9.116, 10.509). The meaning of this adjective is unclear, but Hesychius associates it with the notion of fertility, via the verb λαχαίνω, "dig": εὔσκαφος καὶ εὔγειος· παρὰ τὸ λαχαίνεσθαι, ὅ ἐστι σκάπτεσθαι πυκνῶς ("easy to dig and with good earth, like λαχαίνεσθαι, which means 'dug closely'").[47] If this etymology is correct, then the Grove of Persephone no less than Goat Island possesses the sort of fertile earth that would be good for farming.[48]

Such impressions of a fertile landscape are confirmed when we consider descriptions of the Underworld in Books 11 and 24. In Book 11, having traveled inland from the Grove of Persephone, Odysseus notices a second grove: various fruit trees tempt the ravenous Tantalus (11.588–590). The relevant lines place particular emphasis on the abundance of the fruit. As Odysseus witnesses the scene, the trees "were pouring down fruit from their tops" (κατὰ κρῆθεν χέε καρπόν, 588). Odysseus observes pears, pomegranates, "apple-trees with their glorious fruit" (μηλέαι ἀγλαόκαρποι, 589), "flourishing olives" (ἐλαῖαι τηλεθόωσαι, 590), and "sweet figs" (συκέαι ... γλυκεραί, 590). And again these descriptions of fruit carry with them no suggestion of fertility interrupted.

---

[44] On the fertility of the Greek Underworld in this and other depictions, see Chirassi 1968:96–124 and Vermeule 1979:74–75. Vermeule, commenting on the vegetation growing above Tantalus' head at *Odyssey* 11.588–590, notes that it is "odd indeed in the darkness of Hades." (p. 74).

[45] Cf. Pliny the Elder's explanation of the Homeric epithet at *Natural History* 16.46.

[46] See Stanford 1959 on *Odyssey* 10.508ff.

[47] Hesychius s.v. λάχεια, quoted from Latte 1966.

[48] For the agricultural potentials of Goat Island, see Chapter 5 above.

Rather, this second grove shares the remarkable fertility of the Phaeacian orchards, which likewise boast apples, pears, pomegranates, figs, and olives: in fact, lines 11.589–590 are identical with lines 7.115–116 from the description of those orchards.

The Underworld moreover plays host to floral growth, in the form of meadows of asphodel. These are mentioned three times in the poem. Firstly, the soul of Achilles strides off happily through the meadow after Odysseus describes the valor of Achilles' son Neoptolemus:

> Ὣς ἐφάμην, ψυχὴ δὲ ποδώκεος Αἰακίδαο
> φοίτα μακρὰ βιβᾶσα <u>κατ᾿ ἀσφοδελὸν λειμῶνα,</u>
> γηθοσύνη ὅ οἱ υἱὸν ἔφην ἀριδείκετον εἶναι.

Odyssey 11.538–540

> Thus I spoke, and the soul of the swift-footed grandson of Aeacus
> Wandered off with long strides <u>through the asphodel meadow,</u>
> Happy that I had said his son was conspicuous.

A little later, Odysseus sees the soul of Orion, who is using the asphodel meadow as his eternal hunting ground. There he continues to pursue the (shades of?) beasts that he killed in the course of his life:

> Τὸν δὲ μέτ᾿ Ὠρίωνα πελώριον εἰσενόησα
> θῆρας ὁμοῦ εἰλεῦντα <u>κατ᾿ ἀσφοδελὸν λειμῶνα,</u>
> τοὺς αὐτὸς κατέπεφνεν ἐν οἰοπόλοισιν ὄρεσσι...

Odyssey 11.573–575

> After [Minos] I noticed huge Orion
> Rounding up beasts <u>throughout the asphodel meadow,</u>
> Which he himself had killed in lonely mountains ...

And in the final book of the *Odyssey* the asphodel meadow is home to all the souls of the dead:

> αἶψα δ᾿ ἵκοντο κατ᾿ ἀσφοδελὸν λειμῶνα,
> ἔνθα τε ναίουσι ψυχαί, εἴδωλα καμόντων.

Odyssey 24.13–14

> Straightaway [the souls of the suitors] arrived <u>throughout the asphodel meadow,</u>
> Where souls dwell, images of the dead.

By using the phrase κατ᾽ ἀσφοδελὸν λειμῶνα ("through(out) the asphodel meadow") in these three descriptions of the Underworld, the Homeric poets once more associated one of the most fertile features of the Greek natural environment—its flowery meadows—with the concept of death. In the next chapter, we shall consider the implications of the more general associations of flowers, fertility, and death that we have observed in this and other Homeric images. But for now I would like to focus on the reasons why the Homeric poets might have chosen to focus specifically on the asphodel in our passages from *Odyssey* 11 and 24. In order to get a sense of this, we need to retrace the history of the phrase.

The history of the formula κατ᾽ ἀσφοδελὸν λειμῶνα has been the subject of studies by Steve Reece and Suzanne Amigues. Both scholars propose that it developed from a similar phrase, *κατὰ σποδελὸν λειμῶνα, with the meaning "through the ashen meadow." As Recce explains, the later version, κατ᾽ ἀσφοδελὸν λειμῶνα, could easily have arisen from resegmentation on the part of auditors: the bard sings κατὰσποδελὸνλειμῶνα, and listeners or other performers rationalize the phrase by including the final α of κατὰ with the following word and mis-hearing -π- as -φ- (the addition only of an aspirate). If Reece and Amigues are correct, then, the formula was originally associated not with flowers but with ash.[49]

Reece moreover contends that the formula's later associations with the asphodel were inappropriate for descriptions of the Underworld: for Reece, then, the two versions of the formula are mutually exclusive alternatives. But the evidence that we shall consider below suggests that this is not the case. Firstly, it is possible that different auditors at the same oral performance could have heard either version of the formula or perhaps even both versions at the same time, since they are near-identical in Greek. Secondly, if we consider the connotations of the phrase κατ᾽ ἀσφοδελὸν λειμῶνα, it becomes clear that, in fact, both it and *κατὰ σποδελὸν λειμῶνα would be appropriate for the sorts of contexts exemplified by the passages quoted above. The implications of the two phrases are perfectly compatible with one another and with the Odyssean descriptions of the Underworld: both evoke death and colorlessness, and would thus have helped audiences to imagine the bleak, insubstantial afterlife of the shades.

Two different considerations prompt Amigues and Reece to reconstruct the earlier formula *κατὰ σποδελὸν λειμῶνα. Amigues draws attention to an anomaly in the form and semantics of the Homeric adjective ἀσφοδελός. She notes the difference in accentuation between the oxytone adjective ἀσφοδελός and the proparoxytone noun ἀσφόδελος, which is in keeping with the accentual pattern for Greek plant names, such as θέρμος, "lupin" ("the hot plant"), from

---

[49] Amigues 2002a, Reece 2009:261–271 (≈ Reece 2007).

θερμός, "hot." In such cases, however, the plant name derives from a quality of the plant, conveyed by the corresponding adjective. The adjective ἀσφοδελός, however, clearly means "of asphodel," and thus, if this meaning is any guide, would appear to be derived from the noun ἀσφόδελος, rather than vice versa. Motivated by this anomaly to try to reconstruct an earlier form that might subsequently have been displaced by ἀσφοδελός, Amigues refers to Herodian's notice that some ancient manuscripts preserved an alternative version of the formula in question, κατὰ σφοδελόν. This led some editors to offer the emendation κατὰ σποδελόν, on the supposition that the phrase might originally have referred to the ash (σποδός) from burning pyres.[50]

Reece agrees with Amigues in her reconstruction of an earlier phrase *κατὰ σποδελὸν λειμῶνα and adds a further reason for believing that this was the original version of the formula. According to Reece, of the two versions of the formula, the phrase *κατὰ σποδελὸν λειμῶνα was more appropriate for the gloomy (hence "ashen") Homeric Underworld and would have provided a semantically similar alternative for the phrase ὑπὸ ζόφον ἠερόεντα ("under murky darkness") in cases where a formula starting with a consonant was required by the meter. By contrast, the later version κατ᾽ ἀσφοδελὸν λειμῶνα was inappropriate for such contexts and resulted from the interference of Egyptian depictions of a paradisiacal existence after death. In Reece's opinion, any attempt on the part of critics to argue for the appropriateness of the asphodel to a gloomy Underworld is wishful thinking: its flowers have always been regarded as beautiful and fragrant.[51] To hear the phrase "through(out) the ashen meadow" (*κατὰ σποδελὸν λειμῶνα) was, therefore, automatically to exclude the phrase "through(out) the asphodel meadow" (κατ᾽ ἀσφοδελὸν λειμῶνα).

But as we shall see, the two phrases are, in fact, compatible with one another: both asphodels and ash are associated with death, and only one species of asphodel possesses the bright coloration that Reece associates with the term ἀσφοδελός. The phrase *κατὰ σποδελὸν λειμῶνα would clearly have carried associations with death: like the editors cited by Herodian, early audiences would quite reasonably have associated an adjective σποδελός, "ashen," with the ash from pyres, such as are described by Anticleia at *Odyssey* 11.218–222 (see below). And as both Amigues and Reece note, asphodels are associated with death in wider Greek culture. For instance, Eustathius, commenting

---

[50] Herodian on *Odyssey* 11.539 (Lentz 1868:152): κατ᾽ ἀσφοδελὸν λειμῶνα: ὀξυτόνως. ἄδηλον δὲ πότερον σφοδελόν ἢ ἀσφοδελόν. λέγεται γὰρ καὶ χωρὶς τοῦ ᾰ. τινὲς δὲ γράφουσι σποδελὸν διὰ τὴν σποδὸν τῶν καιομένων νεκρῶν. ἄμεινον δὲ ἀσφοδελὸν διὰ τὸ Περσεφόνης εἶναι λειμῶνα τὸν τόπον. ("κατ᾽ ἀσφοδελὸν λειμῶνα: oxytone; unclear whether it is σφοδελόν or ἀσφοδελόν. For it is also said without the alpha. Some write σποδελόν on account of the ash [σποδός] of burning corpses. But ἀσφοδελόν is better because the place is a meadow of Persephone.")

[51] Reece 2009:266 (= 2007:395).

on the phrase κατ' ἀσφοδελὸν λειμῶνα at 11.539, refers to epigrams that describe mallow and asphodel growing on tombs. Drawing both on the evidence presented by Eustathius and on a Latin version by Ausonius, Reece reconstructs an example of such an epigram:

Νώτῳ μὲν μαλάχην τε καὶ ἀσφόδελον πολύριζον,
κόλπῳ δ' Ἱππόθοόν τ' ἠδὲ Πύλαιον ἔχω.

On my back I hold mallow and many-rooted asphodel;
In my bosom I hold Hippothous and Pylaeus.

Other metrically equivalent names could be substituted in place of Hippothous and Pylaeus.[52] The asphodel is also linked with the concept of death through its chthonic associations: the Suda and the lexicographer Pausanias associate it with Persephone and with other deities of the Underworld.[53] Indeed, despite the fact that his lemma to *Odyssey* 11.539 is cited by Amigues and Reece as a reason to question the primacy of the form ἀσφοδελός, Herodian himself eventually opts for ἀσφοδελός, rather than σποδελός, on the grounds that the asphodel is appropriate for a meadow of Persephone.[54]

Moreover, if we examine the characteristics of individual species of asphodels, we find that there is no necessity to associate the asphodel with brightness.[55] The yellow asphodel, *Asphodeline lutea*, is notable for its brightly colored flowers; Pope's phrase "happy souls who dwell in yellow meads of asphodel,"

---

[52] Reece 2009:267–268 (≈ 2007:396–397), with Reece's Greek text on 2009:268 (2007:396). For Eustathius' text, see Stallbaum 1825:433: νώτῳ μὲν μαλάχην καὶ ἀσφόδελον πολύριζον, κόλπῳ δὲ τὸν δεῖνα ἔχω ("On my back I hold mallow and many-rooted asphodel; in my bosom I hold person X.").

[53] Pausanias (Erbse 1950:166) and Suda (Adler 1928:396) s.v. ἀσφόδελος.

[54] For the associations of the phrase κατ' ἀσφοδελὸν λειμῶνα with flowers and with death, cf. the usage of the similar formula formula ἐς ἀσφοδελὸν λειμῶνα at *Hymn to Hermes* 221 and 344. It is very likely that the Odyssean phrase lies behind the formula in the hymn, which admits of no ambiguity regarding the presence or absence of initial ἀ-, and hence must mean, "to the asphodel meadow" (Amigues 2002a:13–14). Therefore the associations of the phrase κατ' ἀσφοδελὸν λειμῶνα with the asphodel were well established by the time of the composition of the *Hymn to Hermes* (probably in the second half of the sixth century: see Vergados 2017:130–147, Shelmerdine 1986:51 and 51n8, Janko 1982:133–150, Brown 1969:102–132). Early audiences may moreover have connected the asphodel meadows of the hymn directly with those of the Odyssean *Nekyiai*. By leading his stolen cattle over an "asphodel meadow," Hermes anticipates his later career as Psychopompus, the conveyor of souls to the "asphodel meadow" of the Underworld. He is first seen in this role at the opening of *Odyssey* 24, when he leads the dead suitors to their new home κατ' ἀσφοδελὸν λειμῶνα (line 13; see the passage quoted above). For the associations of the meadow of the *Hymn to Hermes* with that of the Underworld, see Motte 1971:240: "Hermès mène son butin d'une très infernale prairie d'asphodèle."

[55] See Irwin 1997:388–390 on the contrasting responses of critics to the perceived brightness or darkness of the asphodel.

quoted by Reece as evidence of the beauty and brilliance of asphodel, might well refer to this species.[56] But the white asphodel, *Asphodelus albus*, is considerably less attractive to the eye. Seen from up close it has "white flowers with dark veins."[57] But from further away, as for instance when one surveys a meadow of asphodel in its entirety, the plant appears to possess a pale, grayish hue—or to put it another way, it takes on the color of ash. In this way, the concept of an "asphodel meadow" is quite compatible with the idea of an "ashen meadow."

The two phrases *κατὰ σποδελὸν λειμῶνα and κατ' ἀσφοδελὸν λειμῶνα, then, not only resemble one another phonetically but would also have shared associations with death and with grayish hues. Building on such observations, I propose that the two hearings of the phrase κατασπ/φοδελὸνλειμῶνα could have existed side-by-side—or even superimposed upon one another—in the minds of at least some of those present at early archaic performances of Homeric poetry. In oral performance, unlike in written texts, audience members are not forced to choose one alternative to the exclusion of the other. The two are able to co-exist, each reinforcing the associations of the other. Seen from a distance, an asphodel meadow is an expanse of gray flowers, which could readily be imagined, through the interference of the similar adjective σποδελός, as "ashen." Audience members would have been encouraged to make this connection from the associations of both asphodels and ash with the dead in wider Greek culture.

They might well, then, have conceived of the asphodel as the "ash-flower." And this would go some way to solving Amigues' difficulty with the accentuation of the ἀσφοδελός: if archaic Greek listeners (mistakenly) imagined that the adjective meant "ashen," they could very well have conceived of the name of the flower as derived from it, picking out one of its most salient characteristics, much as the lupin, θέρμος, was the "hot" or θερμός flower. From its association with the phrase *κατὰ σποδελὸν λειμῶνα, then, the formula κατασπ/φοδελὸνλειμῶνα would have picked up the connotation of "ashen," and when audience members thought they heard ἀσφοδελός, they would have transferred that meaning to the plant with the similar name.

But why did the Homeric poets introduce this "ashen flower" to our scenes from *Odyssey* 11 and 24? We have already seen that Reece associates the notion of an "ashen meadow" with the gloom of the Odyssean Underworld, a concept otherwise captured by the formula ὑπὸ ζόφον ἠερόεντα. And a meadow of "ashen flowers" would likewise be in keeping with the gloom of the place.[58] But

---

[56] Reece 2009:261 (= 2007:389). In the absence of separate Greek terms for the genera *Asphodelus* and *Asphodeline*, we may assume that the lexeme ἀσφόδελος could refer to either.

[57] Irwin 1997:388.

[58] Baumann 1993:65: "the pale, greyish flower ... gives to the landscape a dull appearance matching the sadness and the emptiness of the Underworld."

from the passages quoted above, which represent the sum total of extant usages of the formula κατ' ἀσφοδελὸν λειμῶνα, it appears that the asphodel meadow has more precise associations. In all three passages, it is associated not merely with the Underworld but more specifically with the souls who dwell there. At *Odyssey* 11.538–540 and 573–575, it is the setting for particular shades—those of Achilles and Orion—and at 24.13–14 it is the home of all the souls. We might expect, then, that the phrase κατ' ἀσφοδελὸν λειμῶνα would tell us something about the nature of these souls. But to see what this is we need to consider how the souls are described in the Odyssean *Nekyiai*.

Books 10, 11, and 24 associate the souls with a complex array of characteristics. At times, they are associated with disorderly movement: on Odysseus' arrival they wander "each from a different direction" (ἐφοίτων ἄλλοθεν ἄλλος, 11.42); similarly, Persephone scatters them "each in a different direction" (ἄλλυδις ἄλλῃ, 385). They are also "mindless" ἀφραδέες (476); accordingly, Agamemnon and Anticleia can only recognize Odysseus once they have drunk the blood that he offers them, which apparently restores their consciousness (11.152–154, 390).[59] Still other passages emphasize the great numbers of the souls (11.632) or the strange noises that they make, which resemble the cries of birds or bats (11.605, 24.5–9). And Odysseus alludes to their fame: "they are the celebrated tribes of the dead" (κλυτὰ ἔθνεα νεκρῶν, 10.526, 11.34).[60]

But it is another quality of the souls that is given the greatest emphasis in the Odyssean *Nekyiai*. Several passages and several of the formulae used to describe the souls emphasize their insubstantiality. This concept complements the notion of physical dissolution which, as we have seen, is associated with flowers in the Sirens episode: while bodies on earth lose their form, the concept of insubstantiality implies a lack of definite form—in particular, a lack of clear boundaries or dimensions. The souls are "shadows" (σκιαί, 10.495) or "images (of dead mortals)" (εἴδωλον, 11.83, 602; [βροτῶν] εἴδωλα καμόντων, 11.476, 24.14); and they are described no fewer than four times as "heads without vigor" (ἀμενηνὰ κάρηνα, 10.521, 536, 11.29, 49).

Odysseus, indeed, experiences their insubstantiality directly. At 11.204–208 he tries to embrace the shade of his mother Anticleia, but she slips through his hands three times "like a shadow or even a dream" (σκιῇ εἴκελον ἢ καὶ ὀνείρῳ, 11.207). Consequently, he wonders whether Persephone has sent him a mere "image" (εἴδωλον, 213) in place of his mother. But Anticleia explains the state of mortals after death (218–222): their flesh is burned away on the pyre and their

---

[59] Tiresias, it seems, is exceptional in that he still possesses his wits (10.493).

[60] This formula suggests their celebration in epic songs, such as the Odyssean *Nekyiai*. See Nagy 1999 on the importance to epic poetry of κλέ(ϝ)ος ("fame," from the same root as κλυτός).

souls leave their bones, fluttering "like a dream" (ἠΰτε ὄνειρος, 222).[61] Like the rotting bodies of the Sirens' victims, though in happier circumstances, the body on the pyre dissolves away; but the insubstantial soul travels to the Underworld.

Given the emphasis on the notion of insubstantiality in these Odyssean passages, we can understand why the Homeric poets chose to situate the souls in an ash-gray meadow. The formula κατ' ἀσφοδελὸν λειμῶνα in *Odyssey* 11 and 24 suggests not merely the gloom of the Underworld, as Reece suggests for the similar phrase *κατὰ σποδελὸν λειμῶνα, but more specifically the gray, insubstantial appearance of the souls, who are images, shadows of the dead individual.[62] Listeners familiar both with the asphodel and with Homeric descriptions of the Underworld would have perceived these connections: when they heard of the souls of Achilles and Orion striding through the asphodel meadow at 11.538–540 and 573–575, they would have imagined insubstantial shades. And the notion of insubstantiality is explicitly associated with the phrase κατ' ἀσφοδελὸν λειμῶνα in its third occurrence in the *Odyssey*: the meadow is the setting for "souls, images of the dead" (ψυχαί, εἴδωλα καμόντων, 24.14). In agreement, then, with George Lakoff's and Mark Johnson's theories of metaphor, the Homeric poets used the phrase κατ' ἀσφοδελὸν λειμῶνα (or κατασφοδελὸνλειμῶνα) to help their audiences conceive of something more abstract in terms of something more tangible. They related a concept derived from their physical environment—"asphodel" or "the ashen flower"—to the less accessible notion of the state of souls after death.

In this way, the descriptions of flowery meadows in *Odyssey* 11, 12, and 24 not only complement one another, but also echo the kinds of Iliadic images that we have explored in this chapter. While the Sirens' meadow is associated with the dissolution of bodily form (12.45–46), the asphodel meadow of Books 11 and

---

[61] Similarly, at 11.392–394 the shade of Agamemnon is unable to grasp Odysseus, since the strength (κῖκυς, 393) that was in his limbs is gone. For the separation of the soul and the body, see the distinction between the soul of Elpenor and his body, "unburied and unwept" (11.51–54), or between his soul, which traveled to Hades, and his body, broken by the fall from Circe's roof—a further image of physical disintegration (64–65).

[62] Amigues 2002a:13: "en harmonie avec les ombres des défunts, l'asphodèle [est] sans couleur ni parfum." Irwin (1997:388–390) proposes an alternative reason for the association of death and the asphodel (presumably excluding the genus *Asphodeline*, with its somewhat more impressive flowers): "The ... flowers ... on the terminal spike are small for the height of the stalk and do not open at the same time but, starting from the bottom, bloom and fade progressively" (p. 388). Once all the flowers have fallen off, the bare stalks remain. Irwin therefore suggests that "the asphodel represents continuity and mortality" (p. 390)—the mortality of each individual is set against intergenerational continuity. For Baumann, however (1993:65), the flowerless stalks left by the plant offer an explanation of why they might have been associated specifically with dead soldiers in the Odyssean Underworld (11.40–41, 538–540, 573–575): "The bare stalks of the asphodels in winter have represented for poets the shadowy army which wanders up and down the banks of the Acheron."

24 suggests the insubstantial souls that leave the body as it dissolves on earth. In all these Odyssean passages, moreover, flowers are not only associated with concepts such as these, but also evoke the notion of fertility: the descriptions of the Sirens' island and of the Underworld refer to meadows and hence to the most fertile locales in the Greek world. And our passages from the *Odyssey* thus echo the allusions to flowers and fertility that we discovered in Iliadic descriptions of dying warriors. In the next chapter, we shall seek an explanation for these Homeric associations of flowers with death, dissolution, insubstantiality, and fertility. As will become clear, these concepts evoke a characteristic of death that we have not yet explored: the death faced by the warriors at Troy and by other characters in the Homeric corpus is portrayed as a monstrous horror, which dissolves all the orderliness of life.

9

Homeric Flowers and the Monstrousness of Death

IN THE PREVIOUS CHAPTER, WE FOUND THAT the Homeric floral imagery of death frequently evokes the notion of fertility, at times an exceptional fertility. The Odyssean images that we studied also associate flowers with the notions of insubstantiality and the dissolution of form. As we shall see, these different concepts combine to suggest a particular conception of death. We get a sense of what they might have to do with death when we draw on previous studies that have connected Homeric representations of death with the notion of monstrousness: our Homeric passages and their attendant conceptual associations are best explained as evocations of the monstrous disorder of death: just as monsters are forces of disorder, these floral images depict death as a force that negates the orderliness on which an individual's living identity depends.

To help us understand how death might be conceived as something monstrous, we can refer to discussions of such notions and of their relevance to early Greek culture by Christiane Sourvinou-Inwood and Jean-Pierre Vernant. Sourvinou-Inwood, as noted in the Preamble to Part III, identifies a newfound fear of death in the conceptual systems of archaic Greece, which is reflected in certain passages from the Homeric poems. Death had come to be feared for its dissolution of an individual's identity. In wider Greek culture, such fears were borne out, in part, through associations of death with monstrous figures such as the Gorgon or the Sphinx. These monsters acted as protectors of monuments, but also suggested the horror of death itself.[1]

As we saw in Chapter 7, Vernant contends that certain passages of archaic Greek poetry explore the concept of the beautiful death.[2] But he argues that

---

[1] Sourvinou-Inwood 1995:271–273: "As [the Sphinx] is also a death-bringer, an agent of death, [she] is also, at another level, an image of death" (p. 271).

[2] Vernant 2001.

in other aspects of archaic Greek culture death is portrayed as something horrific. And like Sourvinou-Inwood he associates such concepts both with the monstrous Gorgon and with the loss of an individual's identity. Vernant, however, offers more specific explanations for such associations. Both in the Homeric poems and in other aspects of Greek culture, the Gorgon's mask symbolizes the extreme otherness of death. Death, according to this conception, is "the ultimate horror," which "assume[s] the monstrous mask of the Gorgo so as to embody all that is beyond humanity, the unsayable, the unthinkable, all that is radically other ... ." And death takes on such qualities owing to its dissolution of all the structure and orderliness of life, which undergird an individual's identity. The Gorgon's mask suggests "the horror of chaos, the horror of what has no form and meaning" against which Homeric heroes, while still alive, must "affirm ... the social permanence of [their] human individuality."[3]

In applying these concepts to the Homeric poems, Vernant focuses in particular on two passages from the *Odyssey*. At the end of his visit to the Underworld, Odysseus flees before Persephone can send him the Gorgon's mask: "green fear seized me, lest august Persephone should send me from Hades the Gorgon head of the dread monster" (ἐμὲ δὲ χλωρὸν δέος ᾕρει, / μή μοι Γοργείην κεφαλὴν δεινοῖο πελώρου / ἐξ' Ἄϊδος πέμψειεν ἀγαυὴ Περσεφονεία, *Odyssey* 11.633–635). Vernant points out that Odysseus uses the same language both of his fear of the Gorgon and of his fear of the dead souls that he encounters on his arrival in Hades' realm. As we see from the passage quoted above, Odysseus experiences χλωρὸν δέος, "green fear," at the sight of the Gorgon's mask. The same phrase describes his emotions at the start of the First Nekyia: οἳ πολλοὶ περὶ βόθρον ἐφοίτων / θεσπεσίῃ ἰαχῇ· ἐμὲ δὲ χλωρὸν δέος ᾕρει ("the many [dead] were wandering around the trench / with a marvelous noise; and green fear seized me," *Odyssey* 11.42–43). On the basis of the linguistic parallels between these passages, Vernant concludes that Odysseus fears the same thing in both cases. Odysseus is afraid that he might be trapped in the Underworld and become like the shades he sees before him: lifeless, insubstantial, devoid of human identities.[4] As Vernant explains, the Gorgon has the power to make such fears a reality—she

---

[3]   Vernant 1991a, 1991b, 1996, with quotations from 1996:58 and 61. On the association of the Gorgon with the chaos and formlessness of death, see also Vernant 1991b:144: Gorgons "embody the figure of chaos, the return to the formless and indistinct ... the fact itself of death, of that death which has no visage." Cf. Blaise's description (1992:362–363) of the Hesiodic monster Typhoeus: "il est par la multiplicité interne à son être, la négation de toute forme d'identité." Blaise also associates Typhoeus with human mortality (p. 370). As we shall see, the *Hymn to Demeter* echoes Hesiodic descriptions of Typhoeus in its depiction of the monstrousness of death.

[4]   Vernant 1996:60. For the insubstantiality of the dead in the Odyssean Underworld, see Chapter 8 above.

takes the life of any mortal who attempts to enter the realm of the dead while still alive. The dreadful head of the Gorgon would leave Odysseus like the "heads without vigor" (ἀμενηνὰ κάρηνα), as the dead are described at 10.521, 536, 11.29, 49.[5] According to Vernant, then, Odysseus' "green fear" is a fear of the monstrous otherness of death, of its threat to dissolve all "form and meaning."[6]

Vernant fails to discuss the other Homeric instances of the formula χλωρὸν δέος (or, to be more precise, χλωρὸν δέος plus a part of the verb αἱρέω); he does not, then, offer a complete picture of the kinds of associations that audiences familiar with Homeric poetry would have read into these Odyssean passages. Nevertheless, when we survey other instances of the formula, we find that they do, in fact, support Vernant's conclusions: the phrase χλωρὸν δέος is associated both with a fear of death and with a fear of what is radically other.

The work of John Miles Foley, who does survey all the relevant Homeric passages, helps us to understand the connotations of the formula χλωρὸν δέος more clearly. Foley concludes that the formula always indicates a "supernaturally inspired fear"—that is, a fear of things beyond human control.[7] And this explanation is certainly consistent with a number of the Homeric instances of the phrase. At *Iliad* 7.478–479 and 8.75–77, for instance, "green fear" seizes soldiers who witness meteorological phenomena created by a more-than-mortal force—the thunder and lightning that are sent by Zeus. At *Odyssey* 24.450, the Ithacans experience "green fear" when Medon mentions the divine help that Odysseus received in his battle with the suitors; a little later, the Ithacans feel the same emotion when they hear the voice of Athena (529–535). And at *Hymn to Demeter* 189–190, Metaneira experiences "green fear" when Demeter reveals her true, divine form: "[Demeter] filled the doorway with divine light, and respect, awe, and green fear seized [the mortal Metaneira]" (πλῆσεν δὲ θύρας σέλαος θείοιο. / τὴν δ' αἰδώς τε σέβας τε ἰδὲ χλωρὸν δέος εἷλεν).[8] It is reasonable to conclude, with Foley, that the fear mentioned in these passages amounts to a fear of a divine presence.

Nevertheless, other instances of the phrase χλωρὸν δέος place greater emphasis on the concept of death than on the notion of a supernatural presence. For instance, at *Odyssey* 12.243–244 Odysseus' men experience "green fear" in the face of Charybdis. And while both Circe and Odysseus describe Charybdis as divine (δῖα, 104, 235), Odysseus identifies his companions' "green fear" as a

---

5   Vernant 1991a:121. By this reasoning, if Persephone were to send the mask, Odysseus would be trapped in the Underworld forever. For the "heads" of the dead, see also Chapter 8 above.

6   Vernant 1996:61.

7   J. M. Foley 1999:216–218, 2002:121. Cf. Vernant 1991a:117, 128; the fear inspired by the Gorgon's mask.is something "supernatural" ("surnaturel," Vernant 1985:40, 61).

8   For the emotion of σέβας in the hymn and its relation to divinity, see the comments in Chapter 2 above on *Hymn to Demeter* 10.

fear of death rather than divinity: τοὺς δὲ χλωρὸν δέος ᾕρει. / ἡμεῖς μὲν πρὸς τὴν ἴδομεν δείσαντες ὄλεθρον ("green fear seized them. / We fearing destruction looked towards her"). At *Odyssey* 22.42, moreover, the suitors experience "green fear" when Odysseus threatens them with death. As he puts it, "now the bonds of destruction have been fastened on you all" (νῦν ὑμῖν καὶ πᾶσιν ὀλέθρου πείρατ' ἐφῆπται, 41). Immediately afterwards "each cast about to see where he might flee sheer destruction" (πάπτηνεν δὲ ἕκαστος ὅπη φύγοι αἰπὺν ὄλεθρον, 43).[9] Similarly, at *Iliad* 17.67 the phrase χλωρὸν δέος is associated with dogs who take fright before a lion, much as the Trojans in the main narrative take fright before Menelaus. There is no mention of a supernatural presence in the relevant lines.[10]

From this evidence, then, it seems that the formula χλωρὸν δέος can suggest either fear of a supernatural presence or a fear of death. Early audiences familiar with Homeric poetry would have understood the instances of the formula in *Odyssey* 11 in the light of such usages. And indeed notions both of the supernatural and of death are very much in evidence in our passages from *Odyssey* 11. At 11.43, Odysseus refers to "a marvelous noise" (θεσπεσίη ἰαχῇ) just before mentioning his "green fear." The adjective θεσπέσιος carries associations with divinity: it derives from the roots *θεσ- and σπ-, otherwise attested in the words θεός (< *θεσ-ός, "god") and ἐνι-σπεῖν ("speak"), and would originally have meant "spoken by the gods."[11] But this divine noise is produced by dead souls. In these lines, then, the phrase "green fear" is associated both with a supernatural presence and with the notion of death.

Our second passage from *Odyssey* 11 evokes similar concepts. Odysseus describes how the dead souls thronged around him (632) and goes on to speak of his "green fear" (633). The juxtaposition of this phrase with a description of the shades associates Odysseus' fear with the concept of death. But again, the dead produce a "marvelous (or god-spoken) noise" (ἠχῇ θεσπεσίη, 633), which is mentioned immediately before the formula ἐμὲ δὲ χλωρὸν δέος ᾕρει.

---

[9] J. M. Foley (1999:217–218) explains the "green fear" of the suitors at *Odyssey* 22.42 in terms of Odysseus' reference to the gods at line 39 (οὔτε θεοὺς δείσαντες, οἳ οὐρανὸν εὐρὺν ἔχουσιν, "not fearing the gods, who hold wide heaven"): he infers that the suitors fear divine vengeance for their actions. But in his speech Odysseus does not directly mention divine vengeance. Rather, he alludes "vengeance from mortals" (ἀνθρώπων νέμεσιν, 40), and he follows this phrase with a reference to the doom that awaits the suitors (41).

[10] Likewise, a variant of the formula in question, χλωρὸς/οἳ ὑπαὶ δείους, "green with fear," carries clear associations with death in both its Homeric instantiations; and neither passage alludes to the supernatural. At *Iliad* 10.376, it describes Dolon, who fears death at the hands of Odysseus and Diomedes; at 15.4, it describes the Trojans who are intimidated by the Greeks.

[11] See Beekes 2009 s.v. θεσπέσιος. Elsewhere in Homeric poetry, the adjective is indeed associated with divine utterances: at *Odyssey* 24.49, for instance, it describes the wailing of Thetis and of her fellow Nereids as they mourn for Achilles.

Once more, then, this passage supports Foley's association of the phrase "green fear" with the concept of the supernatural. And that theme is echoed in lines 634–635, with the mention of the Gorgon's head, which is the mask of a deity sent by another deity, Persephone. What is more, a monstrous divinity such as the Gorgon carries particularly strong associations with the supernatural: she is not merely a deity, something more-than-mortal, but also a monster. Audiences familiar with usages of the formula χλωρὸν δέος such as we have considered above would, then, have picked up on the allusions to death and to the supernatural in these passages. They would have concluded that Odysseus' fear amounts to a fear of both these things. And these observations are consistent with Vernant's description of the monstrous otherness of death. As Vernant would have it, Odysseus fears death when he encounters the shades and imagines the Gorgon's mask; but at the same time he fears what is radically other, since death would dissolve all the order that undergirds his living identity.

The notion of the monstrous disorder of death helps to account for the details of the Homeric passages that we studied in Chapter 8 and that we shall consider below. A number of the Homeric floral images of death echo depictions of monsters in other archaic Greek poems. The relevant images either resemble portrayals of specific monsters or recall the wild fertility that the Hesiodic poets attribute to monsters. And in this way, they allude not only to monstrousness but also to the theme of disorder. As mentioned above, monsters are by definition disorderly beings; but the monsters of the Hesiodic tradition, like flowers in Homeric poetry, are also characterized by a disordered fertility that fails to respect regular means of reproduction. Moreover, the irregular fertility of Homeric flowers and of Hesiodic monsters is. in both cases, associated with challenges to established order. Such allusions to disorder are complemented in our Homeric images by descriptions of physical dissolution or of the loss of identity; and these details are likewise consistent with the concept of the monstrous disorder of death.

We should now revisit the relevant passages from Homeric poetry, in order to explore the ways in which they evoke such concepts. The poppy simile from *Iliad* 8.302–308 offers our first example of a floral image alluding to monsters and monstrousness. We might firstly note the γοργ- root in the dying warrior's name, which brings to mind the Gorgon.[12] Lest we think that the resemblance between the two names is fortuitous, the same root is found within fifty lines of Gorgythion's death, where it describes the war-maddened eyes of his half-brother Hector and unambiguously evokes the glare of a Gorgon: Ἕκτωρ δ'

---

[12] For the connotations of monstrousness in Gorgythion's name, see Salvador Castillo 1994:236–238, Kelly 2015:37n81.

ἀμφιπεριστρώφα καλλίτριχας ἵππους, / Γοργοῦς ὄμματ' ἔχων ἠδὲ βροτολοιγοῦ Ἄρηος ("Hector was turning his lovely-haired horses all around; / he had the eyes of Gorgo and of Ares, bane of men," *Iliad* 8.348–349).[13]

The simile that follows, moreover, bears a close resemblance to an image describing a monster in another archaic Greek poem. In the Iliadic passage, Gorgythion "threw his head to one side like a poppy" (μήκων δ' ὡς ἑτέρωσε κάρη βάλεν, 306) when he was struck by Teucer's arrow. Stesichorus associates the monstrous Geryon with similar imagery. When Heracles' arrow strikes the first head of the three-headed monster, it leans to one side like a poppy:

> ἀπέκλινε δ' ἄρ' αὐχένα Γαρ[υόνας
> ἐπικάρσιον, ὡς ὅκα μ[ά]κω[ν
> ἅ τε καταισχύνοισ' ἀπαλὸν [δέμας
> αἶψ' ἀπὸ φύλλα βαλοῖσα γ[

> Stesichorus *Geryoneis* fr. 19.44–47 Davies-Finglass

Ger[yon] then leaned his neck
   to one side, as when a p[o]pp[y
which, shaming its tender [body,
   suddenly casts off its petals ...

We can start to understand what the resemblances between the two passages might signify if we refer to an essay by Jesús Salvador Castillo, who contends that Stesichorus' poem reflects the original context of such images in the Greek poetic tradition. In making this argument, Salvador Castillo adopts a methodology similar to those employed in neo-analytical studies of Homeric poetry.[14] Neo-analysts have identified details in particular passages of the *Iliad* or the *Odyssey* that appear more at home in the equivalent episodes of the Epic Cycle. They have argued that these passages allude to such episodes, and that these allusions lend significance to the relevant portion of the major epics.

The Catalogue of Ships in *Iliad* 2, for example, obtrudes from its immediate context, and critics have argued that it recalls events early in the Trojan Cycle. *Iliad* 2 foregrounds the movements of the Achaean troops: they hurry to the assembly (86–94); they make a rush for the ships (142–154); subsequently, the chieftains re-establish order among them, and they are persuaded to return to the meeting-place (207–210).[15] At this point in the epic, then, we would expect

---

[13] See Vernant 1991a:116–118 on the concentration of a warrior's power of death in the Gorgon device on his shield: according to him, Gorgoneions suggest the eyes of a berserk warrior, like those of Hector in the passage quoted above.

[14] For neo-analysis, see also my Introduction.

[15] For comments on the vegetal imagery in this episode, see Chapter 8 nn. 1 and 37.

any catalogue to list only the soldiers and not the ships that brought them to Troy: even though the ships are mentioned, they are not the primary focus of this episode. In fact, the Catalogue of Ships seems to belong to an earlier episode of the war, when the Achaean fleet was mustering at Aulis. For this reason, neo-analysts have read the relevant lines in *Iliad* 2 as an allusion to such events, which would have been described in the *Cypria*. And this has consequences for our understanding of the Iliadic scene. Benjamin Sammons, for instance, argues that these allusions point up a decline that has taken place in the Achaean army over their time at Troy.[16]

Similarly, Salvador Castillo argues that the image of a poppy leaning its head to one side is a more obvious fit for descriptions of many-headed monsters, such as we find in Stesichorus' poem. He concludes that the Homeric poets are alluding to such passages, so as to enrich their account of Gorgythion's demise. In particular, he argues that allusions to monsters and monstrosity in the relevant lines are important to the portrayal of Gorgythion's death.

In order to demonstrate that the poppy image is more consistent with the description of the many-headed Geryon, Salvador Castillo explores, in particular, the depiction of heads in the two passages. In his discussion of the Iliadic passage, he notes the focus on the heads of both Gorgythion and the poppy. As he observes, such a focus does not seem consistent with the context. Teucer's arrow hits Gorgythion in the chest, not the head, and even if he were struck there we would expect not merely his head to loll but his whole body to crumple under the impact.[17] Stesichorus' image, by contrast, fits its context perfectly—the relevant lines describe the death of the first head of the three-headed monster Geryon. Though Geryon's first head dies, the rest of his many-headed body remains alive, and so we would fully expect it to loll like a poppy-head heavy with seeds. Given that the poppy image is more consistent with the physical details of Geryon's demise, Salvador Castillo proposes that the Iliadic passage does not reflect the original context of such a simile; rather, both Stesichorus and the Iliadic poets were drawing on an earlier image that described the death of a monster.[18]

If we accept the validity of neo-analytical approaches, it is reasonable also to accept Salvador Castillo's idea that our passage from *Iliad* 8 alludes to the death of a monster: the poppy image at *Iliad* 8.302–308, then, would echo the theme of monstrousness introduced by the name Gorgythion. We might,

---

[16] Sammons 2010:135–196.

[17] Kirk 1990 on *Iliad* 8.306–308: "The explanation that [the head] is weighed down with the helmet is hardly necessary, a further piece of poetical pseudo-realistic fantasy—for the body would tend to collapse all at once, and the sagging of the head not stand out from the rest."

[18] Salvador Castillo 1994. Cf. Kauffman 2016, who notes Apollonius Rhodius' use of elements from the Gorgythion and Euphorbus similes to describe the deaths of monsters.

however, query other elements of Salvador Castillo's argument. Firstly, while some neo-analytical studies of the major Homeric epics trace specific allusions to specific linguistic expressions in the relevant poems, others emphasize the fluidity in archaic times, both of the major epics and of the epic cycle.[19] It may be, then, that Stesichorus and the Homeric poets were not drawing on one single image from one single other poem, but rather on a certain kind of image with which they were both familiar. Secondly, we might think not so much in terms of originals and later imitations but of contemporaneous poetic traditions. The Homeric poets used the image of a poppy leaning its head to one side to describe the death of warriors; Stesichorus and other archaic Greek poets employed the same sort of image to describe the death of monsters.

I would also depart from Salvador Castillo in my explanation for the use of such elements in *Iliad* 8. Salvador Castillo suggests that allusions to monstrousness in *Iliad* 8.302–308 liken Teucer's killing of Gorgythion to the slaying of a monster. But this does not seem a very satisfactory interpretation of the Iliadic passage. No previous achievements on the battlefield are attributed to Gorgythion; nor does he play an active role in the events leading up to his death. He seems, then, to be a singularly unlikely candidate for comparison with a terrifying monster. Teucer's feat is, moreover, no great triumph of skill or endurance, such as we would expect from a monster-quest. In fact, he hits Gorgythion by accident, intending instead to kill Hector (*Iliad* 8.300–303).[20]

We can arrive at a better explanation of the allusions to monsters in this passage if we bear in mind Vernant's discussion of the monstrousness of death—after all, Gorgythion's name recalls the Gorgon and hence the very monster that is the focus of Vernant's studies. And indeed it makes more sense to view allusions to monstrousness in the image as providing a comparandum not for the warrior himself, but for the death that he undergoes: if a simile were to compare a warrior with a monster, we would expect him to be the most fearsome of combatants; but death is something that all, both weak and strong, must face.

For a second example of a Homeric floral image resembling an archaic Greek description of a monster, we return to a scene that we have considered twice already, but not yet in connection with the theme of death. As we have seen, the description of the narcissus in the opening lines of the *Hymn to Demeter* is extremely rich in its significations: it contributes to the poem's explorations not

---

[19] For specific allusions, see Currie 2016; for greater fluidity, see Nagy 1999:42–58 and 2004.

[20] Mackie's explorations of Hector's attempts to kill Achilles in terms of a failed monster-quest are rather more convincing (2008:21–50). The victor Achilles takes on characteristics that we would normally expect of a monster, not a warrior, such as the desire to eat human flesh (*Iliad* 22.346–347): had Hector been able to kill the unnatural Achilles, his would have been a feat worthy of comparison with the slaying of a monster.

only of seduction and deception but also of changes to the order of the cosmos.[21] In addition, it is associated with the theme of death. We noted in Chapter 4 that in plucking the flower Korē opens up a passageway between the upper and lower worlds. Hades is thus able to rush up and seize Korē, and shortly afterwards he leads her down into the Underworld. As an immortal, Korē cannot die; nonetheless, her journey below the earth parallels that of the mortal dead.[22] Demeter, moreover, treats Korē's abduction as a kind of death. This much can be seen from her actions, which would have resembled the sorts of rituals of mourning familiar to early audiences: when she hears Korē's despairing cries, she tears her headdress and dons a dark veil (41–42); on arrival at the house of Celeus, she stays seated in silence and unsmiling, and refuses to taste food or drink (197–201).[23]

The characteristics of narcissi in the Greek natural environment, together with the treatment of the narcissus in wider Greek culture, would have encouraged listeners to see suggestions of death also in the opening scene of the hymn. The narcissus often decorated graves and was used as a motif in funerary art.[24] Such practices may have constituted a response to two qualities of the plant: the narcotic properties of its bulb and its blooming at colder times of the year than other Greek flowers. The earliest-flowering narcissi bloom at the start of the spring: at *Historia Plantarum* 6.8.1, for instance, Theophrastus notes that both the narcissus and the lily bloom very early; the *Geoponica*, a Byzantine treatise on agriculture that draws ultimately on ancient sources, transfers the coldness of the narcissus' blooming period to the flower itself (ψυχρότατον δέ ἐστι τὸ ἄνθος αὐτοῦ—"its flower is very cold," 9.25). A belief in the coldness of the flower would readily suggest an association with death:[25] as ancient authorities note, the passing of life is marked by the loss of body heat.[26]

The early Greeks also believed that the narcissus had anesthetic qualities and thought that these explained the name of the plant: they traced the Greek term to the root ναρκ-, which is associated with numbness. According to Plutarch, for instance, the ancients (οἱ παλαιοί) called the plant τὸν νάρκισσον,

---

[21] Chapters 2 and 4 above.

[22] In fact, if we follow Rudhardt (1994) and Clay (2006:202–266), Korē is later able to alleviate the horrific deaths endured by mortals in the Underworld: her annual journeys to and from the upper world allow her to appeal to her husband on behalf of Eleusinian initiates, and thereby to win them the status of "blessed" after death (*Hymn to Demeter* 480); see also Chapter 4n28 above. For the near-death of the gods in Homeric poetry, see Garcia 2013:159–229.

[23] For the associations of Demeter's actions with mourning, see Richardson 1974 on *Hymn to Demeter* 41, 42, and 197–201. For Demeter's treating Korē's abduction by Hades as a kind of death, see DeBloois 1997 and Stehle (Stigers) 1977:94–96, discussed in Chapter 2 above.

[24] Eitrem 1935 col. 1727, Chirassi 1968:146, Richardson 1974 on *Hymn to Demeter* 8, Baumann 1993:68.

[25] Eitrem 1935 col. 1727.

[26] See Aristotle *De Longitudine et Brevitate Vitae* 466a.20–21, *Problems* 909b.29–31.

ὡς ἀμβλύνοντα τὰ νεῦρα καὶ βαρύτητας ἐμποιοῦντα ναρκώδεις ("the narcissus, on the grounds that it dulls the nerves and creates sleepy [*narkōdeis*] heaviness in the body," *Moralia* 647b).[27] The ναρκ- root was, moreover, available to the Homeric poets for the description of numbness: at *Iliad* 8.328, a blow from Hector numbs (<u>νάρκησε</u>) Teucer's hand.[28] Given their knowledge of this verb, the Homeric poets and their audiences might well have understood the origins of the term νάρκισσος in the same way as those mentioned by Plutarch. And although such explanations of the lexeme appear to be no more than folk-etymologies,[29] they may well draw on real qualities of the plant: the bulb of the narcissus contains toxic alkaloids that prove fatal in large quantities. When we take into account these natural characteristics of the narcissus and the resemblance of the first syllable of the plant's name to the ναρκ- root, it would not be at all surprising if the narcissus put archaic Greek audiences in mind of the dulling of the senses in death.[30]

These associations of the narcissus in wider Greek culture would have encouraged listeners to see allusions to the theme of death in the opening scene of the *Hymn to Demeter*, which would then have been reinforced by the references to mourning later in the poem. But early audiences familiar with the Hesiodic tradition would also have perceived an allusion to the theme of monstrousness in the description of the narcissus. Jenny Strauss Clay notes that the many-headed narcissus of the hymn resembles the monstrous Typhoeus from the Hesiodic *Theogony*.[31] And there are, indeed, a number of striking similarities between the description of the flower at *Hymn to Demeter* 8–14 and the Hesiodic depiction of Typhoeus. The goddess Gaia sends up the plant from the Underworld; the same goddess unites with Tartarus, a compartment of the lower world, to produce Typhoeus (*Theogony* 821–822).[32] Like the narcissus, the monster has a

---

[27] Cf. Pliny *Natural History* 21.128, who describes one type of narcissus as *neruis inimicum, caput grauantem et a narce narcissum dictum* ... ("hostile to vigor, weighing down the head, and called *narcissus* from *narce*" [a Greek term for numbness]).

[28] Interestingly, this passage follows shortly after the Gorgythion simile, which as noted in Chapter 8n29 above describes a plant with narcotic qualities—the poppy. It is possible, then, that Homeric audiences, when they heard of this wound to Gorgythion's killer, would still have had in mind the notion of numbness that is latent in the Gorgythion passage.

[29] Chantraine 1984–1990 and Beekes 2009 s.v. νάρκισσος.

[30] On the fatal qualities of alkaloids from bulbs of the genus *Narcissus*, see Bastida and Viladomat 2002, esp. 184–185. On the recognition of these qualities in the Greek associations of the νάρκισσος, see Chirassi 1968:143–144.

[31] Clay 2006:213–214. See also Clay 2003:150 on Hesiodic monsters more generally: they "present a kind of *wild efflorescence* whose continuation might imperil the final stability of the cosmos" (my emphasis). On associations of monsters, flowers, and disorder, see further below. For the engagement of the *Hymn to Demeter* with the story of Typhoeus, see Richardson 1974:40.

[32] Clay 2006:214: "Like many of the prodigious creatures Gaia has brought forth in the past, the narcissus is a monstrosity of nature."

hundred heads: ἐκ δέ οἱ ὤμων / ἦν ἑκατὸν κεφαλαὶ ὄφιος δεινοῖο δράκοντος, / γλώσσῃσι δνοφερῇσι λελιχμότες ("from his shoulders / there were a hundred heads of a dread, glaring snake, / licking with dark tongues," *Theogony* 824–826). The noise of his fight with Zeus carries as far as the scent of the flower—it fills the earth, heaven, sea, and Underworld: ἀμφὶ δὲ γαῖα / σμερδαλέον κονάβησε καὶ οὐρανὸς εὐρὺς ὕπερθε / πόντός τ᾽ Ὠκεανοῦ τε ῥοαὶ καὶ τάρταρα γαίης ("the earth resounded terribly all around, and wide heaven above, / and the sea and the flows of Ocean, and Tartara in the earth," *Theogony* 839–841).

At *Hymn to Demeter* 8–14, then, the Homeric poets described a flower associated with death in terms resembling Hesiodic depictions of monsters. We need not conclude that those poets were thereby alluding to our version of the *Theogony*: again, we may be dealing with two contemporaneous and fluid poetic traditions. Moreover, the Homeric poets may not have had in mind specifically the Hesiodic Typhoeus: the depiction of Typhoeus at *Theogony* 820–880 may reflect a Hesiodic template for describing monsters more generally. But even if this is the case, the Homeric description of the narcissus would have reminded early audiences of the sorts of monsters that they had encountered in performances of Hesiodic poetry. And at the same time, the Homeric poets alluded to a flower that was associated with death in wider Greek culture. If again we refer to Vernant's findings we can posit a reason for these allusions both to death and to monstrousness: the many-headed narcissus suggests the monstrousness of death.

We notice more general similarities between Homeric flowers and Hesiodic monsters when we focus on the notion of fertility, which is given particular emphasis in the relevant passages of Homeric poetry. Both Homeric flowers and Hesiodic monsters possess a wild, disordered fertility whose operations contrast with the more regular reproductive processes associated, for instance, with human beings or with the Olympian gods. And such fertility is not merely disorderly in and of itself: it is associated in both genres with challenges to established order. Again, the combination of such themes with Homeric images of death is consistent with Vernant's explorations of archaic Greek culture: according to him, the early Greeks conceived of death in terms of monstrous disorder.

The wild profusion of the Hesiodic monsters, for instance, contrasts with the more regular successions of divine generations. The *Theogony*'s stories of the gods incorporate the scenes of violent revolution discussed in Chapter 4, but they nonetheless follow a predictable pattern: a succession of brother-sister pairs (Heaven and Earth, Cronus and Rhea, Zeus and Hera) each produces a new generation of gods, and with the exception of Zeus each successive king of the gods is overthrown by one of his sons. By contrast the catalogue of monsters at *Theogony* 270–336 gives an impression simply of wild abundance and multiplicity, sometimes without a clear sense even of which monstrous creature gives birth to which other: in particular, the vague use of the feminine pronoun ἥ at *Theogony* 319 and 326, with no clear referent, creates the sense of a generalized, undifferentiated female fecundity.[33]

Similarly, two of the Homeric passages that we studied in Chapter 8 contrast the regular successions of human generations with descriptions of exceptional floral fertility. Gorgythion is identified as a son of Priam, and the narrative alludes to his mother's fertile body (8.303–305). But lines 306–308 focus on a poppy so heavy with seeds that it can barely hold up its head. In the Gorgythion episode, then, the regular fertility associated with human generations is juxtaposed with vegetal profusion. We notice similar themes in the description of Euphorbus' death in Book 17. Euphorbus is named as the son of Panthous (17.59), which once more reminds us of regular human generations. But a little earlier his death is associated with an image of exuberant floral fertility: the tree in the simile "overflows with white blossom" (βρύει ἄνθεϊ λευκῷ, 56).[34]

Hesiodic monsters and Homeric flowers also employ unconventional modes of reproduction. Within the Hesiodic catalogue of monsters, the Gorgon Medusa, even when decapitated, is able to give birth to Chrysaor and the horse Pegasus (*Theogony* 280–281). Typhoeus, despite seeming to clash with Zeus immediately after his emergence from the lower world, apparently has time to father the monsters Cerberus, Hydra, and Orthus with his mate, the monstrous Echidna (306–318).[35] Critics have, moreover, seen suggestions of mother-son couplings or parthenogenesis in lines 319–332. If such irregular processes are indeed operative in this passage, they would contrast with the modes of reproduction employed by the Olympian gods.[36] Similarly, as we saw in Chapter 6 the Homeric poets associated flowers with a fertility that failed to respect regular modes of reproduction. The archaic Greeks, responding to the sudden burst of color at the start of the Greek spring, believed small flowering plants to be capable of spontaneous generation, without the need for seeds. They thus endowed those plants with a fertility that bypassed the regular means of vegetal reproduction.

And such notions are consistent with some of the details of the Homeric images that we have studied in Part III. André Motte, for instance, notes that the ancient Greeks associated fertile meadows with spontaneous generation; and the images of death in *Odyssey* 11, 12, and 24 allude to just such meadows.[37]

---

[33] See Clay 2003:159–161.

[34] By contrast, Glaucus' simile at 6.146–149, discussed in Chapter 7, likens the alternation of human generations to leaves, not flowers.

[35] At *Theogony* 820–880, a description of Typhoeus' birth passes immediately to an account of his fight with Zeus. Typhoeus is a doublet of the Typhaon mentioned at line 306 of the catalogue of monsters: see West 1966 on *Theogony* 306 (Τυφάονα).

[36] Clay 2003:159–160, with bibliography.

[37] Motte 1971:7–10, 161–162.

Moreover, in the *Hymn to Demeter* Korē's narcissus is not said to emerge from a bulb; rather, it grows under the divine influence of Gaia (*Hymn to Demeter* 8–10).[38] The flower, then, not only resembles Typhoeus, but also, in its unconventional growth, the monsters of the *Theogony* more generally.[39]

Homeric flowers, then, possess an irregular fertility that contrasts with the regular successions of human generations or with more regular modes of reproduction; and Hesiodic monsters possess similar qualities. Such associations of flowers with irregular processes and the echoes thereby of monsters in the Hesiodic tradition are in keeping with the concepts that Vernant associates with death in Homeric poetry and elsewhere—both monstrousness and disorder.

What is more, audiences' knowledge of the associations of flowers in Homeric poetry and of monsters in Hesiodic poetry would have encouraged them to see allusions to monstrous disorder in these Homeric images. The irregular fertility of Hesiodic monsters and of Homeric flowers is in both cases associated with challenges to cosmic order. As we found in Part II, the Homeric poets associated spontaneous growths of flowers with threats to cosmic order. And if we follow Clay, in the Hesiodic *Theogony* the uncontrolled procreation of monsters and the disorderly bodies that result threaten the orderliness of the cosmos.[40] These qualities of Homeric flowers and Hesiodic monsters offer a parallel for death's dissolution of the orderliness of life: as Vernant reminds us, death threatens the orderly structures that undergird an individual's identity.

Lastly, I would like to consider the implications of allusions to formlessness and the dissolution of form in Homeric floral imagery. These are likewise consistent with Vernant's description of the monstrousness of death and would have

---

[38] See Chapter 6 above.

[39] Lowe (2015:205) notes both the resemblance of the narcissus to Typhoeus and the association of Typhoeus' body with "monstrous fecundity." For parallels between the wild fertility of Hesiodic monsters and spontaneous generation, see Clay 2003:150 (such monsters "come into being spontaneously in their exuberant disorder") and Lowe 2015:46. See also Motte 1971:12, who observes that the Greeks associated meadows with both spontaneous generation and the monstrous. In a further connection between spontaneity in nature and monstrousness, spontaneous natural processes were believed, like the reproduction of Hesiodic monsters, to have irregular results. Aristotle, for instance, notes the irregular results of spontaneous (αὐτόματος) generation in animals (*Historia Animalium* 539b.7–14). Theophrastus, whose accounts of spontaneous generation we explored in Chapter 6, notes how "monstrosities" (τέρατα) arise from "spontaneous change" (αὐτομάτην ... μεταβολήν) in plants, which can, for instance, result in a given variety exhibiting the fruit of another variety (*Historia Plantarum* 2.3.1–2). See also *De Causis Plantarum* 5.1–4, 7 on the irregular growths of parts of plants.

[40] See Clay 2003:12–30 and 150–161: while other divine generations in the *Theogony* progress from the disorderly couplings of elemental beings to the regularized sexual unions of anthropomorphized gods, monsters continue to reproduce through unconventional means such as incest or spontaneous generation and to combine different categories of being. For monsters' violation of categories, see Carroll 1990 and Cohen 1996:6–12.

supported associations of fertile flowers with such notions: they associate death with a breakdown of order in the body. Moreover, allusions to the loss of identity in those same lines suggest the consequences of this descent into disorder.

For a first example, we might return once more to the description of the death of Gorgythion. If Vernant's findings are valid, we would expect that the allusions to the monstrousness in the poppy image and in the name of the warrior would suggest the dissolution of Gorgythion's identity at the time of his death. And the details of the passage do, indeed, support such notions. Lines 302–305 describe the warrior's living identity—in particular, through his relationship with his father Priam and mother Castianeira. But audiences familiar with Homeric descriptions of the Underworld would have found suggestions of the loss of identity in lines 306–308, with their focus on the heads of the flower and of the dead warrior. If they bore in mind Homeric descriptions of the dead, they would have been able to posit a reason for such a detail: it anticipates Gorgythion's future among the "heads without vigor" (ἀμενηνὰ κάρηνα), which is the most common description of the dead in the Odyssean *Nekyiai* (10.521, 536, 11.29, 49). As we noted in Chapter 8, this formula suggests the insubstantiality of the shades and hence their lack of a definite physical form. And indeed this is the very fate that, according to Vernant, is symbolized by the head of the Gorgon, the monster recalled by Gorgythion's name.

On this reading, then, there is a tension between the two halves of the Gorgythion passage: the first establishes the warrior's living identity; the second looks forward to the loss of the physical form on which his identity depended.[41] And Gorgythion's name provides the pivot between these two themes: his name, like any other name in the *Iliad*, is a mark of his individuality as a living warrior; but at the same time, with its allusion to the Gorgon it anticipates the loss of his individuality in death.

A second Iliadic poppy image, which we have yet to consider, couples references to a dying warrior's head with more explicit allusions to physical dissolution. Near the end of *Iliad* 14, lines reminiscent of the Gorgythion episode describe Peneleos as he slays Ilioneus. They focus firstly on Ilioneus' mother (as do lines 501–505, where Peneleos boasts that mother and son will have no joyful reunion); in this way, as at 8.302–305 these lines establish the identity that Ilioneus enjoyed while he was still alive. But the narrative goes on to place emphasis on the slain warrior's head; and Ilioneus' head is compared with that of a poppy (κώδεια), the only reference to that plant in our versions of the Homeric poems outside *Iliad* 8. Again, for audiences familiar with Homeric descriptions

---

[41] Cf. Kelly's (2007) idea that floral images in this and other Homeric passages suggest "inevitable faceless mortality" (p. 31; cf. pp. 289–290).

of the Underworld the focus on Ilioneus' head would have suggested his future among the anonymous "heads" of the dead.

But while the Gorgythion simile anticipates the warrior's loss of physical form in death, the Ilioneus episode describes the violation of the warrior's physical integrity. Our passage from *Iliad* 14, with its grisly details, focuses insistently on Peneleos' decapitation of Ilioneus. Peneleos drives his spear through his opponent's eye, tears the eyeball away from its roots, pushes the weapon out through Ilioneus' neck, lops off his head, and displays it to the dead man's comrades with the spear-point still thrust through the eye:

ὁ δ' οὔτασεν Ἰλιονῆα

490   υἱὸν Φόρβαντος πολυμήλου, τόν ῥα μάλιστα
      Ἑρμείας Τρώων ἐφίλει καὶ κτῆσιν ὄπασσε·
      τῷ δ' ἄρ' ὑπὸ μήτηρ μοῦνον τέκεν Ἰλιονῆα·
      τὸν τόθ' ὑπ' ὀφρύος οὖτα κατ' ὀφθαλμοῖο θέμεθλα,
      ἐκ δ' ὦσε γλήνην· δόρυ δ' ὀφθαλμοῖο διαπρὸ
495   καὶ διὰ ἰνίου ἦλθεν, ὁ δ' ἕζετο χεῖρε πετάσσας
      ἄμφω. Πηνέλεως δὲ ἐρυσσάμενος ξίφος ὀξὺ
      αὐχένα μέσσον ἔλασσεν, ἀπήραξεν δὲ χαμᾶζε
      αὐτῇ σὺν πήληκι κάρη· ἔτι δ' ὄβριμον ἔγχος
      ἦεν ἐν ὀφθαλμῷ· ὁ δὲ <u>φὴ κώδειαν</u> ἀνασχὼν
500   πέφραδέ τε Τρώεσσι...

Iliad 14.489–500

and he wounded Ilioneus

490   the son of Phorbas of the many flocks, whom most of
      all the Trojans Hermes loved and granted possessions;
      to him the mother bore Ilioneus alone;
      [Peneleos] wounded him under the eyebrow through the roots of the
          eye,
      and pushed out the eyeball; the spear went
495   right through the eye and through the neck, and he sat down
          spreading
      both hands. And Peneleos drawing his sharp sword
      drove it through the middle of the neck, and he struck off the head
      onto the ground, helmet and all; but the mighty spear
      was still in the eye; and holding it up <u>like a poppy-head</u> [κώδειαν]
500   he showed it to the Trojans ...

While Gorgythion's head remains attached to his body, Peneleos severs Ilioneus' head from his trunk. His action hastens the disintegration of Ilioneus' dead body, its loss of form and orderliness. Peneleos then displays the head to the Trojans as a symbol of the monstrousness of the deaths that he intends to inflict on them. In *Odyssey* 11 the thought of the Gorgon's severed head instills a fear of death in Odysseus and causes him to flee the Underworld. Similarly, at *Iliad* 14.506–507 the Trojans take fright at Peneleos' grisly trophy and seek to escape the doom that it promises: τοὺς δ' ἄρα πάντας ὑπὸ τρόμος ἔλλαβε γυῖα, / πάπτηνεν δὲ ἕκαστος ὅπη φύγοι αἰπὺν ὄλεθρον ("trembling overcame the limbs of all of them, / and each man looked where he might flee sheer doom"). The Trojans, then, experience the kind of horror that Vernant associates with reactions to the monstrousness of death, exhibited by characters such as Odysseus.[42]

Vernant's notion of the monstrous disorder of death is, moreover, consistent with the themes of the Odyssean floral images that we studied in Chapter 8. As with the Gorgythion and Ilioneus episodes, Circe in her depiction of the Sirens' victims focuses firstly on their identities as living men and then passes on to a description of their deaths. Allusions to the relationships of Gorgythion and Ilioneus with their mothers at *Iliad* 8.304–305 and 14.492 help to establish the identities of those warriors. The identities of the Sirens' victims are likewise defined with reference to their familial ties: as Circe warns Odysseus, whoever is beguiled by the Sirens' songs, his wife and children will not welcome him home (*Odyssey* 12.42–43). Circe goes on to place special emphasis on the dissolution of the individuality of those on the Sirens' island. In place of living men, the Sirens' meadow hosts a heap of rotting flesh and bones (45–46). Ilioneus' body is dismembered by Peneleos; but in *Odyssey* 12 Circe offers a more thoroughgoing image of physical dissolution. It is no longer possible even to tell one body from the next, such is their state of decay.

The description of the asphodel meadow at *Odyssey* 24.13–14 also accords with the notions of the loss of individuality and the dissolution of form. At that point, the dead souls who inhabit the meadow are described as "images of the dead" (εἴδωλα καμόντων, 14). And the notion of the εἴδωλον is closely associated with that of insubstantiality. When Odysseus is unable to embrace the shade of his mother, he wonders if Persephone has sent him only an image (εἴδωλον, 11.213) of her. But Anticleia explains that such is the state of souls after death: their bodies dissolve and the soul flits away to the Underworld (219–222). And as noted in Chapter 8, the Homeric poets' choice of a meadow of asphodel, which from a distance would possess a grayish hue, would have offered audiences another way to conceptualize the insubstantiality of the souls. Such a depiction of the souls accords with Vernant's exploration of the monstrousness of death:

---

[42] See also the description of the suitor's "green fear" of death at *Odyssey* 22.42, which is followed by a line identical to *Iliad* 14.507: "each cast about to see where he might flee sheer destruction" (πάπτηνεν δὲ ἕκαστος ὅπη φύγοι αἰπὺν ὄλεθρον, 43).

their insubstantiality reflects the loss of the bodily form that was essential to their identities as living men and women. If Odysseus tarries in the Underworld, he risks losing his physical integrity to the sight of the Gorgon's mask and thereby also his identity. He would become like the insubstantial souls of the asphodel meadow.

* * *

In this chapter and the last, we have laid bare the associations of the Homeric floral imagery of death and have gained a sense of its contributions to the depiction of death in the relevant passages. The allusions to exceptional fertility in these scenes create a parallel both with the characteristics of flowers in the Greek natural environment and with the depiction of monsters in the Hesiodic tradition. And given that both Hesiodic monsters and Homeric flowers are associated with a wild, disorderly fertility, these Homeric images were able to evoke the dissolution of the orderliness on which an individual's living identity depends. Such notions are reinforced by allusions to formlessness and the dissolution of form in the relevant passages. Vernant's work on the monstrous otherness of death helps us to understand the connections between these different concepts. With this rich network of associations, the Homeric poets offered a glimpse of death as a chaotic horror, of its negation of all the orderliness of life.[43] A dying warrior passed into a state of formlessness and disorder, monstrously at variance with the living identity that he had once enjoyed.

---

[43] On Homeric death, horror, and the natural world, see also Redfield 1994:103. According to Redfield, the Iliadic hero steps outside the bounds of civilization to face death in the realm of nature: "For the warrior, culture appears as a translucent screen against the terror of nature."

Conclusion

OVER THE COURSE OF THIS BOOK, we have gained a sense of the particular choices made by the Homeric poets in forming their vegetal images. We have seen that the relevant images draw on some of the most striking characteristics of the Greek flora—the sudden, exceptionally diverse blooms of the Greek spring. And by accessing these phenomena, the Homeric poets were able to draw their listeners' attention to particular aspects of eroticism, order, disorder, and death, and to enhance their understanding of these abstract notions. But none of these choices were forced on the Homeric poets: other archaic poets focused on rather different characteristics of the Greek flora and on different facets of the relevant concepts.

In my concluding remarks, I would like to focus not only on the particular conceptions of eroticism, the cosmos, society, and death facilitated by the Homeric poets' interactions with the natural environment, but also on the place of such conceptions within the wider Homeric corpus. In particular, I shall show that both these images and the Homeric poems more generally offer pessimistic treamtents of these themes. When we survey the concepts that the Homeric poets illustrated with their vegetal images, we might well be struck by their negativity: the vegetal images of other genres celebrate beauty, order-liness, and the joys of youth; but alongside evocations of orderly societies or the strength of warriors, Homeric vegetal images explore deception, disorder, and the monstrousness of death. And the emphasis in these different images on more negative concepts is indicative of the preoccupations of Homeric poetry as a genre: it suggests an interest in the darker aspects of human experience.

The negative tendencies of Homeric poetry as opposed to other genres can be seen in the Homeric poets' treatments of erotic themes. Greek lyric poets explore the beauty of the beloved or the pleasure of erotic encounters. But their Homeric counterparts often portray erotic relationships as unfulfilled, interrupted or otherwise imperfect, and at times these relationships are even a danger to one or other of the partners. The Epic Cycle opens with a wedding—that of Peleus and Thetis—but the event is notable primarily for the intrusion of the goddess Strife, which has dire consequences for mortals: she provokes the quarrel between Athena, Hera, and Aphrodite that leads to the Judgement of Paris, the abduction of Helen, and the Trojan War.[1] In the *Iliad*, Helen and Paris are the only mortal couple whose lovemaking is so much as anticipated: after Aphrodite rescues Paris from the battlefield, she insists that Helen join him in their bedchamber. But Helen's initial resistance to Aphrodite's wishes and her verbal abuse of her new husband sour the occasion (3.383–447). Andromache and Hector, who seem to enjoy a more harmonious relationship, are allowed to meet only once and for the last time as Hector prepares to return to battle (6.390–502).[2]

The *Homeric Hymns* offer a similarly jaundiced portrait of erotic relationships. At *Hymn to Aphrodite* 218–238, for example, the love of the mortal Tithonus and the divine Dawn devolves into a kind of grim comedy: Tithonus wastes away until he cannot move, and Dawn confines her ageing lover to a bedroom, where he babbles away unceasingly (233–238). Aphrodite's own brief relationship with Anchises is from her perspective a source of "dreadful ... pain" (αἰνὸν... ἄχος, 198), which she will commemorate in the name of their son, Aeneas (Αἰνείας, 198). Anchises for his part fears that he will be left "without vigor" from his encounter with a goddess (ἀμενηνόν, 188).[3]

The Homeric floral imagery of the erotic accords with the negative cast of these examples. In Homeric poetry, the alluring surface of erotic bodies associated with flowers conceals the regular appearance of the body in question or hides dangers to which the lover will be exposed. This seems to have unwelcome implications for the nature of erotic encounters. If they are like this, one can never be entirely sure of the identity of one's beloved, nor whether the consequences of such an encounter will be pleasurable or even confined to the sphere of the erotic. By contrast, in archaic Greek lyric, the lover's gaze dominates and safely evaluates the beloved who is associated with flowers (Part I).

Such a distinction, as we have seen, is dependent on two different interactions with the natural environment. Greek lyric poets reminded audiences of the experience of gazing on flowers and judging them beautiful, and thereby illustrated the beauty of erotic bodies, seen from the perspective of

---

[1] See Proclus' summary of the *Cypria* at Bernabé 1996:38–39 lines 4–11. For the Trojan War as a consequence of the Judgement of Paris, see Chapter 2.

[2] Sappho, by contrast, celebrates the wedding of Hector and Andromache (fr. 44 Voigt). This event may not have featured in the Epic Cycle: it is not mentioned in Proclus' summary of the cyclic poems. And the *Iliad* refers to it only in connection with Andromache's widowhood: *Iliad* 22.470–472.

[3] See Chapter 3 above.

the first-person speaker. Their Homeric counterparts, by contrast, drew on the shifting, ποικίλος surfaces of flowers in the Greek spring to suggest the deceptive qualities of bodies decked out for seduction.

Similarly, the Homeric poets incorporate negative elements into their depictions of the cosmos or of human societies. And the relevant passages depart from the treatments of such themes in other genres—if not in their degree of pessimism, then certainly in the kinds of negative elements that they introduce. This becomes clear when we compare Homeric and Hesiodic treatments of order and disorder. The Hesiodic tradition more closely approaches its Homeric counterpart in its handling of those concepts than do other poetic genres in their treatment of the other themes that have formed the focus of this study.[4] And yet the Hesiodic and Homeric poems display different emphases both in their general treatments of order and disorder and in the vegetal images that they use to illustrate those themes.

The Homeric poets depicted a generally stable cosmos, but also suggested that cosmic order was subject to changes and challenges. In the *Homeric Hymns*, Zeus' rulership over the cosmos is well established. But as Jenny Strauss Clay has shown, the hymns explore changes to cosmic order and to the relationships between different gods.[5] The Homeric epics depict a more settled cosmos, likewise governed by Zeus; nonetheless, the good order over which he presides is disturbed by the bickering, intrigue, and insubordination of willful gods and goddesses. In the *Iliad*, Hera accepts Zeus' will only grudgingly and, along with Poseidon, seeks to undermine her husband's plan to favor the Trojans on the battlefield. In the *Odyssey*, Poseidon once more provides a counterweight to Zeus' will: he opposes Zeus' and Athena's plans to return Odysseus to his homeland.[6] The subversive actions of certain divinities, then, provide a point of resistance to Zeus and to the cosmic order that he guarantees, even if they lack the power to overthrow it.

The good order of human societies is likewise subject to challenge in Homeric poetry, and these challenges are if anything more significant than their equivalents on the divine level. Achilles' quarrel with Agamemnon in Book 1 threatens to undermine the political structure of the Achaean camp. Like Zeus, Agamemnon retains his supremacy throughout the *Iliad*; but Achilles' insubordination poses a more serious challenge to his king's position than Hera's

---

[4] As mentioned in the Preamble to Part II, previous studies have explored such intersections between the two genres: Yasumura (2011) identifies similar treatments of divine rebellion in Hesiodic and Homeric poetry; Clay (2003, 2006) traces a continuum from the *Theogony*'s explorations of order and disorder to those of the *Homeric Hymns* and major epics.

[5] Clay 2006.

[6] For Zeus' plans in the *Odyssey* and for the manner in which he responds to Poseidon's opposition, see Marks 2008.

subversive intentions pose to Zeus. Hera lulls Zeus to sleep in the Διὸς ἀπάτη, but he is able quickly to reassert his dominance over her and to regain control of events on earth. Agamemnon, however, is unable to persuade Achilles to rejoin the fighting, even with the promise of lavish gifts (Book 9). It is grief for Patroclus rather than any inducements from Agamemnon that finally convinces him to return to the action. And while Achilles does not choose to overthrow the political structure of the Achaean camp, the *Odyssey* describes just such revolutionary change on Ithaca. The depredations of the suitors and their constant presence in Odysseus' palace have to some extent flattened the hierarchical structure of Ithacan society: a single royal family no longer holds sway over the other nobles, and servants such as Melanthius and Melantho have seized the opportunity to advance their interests at the expense of their former lords.[7]

Hesiodic poetry likewise explores challenges and changes to cosmic and civic order. The *Theogony* depicts Cronus' violent overthrow of Heaven and Zeus' of Cronus, and goes on to describe Zeus' battles against the unruly Titans and Typhoeus. The wild disorder of the Catalogue of Monsters threatens any sense of good order in the cosmos or even of the succession from one divine generation to the next.[8] And just as forces of disorder are present in the cosmos of the *Theogony*, the *Works and Days* incorporates both orderly and disorderly elements into its depictions of human society. The poem describes not only the flourishing of the just city but also the lawless violence of the Age of Iron. And it opens with the narrator's complaints about the unjust behavior of his brother Perses: he is attempting to ingratiate himself with the venal barons who hold sway in the narrator's society, hoping thus to lay claim to a greater share of the brothers' common inheritance (*Works and Days* 37–39).[9]

Nevertheless, the explorations of order and disorder in Homeric and Hesiodic poetry show differences in emphasis. In Homeric poetry, the resistance of the gods to Zeus' will is a constant theme. The Hesiodic *Theogony*'s tales of cosmic strife, mentioned above, are more serious than anything that we find in the Homeric corpus. But the poem goes on to depict the increasing solidification of Zeus' dominance, which is accompanied by increasing orderliness in the

---

[7] See 17.212–253 (Melanthius assaults the disguised Odysseus and wishes Telemachus dead); 20.177–182 (he threatens his disguised king); 22.135–146 (he brings arms to the suitors, in full knowledge that Odysseus has returned); 18.320–325 (Melantho cares nothing for Penelope, despite the queen's kindness to her as a child); 18.326–336, 19.65–69 (she berates the disguised Odysseus).

[8] In Part III, we found that the Homeric poets drew on such Hesiodic themes in their explorations of the monstrous disorder of death.

[9] On the themes of justice and injustice in the *Works and Days*, cf. Erbse 1993, Nelson 1997, Beall 2005/2006, Mordine 2006.

cosmos—even if perfect order is never achieved. By the end of the *Theogony*, we have the sense that Zeus has overcome serious resistance to his rule. He is able to distribute honors to his fellow gods (*Theogony* 881–885) and thus to assert control over their spheres of influence.[10]

Zeus encounters further opposition after this distribution of divine honors; but the dangers that he faces are not as grave as those associated with the Titans or Typhoeus. Among the tales of heroes in the *Catalogue of Women*, we hear of the unruly Salmoneus, who drives cauldrons behind his chariot in an attempt "to be Zeus" (Julian *Oratio* 7.235a/*Catalogue of Women* fr. 15 MW);[11] presumably, he is imitating the sound and light of Zeus' thunderbolt. And yet Salmoneus' challenge is at most a parody of the severe threat posed in the *Theogony* by characters such as Typhoeus, who "would have ruled mortals and immortals" had Zeus not intervened (*Theogony* 837–838). In fact, only in one episode of the *Catalogue of Women* does a divinity challenge Zeus' will. Apollo responds violently when Zeus slays his son, Asclepius (*Catalogue of Women* frr. 51–54(c) MW): he kills the Cyclopes who in the Hesiodic tradition are the manufacturers of the thunderbolt (*Theogony* 141), the very weapon with which Zeus smites Asclepius. But even in this case, Apollo strikes at Zeus' minions rather than at the king of the gods himself.

The *Works and Days* explores the injustices of the current Age of Iron and offers baleful predictions for its moral decline and ultimate destruction by Zeus (*Works and Days* 182–194). Nevertheless, the poem does not describe the sorts of threats to societal order that we find in the Homeric poems. Neither insurrection nor other forms of political instability are major themes of the *Works and Days*. The narrator does not portray dissension among the ranks of the barons who rule the narrator's society: there is no equivalent, then, of the wrangling of Achilles and Agamemnon in the *Iliad*.

And the Hesiodic poets do not offer a parallel for the political situation of *Odyssey* Books 13–21, where the actions of the suitors and of their favorite servants threaten to confuse distinctions between the strata of Ithacan society. If Zeus reacts to the barons' injustice (*Works and Days* 248–269), this does not seem to entail a change in societal structure: he punishes the common people alongside their lords (260–262), and a whole city suffers for the injustice of one bad man (238–247). It does not appear, then, that the people will be able to seize power from their former lords. Nor does the narrator associate his disturbing prophecy for the future of the Iron Race with political upheaval. The Iron Race will be remarkable for its violence and disloyalty, which will lead to the breakdown of familial attachments and of the guest-host relationship. But this is to

---

[10] For such a teleological reading of the *Theogony*, see Clay 2003:12–30.
[11] See also *Catalogue of Women* fr. 30 MW; cf. [Apollodorus] *Library* 1.9.7.

speak only of personal ties: the passage in question does not describe the dissolution of distinctions between the different classes that make up Iron Age society.

The two genres also differ in their use of vegetal images to illustrate such themes. Both the Homeric and the Hesiodic poets associated arboreal growths with good order, whether in the city or the cosmos. But the Homeric poets also drew on natural phenomena to explore the more disorderly elements in civic and cosmic structures. They associated challenges to cosmic order with the apparently spontaneous growth of Greek flowers. And the contrast between the explosive floral growths of the Greek spring and the steadier, more constant growths of trees offered the Homeric poets a way to illustrate the twin concepts of cosmic order and disorder. Those same poets, moreover, cast light on the tensions between forces of civic order and disorder through reference to wild growths and to the managed vegetation that listeners would have encountered in the natural world and in the plantations near human settlements. And while the Hesiodic poets associated wild growths of trees with the flourishing city-state, their Homeric counterparts, in describing the restoration of order on Ithaca, focused specifically on trees governed by the techniques of arboriculture. They thereby suggested that civic order, which was open to challenge from unruly elements, could only be maintained by the careful management of a king.

Which of these explorations of the cosmos and of human society a listener or reader finds more negative will depend on the particular elements of the two genres that s/he chooses to emphasize. The Hesiodic poets offered harrowing tales of cosmic strife; but they also depicted an increasing orderliness in the cosmos, and with their vegetal imagery they emphasized stable structures and flourishing cities. The Homeric poets did not focus on the sorts of tales of cosmic revolution that we find early in the *Theogony*; however, both in the stories that they told and in their vegetal images they stressed constant tensions between forces of order and disorder. Suffice it to say that in their explorations of such themes both Homeric and Hesiodic poetry offer ample justifications for pessimistic readings.

Homeric vegetal images, then, offer negative portraits of the erotic and of civic and cosmic structures, which are in harmony with the Homeric poems' generally pessimistic treatments of such concepts: in the one case, deception mingles with beauty; in the other, disorderly undercurrents pose a challenge to the good order of the cosmos or the city. And these negative elements lend a somewhat darker tone to the relevant passages than would otherwise be the case. But some of the darkest aspects of Homeric poetry are to be found in its descriptions of death in war, many of which focus on the horrors of the battlefield. Again, such a tone is consistent with the associations of Homeric vegetal images: as we have seen, Homeric floral images portray death as a monstrous horror.

In arguing for the importance of horror to Homeric depictions of death, I depart from the findings of a number of other scholars, who have discussed death in the *Iliad* and in the Homeric corpus more generally in terms of tragedy or pathos: and tragedy, though in itself a dark analog to comedy, does not offer so grim an aesthetic as horror. For Jasper Griffin, the *Iliad* depicts the greatness of heroes but also explores the tragic gap between their short lives and the easy existence of the gods. James Redfield draws on Aristotle's definition of tragedy in reading the *Iliad* as "the tragedy of Hector." Yoav Rinon likewise views the *Iliad* as a tragedy in the Aristotelian sense, but applies such an analysis also to the *Odyssey*.[12]

In the concluding section of a book, it is not the place to offer an extensive analysis of the nature of tragedy and horror. But if we are to apply those concepts to the Homeric poems, we should, at least, prepare for such a discussion by noting some of the key distinctions between them. I would like to focus on two important respects in which horrific description, whether in Homeric poetry or elsewhere, departs from Aristotelian notions of the tragic.

The first concerns the emotions that are evoked. Tragedy on an Aristotelian definition elicits both pity and fear from its audiences. We feel pity for someone experiencing misfortune insofar as s/he does not deserve their suffering, and we experience fear insofar as s/he is like ourselves (*Poetics* 1453a3–6). Presumably, we fear that the same might happen to us, given that we resemble the person suffering. Horrific description by contrast elicits only the emotion of fear, and that to a particularly heightened degree.

Secondly, while for Aristotle our feelings of kinship with the tragic hero rest on an appreciation of her/his character (ἦθος), the same could not be said of any such feelings of kinship elicited by horrific description. To the extent that such description does portray an individual's thoughts and emotions, they are frequently reduced to simple terror. And this does not so much provide a basis for sympathetic identification with the victim's suffering as offer a model for listeners' and readers' own reactions. Feelings of kinship with the victim arise not from an appreciation of her/his character, but from reminders of the sheer material facts of the human body, which are emphasized in depictions of the victim's physical degradation: horrific description focuses on blood, flesh, bone, and physical dissolution, and thus invites us to recognize our own corporeality.[13]

---

[12] Griffin 1980, esp. 81–143; Redfield 1994; Rinon 2008; cf. Liebert 2017 on the tragic emotions of the *Iliad*. For Aristotle (*Poetics* 1459b8–17), the Homeric epics follow the same overall forms and are made up of the same components as tragedies, with the exceptions of lyric song and spectacle.

[13] For the focus on the material facts of death in the *Iliad*, cf. Weil 1965. See also Marg 1976:10: "it is characteristic of the *Iliad* that it lets battle speak for itself factually and without pathos so that its basic character, death, shows forth" ("die Ilias eigentümlich sachlich und unpathetisch den

We fear being reduced to these material facts; we fear that we are or will soon be nothing more than them.[14]

It is true that not every one of the Homeric descriptions of death points in the direction of horror: some passages would indeed have encouraged listeners to view them as tragic or pathetic. We noted in Chapter 8 that critics have read Iliadic vegetal images as evocations of a world of peace that introduce notes of pathos to the depiction of warriors' deaths. As we have seen, such notions do not, in fact, dominate the floral and arboreal imagery of the *Iliad*. Nevertheless, it is perfectly possible to find pathos in some of these images: for instance, the focus on Simoeisius' chest and the suggestion of his smooth trunk at 4.480–486 would have invited listeners to sympathize with this young warrior at the time of his death.

Moreover, the depictions of the gods as they witness the battles of the *Iliad* to some extent coincide with Aristotle's descriptions of tragic audiences. The gods do not experience fear when they contemplate mortal suffering. And on an Aristotelian definition of tragedy, this is exactly as we would expect: the gods cannot suffer the same afflictions as mortals and therefore do not fear that the same misfortunes will happen to them. But despite the gulf between mortal and immortal existence, the gods experience the Aristotelian emotion of pity as they witness the events at Troy.[15] For instance, when Hector's corpse is mistreated by Achilles, the gods "pitied him as they looked on" (τὸν δ᾽ ἐλεαίρεσκον … εἰσορόωντες, 24.23).[16] On an Aristotelian reading, such reactions would have provided a model for listeners' own reactions as they contemplated the scene. And indeed, if audiences were inclined to feel pity when they witnessed undeserved suffering, Hector might seem most of all to be worthy of such emotions: in his desire simply to defend his kinsfolk, he appears to deserve such a shameful fate least of all the warriors at Troy.[17]

Kampf für sich sprechen läßt, so daß er bis auf seinen Grundcharakter, das Töten, durchsichtig wird"). For the association of horror with bodily materiality, cf. Kristeva 1982 on the excreta of the living body and the corpse.

[14] Despite the fact that Griffin and Redfield emphasize the tragic aspects of the *Iliad*, both also identify elements of horror in the epic: see Redfield 1994:179–186 on the horror surrounding the unburied body and its materiality. Griffin, however (1980:19–21, 45–47), argues that such elements are downplayed in the *Iliad*, as opposed to other early epic traditions.

[15] For the pity of the Iliadic gods and for their function as a tragic audience, see Griffin 1980:195–196.

[16] Cf. the description of Apollo's motives for preserving Hector's corpse: φῶτ᾽ ἐλεαίρων / καὶ τεθνηότα περ ("pitying the mortal, / even though he was dead" 24.19–20). For the gods' feelings of pity, see also 8.350, 15.12, 44, 16.431, 19.340, 24.332.

[17] Nevertheless, before his mistreatment at the hands of Achilles, Hector is actively involved in the horrors of the Iliadic battlefield. Of all the warriors at Troy, he has a particular association with the madness that descends on a warrior. At 8.299, Teucer likens Hector to a "mad dog" (κύνα λυσσητῆρα), and a little later in Book 8 Hector "ha[s] the eyes of the Gorgon and of Ares, bane of

Certain of the *Odyssey*'s descriptions of death are also consistent with the notions of tragedy and pathos. In the Underworld, for instance, Odysseus employs the same formulaic line to describe his feelings as he beholds the shades of Elpenor, Anticleia, and Agamemnon: τὸν/τὴν μὲν ἐγὼ δάκρυσα ἐλέησά τε θυμῷ ("I wept and pitied him/her in my heart," 11.55, 87, 395). Audiences might have shared Odysseus' emotions as they contemplated the state to which these characters have been reduced.

Listeners were not, however, compelled to regard these passages as tragic. They were free to pass up the opportunity for sympathetic identification with Odysseus in his grief: in particular, they might have borne in mind the rather comic end of Elpenor—he falls drunkenly from Circe's roof (10.551–562)—or the somewhat negative portrayal of Agamemnon in the Homeric poems.[18] And indeed, as we have seen other aspects of the Odyssean *Nekyiai* invite very different reactions to the concept of death, founded on the notion of monstrous horror.

Nor are such horrific elements confined to the Odyssean *Nekyiai*: we find similar portrayals of death in many other episodes of Homeric poetry. Such passages are particularly common in Iliadic battle narrative. The very first description of the Iliadic battlefield mentions the personified emotions Terror and Fear (Deimos and Phobos) and the ground flowing with blood (*Iliad* 4.439–451). Later passages echo the gore of these lines: the battlefield is awash with blood also at 8.65, 15.715, and 20.494; blood, dust, and corpses are said to litter the battlefield at 11.534, 15.118, and 20.499.[19] Such details create a macabre atmosphere in the relevant scenes.[20] What is more, the presence of Terror and Fear on the battlefield at 4.439–451 suggests a possible response to this and other such passages: listeners will experience horror at these gruesome descriptions.

And we find further support for such readings in other passages from the *Iliad*, which likewise incorporate horrific elements into their descriptions of death. This is especially true of Books 13–16 and 20–21, which cover important stretches of battle narrative. Books 13–16 tell the story of the Trojan ascendancy that climaxes with the attack on the Greek ships and then describe the bloody

---

mortals" (Γοργοῦς ὄμματ' ἔχων ἠδὲ βροτολοιγοῦ Ἄρηος, 8.349; see Chapter 9). For Hector's war-madness, see also 9.237–239, 305, 13.53, 15.605–610.

[18] For the negative depictions of Agamemnon, see *Iliad* 1 and 19: he insists on exact compensation for the loss of Chryseis and then deflects blame for his error onto the goddess Delusion. See also Murnaghan 1987 on Agamemnon's misogyny in the *Odyssey*, which distinguishes him from other male characters.

[19] For blood, dust, and corpses on the Iliadic battlefield, see also 11.163–164, 13.393, 16.486, 639–640, 795–796, 17.360–363, 18.538–540.

[20] See Marg (1976:9) on *Iliad* 4.439–451: "Das Bild ist duster und grausig ... Unheimlich ist die Atmosphäre des Schlachtfeldes" ("The image is dark and gruesome ... . The atmosphere of the battlefield is uncanny").

career of Patroclus, which reverses the tide of battle. In the course of these events. we hear of victims' eyes falling out of their sockets (13.615–617, 16.739–750) and of a spear vibrating in a warrior's still-beating heart (13.442–444). The horrors of Peneleos' encounter with Ilioneus (14.489–500) fit this pattern: Peneleos decapitates his opponent and displays the head to his comrades, with the eye still impaled on the spearpoint.[21] The epic reaches a second peak of horror with the account of Achilles' *aristeia* in Books 20 and 21, which dwells on the death and dissolution of his opponents. Tros' liver slips out, and his lap fills with blood (20.469–471); Asteropaeus dies, and the eels and fish busy themselves about the fat on his kidneys (21.203–204). And as a result of the carnage in Book 21, blood and corpses clog the river Scamander (218–220).[22]

What is more, although there are undeniably tragic aspects to Hector's demise the savagery with which Achilles treats his corpse introduces elements of horror that threaten to overmaster the tenderer emotion of pity.[23] Indeed, as Charles Segal has shown, Achilles' treatment of Hector's corpse marks a climactic moment in the *Iliad*'s exploration of bodily degradation. Earlier passages raise the possibility that a warrior's body might suffer further abuse even after his death. Glaucus, for instance, fears that "the Myrmidons will shame the corpse" of Sarpedon (ἀεικίσσωσι δὲ νεκρὸν / Μυρμιδόνες, 16.545–546). But here the possibility is actualized. Achilles bores through the tendons of Hector's feet and drags him behind his chariot (22.395–404).[24] Achilles' actions draw attention away from Hector's desert or lack thereof and onto the sheer materiality of his body: they threaten to make him a figure of horror as opposed to tragedy. It is, perhaps, in this sense that we should understand Apollo's words at 24.44: Ἀχιλεὺς ἔλεον … ἀπώλεσεν, "Achilles has killed pity."[25]

Evidence from the *Odyssey* leads us to similar conclusions: when the epic focuses on death, it indulges in horrific description. We have already noted Circe's description of the "heap / of rotting men" that decorates the Sirens' island (θὶς / ἀνδρῶν πυθομένων, 12.45–46). Horrors likewise attend Odysseus' description of the Cyclops. The monster soaks the ground with the blood and brains of Odysseus' companions as he consumes their bodies (9.290–295). Later, Athena manipulates the appearance of Odysseus' halls in such a way as to anticipate the grisly consequences of the suitors' feasting: "they were laughing with another's jaws, / and were eating meat daubed with blood" (γναθμοῖσι γελώων

---

[21] See Chapter 9 for discussion of this passage.

[22] On the horror of the events in Book 21, see Segal 1971:30–32.

[23] Cf. Nietzsche 1980:784: Achilles' mistreatment of Hector's corpse is "für uns etwas … Grausen Einflößendes" ("for us something that inspires horror").

[24] Segal 1971.

[25] For horror in the *Iliad*, see also Strasburger (1954), who identifies pathos in the poem's portrayals of death alongside a focus on the gruesomeness and inevitability of death.

ἀλλοτρίοισιν / αἱμοφόρυκτα δὲ δὴ κρέα ἤσθιον, 20.347–348). And the prophet Theoclymenus responds with a macabre vision of his own: he imagines walls sprinkled with blood, and night spreading over the hall (351–357).

Shortly afterwards, Odysseus slaughters the suitors amid scenes replete with gore. Indeed, the descriptions of the suitors' deaths recall the grim details of Iliadic battle. When Odysseus slays Antinous "a thick stream of human blood passed through his nostrils" (αὐλὸς ἀνὰ ῥῖνας παχὺς ἦλθεν / αἵματος ἀνδρομέοιο, 22.18–19). Moving on to Eurymachus, Odysseus pierces his chest and fixes an arrow in his liver (83). And like the Iliadic battlefield, the hall is spattered with blood from the slaughter. At line 309, "all the floor was seething with blood" (δάπεδον δ' ἅπαν αἵματι θῦε) and by lines 383–384 the suitors lie together "in the blood and dust" (ἐν αἵματι καὶ κονίῃσι).[26]

Other details in the scene likewise suggest horror rather than tragedy. The suitors are killed to a man, and no distinction is made between those who deserve their fate and those who might not.[27] Amphinomus had earlier received the most sympathetic portrait of any of the suitors, but his death is described like that of the much less pleasant Eurymachus:[28] both die after rushing at Odysseus (22.79–94). Our sympathies are not, then, directed towards the undeserved suffering of particular individuals, which might elicit the Aristotelian emotion of pity. And in place of pity, the narrative emphasizes the emotion of fear: "green fear seized" the suitors as they realized that their death was at hand (χλωρὸν δέος ἕλε, 42). Indeed this phrase, as we saw in Chapter 9, has a particular association in Homeric poetry with the monstrous horror of death. Placed early in Book 22, it establishes the atmosphere for the coming slaughter. And as with the allusion to Terror and Fear in the first description of the Iliadic battlefield, it would have suggested to audiences the kind of reaction appropriate to such gruesome scenes.

A number of the Homeric descriptions of death, then, point not in the direction of tragedy but towards horror. They lay emphasis on the emotion of fear and on the material realities of death. We hear of Terror on the Iliadic battlefield and of the "green fear" of the suitors; we witness the corpses on the battlefield and on the floor of Odysseus' halls; we are presented with the blood, bones, and flesh of violated or decaying bodies.

---

[26] Cf. 22.401–402: Eurycleia "found Odysseus among the dead bodies, / spattered with blood and filth" (εὗρεν... Ὀδυσῆα μετὰ κταμένοισι νέκυσσιν, / αἵματι καὶ λύθρῳ πεπαλαγμένον).

[27] The only characters to be spared, the herald Medon and the bard Phemius, do not number among the suitors.

[28] The characters of Amphinomus and Eurymachus are clearly distinguished from each other in Book 18 through their behavior towards the disguised Odysseus. Amphinomus provides him with food (118–123), but Eurymachus throws a stool at him (387–397).

And it is precisely such concepts that are the focus of the Homeric floral imagery of death and of its particular responses to the Greek natural environment. The poets of the elegiac tradition drew on the brevity of floral blooms in their celebrations of the brief joys of youth. Their Homeric counterparts drew on qualities that flowers shared with monsters in early Greek poetry—many-headedness or a disorderly fertility—to illustrate the monstrous horror of death. The relevant passages, moreover, associate death's monstrous otherness with the negation of the order on which a warrior's living identity depended, and in particular with the dissolution of the physical orderliness of his body. This latter concept is explored not only in Homeric floral images, but also in the horrific descriptions of woundings, of blood coursing through the battlefield, and of decaying corpses that we find in the Homeric poems.

We have seen, then, that the Homeric poets were able to draw on the striking suddenness and proliferation of Greek spring blooms to aid their audiences' understanding of a number of striking concepts. They conjured up images not so much of a floral beauty that, though brief, might still be enjoyed, but of darker notions, such as sudden disappearance, unruly growths, and monstrous profusion. These guided their audiences' conceptions of deceptive surfaces, of insurrection, and of the monstrousness of death. And in turn such images, together with the concepts introduced by them, directed listeners towards darker perspectives on the world and towards the more pessimistic principles on which they were founded: uncertainty, instability, horror.

Plate 1. Spring blooms at the ancient site of Epidaurus, 30 March 2015.
Photo by the author.

Plate 2. Spring blooms at the ancient site of Eleusis, 31 March 2015.
Photo by the author.

Plate 3. Spring bloom on the slopes of the ancient site of
Mycenae, 10 March 2009.
Photo by the author.

Plate 4. *Narcissus tazetta ssp. lacticolor* found at Thebes, from the
herbarium of the Royal Botanical Gardens, Kew.
Photo by the author.

Plate 5. The sanctuary of Apollo and adjacent buildings on Delos, 1 April 2015.
Photo by the author.

Plate 6. The banks of the Scamander north of Ezine, August 30 2008.
Photo by Gebhard Bieg, Troia Project, University of Tübingen.

Appendix
The Semantics of ἄνθος and ἀνθέω

A number of the passages discussed in this book incorporate the noun ἄνθος, which is commonly translated "flower."[1] Linguists have however expressed doubts over the semantics of the lexeme: some have suggested that it originally carried a more abstract meaning, such as "surface" or "that which bursts forth." Therefore, in spite of the usual renderings of ἄνθος by translators, we need to address this controversy if we are to be confident that the relevant Homeric images do indeed refer to flowers.

As we shall see, there are in fact good reasons to endorse more conventional translations of ἄνθος in Homeric poetry. Comparative evidence from other Indo-European languages suggests that the archaic Greek term derived from an earlier Proto-Indo-European root with a floral meaning; and the internal evidence of the Homeric poems offers us still stronger reasons to accept such a meaning for the Homeric noun. While the equivalent verbal root may possess a more general meaning, the primary reference of the Homeric noun ἄνθος is to the concrete concept of "flower(s)."

What is more, George Lakoff's, Mark Johnson's and Mark Turner's analyses of metaphor—and more specifically of the manner in which concrete concepts can be used to explain the more abstract—help us to understand how more abstract connotations of ἄνθος, such as "surface" or "that which bursts forth," might have developed.[2] Given that the lexeme referred to flowers in the Greek natural environment, it was also able to evoke more abstract qualities associated with such flowers—the bright *surfaces* of flowers in spring or early summer, or the flowers that *burst forth* at those times. In this way, the ground was prepared

---

[1] For a second Homeric lexeme commonly translated "flower," the *hapax* θρόνα (*Iliad* 22.441), see Chapter 3 n7.

[2] Lakoff and Johnson 2003; Lakoff and Turner 1989. For discussion of their theories, see my Introduction.

for later, purely metaphorical usages of ἄνθος: it was a relatively easy step for classical authors such as Aeschylus and Pindar to use the noun to evoke surfaces or irruptions more generally.

A number of twentieth-century scholars were led by such classical usages of the noun ἄνθος to doubt that floral meanings were primary for the root ἀνθο/ε-, from which both the noun ἄνθος and the verb ἀνθέω derive. Instead they suggested that the root is associated first and foremost with the notions of "surface" or "top." William Stanford for instance objects to the rendering of Aeschylus' image ἀνθοῦν πέλαγος Αἰγαῖον νεκροῖς (*Agamemnon* 659) as "the deep was all aflower ... with corpses": according to him, associations of corpses with beauty are possible only for "a disillusioned modern *fin de siècle*."[3] He suggests that this and other attestations of the root ἀνθο/ε- do not, in fact, convey the meaning "flower" but rather "that which rises to the surface." Drawing on Stanford's observations, Kerr Borthwick argues that the image τρίβῳ κατέξαινον ἄνθος Ἀργείων at *Agamemnon* 197–198 ("[winds] were wearing away the *anthos* of the Argives with their attrition") evokes the nap (i.e., the top) of a cloth, and that the metaphor at line 659 refers in fact to the foam of the sea.[4]

Some linguists have drawn similar conclusions from the Homeric uses of ἄνθος. Rahim Raman for instance builds on Stanford's conclusions in a study of Homeric and classical poetry. In a homogenizing reading of the terms ἄωτος, ἄνθος, χνόος, and ἀκμή, he argues that they all underwent a development from a Homeric meaning of "surface-growth" to a later metaphorical sense of "excellence," and that at no point were ἄνθος or any of these other nouns primarily associated with flowers. In his opinion, ἄνθος only refers to flowers in the sense of "surface of a landscape" or "top of a plant," and we should not see instances where the term refers to other types of thing as floral metaphors.[5] Likewise J. M. Aitchison, in an essay focused on Homeric poetry, argues that ἄνθος is not primarily associated with flowers. According to him, a meaning of "growth (up from)" best accounts for all the Homeric usages of the root ἀνθο/ε-.[6] Michael Clarke has recently revisited Aitchison's interpretation. He argues that early Greek uses of ἄνθος convey the concept of "burgeoning, swelling, upward-spreading motion or growth that bursts into a spreading excrescence."[7]

---

[3] Stanford 1936:112–114, with quotation from p. 112.
[4] Borthwick 1976. Silk (1974:162–163) is likewise at pains to disassociate the use of ἀνθο/ε- at *Agamemnon* 659 from the connotations of the English word "flower," but unlike Stanford and Borthwick he believes that the Aeschylean image focuses primarily on a notion somewhat closer to the vegetal realm—that of growth. For the suggestion that ἄνθος means "growth" also in Homeric poetry, cf. Aitchison 1963, Raman 1975, and Clarke 2005, whose essays are discussed below.
[5] Raman 1975.
[6] Aitchison 1975.
[7] Clarke 2005, with quotation from p. 25.

As we can see from this summary, while some of these scholars associate the root ἀνθο/ε- with the concept of growth, they all cast doubt on the floral associations of the root. However, when we study evidence from historical linguistics and review the testimony from our Homeric texts, we find good reasons to believe not only that the primary and original meaning of the root ἀνθο/ε- was vegetal, but also that the noun from this root, ἄνθος, has the specific meaning of "flower" in Homeric poetry.

Firstly, the possible cognates of ἄνθος in other Indo-European languages do not point in the direction of abstractions such as "what lies on the surface," but towards more concrete meanings. They include Frisian *åndul*, "marsh grass"; Armenian *and*, "field"; Sanskrit *ándhas-*, "a herb; the soma plant; grassy ground"; and, most strikingly, Albanian *ëndë*, "flower."[8] The semantics of some of these proposed cognates are uncertain.[9] Nevertheless, they are all associated in one way or other with vegetation. What is more, the chief Albanian grammars, which are not always cited by linguists working on this question, confirm the existence of a cognate of Greek ἄνθος with a floral meaning.[10]

On the basis of such evidence, linguists have suggested Proto-Indo-European roots with vegetal meanings. Robert Beekes tentatively offers an original verbal root *h_2endh- with the meaning "sprout."[11] James Mallory and Douglas Adams reconstruct a nominal stem *$h_2endhes$- with the meaning "± flower": that is, "flower" offers the best approximation of the original meaning of this Proto-Indo-European root, but a more general, vegetal meaning is also possible.[12] What

---

[8] I quote these possible cognates and their meanings as they are given by Mallory and Adams (2006:161–162). Boisacq (1938 s.v. ἄνθος) and Pokorny (1959 s.v. *andh-, anedh-*) also point to a number of possible cognates in the Celtic languages, most of which refer to young women or to young animals. If this is correct, the metaphor of the "flower of youth" discussed in Chapter 7 could be of very early provenance. But it might also be the case that the metaphor developed independently in the Greek and Celtic branches of the Indo-European family.

[9] See Frisk 1960–1972 s.v. ἄνθος; Chantraine 1984–1990 s.v. ἄνθος on Skt. *ándhas-*; Mallory and Adams 2006:161, who note the "vague meanings" of the proposed cognates; Beekes 2009 s.v. ἄνθος, who lists the Albanian form "*endë*" "'flour'" [*sic*]. But see n10 below on the semantics of the proposed Albanian cognates. Some scholars have expressed doubts concerning the relationship of the various possible cognates with Greek ἄνθος: Beekes 2009 s.v. ἄνθος.

[10] Meyer (1891 s.v. *qj*) cites "*ënde* f. 'Blütenkelch, Blume des Weines,' auch 'Freude, Annehmlichkeit'"; Demiraj (1997 s.v. *end* (t.)/*ën(d)* (g.)) includes forms that cover both the meanings "flour" ("*ënde*"—"'Kernmehl'"; cf. n9 above on Beekes 2009 s.v. ἄνθος) and "flower" ("*énd(ë)*"—"'Blüte,'" "*ënd*"—"'Blütenstaub, Pollen,'" "*éndëz*"—"'Sproß; Blume,'" "*endëzón*"—"'blühen'"); Orel (1998) lists "*end*" "'pollen'" and "*end*" "'to blossom.'" On the basis of such evidence, the Albanian expert Brian Joseph informs me *per litteras* that there are "good authorities ... for maintaining the connection between *an* [his emphasis] Albanian word having to do with flowers and Greek *anthos*."

[11] Beekes 2009 s.v. ἄνθος.

[12] Mallory and Adams 2006:161–162. Similarly, Pokorny (1959 s.v. *andh, anedh*) reconstructs earlier forms with either specifically floral or generally vegetal meanings. He lists two forms: a root *andh-/anedh-* meaning "hervorstechen, spießen, blühen" and a noun *andhos* meaning "Blume, Kraut."

is more, as Adams has pointed out to me *per litteras*, even if we cannot be certain that Proto-Indo-European *$h_2endhes$- meant "flower," the presence of cognates with that meaning in geographically adjacent regions, Greek and Albanian, indicates that at the very least these two branches of the Indo-European family shared an early noun meaning "flower."[13]

This evidence, then, suggests that the floral meaning of the Greek noun ἄνθος is not a later development but rather reflects the early semantics of the term. And as we shall see, the internal evidence of Homeric poetry likewise points us towards more concrete referents for the root ἀνθο/ε-, as opposed to abstractions such as "burstings forth." Specifically, we observe a distinction between a verbal root associated with vegetation in general and substantival stems referring to flowers. The verbal root ἀνθε-, usually found in participial form, has either a general, vegetal meaning of "flourishing" or a more specific meaning of "blooming," while in all but a few instances the adjective ἀνθεμόεις and the noun ἄνθος clearly mean "flowery" and "flower" respectively. We have, then, a distinction between verbal and nominal roots similar to that between the verbal root *h_2endh-, tentatively proposed by Beekes, and the nominal root *$h_2endhes$-, reconstructed by Mallory and Adams, which have the meanings "sprout" and "± flower" respectively: it is possible that these Homeric roots reflect the semantics of the original Proto-Indo-European forms.

There are three cases in our versions of the Homeric poems where the noun ἄνθος might carry a more general meaning of "vegetal growth"—though in all of these instances a floral meaning is still very much a possibility. It might seem at first sight that the phrase ἄνθεα ποίης at *Odyssey* 9.449 and *Hymn* 30.15 has a more general vegetal meaning—"grassy growths" vel sim. But audiences familiar with early hexameter might not have understood it in this fashion. At *Theogony* 576 the phrase refers to material used for a garland, which we would expect to be made up of flowers.[14] This suggests that it could carry the meaning "flowers of the grassland."[15] At *Odyssey* 7.125–126, a general vegetal sense of ἄνθος is likewise possible: πάροιθε δέ τ' ὄμφακές εἰσιν / ἄνθος ἀφιεῖσαι ("before them were unripe grapes / sending a bloom [?] around them"). The juxtaposition of

---

[13] The Albanian and Greek nouns would either represent a development from a common lexeme shared by the Balkan branches of Proto-Indo-European or a borrowing from one of the branches into the other. Adams (*per litteras*) wonders, in particular, whether the Albanian term might have been borrowed from a northern dialect of Greek. But if this were the case, "[i]t's hard to date this early stratum of borrowing." Nevertheless, "it almost certainly antedates the 'final' Ionic recension of Homer."

[14] Cf. the garlands of violets and roses described at Sappho fr. 94.12–13 Voigt. For this poem, see also Chapter 1.

[15] For ποίη as "grassland" rather than simply "grass," see LSJ s.v. πόα 1.4: "a grassy place."

ἄνθος with a reference to ripening grapes is surprising: we would expect the flowers to fall off the vine before any fruit appeared. It may be, then, that these lines attribute some general notion of vegetal flourishing to the grapes. But we should remember that the Phaeacian plantations are no ordinary allotments: as we saw in Chapter 5, their plants grow constantly throughout the year, without the need for human tendance; and the description of unripe grapes in lines 125–126 is immediately followed by a reference to mature grapes. Audiences could readily have imagined that such plants, which are not subject to seasonal variation, would exhibit flowers and fruit *at the same time*.

In other passages, the Homeric noun ἄνθος clearly evokes flowers. In a number of cases, the noun is coupled with references to particular flowering plants. At *Hymn to Demeter* 6, for instance, Korē is gathering ἄνθεα, specified as roses, crocuses, and violets; later in the hymn the daughters of Celeus are said to have hair like the saffron flower (κροκηΐῳ ἄνθει, *Hymn to Demeter* 178); at *Odyssey* 10.304, Hermes digs up the herb μῶλυ, which has γάλακτι ... εἴκελον ἄνθος ("a flower like milk"); and at *Odyssey* 6.231 and 23.158, Athena adorns Odysseus' head with locks like the flower of the hyacinth (ὑακινθίνῳ ἄνθει).[16]

Similarly, in the relevant passages of Homeric poetry the adjective ἀνθεμόεις is most readily translated "flowery." It is often used to describe man-made objects: cauldrons (*Iliad* 23.885, *Odyssey* 3.440), a mixing-bowl (*Odyssey* 24.275), and Aphrodite's earrings (*Hymn* 6.9). It is very likely that these passages focus on decorative, floral motifs, rather than conveying the more vague notions of "surfaces" or "burstings forth."[17]

The noun ἄνθος and the adjective ἀνθεμόεις, then, mean "flower" or "flowery" in the majority of instances in Homeric poetry, and even in those cases where they seem at first sight not to do so, audiences might well have perceived a reference to flowers. The verb ἀνθέω in Homeric poetry can also

---

[16] For Odysseus' hyacinthine hair, see Chapter 2. For ἄνθος = "flower," see also *Hymn to Demeter* 425 (flowers gathered by Korē); *Hymn to Apollo* 139 (the flowers that bloom when Apollo steps on Delos, discussed in Chapter 4); *Hymn* 7.41 (ivy flowers); *Iliad* 2.89, 2.468, 9.51 (spring flowers); *Hymn to Demeter* 401, 472 (also spring flowers, if as suggested in Chapter 4 Korē's return marks the coming of spring). The noun can also refer to blossom: see *Iliad* 9.542, 17.56 (the Euphorbus simile, studied in Chapter 8). Given that ἄνθος has the primary meaning of "flower" or "blossom" in these passages and in those listed in the main text, which represent the majority of the Homeric usages of the noun, the other occurrences of the lexeme can be understood in a similar fashion. For example, when ἄνθος refers to the youthful flourishing of humans or gods (*Hymn to Demeter* 108, *Hymn to Hermes* 375, *Hymn* 10.3, *Iliad* 13.484; see also the similar usage of ἀνθέω at *Odyssey* 11.320), we should treat the relevant phrases as floral metaphors. Cf. Chapter 7 on the image of the "flower of youth" in Homeric poetry and elsewhere.

[17] Given the floral associations of the ἀνθεμο- root in these passages, it is reasonable to follow Bakker (2002:25) in treating the name Ἀνθεμίων, Simoeisius' father at *Iliad* 4.473 and 488, in a similar fashion (Bakker renders it "Flowerman"; see also Chapter 8 n14).

be associated with flowers, but more often it carries general vegetal meanings.[18] In two of the Homeric instances of the verb, a generally vegetal translation of "flourish" seems appropriate: ὄρος ἄνθεον ὕλη, "a mountain flourishing with forest" (*Hymn* 1.9), and ἀνθοῦσαν ἀλωήν, "flourishing vineyard" (*Hymn to Hermes* 87). In contrast with the vines of *Odyssey* 7, the vineyard in the *Hymn to Hermes* is a regular plantation tended by a farmer: we would not expect that its flowers and fruit would appear at the same time. But owing to its associations with flowers, the noun ἄνθος is able to bring out similar connotations in the verb ἀνθέω. At *Hymn to Apollo* 139, for instance, the juxtaposition of the aorist form ἤνθησ' with the noun ἄνθεσιν suggests a specifically floral meaning for the verb: "[Delos] bloomed ... with flowers."

From this evidence it seems best to conclude that in Homeric poetry the root ἀνθο/ε- has either a specifically floral or a generally vegetal meaning. Depending on context the verb ἀνθέω can be translated either "bloom" or "flourish." And in most if not all instances, the substantival forms ἄνθος and ἀνθεμ- refer specifically to flowers.

It is, however, true that in a restricted range of passages the noun ἄνθος and the adjective ἀνθεμόεις might evoke not merely "flowers" but "flowery surfaces"—the sorts of bright, colorful surfaces that carpet Greek spring landscapes. And these passages point us in the direction of a compromise with the findings of scholars such as Stanford and Borthwick. In the *Iliad*, for instance, the two lexemes describe flowers by the River Scamander:

> ἔσταν δ' ἐν λειμῶνι Σκαμανδρίῳ ἀνθεμόεντι·
> μυρίοι, ὅσσα τε φύλλα καὶ ἄνθεα γίγνεται ὥρῃ.
>
> *Iliad* 2.467–468

> They stood on the flowery meadow of the Scamander,
> Countless as the leaves and flowers that grow in season.

An onlooker—or an audience member imagining the scene—might perceive not merely the individual flowers (captured by the plural ἄνθεα) but also their collective effect as they cover the meadow of the Scamander (suggested by the adjective ἀνθεμόεντι).[19]

The root ἀνθεμ- evokes "flowery" fields in three other passages, perhaps again with suggestions of "flowery surfaces." At *Odyssey* 12.159. we once more find the phrase λειμὼν ἀνθεμόεις (this time in the accusative case) in the

---

[18] Cf. Beekes' (2009 s.v. ἄνθος) tentative reconstruction of a Proto-Indo-European verbal root with a vegetal meaning: *$h_2$endh-, "sprout."

[19] For discussion of this passage, see Chapter 8 n37.

description of the island of the Sirens; at *Hymn to Hermes* 96, we encounter "flowery plains" (πεδί᾿ ἀνθεμόεντα), which appear to anticipate the asphodel meadows of lines 221 and 344; and the "flowery pastures" (νομοὶ ἀνθεμόεντες) of *Hymn to Aphrodite* 169 contrast with the "grassy pastures" (νομοὶ ποιήεντες) of line 78.[20] A translation simply of "surface" or "with surfaces" would not do for ἀνθεμόεις in any of these descriptions of fields; but "(with) flowery surface(s)" is certainly possible.

I suggest, therefore, that the meaning simply of "surface" (as opposed to "flowery surface") attributed by Stanford and Borthwick to the root ἀνθο/ε- in Aeschylus represents not an earlier sense of the ἀνθο/ε- root that was then *transferred* to flowers, but rather a metaphorical development from an original, floral meaning of the term. Flowers carpeted Greek spring landscapes, and this concept of bright surfaces may well have been present in some early uses of the term, including the Homeric descriptions of fields listed above; classical authors would therefore have been able to use the concept of flowers to evoke surfaces more generally. And if as Clarke suggests, the noun ἄνθος conveys the notion of bursting forth in other passages of classical Greek literature, this would represent a metaphorical development from a second characteristic of Greek flowers—their bursting forth in the spring and early summer.[21] These developments would be in keeping with Lakoff's, Johnson's and Turner's analysis of the formation of metaphor: as they show, metaphors map from the more concrete to the more abstract and thereby aid our understanding of abstract concepts.[22]

---

[20] See Chapter 8 for the Sirens' flowery meadow and Chapter 5 for a discussion of *Hymn to Aphrodite* 78 and 169. I comment on *Hymn to Hermes* 221 and 344 in Chapter 8 n54.

[21] The metaphorical development of ἄνθος to embrace the meanings "X covering a surface" or "X bursting forth" also explains the later use of ἐξανθέω to describe eruptions of disease on skin: see Garvie 1986 on Aeschylus *Choephori* 282, Schironi 2010:344, and LSJ s.v. ἐξανθέω: I.1: "*put out flowers*"; I.2: "metaph., *burst forth from* the surface, like an efflorescence"; I.3: "of ulcers, etc., *break out.*"

[22] Raman's (1975) study of ἄωτος, ἄνθος, χνόος, and ἀκμή, mentioned above, likewise imagines a development from more concrete to more abstract, metaphorical meanings. He argues that ἄνθος originally carried a sense of "surface-growth," which later developed into the meaning "excellence" in the metaphorical sense of "topmost."

Bibliography

Adkins, A. W. H. 1983. "Orality and Philosophy." In *Language and Thought in Early Greek Philosophy*, ed. K. Robb, 207–227. La Salle, IL.

Adler, A. 1928. *Suidae Lexicon*. Vol. 1. Leipzig.

Ahl, F., and H. M. Roisman. 1996. *The* Odyssey *Reformed*. Ithaca.

Aitchison, J. M. 1963. "Homeric ἄνθος." *Glotta* 41.3/4:271–278.

Alexiou, M. 2002. *The Ritual Lament in Greek Tradition*. Lanham, MD.

Allen, A. 1993. *Mimnermus: Text and Commentary*. Stuttgart.

Allen, T. W. 1912–1920. *Homeri Opera*, 5 vols. Oxford.

Allen, T. W., W. R. Halliday, and E. E. Sikes, eds. 1963. *The* Homeric Hymns. Amsterdam.

Amigues, S. 1988–2006. *Théophraste: Recherches sur les plantes*. 5 vols. Paris.

———. 1992. "*Hyakinthos*: Fleur mythique et plantes réelles." *Revue des études grecques* 105:19-36.

———. 2002a. "La 'prairie d'asphodèle' de l'Odyssée et de l'Hymne Homérique à Hermès." *Revue de philologie* 76.1:7-14.

———. 2002b. "Les traités botaniques de Théophraste." In *Études de botanique antique*, 11-43. Paris.

———. 2012–17. *Théophraste: Les causes des phénomènes végétaux*. 3 vols. Paris.

Amory, A. 1963. "The Reunion of Odysseus and Penelope." In *Essays on the* Odyssey: *Selected Modern Criticism*, ed. C. H. Taylor, 100–121. Bloomington, IN.

Arthur (Katz), M. B. 1991. *Penelope's Renown: Meaning and Indeterminacy in the* Odyssey. Princeton.

———. 1994. "Politics and Pomegranates: An Interpretation of the *Homeric Hymn to Demeter*," in *The* Homeric Hymn to Demeter, ed. H. P. Foley, 214–242. Princeton. Orig. pub. *Arethusa* 10:7-47. 1977.

Bakker, E. J. 2001. "The Greek *Gilgamesh*, or the Immortality of Return." In *Eranos: Proceedings of the 9th International Symposium on the* Odyssey, ed. M. Païsi-Apostolopoulou, 331–353. Ithaca.

———. 2002. "*Khrónos, Kléos*, and Ideology from Herodotus to Homer." In *Epea pteroenta: Beiträge zur Homerforschung; Festschrift für Wolfgang Kullmann zum 75. Geburtstag*, ed. M. Reichel and A. Rengakos, 11–30. Stuttgart.

———. 2005. *Pointing at the Past*. Cambridge, MA.

Balme, D. M. 1962. "Development of Biology in Aristotle and Theophrastus: Theory of Spontaneous Generation." *Phronesis* 7:91–104.

Bastida, J., and F. Viladomat. 2002. "Alkaloids of Narcissus." In *Narcissus and Daffodil: The Genus Narcissus*, ed. G. R. Hanks, 141–214. London.

Baumann, H. 1993. *Greek Wild Flowers and Plant Lore in Ancient Greece*. Trans. and augmented by W. T. Stearn and E. R. Stearn. London. (= *The Greek Plant World in Myth, Art and Literature*. Portland, 1993.) Orig. pub. as *Die griechische Pflanzenwelt in Mythos, Kunst und Literatur*. Munich, 1982.

Beall, E. F. 2006. "Hesiod's Treatise on Justice: *Works and Days* 109–380." *Classical Journal* 101.2:161–182.

Beekes, R. S. P. 2009. *Etymological Dictionary of Greek*. Leiden.

Berardi, E., F. L. Lisi, and D. Micalella, eds. 2009. *Poikilia: Variazioni sul tema*. Rome.

Bernabé, A. 1996. *Poetae Epici Graeci: Testimonia et Fragmenta; Pars I*. 2nd ed. Leipzig.

———. 2015. "Language and Meter of the Epic Cycle." In *The Greek Epic Cycle and its Ancient Reception: A Companion*, ed. M. Fantuzzi and C. Tsagalis, 139–153. Cambridge.

Bierl, A. 2016. "Visualizing the Cologne Sappho: Mental Imagery through Chorality, the Sun, and Orpheus." In *The Look of Lyric: Greek Song and the Visual,* ed. V. Cazzato and A. Lardinois, 307–342. Leiden.

Blaise, F. 1992. "L'épisode de Typhée dans la Théogonie d'Hésiode (v. 820–885): La stabilisation du monde." *Revue des études grecques* 105:349–370.

Boehringer, S., and A. Chabod. 2017. "Sotto il rischio di *eros*: Genere e poesia melica in una società che precede la sessualità." In Caciagli 2017:23–50.

Boisacq, E. 1938. *Dictionnaire étymologique de la langue grecque*. Paris.

Bolling, G. M. 1958. "ΠΟΙΚΙΛΟΣ and ΘΡΟΝΑ." *American Journal of Philology* 79:275–282.

Bonnafé, A. 1984–1987. *Poésie, nature et sacré*. 2 vols. Lyon.

Borgeaud, P. 1988. *The Cult of Pan in Ancient Greece*. Trans. K. Atlass and J. Redfield. Chicago. Orig. pub. as *Recherches sur le dieu Pan*. Rome, 1979.

Borthwick, E. K. 1976. "The 'Flower of the Argives' and a Neglected Meaning of ἄνθος." *Journal of Hellenic Studies* 96:1–7.

Bowdle, B. F., and D. Gentner. 2005. "The Career of Metaphor." *Psychological Review* 112.1:193–216.

Bowman, L. 2004. "The 'Women's Tradition' in Greek Poetry." *Phoenix* 58.1/2:1–27.

Braudel, F. 1972. *The Mediterranean and the Mediterranean World in the Age of Philip II*. Trans. S. Reynolds. Vol. I. New York. Orig. pub. as *La Méditerranée et le monde méditerranéen à l'époque de Philippe II*. Paris, 1966.

———. 2001. *The Mediterranean in the Ancient World*. Trans. S. Reynolds. London. Orig. pub. as *Les Mémoires de la Méditerranée*. Paris, 1998.

Brillet-Dubois, P. 2001. "Les liaisons dangereuses: Dieux et mortels dans l'*Hymne homérique à Aphrodite*." *Europe* 865:250–260.

———. 2011. "An Erotic *Aristeia*: The *Homeric Hymn to Aphrodite* and its Relation to the Iliadic Tradition." In Faulkner 2011:105–132.

Broodbank, C. 2013. *The Making of the Middle Sea: A History of the Mediterranean from the Beginning to the Emergence of the Classical World*. Oxford.

Brown, N. O. 1969. *Hermes the Thief: The Evolution of a Myth*. New York. Orig. pub. 1947.

Bruneau, P. 1970. *Recherches sur les cultes de Délos à l'époque Hellénistique et à l'époque impériale*. Paris.

Budelmann, F., and P. A. LeVen. 2014. "Timotheus' Poetics of Blending: A Cognitive Approach to the Language of the New Music." *Classical Philology* 109.3:191–210.

Burgess, J. S. 2001. *The Tradition of the Trojan War in Homer and the Epic Cycle*. Baltimore.

———. 2009. *The Death and Afterlife of Achilles*. Baltimore.

Burkert, W. 1979. "Kynaithos, Polykrates and the *Homeric Hymn to Apollo*." In *Arktouros: Hellenic Studies Presented to Bernard M. W. Knox*, ed. G. W. Bowersock, W. Burkert, and M. C. J. Putnam, 53–62. Berlin.

Burrow, C. 2002. *William Shakespeare: The Complete Sonnets and Poems*. Oxford.

Buschor, E. 1944. *Die Musen des Jenseits*. Munich.

Butterworth, E. A. S. 1970. *The Tree at the Navel of the Earth*. Berlin.

Buxton, R. 2004. "Similes and Other Likenesses." In *The Cambridge Companion to Homer*, ed. R. Fowler, 139–155. Cambridge.

Caciagli, S., ed. 2017. *Eros e genere in Grecia arcaica*. Bologna.

Calame, C. 1997. *Choruses of Young Women in Ancient Greece: Their Morphology, Religious Role, and Social Function*. Trans. D. Collins and J. Orion. Lanham, MD. Orig. pub. as *Les chœurs de jeunes filles en Grèce archaïque*. Rome, 1977.

———. 1999. *The Poetics of Eros in Ancient Greece*. Trans. J. Lloyd. Princeton. Orig. pub. as *I Greci e l'eros: Simboli, pratiche e luoghi*. Rome, 1992.

———. 2016. "The Amorous Gaze: A Poetic and Pragmatic *Koinê* for Erotic *Melos*?" In *The Look of Lyric: Greek Song and the Visual*, ed. V. Cazzato and A. Lardinois, 288–306. Leiden.

Campbell, D. A. 1982–1993. *Greek Lyric*. 5 vols. Cambridge, MA.

Cardete del Olmo, M. C. 2016. *El dios Pan y los paisajes pánicos: De la figura divina al paisaje religioso.* Seville.

Carroll, N. 1990. *The Philosophy of Horror, or, The Paradoxes of the Heart.* New York.

Càssola, F. 1975. *Inni omerici.* Milan.

Chantraine, P. 1984–1990. *Dictionnaire étymologique de la langue grecque.* Paris.

Chiappe, D. L. 1999. "Aptness Predicts Preference for Metaphors and Similes, as well as Recall Bias." *Psychonomic Bulletin and Review* 6:668–676.

Chiappe, D. L., and J. M. Kennedy. 2000. "Are Metaphors Elliptical Similes?" *Journal of Psycholinguistic Research* 29:371–398.

Chiappe, D. L., J. M. Kennedy, and T. Smykowski. 2003. "Reversibility, Aptness and the Conventionality of Metaphors and Simile." *Metaphor and Symbol* 18.2:85–105.

Chirassi, I. 1968. *Elementi di culture precereali dei miti e riti greci.* Rome.

Clader, L. L. 1976. *Helen: The Evolution from Divine to Heroic in Greek Epic Tradition.* Leiden.

Clarke, M. 2005. "Etymology in the Semantic Reconstruction of Early Greek Words: The Case of ἄνθος." *Hermathena* 179:13–37.

Clay, J. S. 1980. "Goat Island: *Od.* 9.116–141." *Classical Quarterly* 30:261–264.

———. 2003. *Hesiod's Cosmos.* Oxford.

———. 2006. *The Politics of Olympus: Form and Meaning in the Major* Homeric Hymns. London. Orig. pub. Princeton, 1989.

———. 2011. "The *Homeric Hymns* as Genre." In Faulkner 2011:232–253.

Cohen, B. 1995. *The Distaff Side: Representing the Female in Homer's* Odyssey. New York.

Cohen, J. J. 1996. "Monster Culture (Seven Theses)." In *Monster Theory: Reading Culture,* ed. J. J. Cohen, 3–25. Minneapolis.

Colli, G., and M. Montinari, eds. 1980. *Friedrich Nietzsche: Sämtliche Werke; Kritische Studienausgabe in 15 Banden.* Vol. 1. Berlin.

Comrie, B. 1976. *Aspect: An Introduction to the Study of Verbal Aspect and Related Problems.* Cambridge.

Crowther, P. 2003. "Literary Metaphor and Philosophical Insight: The Significance of Archilochus." In *Metaphor, Allegory, and the Classical Tradition: Ancient Thought and Modern Revisions,* ed. G. R. Boys-Stones, 84–100. Oxford.

Currie, B. 2016. *Homer's Allusive Art.* Oxford.

Curtis, P. 2011. *Stesichoros's Geryoneis.* Leiden.

Davies, M., and P. J. Finglass. 2015. *Stesichorus: The Poems.* Cambridge.

Deacy, S. 2013. "From 'Flowery Tales' to 'Heroic Rapes': Virginal Subjectivity in the Mythological Meadow." *Arethusa* 46.3:395–413.

DeBloois, N. A. 1997. "Rape, Marriage, or Death? Perspectives in the *Homeric Hymn to Demeter.*" *Philological Quarterly* 76.3:245–262.

Demiraj, B. 1997. *Albanische Etymologien: Untersuchungen zum albanischen Erbwortschatz.* Amsterdam.

Deonna, W. 1946. "La végétation à Délos." *Bulletin de correspondance hellénique* 70:154–163.

Detienne, M., and J.-P. Vernant. 1978. *Cunning Intelligence in Greek Culture and Society.* Trans. J. Lloyd. Hassocks. Orig. pub. as *Les Ruses de l'intelligence: La Mêtis des Grecs.* Paris, 1974.

Diels, H. 1882. *Simplicii in Aristotelis Physicorum libros quattuor priores commentaria.* Commentaria in Aristotelem Graeca 9. Berlin.

Diels, H., and W. Kranz. 1954. *Die Fragmente der Vorsokratiker.* Berlin.

Doherty, L. E. 1995a. *Siren Songs: Gender, Audiences, and Narrators in the* Odyssey. Ann Arbor, MI.

———. 1995b. "Sirens, Muses, and Female Narrators in the *Odyssey*." In Cohen 1995:81–92. Oxford.

Dougherty, C. 2015. "Nobody's Home: *Metis*, Improvisation and the Instability of Return in Homer's *Odyssey*." *Ramus* 44.1–2:115–140.

DuBois, P. 1995. *Sappho is Burning.* Chicago.

Dué, C. 2002. *Homeric Variations on a Lament by Briseis.* Lanham, MD.

———. 2006. *The Captive Woman's Lament in Greek Tragedy.* Austin.

———. 2010. "Agamemnon's Densely-Packed Sorrow in *Iliad* 10: A Hypertextual Reading of a Homeric Simile." *Trends in Classics* 2:279–299.

Duigan, M. 2004. "Pretending To Be What They Are Not: Colour and the Deceptive Gift." In *Colour in the Ancient Mediterranean World*, ed. L. Cleland and K. Stearns, 78–84. Oxford.

Eck, J. van. 1978. *The* Homeric Hymn to Aphrodite. *Introduction, Commentary and Appendices.* Utrecht.

Eckerman, C. Forthcoming. "I Weave a Variegated Headband: Metaphors for Song and Communication in Pindar's Odes." *Harvard Studies in Classical Philology* 110.

Edwards, G. M. 1991. *The* Iliad: *A Commentary.* Vol. 2, *Books 17–20.* Cambridge.

Einarson, B., and G. K. K. Link. 1976–1990. *Theophrastus:* De Causis Plantarum. 3 vols. Cambridge, MA.

Eitrem, S. 1935. In *Pauly-Wissowa* 2te Reihe, Vol. XXXII, col. 1721–1732, s.v. *Narkissos.*

Eliade, M. 1959. *The Sacred and the Profane.* Trans. W. R. Trask. San Diego. Orig. pub. as *Le sacré et le profane.* Paris, 1956.

———. 1963. *Patterns in Comparative Religion.* New York. Orig. pub. as *Traité d' histoire des religions.* Paris, 1959.

———. 1988. *Shamanism: Archaic Techniques of Ecstasy*. Trans. W. R. Trask. London. Orig. pub. as *Le chamanisme et les techniques archaïques de l'extase*. Paris, 1951.

Elliger, W. 1975. *Die Darstellung der Landschaft in der griechischen Dichtung*. Berlin.

Enright, M. J., and A. J. Papalas. 2002. "The Cosmic Justice of Hanging Hera." *Syllecta Classica* 13:19–33.

Erasmo, M. 2012. *Death: Antiquity and its Legacy*. New York.

Erbse, H. 1950. *Untersuchungen zu den attizistischen Lexica*. Berlin.

———. 1993. "Die Funktion des Rechtsgedankens in Hesiods 'Erga'." *Hermes* 121:12–28.

Evans, A. 1901. "Mycenean Tree and Pillar Cult." *Journal of Hellenic Studies* 21:99–204.

Fauconnnier, G., and M. Turner. 2002. *The Way We Think: Conceptual Blending and the Mind's Hidden Complexities*. New York.

Faulkner, A. 2008. *The* Homeric Hymn to Aphrodite. Oxford.

———, ed. 2011. *The* Homeric Hymns: *Interpretive Essays*. Oxford.

Felson(-Rubin), N. 1997. *Regarding Penelope: From Character to Poetics*. Norman, OK.

———. 2011. "Children of Zeus in the *Homeric Hymns*: Generational Succession." In Faulkner 2011:254–279.

Fenno, J. 2005. "'A Great Wave against the Stream': Water Imagery in Iliadic Battle Scenes." *American Journal of Philology* 126.4:475–504.

Ferrari, F. 2010. *Sappho's Gift: The Poet and her Community*. Trans. B. Acosta-Hughes and L. Prauscello. Ann Arbor, MI. Orig. pub. as *Una mitra per Kleis: Saffo e il suo pubblico*. Pisa, 2007.

———. 2017. "Sapph. fr. 1,18–24 e la grammatica dell'*eros*." In Caciagli 2017:85–106.

Finné, M., K. Holmgren, H. S. Sundqvist, E. Weiberg, and M. Lindblom. 2011. "Climate in the Eastern Mediterranean, and Adjacent Regions, During the Past 6000 Years—A Review." *Journal of Archaeological Science* 38.12:3153–3173.

Foley, H. P., ed. 1994. Homeric Hymn to Demeter: *Translation, Commentary and Interpretative Essays*. Princeton.

———. 2009. "'Reverse Similes' and Sex Roles in the *Odyssey*." In *Oxford Readings in Homer's* Odyssey, ed. L. E. Doherty, 189–207. Oxford. Orig. pub. *Arethusa* 11:7–26, 1978.

Foley, J. M. 1999. *Homer's Traditional Art*. University Park.

———. 2002. *How to Read an Oral Poem*. Urbana.

Ford, A. 1992. *Homer: Poetry of the Past*. Ithaca.

Friedrich, W.-H. 2003. *Wounding and Death in the* Iliad: *Homeric Techniques of Description*. Trans. G. Wright and P. Jones. London. Orig. pub. as *Verwundung und Tod in der Ilias: Homerische Darstellungsweisen*. Göttingen, 1956.

Frisk, H. 1960–1972. *Griechisches etymologisches Wörterbuch.* Heidelberg.

Frontisi-Ducroux, F. 1975. *Dédale: Mythologie de l'artisan en Grèce ancienne.* Paris.

Gallet de Santerre, H. 1958. *Délos primitive et archaïque.* Paris.

Garcia, L. F. 2013. *Homeric Durability: Telling Time in the* Iliad. Washington, DC.

Garland, R. 1985. *The Greek Way of Death.* Ithaca.

Garvie, A. F. 1986. *Aeschylus:* Choephori. Oxford.

Gentili, B. 1958. *Anacreon.* Rome.

Germany, R. 2005. "The Figure of Echo in the *Homeric Hymn to Pan.*" *American Journal of Philology* 126.2:187–208.

Giacomelli, A. 1980. "Aphrodite and After." *Phoenix* 34.1:1–19.

Giannini, P. 2009. "La *poikilia* nell'età arcaica e in Pindaro." In Berardi, Lisi, and Micalella 2009:65–82.

Glenn, J. 1998. "Odysseus Confronts Nausicaa: The Lion Simile of *Odyssey* 6.130–36." *Classical World* 92.2:107–116.

Glucksberg, S., and C. Haught. 2006. "On the Relation between Metaphor and Simile: When Comparison Fails." *Mind & Language* 21.3:360–378.

Glucksberg, S., and B. Keysar. 1990. "Understanding Metaphorical Comparisons: Beyond Similarity." *Psychological Review* 97.1:3–18.

——. 1993. "How Metaphors Work." In Ortony 1993a:401–424.

Gnoli, G. and J.-P. Vernant, eds. 1982. *La mort, les morts dans les sociétés anciennes.* Cambridge.

González, J. M. 2013. *The Epic Rhapsode and his Craft: Homeric Performance in a Diachronic Perspective.* Cambridge, MA.

Greene, E., ed. 1996. *Reading Sappho: Contemporary Approaches.* Berkeley.

——. 2002. "Subjects, Objects and Erotic Symmetry in Sappho's Fragments." In *Among Women: From the Homosocial to the Homoerotic in the Ancient World*, ed. N. S. Rabinowitz and L. Auanger, 82–105. Austin.

——. 2008. "Masculine and Feminine, Public and Private, in the Poetry of Sappho." In *Dialogism and Lyric Self-Fashioning: Bakhtin and the Voices of a Genre*, ed. J. Blevins, 23–45. Selinsgrove, PA.

——. 2010. *The Erotics of Domination: Male Desire and the Mistress in Latin Love Poetry.* Norman, OK. Orig. pub. 1998.

Gregorio, L. di. 1975. *Scholia vetera in Hesiodi Theogoniam.* Milan.

Gregory, A. 2016. *Anaximander: A Re-Assessment.* London.

Grethlein, J. 2018. "The Eyes of Odysseus: Gaze, Desire and Control in the *Odyssey.*" In *Gaze, Vision, and Visuality in Ancient Greek Literature*, ed. A. Kampakoglou and A. Novokhatko, 33–60. Berlin.

Griffin, J. 1976. "Homeric Pathos and Objectivity." *Classical Quarterly* 24:161–187 (≈ Griffin 1980:103–143).

———. 1977. "The Epic Cycle and the Uniqueness of Homer." *Journal of Hellenic Studies* 97:39–53.

———. 1980. *Homer on Life and Death*. Oxford.

Griffith, M. 1975. "Man and the Leaves: A Study of Mimnermos fr. 2." *California Studies in Classical Antiquity* 8:73–88.

Hague, R. 1984. "Sappho's Consolation for Atthis, fr. 96 LP." *American Journal of Philology* 105.1:29–36.

Hahn, R. 2001. *Anaximander and the Architects*. Albany.

Hamilton, J. T. 2001. "*Hymnos/ Poikilos*." *Helios* 28.2:119–140.

Hansen, P. A., and I. C. Cunningham, eds. 2009. *Hesychii Alexandri Lexicon*. Vol. 4, *T-Ω*. Berlin.

Harsh, P. W. 1950. "Penelope and Odysseus in *Odyssey* XIX." *American Journal of Philology* 71.1:1–21.

Haught, C. 2013. "A Tale of Two Tropes: How Metaphor and Simile Differ." *Metaphor and Symbol* 28:254–274.

Heinemann, G. 2005. "Die Entwicklung des Begriffs 'Physis' bis Aristoteles." In *Physik/ Mechanik*, ed. A. Schürmann, 16–60. Vol. III of *Geschichte der Mathematik und der Naturwissenschaften*, ed. G. Wöhrle. Stuttgart.

Heitman, R. 2005. *Taking Her Seriously: Penelope and the Plot of Homer's* Odyssey. Ann Arbor, MI.

Henderson, J. 1997. "The Name of the Tree: Recounting *Odyssey* XXIV 340–2." *Journal of Hellenic Studies* 117:87–116.

Höhfeld, V., ed. 2009. *Stadt und Landschaft Homers: Ein historisch-geografischer Führer für Troia und Umgebung*. Mainz.

Holmberg, I. E. 1990. "Gender and Deceit in Early Greek Hexameter Poetry." PhD diss., Yale University.

Hopman, M. G. 2012. *Scylla: Myth, Metaphor, Paradox*. Cambridge.

Horden, P., and N. Purcell. 2000. *The Corrupting Sea: A Study of Mediterranean History*. Oxford.

Holst-Warhaft, G. 1992. *Dangerous Voices: Women's Laments and Greek Literature*. London.

Horn, F. 2015a. "'Sleeping the Brazen Slumber'—A Cognitive Approach to Hom. *Il.* 11.241." *Philologus* 159.2:197–206.

———. 2015b. "Visualising *Iliad* 3.57: 'Putting on the Shirt of Stone.'" *Rheinisches Museum* 158.1:1–7.

Hughes, J. D. 2014. *Environmental Problems of the Greeks and Romans: Ecology in the Ancient Mediterranean*. Baltimore (rev. ed. of *Pan's Travail: Environmental Problems of the Greeks and Romans*, 1994).

Huxley, A., and W. Taylor. 1977. *Flowers of Greece and the Aegean*. London.

Irwin, M. E. 1974. *Colour Terms in Greek Poetry*. Toronto.

———. 1984. "The Crocus and the Rose." In *Greek Poetry and Philosophy: Studies in Honour of L. Woodbury*, ed. D. E. Gerber, 147–168. Chico, CA.

———. 1990. "Odysseus' 'Hyacinthine hair' in *Odyssey* 6.231." *Phoenix* 44:205–218.

———. 1994. "Roses and the Bodies of Beautiful Women in Greek Poetry." *Echos du monde classique*, 13:1–13.

———. 1997. "Flowers in the Landscape of Greek Epic." *Echos du monde classique*, 16.3:375–390.

Jackson, P. 2002. *Verbis pingendis: Contributions to the Study of Ritual Speech and Mythopoeia*. Innsbruck.

Janko, R. 1982. *Homer, Hesiod and the Hymns: Diachronic Development in Epic Diction*. Cambridge.

———. 1994. *The* Iliad: *A Commentary*. Vol. 4, *Books 13-16*. Cambridge.

———. 1998. "The Homeric Poems as Oral Dictated Texts." *Classical Quarterly* 48:1–13.

Jean, J. de. 1987. "Female Voyeurism: Sappho and Lafayette." *Rivista di letterature moderne e comparate* 40:201–215.

Jeanmaire, H. 1939. *Couroi et courètes: Essai sur l'éducation spartiate et sur les rites d'adolescence dans l'antiquité hellénique*. Lille.

Jong, I. J. F. de. 1989. "The Biter Bit: A Narratological Analysis of *H. Aphr.* 45–291." *Wiener Studien* 102:13–26.

———. 2001. *A Narratological Commentary on the* Odyssey. Cambridge.

Jouanna, J. 1999. "Le trône, les fleurs, le char et la puissance d'Aphrodite (Sappho I, v. 1, 11, 19 et 22): Remarques sur le texte, sur les composés en -*thronos* et sur les homérismes de Sappho." *Revue des études grecques* 112.1:99–126.

Kaniewski, D., E. Paulissen, E. van Campo, H. Weiss, T. Otto, J. Bretschneider, and K. van Lergerghe. 2010. "Late Second-Early First Millennium BC Abrupt Climate Changes in Coastal Syria and their Possible Significance for the History of the Eastern Mediterranean." *Quaternary Research* 74:207–215.

Kauffman, N. 2016. "Monstrous Beauty: The Transformation of Some Death Similes in Apollonius' *Argonautica*." *Classical Philology* 111:372–390.

Kelly, A. 2007. *A Referential Commentary and Lexicon to* Iliad *VIII*. Oxford.

———. 2015. "Stesichorus' Homer." In *Stesichorus in Context*, ed. A. Kelly and P. Finglass, 21–44. Cambridge.

Kern, O. 1922. *Orphicorum fragmenta*. Berlin.

Kirk, G. S. 1985. *The* Iliad: *A Commentary*. Vol. 1, *Books 1-4*. Cambridge.

———. 1990. *The* Iliad: *A Commentary*. Vol. 2, *Books 5-8*. Cambridge.

Konstan, D. 1994. *Sexual Symmetry: Love in the Ancient Novel and Related Genres*. Princeton.

Kristeva, J. 1982. *Powers of Horror: An Essay on Abjection*. Trans. L. S. Roudiez. New York. Orig. pub. as *Pouvoirs de l'horreur*. Paris, 1980.

Kurke, L. 1999. *Coins, Bodies, Games, and Gold: The Politics of Meaning in Archaic Greece*. Princeton.

Lacan, J. 1977. *The Four Fundamental Concepts of Psycho-Analysis*. Ed. J.-A. Miller. Trans. A. Sheridan. Harmondsworth.

Lakoff, G., and M. Johnson. 1999. *Philosophy in the Flesh*. New York.

———. 2003. *Metaphors We Live By*. Chicago. Orig. pub. 1980.

Lakoff, G., and M. Turner. 1989. *More Than Cool Reason: A Field Guide to Poetic Metaphor*. Chicago.

Lardinois, A. P. M. H. 1989. "Lesbian Sappho and Sappho of Lesbos." In *From Sappho to de Sade: Moments in the History of Sexuality*, ed. J. N. Bremmer, 15–35. London.

———. 1996. "Who Sang Sappho's Songs?" In Greene 1996:150–172. Berkeley.

———. 1998. Review of *Sappho's Sweetbitter Songs*, by L. H. Wilson. http://bmcr.brynmawr.edu/1998/1998-07-03.html.

———. 2001. "Keening Sappho: Female Speech Genres in Sappho's Poetry." In *Making Silence Speak*, ed. A. P. M. H. Lardinois and L. McClure, 75–92. Princeton.

Latte, K. 1966. *Hesychii Alexandrini Lexicon*. Vol. 2, E-O. Copenhagen.

Lattimore, R. 1962. *Themes in Greek and Latin Epitaphs*. Urbana.

Lazzeri, M. 2008. *Studi sulla Gerioneide di Stesicoro*. Quaderni del Dipartimento di Scienze dell' Antichità, Università degli studi di Salerno, 35. Naples.

Lentz, A. 1868. *Herodiani Technici reliquiae*. Leipzig.

Leo, G. M. 2015. *Anacreonte: I frammenti erotici; Testo, commento e traduzione*. Rome.

Levaniouk, O. 2011. *Eve of the Festival: Making Myth in* Odyssey *19*. Washington, DC.

Levine, D. B. 1983. "Penelope's Laugh: *Odyssey* 18.163." *American Journal of Philology* 104.2:172–178.

Liebert, R. S. 2017. *Tragic Pleasure from Homer to Plato*. Cambridge.

Lincoln, B. 1981. *Emerging from the Chrysalis*. Cambridge, MA.

Loraux, N. 1982. "Mourir devant Troie, tomber pour Athènes: De la gloire du héros à l'idée de la cité." In Gnoli and Vernant 1982:27–43.

Lord, A. B. 2000. *The Singer of Tales*. 2nd ed. Cambridge, MA. Orig. pub. 1960.

Lovatt, H. 2013. *The Epic Gaze: Vision, Gender and Narrative in Ancient Epic*. Cambridge.

Lowe, D. 2015. *Monsters and Monstrosity in Augustan Poetry*. Ann Arbor, MI.

LSJ = Liddell, H. G., R. Scott, H. S. Jones, and R. McKenzie, eds. 1996. *A Greek-English Lexicon*. Oxford.

Mackie, C. J. 2008. *Rivers of Fire: Mythic Themes in Homer's* Iliad. Washington, DC.

Maggiulli, G. 1989. "Amore e morte nella simbologia floreale." *Maia* 41:185–197.

Mallory, J. P. and D. Q. Adams. 2006. *Oxford Introduction to Proto-Indo-European and the Proto-Indo-European World*. Oxford.

Marg, W. 1976. "Kampf und Tod in der *Ilias.*" *Würzburger Jahrbücher für die Alter-tumswissenschaft* 2:7–19 (expanded version of *Antike* 18 (1942), 167–179).

Marks, J. 2008. *Zeus in the* Odyssey. Washington, DC.

Marquardt, P. 1985. "Penelope 'πολύτροπος.'" *American Journal of Philology* 106.1:32–48.

Martin, R. P. 1989. *The Language of Heroes: Speech and Performance in the* Iliad. Ithaca.

———. 2000. "Synchronic Aspects of Homeric Performance: The Evidence of the *Hymn to Apollo.*" In *Una nueva vision de la cultura griega antigua hacia el fin del milenio,* ed. A. M. González de Tobia, 403–432. La Plata.

———. 2001. "Rhapsodizing Orpheus." *Kernos* 14:23–33.

McEvilley, T. 2008. *Sappho.* Putnam, CT.

Merkelbach, R., and M. L. West. 1967. *Fragmenta Hesiodea.* Oxford.

Meyer, G. 1891. *Etymologisches Wörterbuch der albanesischen Sprache.* Strasburg.

Michelini, A. 1978. "'Ύβρις and Plants." *Harvard Studies in Classical Philology* 82:35–44.

Minchin, E. 2001. *Homer and the Resources of Memory.* Oxford.

———. 2007. *Homeric Voices: Discourse, Memory, Gender.* Oxford.

Mirto, M. S. 2012. *Death in the Greek World.* Trans. A. M. Osborne. Norman, OK (revised from Italian version, *Morte nel mondo greco.* Rome, 2007).

Mordine, M. J. 2006. "Speaking to Kings: Hesiod's αἶνος and the Rhetoric of Allusion in the *Works and Days.*" *Classical Quarterly* 56.2:363–373.

Morris, I. M. 1989. "Attitudes toward Death in Archaic Greece." *Classical Antiquity* 8.2:296–320.

Morris, S. P. 1992. *Daidalos and the Origins of Greek Art.* Princeton.

Most, G. W. 2006. *Hesiod:* Theogony, Works and Days, *Testimonia.* Cambridge, MA.

Motte, A. 1971. *Prairies et jardins de la Grèce antique de la religion à la philosophie.* Brussels.

Muellner, L. 1990. "The Simile of the Cranes and the Pygmies: A Study of Homeric Metaphor." *Harvard Studies in Classical Philology* 93:59–101.

Mulvey, L. 1989a. "Afterthoughts on 'Visual Pleasure and Narrative Cinema' Inspired by King Vidor's *Duel in the Sun* (1946)." In *Visual and Other Pleasures,* 29–38. Bloomington, IN. Orig. pub. in *Framework* 1981.

———. 1989b. "Visual Pleasure and Narrative Cinema." In *Visual and Other Pleasures,* 14–25. Bloomington, IN. Orig. pub. in *Screen* 1975.

Murr, J. 1969. *Die Pflanzenwelt in der griechischen Mythologie.* Groningen.

Murnaghan, S. 1987. *Disguise and Recognition in the* Odyssey. Princeton.

———. 1999. "The Poetics of Loss in Greek Epic." In *Epic Traditions in the Contemporary World: The Poetics of Community,* ed. M. Beissinger, J. Tylus, and S. Wofford, 203–220. Berkeley.

Nagler, M. N. 1996. "Dread Goddess Revisited." In Schein 1996:141–161. Princeton.

Nagy, G. 1974. *Comparative Studies in Greek and Indic Meter*. Cambridge, MA.

———. 1982. "Hesiod." In *Ancient Writers: Greece and Rome*. Vol. 1, ed. T. J. Luce, 43–73. New York.

———. 1985. "Theognis and Megara: A Poet's Vision of His City." In *Theognis of Megara: Poetry and the Polis*, ed. T. J. Figueira and G. Nagy, 22–81. Baltimore.

———. 1990. *Pindar's Homer: The Lyric Possession of an Epic Past*. Baltimore.

———. 1996. *Homeric Questions*. Austin.

———. 1999. *The Best of the Achaeans*. Baltimore. Orig. pub. 1979.

———. 2004. *Homer's Text and Language*. Urbana.

———. 2010. *Homer the Preclassic*. Berkeley.

———. 2013. *The Ancient Greek Hero in 24 Hours*. Cambridge, MA.

Naiden, F. 1999. "Homer's Leopard Simile." In *Nine Essays on Homer*, ed. M. Carlisle and O. Levaniouk, 177–203. Lanham.

Nelson, S. 1997. "The Justice of Zeus in Hesiod's Fable of the Hawk and the Nightingale." *Classical Journal* 92.3:235–247.

Neumann, J. 1993. "Climatic Changes in Europe and the Near East in the Second Millennium BC." *Climatic Change* 23:231–245.

Nieto Hernández, P. 2000. "Back in the Cave of the Cyclops." *American Journal of Philology* 121:345–366.

Nooter, S. 2019. "The Wooden Horse and the Unmaking of the *Odyssey*." In *Thinking the Greeks: A Volume in Honour of James M. Redfield*, ed. B. M. King and L. Doherty, 38–52. Abingdon.

Nortwick, T. van. 1979. "Penelope and Nausicaa." *Transactions of the American Philological Association* 109:269–276.

Olson, S. D. 2012. *The* Homeric Hymn to Aphrodite *and Related Texts*. Berlin.

Orel, V. 1998. *Albanian Etymological Dictionary*. Leiden.

Ortony, A. 1979. "Beyond Literal Similarity." *Psychological Review* 86.3:161–180.

———, ed. 1993a. *Metaphor and Thought*. 2nd ed. Cambridge. Orig. pub. 1979.

———. 1993b. "The Role of Similarity in Similes and Metaphors." In Ortony 1993:342–356.

Ory, T. 1984. "L'animal et le végétal dans l'*Hymne homérique à Aphrodite*." *Les études classiques* 52:251–254.

Parker, H. N. 1993. "Sappho Schoolmistress." *Transactions of the American Philological Association* 123:309–351.

Parker, R. 1991. "The *Hymn to Demeter* and the *Homeric Hymns*." *Greece & Rome* 38:1–17.

Parry, A., ed. 1971. *The Making of Homeric Verse: The Collected Papers of Milman Parry*. Oxford.

Patzer, H. 1993. *Physis: Grundlegung zu einer Geschichte des Wortes*. Stuttgart.

Pignatti, S. 1983. "Human Impact on the Vegetation of the Mediterranean Basin." In *Man's Impact on Vegetation*, ed. W. Holzner, M. J. A. Werger, and I. Ikusima, 151–162. The Hague.

Pokorny, J. 1959. *Indogermanisches etymologisches Wörterbuch*. Vol. 1. Bern.

Polunin, O. 1980. *Flowers of Greece and the Balkans: A Field Guide*. Oxford.

Prier, R. A. 1989. *Thauma Idesthai: The Phenomenology of Sight and Appearance in Archaic Greek*. Tallahassee, FL.

Pucci, P. 1979. "The Song of the Sirens." *Arethusa* 12:121–132. Republished in *The Song of the Sirens*. Lanham, 1997:1–9.

———. 1987. *Odysseus Polutropos: Intertextual Readings in the* Odyssey *and the* Iliad. Ithaca.

———. 1996. "Between Narrative and Catalogue: Life and Death of the Poem." *Mètis* 11:5–24.

Purves, A. 2006. "Unmarked Space: Odysseus and the Inland Journey." *Arethusa* 39.1:1–20.

———. 2010. *Space and Time in Ancient Greek Narrative*. Cambridge.

———. 2014. "Who, Sappho?" In *Defining Greek Narrative*, ed. R. Scodel and D. Cairns, 175–196. Edinburgh.

Quinn, F. X. 1964. "Theory of Spontaneous Generation According to the Ancients." *Classical Bulletin* 40:52–55 and 57–59.

Rackham, O., and J. Moody. 1996. *The Making of the Cretan Landscape*. Manchester.

Raman, R. A. 1975. "Homeric ἄωτος and Pindaric ἄωτος: A Semantic Problem." *Glotta* 53:195–207.

Rankin, A. V. 1962. "Penelope's Dreams in Books XIX and XX of the *Odyssey*." *Helikon* 2.3–4:617–624.

Ready, J. L. 2004. "A Binding Song: The Similes of Catullus 61." *Classical Philology* 99.2:153–163.

———. 2011. *Character, Narrator, and Simile in the* Iliad. Cambridge.

———. 2018. *The Homeric Simile in Comparative Perspectives*. Oxford.

Redfield, J. M. 1994. *Nature and Culture in the* Iliad. Durham, NC. Orig. pub. 1975.

———. 2009. "The Economic Man." In *Homer's* Odyssey: *Oxford Readings in Classical Studies*, ed. L. E. Doherty, 265–287. Oxford.

Reece, S. 2007. "Homer's Asphodel Meadow," *Greek, Roman and Byzantine Studies* 47.4:389–400 (≈ Reece, S., *Homer's Winged Words: The Evolution of Early Greek Epic Diction in the Light of Oral Theory*. Leiden, 2009:261–271.)

Richardson, N. J. 1974. *The* Homeric Hymn to Demeter. Oxford.

———. 1993. *The* Iliad: *A Commentary*. Volume VI, *Books 21–24*. Cambridge.

———. 2010. *Three* Homeric Hymns: *To Apollo, Hermes, and Aphrodite*. Cambridge.

Rinaudo, M. 2009. "Sviluppi semantici e ambiti d'uso di ποικίλος e derivati da Omero ad Aristotele." In Berardi, Lisi, and Micalella 2009:25–64.

Rinon, Y. 2008. *Homer and the Dual Model of the Tragic*. Ann Arbor, MI.

Rissman, L. 1983. *Love as War: Homeric Allusion in the Poetry of Sappho*. Beiträge zur Klassischen Philolgie 157. Königstein.

Romilly, J. de. 1993. "Trois jardins pardisiaques dans *l'Odyssée*." *Scripta Classica Israelica* 12:1–7.

Rood, N. 2008. "Craft Similes and the Construction of Heroes in the *Iliad*." *Harvard Studies in Classical Philology* 104:19–43.

Rose, P. W. 2012. *Class in Archaic Greece*. Cambridge.

Rosenmeyer, P. A. 1997. "Her Master's Voice: Sappho's Dialogue with Homer." *Materiali e discussioni per l'analisi dei testi classici* 39:123–149.

———. 2004. "Girls at Play in Early Greek Poetry." *American Journal of Philology* 125:163–178.

Rudhardt, J. 1994. "Concerning the *Homeric Hymn to Demeter*." In *The Homeric Hymn to Demeter*, ed. H. P. Foley, 198–211. Trans. L. Lorch and H. P. Foley. Princeton. Orig. pub. as "A propos de l'hymne homérique à Déméter." *Museum Helveticum* 35:1–17, 1978.

Russo, J. 1982. "Interview and Aftermath: Dream, Fantasy, and Intuition in *Odyssey* 19 and 20." *American Journal of Philology* 103.1:4–18.

Salvador Castillo, J. A. 1994. "El símil homérico de la μήκων (*Il*. 8.302–308)." *Cuadernos de filología clásica: Estudios griegos e indoeuropeos* 4:227–245.

Sammons, B. 2010. *The Art and Rhetoric of the Homeric Catalogue*. Oxford.

———. 2017. *Device and Composition in the Greek Epic Cycle*. Oxford

Scheid, J., and J. Svenbro. 1996. *The Craft of Zeus: Myths of Weaving and Fabric*. Trans. C. Volk. Cambridge, MA.

Scheijnen, T. 2017. "Ways to Die for Warriors: Death Similes in Homer and Quintus of Smyrna." *Hermes* 145.1:2–24.

Schein, S. L. 1976. "The Death of Simoeisios, *Iliad* 4.473–489." *Eranos* 74:1–5.

———, ed. 1996. *Reading the Odyssey: Selected Interpretive Essays*. Princeton.

———. 2012. "Divine and Human in the *Homeric Hymn to Aphrodite*." In *Hymnes de la Grèce antique: Approches littéraires et historiques*, ed. R. Bouchon, P. Brillet-Dubois, and N. Le Meur-Weissman, 295–312. Lyon.

Schironi, F. 2010. "Technical Languages: Science and Medicine." In *A Companion to the Ancient Greek Language*, ed. E. J. Bakker, 338–352. Malden.

Schmidt, M. A. 1976. *Die Erklärungen zum Weltbild Homers und zur Kultur der Heroenzeit in den bT-Scholien zur Ilias*. Zetemata 62. Munich.

Scott, W. C. 1974. *The Oral Nature of the Homeric Simile*. Leiden.

———. 2009. *The Artistry of the Homeric Simile*. Lebanon, NH.

Segal, C. 1971. *The Theme of the Mutilation of the Corpse in the* Iliad. Mnemosyne Supplement 17. Leiden.

———. 1974. "The *Homeric Hymn to Aphrodite*: A Structuralist Approach." *Classical World* 67:205–212.

———. 1986. "Tithonus and the *Homeric Hymn to Aphrodite*: A Comment." *Arethusa* 19:37–47.

Serrao, G. 1968. "L'ode di Erotima: Da timida fanciulla a donna pubblica (Anacr. fr. 346, 1 P. = 60 Gent.)." *Quaderni urbinati di cultura classica* 6:36–51.

Shelmerdine, S. C. 1986. "Odyssean Allusions in the Fourth *Homeric Hymn*." *Transactions of the American Philological Association* 96:49–63.

Silk, M. S. 1974. *Interaction in Poetic Imagery with Special Reference to Early Greek Poetry*. Cambridge.

Skinner, M. 1993. "Woman and Language in Archaic Greece, or, Why is Sappho a Woman?" In *Feminist Theory and the Classics*, ed. N. Sorkin Rabinowitz and A. Richlin, 125–144. London.

Slatkin, L. M. 1986. "Genre and Generation in the *Odyssey*." *Mètis* 1:259–286.

Smith, A. 1993. *Porphyrii philosophi fragmenta*. Stuttgart.

Smith, P. 1981. *Nursling of Mortality: A Study of the* Homeric Hymn to Aphrodite. Frankfurt.

Snell, B. et al., eds. 1955–2010. *Lexicon des frühgriechischen Epos*. Göttingen.

Snell, B., and H. Maehler. 1984–1989. *Pindari carmina cum fragmentis*. 2 vols. Leipzig.

Snyder, J. M. 1997. *Lesbian Desire and the Lyrics of Sappho*. New York.

Sourvinou-Inwood, C. 1995. *"Reading" Greek Death to the End of the Classical Period*. Oxford.

Sowa, C. A. 1984. *Traditional Themes and the* Homeric Hymns. Chicago.

Stallbaum, G. 1825. *Eustathii, Archepiscopi Thessalonicensis, Commentarii ad Homeri Odysseam*. Vol. 1. Leipzig.

Stanford, W. B. 1936. *Greek Metaphor*. Oxford

———. 1959. *Homer:* Odyssey Books I–XII. London.

Stehle (Stigers), E. 1977. "Retreat from the Male: Catullus 62 and Sappho's Erotic Flowers." *Ramus* 6:83–102.

———. 1981. "Sappho's Private World." *Women's Studies* 8:47–63.

———. 1996. "Sappho's Gaze: Fantasies of a Goddess and Young Man." In Greene 1996:193–225.

———. 1997. *Performance and Gender in Ancient Greece: Nondramatic Poetry in its Setting*. Princeton.

———. 2009. "Greek Lyric and Gender." In *The Cambridge Companion to Greek Lyric*, ed. F. Budelmann, 58–71. Cambridge.

Strasburger, G. 1954. *Die kleinen Kämpfer der* Ilias. Frankfurt-am-Main.

Strid, A., and K. Tan, eds. 1997–2002. *Flora Hellenica*. 2 vols. Königstein.

Suter, A. 2002. *The Narcissus and the Pomegranate*. Ann Arbor, MI.

Sutherland, E. H. 2003. "How (Not) to Look at a Woman: Bodily Encounters and the Failure of the Gaze in Horace's *C.* 1.19." *American Journal of Philology* 124.1:57–80

Taplin, O. P. 2007. "Some Assimilations of the Homeric Simile in Later Twentieth-Century Poetry." In *Homer in the Twentieth Century, Between World Literature and the Western Canon*, ed. B. Graziosi and E. Greenwood, 177–190. Oxford.

Thalmann, W. G. 1992. *The* Odyssey: *An Epic of Return.* New York.

Thiel, H. van. 2000. *Scholia D in Iliadem.* http://kups.ub.uni-koeln.de/1810/.

Thomas, O. 2011. "The *Homeric Hymn to Pan.*" In Faulkner 2011:151–172.

Tsagalis, C. 2012. *From Listeners to Viewers: Space in the* Iliad. Washington, DC.

Vergados, A. 2017. *The* Homeric Hymn to Hermes: *Introduction, Text and Commentary.* Berlin.

Vermeule, E. 1979. *Aspects of Death in Early Greek Art and Poetry.* Berkeley.

Vernant, J.-P. 1965. *Mythe et pensée chez les Grecs.* Paris.

———. 1974. "Le mythe prométhéen chez Hésiode." In *Mythe et société en Grèce ancienne*, 177–194. Paris.

———. 1989. "At Man's Table: Hesiod's Foundation Myth of Sacrifice." In *The Cuisine of Sacrifice among the Greeks*, ed. M. Detienne and J.-P. Vernant, 21–86. Trans. P. Wissing. Chicago. Orig. pub. as "À la table des hommes. Mythe de foundation du sacrifice chez Hésiode." In *La cuisine du sacrifice en pays grec.* Paris, 1979:37–132.

———. 1991a. "Death in the Eyes: Gorgo, Figure of the Other." In Vernant 1991c:111–138. Trans. F. I. Zeitlin. Orig. pub. as *La mort dans les yeux: Figures de l'autre en Grèce ancienne.* Paris, 1985:28–82.

———. 1991b. "In the Mirror of Medusa." In Vernant 1991c:141-150. Trans. F. I. Zeitlin. Orig. pub. as "Dans l'oeil du miroir: Méduse." In *Lo specchio e il doppio: Dallo stagno di Narciso allo schermo televiso*, ed. G. Macchi and M. Vitale. Milan, 1987:26-32.

———. 1991c. *Mortals and Immortals: Collected Essays*, ed. F. I. Zeitlin. Princeton.

———. 1991d. "*Panta kala*: From Homer to Simonides." In Vernant 1991c:84-91. Trans. F. I. Zeitlin. Orig. pub. as "ΠΑΝΤΑ ΚΑΛΑ: D'Homère à Simonide." *Annali della Scuola Normale Superiore di Pisa* 9:1365–1374, 1979.

———. 1996. "Death with Two Faces." In Schein 1996:55–61. Trans. J. Lloyd. Princeton. Orig. pub. as "Mort grecque, mort à deux faces." *Le Débat* 12:51–59, 1981.

———. 2001. "A 'Beautiful Death' and the Disfigured Corpse in Homeric Epic." In *Oxford Readings in Homer's* Iliad, ed. D. L. Carins, 311–341. Trans. A. Szegedy-Maszak. Oxford. Orig. pub. as "La belle mort et le cadavre outragé." In Gnoli and Vernant. 1982:45–76.

Vernant, J.-P., and F. Frontisi-Ducroux. 1997. *Dans l'oeil du miroir.* Paris.

Vidal-Naquet, P. 1996. "Land and Sacrifice in the *Odyssey*: A Study of Religious and Mythical Meanings." In Schein 1996:33–53. Orig. pub. as "Valeurs religieuses et mythiques de la terre et du sacrifice dans l'Odyssée." *Annales: économies, sociétés, civilisations* 25:1278–1297, 1970.

Villarrubia, A. 1997. "Una lectura del Himno Homérico a Pan." *Habis* 28:7–13.

Voigt, E.-M. 1971. *Sappho et Alcaeus*. Amsterdam.

Voliotis, D. 1984. "A Phenological Study of Flowering Period and Flower Colours of Aromatic Plants in Greece." *Vegetatio* 56:129–137.

Waern, I. 1999. "Flora Sapphica." *Annales Musei Goulandris* 10:171–180.

Weiss, B. 1982. "The Decline of Late Bronze Age Civilization as a Possible Response to Climate Change." *Climatic Change* 4:173–198.

Wendel, C. 1966. *Scholia in Theocritum vetera*. Stuttgart.

Weil, S. 1965. "The *Iliad*, or the Poem of Force." *Chicago Review* 18.2:5–30. Trans. M. McCarthy. Orig. pub. as "L'Iliade ou le poème de la force." *Cahiers du sud* Dec. 1940:561–574, Jan. 1941:21–34.

West, M. L. 1966. *Hesiod:* Theogony. Oxford.

———. 1978. *Hesiod:* Works and Days. Oxford.

———. 1992. *Iambi et elegi Graeci. Editio altera*. 2 vols. Oxford (= West²).

———. 1993. "Simonides Redivivus." *Zeitschrift für Papyrologie und Epigraphik* 98:1–14.

———. 2001. "The Fragmentary *Homeric Hymn to Dionysus*." *Zeitschrift für Papyrologie und Epigraphik* 134:1–11.

———. 2003. *Homeric Hymns, Homeric Apocrypha, Lives of Homer*. Cambridge, MA.

———. 2005. "The New Sappho." *Zeitschrift für Papyrologie und Epigraphik* 151:1–9.

———. 2011. *The Making of the* Iliad: *Disquisition and Analytical Commentary*. Oxford.

———. 2013. *The Epic Cycle: A Commentary on the Lost Troy Epics*. Oxford.

———. 2014. *The Making of the* Odyssey. Oxford.

Whitman, C. H. 1958. *Homer and the Heroic Tradition*. Cambridge, MA.

Wilson, L. H. 1996. *Sappho's Sweetbitter Songs*. London.

Winkler, J. J. 1990. *The Constraints of Desire: An Anthropology of Sex and Gender in Ancient Greece*. New York.

———. 1996. "Gardens of Nymphs: Public and Private in Sappho's Lyrics." In Greene 1996:89–109.

Wofford, S. L. 1992. *The Choice of Achilles: The Ideology of Figure in the Epic*. Stanford.

Yasumura, N. 2011. *Challenges to the Power of Zeus in Early Hexameter Poetry*. London.

Young, D. C. 1968. "Three Odes of Pindar: A Literary Study of *Pythian 11, Pythian 3*, and *Olympian 7*." *Mnemosyne Supplement* 9:69–105.

Zanetto, G. 1996. *Inni Omerici*. Milan.

Zeitlin, F. I. 1995. "Figuring Fidelity in Homer's *Odyssey*." In Cohen 1995:117–152.

Zusanek, H. 1996. *Kalypso: Untersuchungen zum dios-Begriff 1*. Frankfurt.

Index of Subjects

Greek Terms

ἀνθο/ε-, 124–126, 133, 198–199, 249–255

ἄνθος ἥβης. *See* flower of youth

ἀρο-, 163–172

ἀσφόδελος/ἀσφοδελός, 212–218

ἄφθιτος, 189

βρύω, 203

δρῦς, 2

ἔρνος, 200–203

ἥβης ἄνθος. *See* flower of youth

θαλερός, 198–199, 203

θαῦμα, 47–49, 136–138, 143–145

θρόνα, 76–77

ἴον, 2

λειμών, 208

νάρκισσος, 2–3, 227–228

ὀμφαλός, 95–98, 135–136

ποικίλος, 75–83

ὑάκινθος, 58, 118

ὑβρίζω, 165

φυ-, 93–94, 155–172, 181–182, 197

φυτο/ε-, 163–172

Names and Terms

Achilles, 54, 64–67, 120, 125, 140, 151, 170, 179, 181, 187–189, 194, 198, 201, 209, 211, 216–217, 222, 226, 239–241, 244–246

Aeneas, 140, 184, 187–189, 238

Agamemnon, 125, 140, 192, 216–217, 239–241, 245

agriculture, 126–128, 139–142, 145, 154–172, 192, 209–210

Aias, 120, 195–199

Anchises, 77–79, 128–134, 168, 238

Andromache, 76–77, 238

Anticleia, 213, 216, 234, 245

Aphrodite, 22, 26–29, 31, 33–34, 42, 51–56, 58, 61, 64, 66–67, 70, 72, 76–81, 83, 115–116, 119, 128–134, 168, 184, 188–189, 238, 253

Apollo, 53, 65–66, 92, 98, 105–114, 120, 158, 161, 184, 241, 244, 246, 253

apple, 33–34, 142–145, 150–153, 210–211

arboriculture, 139–172

Asclepius, 92, 106, 241

Asius, 192–194, 204

asphodel, 207, 209–218, 234–235, 255; *Asphodeline lutea*, 214–215; *Asphodelus albus*, 214–218

Athena, 42, 51–54, 56–72, 135–138, 145–149, 158, 184, 203, 221, 238–239, 246–247, 253

Atlas, 95–98

axis mundi, 95–99, 117

beauty, 10, 12–15, 22–39, 51–73, 77–81, 125, 146–147, 179–189, 192, 237–239, 250

Index Locorum